The Spirit of Solitude

The Spirit of Solitude

Conventions and Continuities in Late Romance

Jay Macpherson

Yale University Press
New Haven and London

Published with assistance from the Mary Cady Tew Memorial Fund.

Designed by Nancy Ovedovitz and set in IBM Palatino type.
Printed in the United States of America by
The Murray Printing Company, Westford, Massachusetts.

Library of Congress Cataloging in Publication Data

Macpherson, Jay.
  The spirit of solitude.

  Bibliography: p.
  Includes index.
  1. Literature, Modern—History and criticism.
2. Romanticism.   I. Title.
PN701.M33   809'.9145   81-11462
ISBN 0-300-02632-3   AACR2

10   9   8   7   6   5   4   3   2   1

to my father
Major James Ewan Macpherson
champion of Ossian

But he who is unable to live in society, or who has no need to because he is sufficient to himself, is no part of a state, being either a wild beast or a god.
— *Aristotle,* Politics

It had been hard for him that spake it to have put more truth and untruth together, in few words, than in that speech: "Whosoever is delighted in solitude, is either a wild beast, or a God."
— *Bacon,* "Of Friendship"

These men are Devils alone, as the saying is . . . : a man alone, is either a Saint or a Devil; and Vae soli *in this sense, woe be to him that is so alone!*
— *Burton,* Anatomy of Melancholy

Du trittst hier gleichsam aus dem Kreise der Menschheit— entweder musst du ein höherer Mensch sein oder du bist ein Teufel.
— *Schiller,* Die Räuber

Contents

Illustrations

Preface

> *What vitiates life in the present is that it must be lived before it can be remembered. Not so in the art of pastoral.*
> —*Richard Cody*, The Landscape of the Mind

"Unfortunately," said Schiller of pastoral idylls, "they set behind us the goals towards which they ought to lead us, and so they can suggest to us only the sad sense of a loss, not the joyful one of hope." He is speaking in *On Naïve and Sentimental Poetry* of the alienation from nature, the self, perhaps too one's fellow man, that pervades modern consciousness and writing. Certain sturdy characters and authors have managed to live among realities by the light of the ideal: these are the heroes of natural supernaturalism, plungers in the sacred fount rather than lingerers in the ivory tower. For others, the vision has proved desolating: desiring to move forwards, they have been drawn either backwards into states parodying the tyrannical self-completeness of childhood, or along circular paths towards ironic discoveries. The alternatives are perhaps symbolized in some familiar Romantic myths of poetic creation. For Wordsworth the process moves forwards, with the original upsurge of feeling requiring completion by the gentler, more leisurely powers that belong to tranquillity; while Coleridge and Shelley have imaged it as a forever unsuccessful struggle to recapture a vanishing vision or a glow no sooner glimpsed than fading.

This study will follow, in the main, the nonheroic, or elegiac, line, sprung not from epic and drama but from pastoral, to which it remains close—not Faust and Prometheus, so to speak, but Werther and the Poet of *Alastor*—with its myths of solitude and retribution, Narcissus and Cain. Less, however, "follow" than cast about after; and less a line than a loose and ramifying cluster of images and structures that center in a body of secondary, or "sentimental," romance, in both Schiller's senses: it is late, which here means post-Miltonic, and it draws on a subjective mental world of reflection and dream, as well as on earlier authors, rather than on a direct experience of "nature," reality inward and outward. Its literary materials, of varied and often quite ancient origin, are largely gathered together by Milton and English eighteenth-century poetry and verse drama, and carry over into fiction with Rousseau, Goethe, and English

Romantic and later novelists. In the late twentieth century, secondary romance has taken on new life in popular novel and movie versions and in the work of serious writers interested in these.

The book's method, loose and ramifying to match its subject, will alternate between following out particular motifs and looking at their interaction with others in works by, to name some, Goethe, William Godwin, the Shelleys, James Hogg, Bulwer Lytton, Tennyson, Gérard de Nerval, Rider Haggard, George MacDonald, Oscar Wilde, W. H. Hudson, and Thomas Mann. We shall pursue thematic connections rather than interpretation and the history of ideas; notes and an index of motifs extend the range of continuities as far as has seemed feasible. "Pastoral" and "elegiac" will usually refer not so much to the traditional genres as to modes and patterns descended from them. "Descent" may seem a keynote also in the progression from Milton and Goethe to *Dracula* and *The Phantom of the Opera*. It should not in the Canadian epilogue, which moves cautiously towards a reconciliation of naïve and sentimental, exile and pioneer: the end of the golden string has to start from where one sits writing.

A Note on Books Referred To

The date accompanying the first mention of a book is usually that of first publication. For editions to which page references are made, please check the finding list at the end. A very few books whose chapters are renumbered in some single-volume editions are cited both ways, as, *Frankenstein* (III.i; xviii). Translations unless otherwise identified are approximately my own.

A Further Note

Among the various puzzles this book threw up in the course of writing, only one has seriously troubled me: why, when we begin with Narcissus (from whom the MS was named till barely yesterday), do we end with Cain? The transition is only to a slight extent chronological: there are plenty of Romantic Cains and modern Narcissuses, had they chosen to float to the top. A colleague's article recently offered a clue: Vincent A. De Luca ("The Lost Traveller's Dream," *Ariel* 11 [January 1980]: 49–69), analyzing a passage from *The Four Zoas*, remarks, " . . . it would seem that in human development a predominant consciousness of place yields inevitably to a predominant consciousness of time." In that light, Narcissus gazes into a paradise that is his own but that he can't enter, while Cain, born into a world of continuity rather than contiguity, goes wandering through the shades of night uncertain where, or whether, paradise ever was. To say this is not to resolve the puzzle, but merely to indicate an approach.

Acknowledgments

My first and greatest debt of gratitude is to my successive thesis supervisors, Northrop Frye (1955–59) and Milton Wilson (1960–64); like Satan I can't quit it in a moment, and I'm not going to try. I want also to thank friends and colleagues (academic and other) Margaret Atwood, Laurel Braswell, James Carscallen, Eleanor Cook, Julian Patrick, and James Polk, besides others unnamed, including many students, for interest and encouragement that was not just welcome but vital; Jane Widdicombe and Marilyn (Baxter) Chapman, typist and checker, who proved also very friendly early readers; next Harold Bloom, without whose generous and active involvement this package would still be rankling in my bottom drawer; all members of my classes of 1980–81, 206 and 4300, for their remarkable courtesy in tolerating late return of papers; and last—this sequence is purely chronological—Ellen Graham of the Press, who supplied in Lawrence Kenney a copy editor both correct and sympathetic, and who has never asked me to disguise either the long-ago date at which most of the writing was done or the arrant Canadianism of its epilogue. It gives me very great satisfaction to have by convention a page on which to at least shadow forth my debts. While solitude is balm to the writer of a fat and obsessive book, it is not enough; one needs one's community to fend off the ghosts, and I have been very happy in mine.

Victoria College
Toronto

Part One

One   The Pastoral Landscape

The gladsome shepherds on the mountain side,
Array'd in all their rural pride,
Exalt the festive note,
Inviting Echo from her inmost grot—
But ah! the landscape glows with fainter light,
It darkens, swims and flies for ever from my sight.
                                                   —James Beattie

Goethe's play *Torquato Tasso*, 1789, handles several suggestive motifs, most of them gathered out of contemporary English poetry. These motifs, brought together for the first time by Goethe, seem intrinsically related, and make up a complex that is pastoral-elegiac in its nature as well as in its background, as will be seen in the next chapter when the play is discussed in detail. Goethe apparently realized certain implications in contemporary English elegy before the English themselves did; the next generation of English poets were fully aware of them. All the motifs in question were repeatedly worked over by Romantic writers, and survive, often with startling modifications, through the nineteenth century and even into our own, shape-changing as they go. Without attributing to Goethe or his play any direct historical influence, we can still say that Tasso as web-spinner becomes the spider artist, mad scientist, or demon magician; that the "treasure" he seeks becomes the secret of life, alchemical or scientific; that the princess he loves becomes the soulmate-figure, whether phantom, dummy, or fatal woman; and that the play's setting of Belriguardo becomes the unstable paradise, the palace of art or house built on water.

The feature in *Tasso* closest to the tradition of pastoral elegy is the metaphorical setting, shifting from the garden scene via river and wilderness to the destructive element of the sea. One might say that a drowning is almost the standard pastoral catastrophe, thinking of Ophelia, Jonson's Earine (*The Sad Shepherd*), and Lycidas. Not, it is true, in Spenser, who prefers irruptions of boars and pirates, on the model of Greek romance and of the myth of Adonis: the "rough boar" chained under the mountain in the Gardens of Adonis is the destructive principle of Spenser's Eden. In "Lycidas," the presence of the "western sea" of death balances and even threatens the security of the inland pastoral life Milton depicts. In *Paradise*

3

Lost the pastoral scene is carried back to its biblical archetype, the myth of Eden, and the forces threatening it are symbolized by water. The Flood in Milton is a later and final version of the fall of man, but its occurrence is already suggested in the Garden, both in the night of storm following the tasting of the apple and in the storm of tears in which the guilty couple indulge. Their recovery from it is accompanied by a simile recalling the landing of Deucalion and Pyrrha following the deluge that destroyed their world.

Water of course has its place in the smiling pastoral scene, which it nourishes and freshens; it may be in fact the source of life, the fountain in the garden. Milton, in accordance with Ovid's order of the elements,[1] in *Paradise Lost* places it beneath:

> Southward through Eden went a River large,
> Nor chang'd his course, but through the shaggie hill
> Pass'd underneath ingulft; for God had thrown
> That Mountain as his Garden mould high rais'd
> Upon the rapid current, which through veins
> Of porous Earth with kindly thirst updrawn
> Rose a fresh Fountain, and with many a rill
> Waterd the Garden . . .
>
> [IV. 223-30]

He elsewhere uses the same order with some point, as in Book Nine. Eve has dreamed of flying, which means mounting above her place in the chain of being: when Adam tastes the apple, she and he "swim in mirth" (1009),[2] implying that in fact they have moved downwards. Or, to put it another way, that the inferior element has risen:

> They sate them down to weep, nor onely Teares
> Raind at thir Eyes, but high Winds worse within
> Began to rise, high Passions, Anger, Hate,
> Mistrust, Suspicion, Discord, and shook sore
> Thir inward State of Mind, calm Region once
> And full of Peace, now tost and turbulent:
> For Understanding rul'd not, and the Will
> Heard not her lore, both in subjection now
> To sensual Appetite, who from beneathe
> Usurping over sovran Reason claimd
> Superior sway. . . .
>
> [IX. 1121-31]

That is, the rebellion of Appetite over Will and its controlling power of Reason or Understanding is compared to the threatening of a "calm Region" by tempest and flood—the fate that eventually overtakes Eden. This theme (ultimately biblical) of the need for control of the waters, associated with disorder and passion, is prominent also in *The Faerie Queene*,[3] *The Tempest*, and "Lycidas." Controlled and kept in their proper place, the waters are a source of life and power; if they break out, they can only destroy.

In *Paradise Lost*, settings are symbolic: beings inhabit the places appropriate to their natures, and outward worlds are projections of inner states. The order of heaven reflects that of the mind of God, and the beings next down in order from the heavenly spirits inhabit the next highest place. The order of the garden is a paradigm of Adam's state: the high point of the created world, founded in the material elements and looking toward heaven. It is in fact an image of his physical and moral nature, and at the same time a microcosm of the hierarchy of settings in the poem.

sky	heaven	reason
garden	unfallen world	will
mountain	fallen world, chaos	appetite, passion
river	hell	illusion, dream

The hierarchy corresponds to that of the elements: fire, air, earth, water. We can add: summer, spring, autumn ("fall"), winter.

"The" pastoral setting of *Paradise Lost*, as next under heaven, occupies the second level of our diagram. However, the entire scheme of locales of the poem can be seen in pastoral terms, on the four levels indicated. Heaven, the source and pattern of all the good things in the lower worlds, has the best of pastoral as of other treasures: the city that is at the same time a garden, the river of life, the immortal plants of the amaranth and later the tree of life. Below it is the happy garden of the Earthly Paradise, the arch-typical *locus amoenus*. It enjoys a perpetual spring and spontaneous fruitfulness, and is a place of happy love where the animals are at peace with one another and the rose blooms without a thorn. Below it in the poem's scheme is the fallen world, sharing something of the nature of Chaos. This is the wilderness where Adam labors for his bread, where nature is fruitful only under coercion, tares and thistles mix with the wheat, and the weather is more often bad than good. Below that again is the landscape of hell, hostile to life, where existence is a torment. Its appropriate and only vegetable life is the tree of death or delusion bearing apples of Sodom.

The top and bottom states, heaven and hell, are beyond time, for better or worse as the case may be. The unfallen and fallen worlds are ruled by the course of the seasons and the other natural cycles, again for better or worse: "better" in Paradise, with its alternation merely of seedtime and harvest, spring and autumn dancing hand in hand without the harsh extremes of summer and winter. Time here is experienced as a creative rhythm of energy and repose. In the fallen world there is more awareness of the harshness of the course of time, the presence of labor, pain, age, and death.

This scheme is derived from *Paradise Lost* viewed in its pastoral aspect; at the same time, the pastoral elements in the poem naturally rest on the conventions of literary pastoral, so that the scheme should carry over. In fact it does, at any rate by sections. Milton is nearly alone in his heaven; that belongs to the level of pure myth that few have attempted, and comes straight from the Bible, mostly the last chapter of Revelation. Milton's second level is the more familiar literary landscape of ideal or romance-pastoral, typified by happy love, spontaneous song, and the sympathy of nature. It is here that we tend to locate the home ground of pastoral. It is the fruitful, benevolent world indicated in the Song of Songs, Prospero's wedding-masque, the "broad fields of the sky" in *Comus*. It is there that Sidney's shepherd-boy is heard piping as if he should never be old, and the Passionate Shepherd issues his invitation. Raleigh's Nymph in reply-ing shows herself a "realist"; but then she belongs to the next world down, where nature is no longer in sympathy with man and we are more conscious of the dark or declining side of the cycles of nature, of love, of human life.

In the two middle worlds, what we might call the levels of fair-weather and foul-weather pastoral, there are few clear extremes of good and evil. The course of the seasons that is their governing condition of life is am-biguous, bringing pleasure or grief according to one's standpoint. The poet who asks, "If winter comes, can spring be far behind?" is taking the hopeful view, whereas the chorus at the end of *Hellas* asks spring not to come in order to spare us the following winter, in a pessimistic application of the cyclical pattern of nature to the life of civilizations. On the lowest level, time expresses grief as a fixed condition. In the world of the Waste Land, April is the cruellest month because the outward renewal of the earth is a mockery to the man whose state is spiritual death. The hells of pastoral, where not theologically conceived, usually feature those aspects of nature farthest from the happy and fertile: desert, sea, icecap. Their vegetation is selected on the same principle: the pricklypear, Cain's thornbush, the bloody rose of *Maud*, the upas, the gallows tree glooming over a blasted heath.

As we progress down the series of levels, we notice an increasing alienation between man and his object-world, whose relation, with Na-ture as the object, is one of the things pastoral appears to be about. On the top level there is total mythical identity: the living water and tree are identified with the blood and body of the God-Man who is "all in all"—there is no "outside world" at all. This means, for example, that in an unequivocal heaven there is no echo. The next level is distinguished by the sympathy of Nature—"fanning their joyous Leaves to thy soft layes." The third level can be described perhaps as that of "sensibility." Nature and man no longer run on parallel lines and reflect each other's joys and sorrows; yet man is moved by a Nature that has become mysterious and has moments at which it appears to "speak" or convey significance to him, if he could only understand its language. On the bottom level man's situation is that of solitude utter and complete, a parody of the pure self-completeness of the top level; his state excludes, rather than includes, a Nature that has become alien, hostile, or dead.

Where the relationship of man and object is seen in terms of love the terms are analogous—"Wyf is mannes garden," as Chaucer says. Again we meet identity on the top level: the divine bride as the Church is also the divine body. The idyllic pastoral scene is usually characterized by happy love, the foul-weather scene by unhappy, owing to natural conditions like the limitations of the flesh and the imperfections of human communication. The hells of love—states of possessiveness, jealousy, parasitic self-love like Satan's for Sin—everything that makes the object *mere* object—lead to a solitude that is not just physical aloneness but ultimately the egoist's gnawing of his own heart.[4]

The state of man himself varies according to the level he is on, though putting it that way we reverse the real state of things. The top level, the world of pure myth, is the world of the god, the full embodiment of all the powers of life. The idyllic pastoral scene is the place of the innocent and youthful. On the foul-weather level,[5] innocence gives place to ignorance and wandering confusion. At the bottom of the scale, the protagonist is regularly outlaw or exile, fleeing from or towards an object of remorse or of delusive desire.

As the action of *Paradise Lost* would suggest, our diagram is not static, and the action of a work may consist in movement from level to level. Pastoral elegy, and the forms we are taking as related, usually involve a passage from an ideal or sympathetic scene to an unsympathetic or definitely hostile one: from Peele Castle in a calm to Peele Castle in a storm, or, to note a pastoral strain in an unpastoral work, from the first stanza of "The flowers that bloom in the spring, tra-la" to the second. The transition is usually from level two to three or four, and can conveniently be called "the pastoral fall."

Traditional pastoral elegy, reduced to its barest essentials, tends to be a lament for a "fall," analogous to the Fall of Christian teaching if not usually expressed in religious terms. The shepherd-mourner complains of the loss of a particular harmonious relation of man to the natural order that is regularly symbolized by the presence in the pastoral scene of the Muses and other divine or imaginative figures, by the sympathy of Nature to man's joys and griefs, and by the companionability of Echo. With the death of the person mourned for, all this is lost as well: the gods desert the fields, song no longer rises spontaneously to the shepherd's lips, wolves threaten the flock, and the weather takes a turn towards winter.

The reconciliation will not come until a different kind of harmony has been reached and the poet is able to see Nature, not as complete and self-sufficient as she seemed before, but in relation to a larger order that is more adequate to human desires and capacities—ordinarily that of grace or its secular analogue, art.

To illustrate briefly from "Lycidas," which for our purposes can be taken as definitive. The death of Lycidas is compared to various kinds of natural blight that affect the landscape, which itself is characterized by "Woods, and desert Caves" ("woods" in Milton almost invariably has overtones of desolation), the pastoral music and its response are now lacking, and the traditional question "Where were ye Nymphs . . . ?" becomes a question about the presence and even the efficacy of pastoral inspiration. The poet at the beginning complains that his garland, the poetic tribute, is plucked "with forc'd fingers rude," and only after the consolation is he seen "with eager thought warbling." The pastoral scene at its most bleak and forsaken is described by St. Peter, who implies that this will be its condition now that the good pastor is gone. The poem's nadir is "the bottom of the monstrous world," the depths of the sea. Consolation comes about "through the dear might of him that walk'd the waves," transforming the waters of death (via the ocean of the sun's repose, "other streams," and "Nectar pure") into those of life and comfort, renewing in the mourner's sight the woods and pastures of earth.

Man's alienation from the life of nature has been a consistent theme of pastoral elegy, beginning with the first pastoral lament for a figure not half-divine like Adonis (or Theocritus's Daphnis) but human, the anonymous elegy for the poet Bion: "Alas, when the mallows and green parsley and curly-tendrilled anise perish in the garden, they live once more and grow up another year; but we men . . . " (99–104).[6] The theme, more or less developed from this point, remains a feature of pastoral elegy down to the "Epitaphium Damonis," where Milton devotes a stanza to it (94–111): the birds and beasts, if they lose a mate, seek out another from the flock, but we men are a hard race. . . .

In the First Idyll of Theocritus, the complaint is spoken by the dying shepherd Daphnis himself and consists mostly of his farewell to the pastoral scene, ending with an *adynaton,* or catalogue of impossibilities, that amounts here to a curse of disorder and confusion: "Now violets bear, ye brambles, ye thorns bear violets . . . . Let the stag drag down the hounds, let owls . . . contend in song with nightingales" (132–36). Virgil adapts this motif in the lament for Daphnis, Eclogue 5, but has naturalized it by combining it with what was originally a different theme—the land's showing the marks of human neglect occasioned by unhappy love, beginning in the Eleventh Idyll of Theocritus and developed in Virgil's Second Eclogue; in the Fifth, after the gods leave the fields: "oft in the furrows to which we have committed great grains of barley, unfruitful darnel and barren wild oats spring; instead of the gentle violet, instead of the bright narcissus, the thistle rises up, and the thorn with prickly spikes" (36–39).[7]

To the desolation of the pastoral landscape we can relate the theme of its loss. In the Tenth Eclogue, as in the First Idyll, it is again the languishing swain who speaks: Gallus renounces the pastoral-poetic landscape of Arcadia to wander an exile in harsher climes, enduring the frosts of Thrace and the cruel sun of Ethiopia. The Tenth is the last of the Eclogues, and shows, not a death, but essentially the loss of the pastoral scene, here brought about through love. This loss is not, as in the ritual laments from which the form originates, a yearly recurring phase of the generative and undifferentiated love that sustains flocks and crops alike, but a personal and final event. Already there is present the note of nostalgia that later comes into almost invariable association with pastoral poetry—"Nymphs and Shepherds dance no more," "Nous n'irons plus aux bois, les lauriers sont coupés":

> "Yet you, O Arcadians," he said, "will sing of this to your mountains, Arcadians who alone are skilful in song. O how softly would my bones then rest, if ever your pipes should tell of my loves! And would that I had been one of you, a keeper of one of your flocks or a dresser of your ripe grapes!... Then my dear would be lying beside me...."   [31–36, 40]

The theme of the loss or desolation of the pastoral scene, whatever its actual origin, soon finds its mythical archetype in the passing of the Golden Age, the perpetual spring when the earth was fertile without man's labor and man and the animals all lived at peace. Something of the process can be seen in Virgil, as in the Fifth Eclogue. In the Fourth the *adynaton*, equivocal in Theocritus and negative elsewhere in Virgil, takes a positive form:

> The earth shall begin to pour forth ... without cultivation her simple gifts ... , the herds shall not fear the mighty lions ... , the serpent shall perish, and the treacherous poison-plant.... Next ... the soil shall not feel the hoe, nor the vineyard the pruning-hook ... and wool shall not learn to counterfeit various colours, but of himself the ram in the meadows shall now begin to change the whiteness of his fleece for sweetly-blushing crimson, and for saffron dye; scarlet of its own accord shall dress the browsing lambs. [18–45]

To all aspects of the theme close parallels are to be found in the Bible. Job protesting his innocence says, "If my land cry against me, or that the furrows likewise thereof complain; ... Let thistles grow instead of wheat, and cockle instead of barley" (31 : 38, 40). Isaiah prophesying the coming of the Messiah declares that the city of Bozrah shall become a place of thorns, nettles, and brambles, while on the other hand "the desert shall rejoice, and blossom as the rose" (34:13, 35:1). The focus of such expressions is the biblical myth of the loss of Eden and the cursing of the ground, corresponding to the end of the Golden Age, and the promise of its eventual restoration to man.

The Genesis account of the loss of Eden is twofold. First God pronounces to Adam in Eden the curse on the ground: "Cursed is the ground for thy sake; . . . Thorns also and thistles shall it bring forth to thee." Then Adam is expelled from the garden, "to till the ground whence he was taken." Thus the garden is first desolated, then shut away from man. So in Milton: first within the garden itself there comes a rainstorm and dismal weather, and the beasts begin to prey on one another, and then Adam and his wife are dismissed into the "waste Wilderness" of the outside world. Milton exploits also a third possibility, whereby the garden is afterwards ravaged by the Flood and its original site becomes "an Iland salt and bare" (XI.834); this underlines Milton's point that the true Eden is not a place in the physical world but a state within the breast of man.

Thus pastoral elegy and its mythical archetypes turn on the juxtaposition of two worlds. The world of the unspoiled pastoral setting with which man is in harmony reflects his own tranquillity, and is in fact a projection or outward realization of his inward state. Following the crisis or catastrophe, the scene comes to mirror his own desolation or, more radically, to appear unfeeling, alien, terrible, or dead. The passage from a sympathetic to an unsympathetic natural world is the pastoral "fall," and once it has come about, the desolated present is seen as the real world and the idyllic past rejected as illusory or a dream.

To the Christian Renaissance poet, "sympathetic" Nature means an unfallen or Eden-world where man participates in a divinely ordered reality, expressed in spontaneous song and happy love and all the blessings that characterize fair-weather pastoral. It is that transcendent order of Nature that the artist seeks to imitate or to recreate, the source not so much of things as of standards and ideals, fertile and fertilizing. Foul-weather pastoral, on the other hand, where "time leads the flocks from field to fold," is the world of the infirmities produced by the Fall, the real as distinct from the idyllic or ideal order of God's original creation, and is typified mythically by such incidents as the rape of Philomela and the *sparagmos* of the divine poet—"the young man mutilated, / The torn girl trembling by the millstream," as *Murder in the Cathedral* puts it.

We have already noted the way in which the order of the Miltonic pastoral setting is connected with that of the human faculties—explicitly in *Paradise Lost*, implicitly elsewhere. For Milton, the powers of inspiration and insight come to man from above and inform his own highest powers. As the work of the Holy Spirit, they are man's link with heaven. The hermetic student of "Il Penseroso" speculates on immortality "in some high lonely Towr"; the scene of "Lycidas" is crowned by the hills of the Muses, the Druids, and the sentinel Angel; the mount of Eden faces the gate of Heaven and is joined to it by the angelic stairway. In fact Eden is an unusually favored place, being inaccessible from below. Following the Fall, the direct communication of Earth and Heaven is broken off and the causeway linking Earth to Hell comes into use—so to speak, the upper gate is closed up and a lower one opened.

This is the usual pattern of the pastoral catastrophe: the forces of disorder and death invade from below, and personages embodying man's link with higher powers—Astraea, the fairies of England, or most typically the Muses—depart. At the opening of "Lycidas," not only has the shepherd's premature death broken the ordinary rhythm of nature, but poetry itself has somehow failed the poet. It is pastoral music—"Shepherds ear"—that the loss most strikingly affects. Moreover the "Nymphs," here clearly Muses, were absent at the time of the catastrophe, and even if they had been present would have been powerless to prevent it: a suggestion which foreshadows Milton's later dismissal of the Classical Muse as "an empty dreame." This first part of "Lycidas" ends with the first of the poem's consolations, the words of Phoebus reconciling the poet with the powers of a classical-poetic heaven. As a consolation it is incomplete, and cannot keep his thoughts from straying a second time out to sea. The second consolation, that of the flowery vales led on by the Sicilian Muse, is similarly incomplete, even faintly delusive, and is followed by the deepest of the poem's plunges into the sea. The last consolation, the only complete one, washes away the taint of death and salt water, makes heaven the apotheosis of the happy pastoral scene, and suggests that it too is a place of spontaneous song. The small enclosed classical-pastoral inland scene of the opening was threatened by its outside opposing element, the destructive sea. The consolation introduced by the cycle of the "day-star" offers a larger harmony including the threatening element as a part of its wholeness, and provisionally binds up the breach caused by the Fall and the attendant facts of mortality. The traditional guardianship of fields and flocks becomes one of "the shore" and of wanderers in the perilous flood: the whole lower world is now seen as, metaphorically, both of these. The sea is the world of all the forces of time and death that threaten man with loss of faith or poet with loss of inspiration. Thus the link with Heaven is restored and even strengthened by a truer understanding of the place of the pastoral scene and its limited heaven in the scheme of Providence.

Pastoral, centering as it does on a scene innocent or unfallen, tends to appear one of the most artificial of literary modes, or at very least the product of a deliberate restriction of experience. As Milton in the first part of "Lycidas" lets us see that the happy pastoral scene is not really self-sufficient, and in his description of Eden subtly foreshadows the approaching Fall, pastoral elegy can exploit the limitation and fragility of the pastoral scene, allowing it to be broken in on by an element it has excluded, usually the fact of death, which it has to assimilate before its wholeness can be restored in an expanded form. After the catastrophe the original wholeness and completeness of the scene may appear as delusive, and the restored order itself perhaps as temporary and provisional, maintained by Providence or faith or will or art until the boar breaks his chain or the raging waters have their day. The question about all paradises is the one Satan asks as he watches Adam and Eve: "And do they onely stand By Ignorance?"—pessimistically answered by Gray in "Eton College." Not until the innocents stand by enlightened reason, which Adam was always free to do, can they be assured of a paradise perhaps invisible but at least not hollow.

If we turn now from Miltonic pastoral to "Kubla Khan," we find a comparable order. Kubla's walled paradise is situated on a hill, with the pleasure-dome at the center, midway between fountain and caves, and presumably crowning all. (I am assuming, with whatever physical improbability, that the river is "flung up" on one side of the hilltop and descends on the other.) The sacred river, traversing the hill, is thrown up from and descends back into a bottom level of caverns and "lifeless ocean." The pleasure-dome is a microcosm of the whole, with river and "caves of ice" at its foot and imprisoned sunlight above. The river embodies the life of the whole scene and supplies its music; it also seems linked with the "waning moon" rather than the sunlit side of the picture—the demonic desolation of the "chasm," the instability of Kubla's triumph over the elements, the prophecies of war. If the river sustains the scene, it is equally a threat to it. At the end of the poem, although we have been shown no catastrophe, the vision has been snatched away, and the poet implies his inability to recapture it.

The vision of "Kubla Khan" is largely built up out of Miltonic echoes, but its relation to Milton's Eden is somewhat ironic. "Cambalu, seat of Cathaian Can" is one of the kingdoms of a fallen earth that Michael shows Adam, and Coleridge connects it with the delusive paradise of Mount Amara (which becomes that also of *Rasselas*). The placid "haunted stream" of "L'Allegro," where throughout the eighteenth century poets had continued to court inspiration,[8] becomes the "romantic chasm" where woman wails for her demon lover. Milton inserts a demon lover in his description of Eden, in the reference to Asmodeus and "the Spouse of Tobits Son" (IV.166–71), which hints at Satan's coming seduction of Eve: in "Kubla Khan" the victim is accustomed and dependent. The "cedarn cover" is also Miltonic (cf. *PL* IX.434–35), and connected with Adam's lament at the end of Book Nine:

> O might I here
> In solitude live savage . . .
>   . . . Cover me ye Pines,
> Ye Cedars . . .   [1084–85, 1088–89][9]

The difference from Milton's world is apparent in the linking of "holy" with "savage," "enchanted," "haunted" and "demon lover," and in the founding of any kind of order on so mantic and underworld a force as this particular river, forced up from below, not "updrawn." The stress is less on an upper world of illumination than on a lower one of passion and instinct, and the "inspiration" of such a scene belongs more to a possessed sibyl than to a serene Muse. As it appears at the end, making the beholders cry, "Beware," it seems close to both magic and mania.

This difference might be described as a matter of "Kubla Khan's" romantic primitivism. Such primitivism as Milton shows is religious, not romantic:[10] to him the "savage" is the fallen, inseparably attainted with a melancholy deriving from the sense of glories lost.

> How shall I behold the face
> Henceforth of God or Angel, earst with joy
> And rapture so oft beheld? those heav'nly shapes
> Will dazzle now this earthly, with thir blaze
> Insufferably bright. O might I here
> In solitude live savage, in some glade
> Obscur'd, where highest woods, impenetrable
> To Starr or Sunlight, spread thir umbrage broad
> And brown as Evening: Cover me ye Pines,
> Ye Cedars, with innumerable boughs
> Hide me, where I may never see them more.   [IX.1080–90]

Again:

> Those Leaves
> They gatherd, broad as Amazonian Targe,
> And with what skill they had, together sowd,
> To gird thir waste—vain Covering if to hide
> Thir guilt and dreaded shame; O how unlike
> To that first naked Glorie. Such of late
> Columbus found th'American, so girt
> With featherd Cincture, naked else and wilde
> Among the Trees on Iles and woodie Shores.   [1110–18]

The Miltonic savage has no romantic nobility, but much rather a furtively skulking secrecy, induced by guilt and shame. Guilt and shame if present in Coleridge's scene have a certain fascination and even splendor, decking the heir of Tartar warlords. Kubla's enclosed and threatened paradise is what Milton's explicitly is not—the tyrant's solitude, an ironic form of the *locus amoenus* constantly to recur in nineteenth-century literature.[11] His power and his knowledge, so far from coming from above, rest on an underworld force that is inscrutable, unpredictable, and potentially immensely destructive.

We may say generally that such a diagram corresponds to the changed world picture of Romanticism at large, a change deriving largely from Rousseau. He described a happy "natural" state of mankind, not withdrawn into heaven or sequestered away by an angelic guard, but buried beneath the weight of artificial social institutions and expecting its chance to break up through, like spring in the shepherd chorus in *Prometheus Unbound* (end of act I). We may compare the diagram of that poem: above, Jupiter reigns among his flunkies in the vulture-delighting sky; the next level is Prometheus's place of torment, and below that is the Caucasian vale and the natural life of earth; at the very bottom is the oracular pit of Demogorgon, the ambiguous sustaining power.[12] Such a change in emphasis follows in part also from the "pre-Romantic" interest in the oracular, the bardic—an altogether more visceral view of the imagination than would have made sense to Milton. A generation of *poètes maudits* has replaced the Apollonian spotless robe with the ivy wreath of insobriety and the gestures of frenzy; hence, perhaps, the appeal of Tasso's distresses not only to Goethe but from Shelley and Byron down to Browning. The poetic art is like Goethe's Pandora in the "Elegy": "so rich in gifts, in perils richer far."

The original central figure in the literary tradition of pastoral elegy is Adonis, the dying and reviving god of the natural cycle, beloved and mourned by the great goddess of fertility. Partly through the literary figment of Theocritus's Daphnis, the shepherd and sweet singer destroyed by the same goddess out of jealousy, the archetype modulates to the divine poet Orpheus torn to pieces by angry women in a landscape already desolated by the loss of Eurydice. Orpheus is central in Virgilian and Miltonic pastoral elegy, and with him the form takes on a new inwardness. The identity in his myth of mourning poet and the one mourned for clarifies and justifies the old inclination of the pastoral-elegiac poet in another's fate to weep his own. In literary terms, the complaint that Milton in"Lycidas" talks more about himself than about his "subject" means that he is stressing the core of the pastoral-elegiac lament, the fall of the pastoral landscape, for which the death of Lycidas is the particular occasion. From the publication of "Lycidas" it is just a matter of time until the dead shepherd drops out and only the mourner is left, and that mourner specifically a poet exiled from a paradise that was also the hill of the Muses. The identity of mourner and mourned-for, whether in a religious sense or in the community of art, towards which the form tends is appropriate to a mode turning on the mythos of a fall, whether Adam's or another's. Once this identity becomes established, the fictional situation of one man dead and another lamenting him is no longer necessary, and the pastoral-elegiac mode is free to detach itself from pastoral elegy as a form. If this is granted, we can characterize as "pastoral-elegiac" a number of works that certainly are not pastoral elegies, notably "Ode: Intimations," "Kubla Khan," "Dejection," *Alastor*, and some that are not even poems, including *Werther* and (up to a point) *Tasso*. In all of them we meet the Poet (or artist) lamenting his own desolation, partly in terms of his relation to a landscape.

In Renaissance and older pastoral elegy, the consolation usually restores to the mourner what he has lost, through the agency of natural recurrence: "Farewell, dear Adonis, and may you find us all flourishing when you come again next year" (Theocritus); of art: "To others didst thou leave thy wealth, to me thy minstrelsy" (elegy on Bion); or of religious faith: "Lycidas your sorrow is not dead." In Romantic elegiac poems, although these themes may be touched on, usually the poet insists that some essential element has departed from his world and cannot be restored. In "Ode: Intimations" as in *Adonais*, though "desolation" is too strong a word, the natural scene has lost in stature, while storm dominates the endings of "Elegiac Stanzas" ("Peele Castle") and "Dejection."

It is Milton who makes another pastoral development possible, the interiorization of the outward pastoral scene. He does this in his treatment of the theme of Eden in *Paradise Lost*, where the unfallen pastoral setting moves inward when its physical embodiment is laid waste. Thus Michael, dismissing Adam to the wilderness, can promise him "a paradise within thee, happier farr" than the original outward one. Henceforth the pastoral realm is most fruitfully understood as a mental, almost a psychological, realm of happiness, distinct from particular time and place, and the object of every man's effort and desire. For Milton the context is the fully religious one of obedience, self-discipline, and the direction of Providence. The Romantic writers, as we should expect, are interested more in the individual and his own creative powers.

In Romantic literature, the religious context having dropped into the background, the distinction between two worlds is less that of unfallen and fallen than of *natura naturans* and *naturata*—a subjective realm of divinely creative powers in which the poet participates with the great force of Nature, and an object realm of a nature cruel, mindless, or dead, from which the unearthly light has passed away and in which the poet no longer sees any guarantee of his inspiration. Hence the focus is regularly on the passage from childhood, innocent vision, and spontaneous creativity to self-conscious adulthood with the ambiguities, confusions, and inhibitions that attend it: from the *Songs of Innocence* to those of *Experience,* from Goethe's joyful Musensohn to Hölderlin's troubled singer of "Hyperions Schicksalslied." It is this passage that most usually constitutes the Romantic "fall." However, although in terms of ideas the context has changed, the essential pattern of images remains the same.

In what we are calling Romantic elegiac poems and romances, the protagonist is not Man as such, or Adam, but Poet. Nor, although he may have connections with both, is he exactly an Adonis or Orpheus. Adonis, the fertility daemon torn by the forces of winter and death from the life-goddess Venus, is a comparatively simple figure. As an image of the self's relation to Nature, he represents instinctive man without self-awareness, walking blindly through the round of natural process. Some features of his myth are shared with that of Orpheus, a more developed and individualized figure and one not obviously attached to an annual ritual. Orpheus's bereavement, failure, and death are particular and unique events, and he suffers the agony of a man, not the pathos of a daemon. Nature in his myth is not single and all-encircling but separated into upper and lower realms, one of order and harmony, soon lost, and the savage one that replaces it. Eurydice, the nymph of flowering meadows destroyed by a snake that lay among the flowers, is another Proserpina, whose loss desolates the scene like the fall of Eve. For the Renaissance writer, Orpheus in his desolation is still the divine poet, charged with an ethical burden: he is the man overwhelmed by a personal winter who remembers the eternal spring of the Golden Age and is able by his song to recreate its condition around him, taming the savage hearts of beasts and men. Thus he is the type of the poet's eternal task, and the figure of Eurydice, standing for the lost ideal that inspires his mournful song, embodies the harmony of man with a divinely ordered Nature.

The protagonist of our third phase of pastoral-elegiac is the Poet as exile and wanderer through mournful scenes: if an Orpheus, one overwhelmed by his failure and threatened with silence. The type has been characterized as "the gloomy egoist":[13] we shall call him by the name of Narcissus, the beautiful youth who fell into indolence, madness, and death through gazing at his own likeness in a pool. Narcissus's error is the passive and sterile acceptance of shadow for substance, and he becomes a parable of the self-absorbed artist who falls into doting on his own powers until they become sapped. A long history of commentary on the myth, including its exegesis by Plotinus as representing the fall of spirit into the flux of matter (*Enneads* i.6.8), precedes this development, which is seen in English literature perhaps most clearly in Blake, Shelley, and Poe.

Unlike the myths of Adonis and Orpheus, that of Narcissus has nothing to do with recurrent ritual acts. In its classic formulation, that of the *Metamorphoses*, Ovid may well be influenced almost equally by the primitive folklore theme of the water fairy who seizes man's soul in his reflection and leaves him without it to die, familiar in German Romantic elaboration, and by philosophical parables about the soul's descent into matter. Once Ovid has introduced her, the nymph Echo standing neglected beside the youth is an integral part of the myth, and of its exegesis. Compare, for example, the remark of the Christian Neoplatonist Landino that Narcissus is the man who yearns after earthly beauty, the shadow, while his own soul, the substance, fades away within him. [14] Landino's explanation goes back to ancient sources: Narcissus has quickly become a parable of the vain pursuit of spiritual qualities in the external world of Nature, whose apparent responsiveness can offer only a deluding reflection of himself, no fit object for love. It is, by the way, substantially Landino's account of Narcissus that is given so late as 1810–12 by the German Romantic mythographer Friedrich Creuzer in his *Symbolik und Mythologie der alten Völker*. [15]

Adonis, tossed about by forces more powerful than himself, is not the hero of any quest. Orpheus has a quest in his search for the lost Eurydice, but as is well known he fails in it. Narcissus in Christian and Platonic exegesis seeks vainly in the outward, material world the spiritual reality; in the poetic tradition of modern Europe he seeks the springs of individuality, creation, love. Led on by a deluding vision, of himself or of an ideal companion, he is engaged in a false quest which eventually weakens and destroys him. As a philosophical or a religious parable, Narcissus represents the soul's subjection to matter; a later age makes of him a parable of art, representing something like the passive surrender of the imagination to the natural world, the ascribing to outward nature of powers that belong to the creative mind.

In all three of the myths discussed, incidentally, water is associated with the pastoral catastrophe. The river Adonis runs red with blood at the annual death of the god, and his ritual requires that his body or an effigy of it, along with growing flowers and corn, be thrown with lamentations into the sea, to be drawn out with rejoicing far away. The scattered limbs of Orpheus were thrown into running water and borne "down the swift Hebrus to the Lesbian shore." To Narcissus, the water is itself the dangerous element, and in all versions but the sophisticated ones of Ovid and Pausanias, it is by drowning that he meets his death.

In relation to the scheme or cosmology of pastoral, then, we can say, first, that the pastoral world of which Adonis is the embodiment is a unified one, its contrasts belonging to the course of the seasons, and its destructive features being part of the wholeness of the landscape. In Orpheus's story the snake among the flowers plays a similar part to the boar in Adonis's; but we see Orpheus after his intensified loss as the inhabitant of a different kind of scene, having exchanged meadows for mountains and spring for an endless winter. Narcissus's world is again single, but contrast has concentrated itself into ambiguity. The hero's egregious trait, his beauty, is what destroys him; and whether the scene is delightful or malignant cannot be objectively decided, as it depends on the character of the person for whom it forms a setting. In the Romantic works we shall look at, landscape is charged with a significance that rests in its beholder: "In our life alone does Nature live," we can say, or more briefly, "The difference to me!"

Two   Tasso: *A Late-Pastoral Design*

> *... Torquatum cepit Leonora Poëtam,*
> *Cujus ab insano cessit amore furens.*
>
> —*John Milton*
>
> *Are the green fields gone? What do they here?*
>
> —*Herman Melville*

Goethe's *Torquato Tasso* is a simply constructed play, adhering strictly to the unities of place, time, and action. The scene is Belriguardo, a country residence built by the d'Este family and at present in the possession of Tasso's patrons, Alfons the Duke of Ferrara and his sister, the princess Leonore. The remaining two characters are Antonio, secretary of state and the duke's trusted friend, and the princess's confidante, Leonore Sanvitale.

The play's five characters show a certain symmetry in their rôles. The impression given is not that of a group surrounding the central character Tasso. Rather, the central position is that occupied by Alfons and his sister, supported respectively by Antonio and Leonore, and this grouping provides the center towards and away from which Tasso in the course of the action moves. The four constitute the inner circle, troubled by no disharmony; Tasso, their dependent, is both socially and temperamentally an outsider.

The action is a very simple one. Tasso at the opening of the play has completed his great work *Jerusalem Delivered*, and he presents it to his patrons and enjoys a brief moment of congratulation and felicity. The scene is interrupted by the arrival of Antonio, who has successfully completed a mission for the duke and in his turn is congratulated. In the second act, in the course of conversations with the princess and Antonio, Tasso indicates that Antonio's arrival has disturbed him, effects a closer rapprochement with the princess on the basis of a hitherto undeclared sympathy between them, to please her tries to begin a friendship with Antonio, ends by picking a quarrel with him, and is confined to his own room by Alfons. In the third act, Tasso's case is discussed at length by Leonore and the distressed princess. They agree that Leonore is first to bring about a reconciliation between Tasso and Antonio and then to take Tasso away with her until he has recovered himself, and she accordingly

wins over the indignant Antonio. In the fourth act she addresses herself to Tasso, who pretends to believe her; when Antonio comes to see
him, as a test of friendship he makes him promise to ask the duke to let
Tasso go to Rome. Alfons in the fifth act reluctantly agrees, but refuses
to return Tasso his manuscript for correction. Tasso, whose mental state
has been becoming more and more unstable, imagines that Antonio has
played him false and influenced the duke against him. The princess
comes to see him and expresses her compassion and grief for his condition, and he, overcome by intense feeling, tries to take her in his arms:
she repels him and hurries away. The last scene is between Tasso and
Antonio. Tasso undergoes one final revulsion, seeing now even the princess as deceiving and corrupted. Emerging from this most severe of all
his crises, he declares that he has now lost or ruined everything but
his God-given poetic power, and in a final gesture he embraces Antonio.

The characters of the play are carefully grouped according to a principle
of complement. This is perhaps evident from the opening speeches:
Leonore is amused to notice that while she herself has woven a garland
of flowers to deck the bust of Ariosto, the princess has prepared one of
laurel and honors Virgil. The princess and her brother belong respectively
to the realms of contemplation and action, the ideal and the practical,
the passive and the self-exerting. The two supporting figures are both
presented as types of the practical life, in order more effectively to iso-
late Tasso and the princess; but they also are complementary, in that
Antonio, like his master, is detached and entirely disinterested, sometimes to the point of seeming cold, whereas Leonore, plunged into and
deeply involved in the life around her, is dominated by self-interest. In
this she is a kind of reversed reflection of her mistress, seeing that the
princess, through her evident love for Tasso "interested" in his fate as
her brother is not, is at the same time committed by her strange temperament to absolute nonintervention.

The complementary relation of the princess and her brother is once
casually alluded to by him (I.ii.283–86): it is somewhat that of a moon and
a sun. Much more important, however, is that existing between Tasso
and Antonio, and once it is established we are never allowed to forget
it. Tasso himself first states it, early in the second act:

> He possesses,
> I well might say, all that I lack myself.   [II.i.943–44]

Leonore makes it more explicit:

> They are two men, I've long perceived it so,
> Whom Nature set at odds because she failed
> To mingle both their qualities in one.   [III.ii.1704–06]

The combination would have represented the ideal relationship of the contemplative spirit with the active, or, in Tasso's terms, of poet and hero; but as things are the two are bound to come again and again into conflict. Tasso's appeal in the second act for Antonio's friendship is on the basis of the lack in himself which he feels Antonio's stability and experience might enable him to make up; and when Antonio, clearly bewildered by his impetuosity, replies rather coolly, it is in terms of the difference between Tasso's poetic garland and the reward which crowns heroic endeavor (II.iii.1298–1302).

Tasso recognizes in the princess a poetic nature like his own. She is not his complement but his counterpart, though with important differences. She is an extraordinarily withdrawn figure, like Tasso participating only indirectly in the concerns of the world. Her way of life is made possible by her unusual gift of sympathy and by her capacity to demand nothing for herself, so that she is strong precisely where Tasso is weak. One might see in the princess an embodiment of Tasso's own ideals without his saving admixture of human weakness. She is more conscious of her principles than he and more consistent in them; at the same time her passions are more ambiguous than his, and her whole figure carries in its extreme refinement something almost morbid. Contrasted with her, besides the practical Leonore Sanvitale, is her sister, whose warmth and vitality and outward-goingness are frequently mentioned. A "veil" of ill health and emotional withdrawal hangs between the princess and the "bright colors" of the world (II.i.856–58), and fate has taken away from her the consolation of self-expression in her singing (III.ii.1806–16). This enforced silence seems the appropriate concomitant to her reserve and passivity, and suggests that it may indeed be Tasso's comparative weakness of character that will save him not only as man but even as poet.

It is at the opening of the play that Tasso and the princess are most clearly presented as counterparts. In the first scene, the princess talks about her own nonparticipating relation to life and then speaks of Tasso's elusiveness; Alfons enters, complaining that he can never find Tasso and that the poet's love of solitude should not go so far as to make him shun his friends, as he appears to. Tasso's ideal love described in the first scene, not so much attached to earthly forms as transfiguring them in the light of a spiritual love, is comparable to the princess's doctrine, described in act II, of a love based on *Entbehren*, renunciation. With this shared idealism we may associate Tasso's reluctance in I.iii to have his heavenly reward of poetic fame forced upon him in the form of a tangible (though symbolic) sign—the laurel wreath with which Alfons and the princess want to crown him, and which he at first refuses.

Tasso's consistency to his ideal principles in the first act, even though at least once it makes him speak in a way that comes close to raving, gives him a certain moral stature. It is when he departs from it in the sphere of love that we see his character as beginning to disintegrate. At first his relation to love is like his relation to heroism; he is able to comprehend and to glorify both through his poetry and seems not to need to desert his own realm of the ideal. Early in the second act (II.i.979-94) his words to the princess identifying the condition of the Golden Age with complete sexual freedom show that his attitude is changing. Here the moral superiority lies with the princess, who warns him that he is now in danger of sacrificing an inner good for an outward and less real one—of doing precisely the opposite of what his refusal of the garland signified.

The contrast between womanly and manly ideals that the princess goes on to outline (1024-47) turns on the theme of inner and outer worlds that is central to the play. The man's desires press outward into the wide expanses of the world, whereas the woman's, intensive rather than extensive, turn in upon a severely limited area of possible happiness. Men are slow to recognize the inward treasure of a woman's love, and once it is possessed it loses its value to them. Their choice is too lightly determined by outward qualities, good and bad, and they are rarely content to rest with what they have once gained. Since the play is less about sexual love than about the relation of ideal and practical realms, we may notice that the "masculine" attitude the princess describes is point for point the opposite of that which Tasso at the beginning of the play showed towards the objects of his ideal desires. Then, inwardness was everything—the small circle of friends, the intensely realized force of endless gratitude and love, the refusal to allow the realization of his desires to be forced on him in any physical form, even a symbolic one. On the one hand there is something extremely feminine in such an account of the poet's temperament: on the other, the princess's words, apart from their bearing on her own strikingly equivocal psychological state, seem in their context to carry a warning that if Tasso lets his ideal desires rest in physical objects he will actually be giving the substance for the shadow. The contrast, then, is less between the sexes than between two ways of life.

Tasso's problem, which develops to crisis in the course of the play, is that of the relation of ideal and practical, inner and outer worlds. As the play opens, the problem is not immediately apparent. Tasso seems completely satisfied with his surroundings and his manner of life. While taking no part himself in the active striving of the world, he is able to embody his patron's heroic qualities in his poem, and for himself feels no lack. Alfons, who with Antonio represents the active side of life that is contrasted to the peace of Belriguardo, is appreciative of Tasso's gifts and accomplishments. At the same time, he feels that Tasso needs experience of the outside world to make a man of him—that his remaining at Belriguardo in attendance on the ladies is a retreat from reality. However, about to offer Tasso the garland, he speaks warmly of the hero's need of the poet and unenvying delight at seeing him appropriately crowned. In his ecstasy at the moment of his triumph, Tasso takes up these words, seeing in vision the poet and hero bound together by a glorious necessity, though his exuberance and exaggeration suggest that there is something unbalanced in his conviction. The theme of the relation of action and contemplation, or of heroism and poetry, is another form of the dialectic of outer and inner worlds around which the play is built.

Tasso's triumph is interrupted by the arrival of Antonio, for whom the center of reality is in the world of practical affairs and who seems unable, anyway at this moment, to take the poet's claim to attention very seriously. He will honor Ariosto willingly enough, but in such a way as faintly to slight Tasso. It is not this, though, that disturbs Tasso; as he tells the princess at the opening of act II, it is Antonio's talk of a wider world that troubles his sense of his own reality:

> But ah! the more I listened, more and more
> To my own eyes I seemed to fade from sight,
> And feared like Echo in the rocks to vanish,
> An answering cry, a naught, to die away.   [II.i.797–800]

The poet, previously the inhabitant of a complete and self-sufficient world, now fears that it is becoming phantasmal and shadowy as he sees it through the eyes of another. (Compare the dialogue in III.iv between Leonore and Antonio, where Tasso's realm does in fact appear phantasmal.) However, repulsed in his effort to grasp Antonio and his world, Tasso retreats farther into his own inner life, eventually, in his interview with Alfons in V.ii, claiming self-sufficiency for the poetic impulse that "alternates day and night" in his breast. He goes on:

> Forbid the silkworm to continue spinning,
> Though spinning brings him nearer to his death:
> The precious thread he patiently unwinds
> Out of his inner self, nor will leave off
> Until he's wrapped himself in his own coffin.
> O may a kindly god to us one day
> Accord that enviable insect's fate,
> In a new sunny valley to unfold
> His wings with eager joy!   [V.ii.3083–91]

Thus he rejects the opposition implied by Alfons and Antonio, who see him as having taken the wrong direction in a simple choice between fantasy and reality, morbidity and right-mindedness. He would reject also their suggestion that he is sacrificing the "man" to the "poet":

> I beg you, tear yourself out of your self!
> The man will gain all that the poet lost.   [V.ii.3077–78]

For him the opposition does not exist in that form, because his entire world is an inward one: what is external is only the perfected expression, the shimmering web. It has been indicated much earlier in the play that Tasso's hold on reality is entirely through his power of expression, the externalization of his inward world, and his words about the silkworm are quite consistent. Antonio has in his own way already touched on this in a piece of psychological analysis (III.iv.2116-39). Tasso, he says, is as absorbed in himself as if he carried the world in his bosom, and when he turns outward it is in a violent effort to force the outer world immediately into the shape of his inner one; when he fails, as in practical terms he is bound to do, he sinks back into himself. Naturally: it is only in the realm of poetry that his desires can effectively be realized. He does indeed carry a whole world in his breast, by virtue of the poetic impulse that "alternates day and night" there. The sunlight of which he speaks signifies, not release from the dark world of his own subjectivity and emergence into an outward life, but again an inward condition, the realization of poetic achievement that is Tasso's main goal. In that sense the inward life is complete and self-sustaining: darkness and light, a deathlike condition and renewal of life, equally belong, not to an opposition of inner and outer, but to the creative rhythm of inwardness itself. Accordingly, Tasso is protesting the self-sufficiency of poetry as a way of life. Even so the passage remains somewhat ambiguous, tinged with a romantic morbidity. Creative activity not only brings the creator into a seeming death: as with the insect, the moment at which his vital strength is released also sets a number to his days. This passage is at once the most complete and the most disturbing exposition of the basis of Tasso's way of life; and it is only the more ironic for Tasso's declaration almost immediately following that the series of statements within which it occurs was a piece of self-falsification designed to deceive his enemies.

In attempting to give physical expression to his relationship with the princess, Tasso tries to embrace the image of his own inward life. In terms of the play's action the attempt is disastrous, notwithstanding the reality and importance for both of their relationship, because of the princess's nature: fragile, withdrawn, inaccessible to any but metaphorical approaches. The taboos that surround her are the conditions necessary to her life, and she has already gone as far towards Tasso as she can possibly go. In terms of the play's theme of outward and inward, Tasso loses the treasure he possesses—an ideal harmony with an unmistakable soulmate—by attempting to confirm his possession by means not ideal. He thus loses the substance by an attempt to grasp at the shadow. If, as I suggest, the princess can be seen further as a figure of his own inward world, the implication is, not so much that Tasso is excluding one half of life, but that in clinging to the other half he is demanding of it functions and fulfillments that it cannot of its nature supply. The imagination is the source of poetry and ideal joys, but love and experience come to us, at least in part, from outside.

When the princess, to save her own equilibrium, has fled from him, Tasso in the play's other climactic embrace chooses Antonio. Goethe changes the historical end of the story: by closing the play with this gesture and Tasso's words about it, he indicates that Tasso has thereby saved himself as a man. This time he reaches towards an embodiment, not of his imaginative life in a soulmate or counterpart, but of the complement, the world of outward reality and experience. His earlier attempt to gain Antonio's friendship failed because he never really turned outward to make it; endeavoring to please the princess, and carried on a wave of enthusiasm and self-confidence, he was still self-absorbed and unconvinced of the reality of what he pretended to confront. Now, with his inner life all but overthrown through his sufferings, he is no longer confined by it. The palace still stands, but the prison walls are down.

The dimensions of *Tasso* are widened for its reader through the use of a sweeping imagery that opens out a larger world surrounding the pleasure-castle of Belriguardo, reflecting and supporting the play's theme of the equilibrium between inner and outer worlds.

Belriguardo is presented at the opening as a classical-poetic garden scene with appropriate suggestions of the pastoral Golden Age, the Hesperides, and Elysium. Setting and imagery bear each other out in introducing Tasso as the genius of a laurel-crowned island of poetry removed from the troubles of the outside world: here and elsewhere in the play, poetry is spoken of as if it were itself a landscape. The relation of this contemplative scene to the world of action is felt differently by the different characters. To Alfons and Antonio, their privileged position is one of responsibility, and Belriguardo represents the deserved rest that refreshes for further labors; both use the figure of a shady garden to which one returns after toil. To the princess, withdrawn as she is from ordinary life, it is a natural setting for the serene life appropriate to a lady of her rank and temperament. The different views of Tasso's place in the scene are much more complex, and their development mirrors the action of the play. It is to the two women that he is an integral part of the spiritual atmosphere of Belriguardo; his otherworldliness seems to be counterbalanced by the gracious artificiality of the princess's mode of life.

To Tasso the contemplative paradise of Belriguardo *is* the world; and the shock that brings his emotional difficulties first to expression and then to crisis is the reminder through Antonio of the "real" world of struggle and achievement. The relation of Belriguardo and the surrounding world of policy and action in the setting and practical discourse of the play is exactly parallel to that of poetry and heroism in the mental realm established by the imagery.

A theme which might bind these severed halves together, and at the conclusion of the play perhaps does so, is that of the quest. Tasso is repeatedly seen as in search of something;[1] and the introduction of this motif early begins to disrupt the sense of a small, secluded, self-contained and self-sufficient world that is established in the opening scene. The poet seems to be searching through the world for a treasure, some miraculous fulfillment that always eludes him. There is considerable ambiguity as to the object of the search, and the suggestion is made that he seeks in vain in the outside world what he has failed to recognize as present either in his familiar surroundings or in himself. As the action develops and the tragic notes deepen, a variation of this enters: the pursuit of an alluring object that leads on like a will-o'-the-wisp until it has drawn the pursuer to his death. It is such an object that the laurel garland, at first the object of his real and lifelong striving, becomes for Tasso in his final disillusionment, and some of his descriptions of the pursuit of poetry carry a similar suggestion.[2] The most striking image of this kind relates, however, not to Tasso's fate but to that of the princess:

> Indeed the world is fair! In her expanses
> So many a joy goes straying here and there.
> Alas, each always seems to glide beyond us
> Just one step further, and beguile our longing
> Step after step that brings us to the grave!   [III.ii.1900–05]

As her temperament is a more extreme and tragic version of Tasso's own, it is appropriate that she formulates this motif most sharply. Her further words are close to others applied elsewhere to Tasso's search for contentment or fulfillment:

> So rarely comes it that men ever find
> The treasure that once seemed appointed for them,
> So rarely that they can long hold the good
> That once their lucky hands made bold to grasp!
> What earlier gave itself to us, breaks free,
> And we let slip what our desire once seized on.
> True joy there is, but still we fail to know it,
> Or knowing it, we fail to prize it right.   [1906–13]

Through the introduction of the theme of the quest and at the same time the split between inner and outer worlds, the poet begins to be seen less as the embodiment and genius of an enclosed pastoral-poetic landscape than as a wanderer through scenes not particularly friendly. This is not a matter of the imagery alone, since Tasso's increasing disturbance at Belriguardo makes him determine to leave it, and his friends warn him of the distress he is bound to suffer in the world outside. Accordingly, though the action of the play never leaves Belriguardo, the mental scene, so to speak, undergoes gradual alteration. A key passage of the play, from the scene of the princess's long discussion with Tasso, runs as follows:

> Such ways as those I fear will never bring
> Companionship, my Tasso! That path leads
> One's lonely steps through desert thickets on,
> To stray through silent valleys; more and more
> The spirit will grow fretful, and will strive
> To raise in its own world that golden time
> It cannot find without, but strive in vain.   [II.i.970–77]

The princess is reproaching Tasso for his reservations about Antonio and Leonore. Tasso is aware at this stage of the poet's need at least for models of heroism and virtue; but he is a solitary spirit, as yet unaware of the human need for companionship which the princess, reserved as she is, nevertheless assumes. Her words unite three motifs we have noted, all of them at the same time images, that is, creations of the poetic language, and deeply involved in the explication of Tasso's problem that constitutes the plot. The Golden Age of pastoral-poetic happiness, again partly related to the physical scene and partly a mental state, has been replaced by a desolate and solitary landscape, and now is identified with the treasure vainly sought in the outside world—vainly, because it is susceptible only of internal possession.

Tasso's second long scene with the princess, V.iv., which ends with the disastrous embrace, develops the pastoral theme farther. After talking about his projected journey to Rome, Tasso in one of his more extravagant outbursts sees himself on a visit to his sister in Sorrento. Disguised as pilgrim or shepherd, he will pass through the city of Naples, forbidden to members of his family, and on the shore find a boat that will carry him to Sorrento with peasants returning from market. Arriving, he will enquire for Cornelia, spinning-women will show him the way, and, surrounded by children who stare at the mournful stranger with the unkempt hair, he will reach her doorstop. . . . Recalled by the princess from this dream, he implores her to persuade the duke to dismiss him to one of his remoter and more rarely visited castles, where he will act as gardener and caretaker, opening the windows to air the rooms, setting out flowers in the beds, clearing and smoothing the walks. . . . These visions represent a different level of pastoral from that on which the play opened: there everything was aristocratic and "artificial," here the idyllicism is of a more "natural" and humble kind, comparable to that of the Wahlheim scenes in the early part of *Werther*. In the first of these speeches, Tasso is longing to go "back" to a past that never was his. Tasso was born in Sorrento as the child of a nobleman who later was outlawed and lost all his possessions but who found places for himself and his son at the courts of other nobles.

Cornelia's marriage into obscurity has been a different kind of adaptation to circumstances. Too clearly the natural and simple life is not for Tasso, as the melodrama in his vision of himself as romantic wanderer shows. The second speech is also idyllic and nostalgic: if he is exiled from his accustomed life of courts and castles, he will devote himself to tending the setting for those who still belong to it. Again, his enthusiasm is extravagant and misplaced: even if Alfons could allow such an arrangement, Tasso is not fitted for it. Tasso's proper rôle as garden genius and pastoral shrine-tender, namely through his poetry, has been fully described in the play's opening scene, and any transposition of it into other terms would necessarily prove ill-judged.

With the introduction of the wanderer and the quest of a lost Golden Age at the opening of act II, time and change became factors in the development of the play. We have by now moved far out of the seemingly timeless world of Belriguardo's garden; the wanderer has left it behind, and the Golden Age of the pastoral scene now belongs to a lost past, to which no return is possible. The play's movement is thus continually downward, like an expulsion from Eden into a wilderness characterized by rocks and abysses, with which exiled man has to come to terms.[3]

Sometimes the imagery of *Tasso* indicates that the scene in which the play opened has been left behind and its inhabitant transformed to a wanderer and exile; sometimes, however, the garden and palace have themselves been defaced. At the end of the play Tasso for an instant even imagines that the palace has fallen in ruins, though he quickly recovers himself. However, whether Paradise has been desecrated or abandoned, Tasso's mental world by the end of the play is the ultimate form of the wilderness, the open sea.[4]

There are many suggestions throughout the play that the presence of the sea somehow balances the pastoral "island of poetry" (I.i.140–41), starting with one of *Tasso's* sharpest formulations in Leonore's words:

> A talent best can shape itself in stillness,
> A character, best in the world's main stream.   [I.ii.305–06]

The princess at the beginning of the next act, reminding the disturbed Tasso of his own words about the relation of poet and hero, assures him that he may be content to watch the rough course of the world from this small state as from the shore (II.i.805–10); and he at the end of the same scene (1071–84) sees her as a divine figure oblivious to the storms in which ordinary mortals are tossed.[5] Tasso already in the second act (II.iii.1255–56) sees Antonio as possessing a constant heart on the unsteady waves of life. Two related expressions show a slightly different tendency: in III.ii.1875–77, the princess laments that life has up to now been a pleasant drifting down the stream, but now all is changed; and in V.ii.3068–71,

Tasso tells Alfons that he is not constituted to let the yielding element
the days bear him cheerfully out into the wide sea of time. The image
varies, but sea or river is never far out of sight. The sea is contrasted to the
smooth river down which one drifts in the same way as it is to the secure
pastoral state that it surrounds as the outside world does Belriguardo; and
it is in this sea and among its rocks that Tasso in the end embraces his
necessary complement and is saved from destruction.

An image not directly related to the pastoral complex, but worth exam-
ining because of its final development, is that of the "web" that meets the
reader several times in the second half of the play. Its first mention is in
the quarrel scene (II.iii.1358–61), where Tasso sees envy as a dirty cobweb
defacing the palace's marble walls. Elsewhere the web becomes an entanglement like the Gordian knot, and he has no weapon to cut his way
through (IV.ii.2270–71). Leonore picks up the image:

> As once for others' pleasure
> You would compose, this time you are contriving
> A curious web, alas! to your own grief.
> I am resolved to tear its windings from you,
> And let you freely walk in life's fair way.

Tasso later thinks he recognizes "the artifice of all this courtly web"; but
Leonore's wordplay and the suggestion that Tasso himself is the creator
of the web foreshadow the further development of the image in Tasso's
strange outburst to Alfons about his poetry, with its image of the poet as a
silkworm spinning its precious thread out of itself, regardless that it is
creating its own shroud. Here all the previous suggestions about the
web—that it is something deadly, that Tasso is involved in it to his destruction, that nevertheless he has produced it himself and as something
integral to his own being—are drawn together and made to appear positive (by the substitution of silkworm for spider) in a few impressive but
still equivocal lines, troubling especially in their suggestion of an activity
not free but inwardly compelled.

The web appears first as the envy and plots with which Tasso feels
himself surrounded. Next, through Leonore's speech and Tasso's response to it, all this entanglement is seen as Tasso's own mental creation.[6]
Next, Tasso himself applies the image to his own work as artist, the
productive process in which he is so deeply involved. Last in the sequence come Tasso's words to the princess about his art, developing
directly from the silkworm image though not referring to it:

> I feel - I feel it true, the mighty art
> Nourishing all, that strengthens and sustains
> The healthy spirit, will be my overthrow
> And drive me forth from here.   [V.iv.3133–36]

These words confirm the fatal opposition implied throughout the play between man and poet. What is enough for the poet is not enough for the man, and has led to a morbidly romantic view of poetry itself.

If Tasso's art is a "web," shimmering and entrancing but drawing parasitically on the life of its maker, the sensibility from which it proceeds is a "mirror."

> How charming, when so fine a soul as his
> Reflects one's image back!   [III.iii.1928–29]

exclaims the self-centred Leonore. More striking is Tasso's rhapsody at the moment of his triumph. Crowned with the laurel garland, he will wander in the deep groves surrounding the palace, not as previously with his sorrows:

> And if in its pure mirror some clear spring
> Shows me a man who, strangely garlanded,
> Amid reflected heaven and trees and rocks
> Stands pensively, then I shall think I see
> Elysium figured on the magic surface.
> Thoughtful I ask, Who is that soul in bliss,
> That stripling from past times, with glory crowned?
> How may I learn his name, his merit's worth?
> Long sunk in thought I dream, Oh that there came
> Another and another, that they joined
> With him in friendly converse as I watched them!
> Oh, might I see the heroes and the poets
> Of ancient time around this spring assembled!
> Oh, might I see them in eternal friendship,
> As when they lived their minds were undivided!   [I.iii.532–48]

Like other watery otherworlds in Romantic literature, this vision presents a life more fair and desirable than our own. The world of the mirror here is that of the ideal union of poetry and heroism dominated by the poetic (that is, literary) conception of immortal fame. What is shown is as much a poetic landscape as is the laurel-crowned island of poetry in an earlier passage, but the latter's quality of existence beyond time and space is here carried further; though the Elysian vision is pictured in a pool in one of the groves around Belriguardo, the natural scene contributes only the reflecting surface. Further, the scene relates to antiquity as belonging to a lost past, its central figure the "stripling from past times"; more specifically, it concerns the afterlife of that past, already itself a creation of the poets.

If we turn from Tasso's vision-at-several-removes directly to Tasso, something can be said about its significance for him. For the poet, the union of action and contemplation is possible precisely in the realm of poetry itself, not in "life" as such. In the play, poetry is clearly not something Tasso does so much as the ruling condition of what he is. The poetic personality is essentially devoted and passive—"Homer forgot himself . . ." (I.iii.552)—providing the magic glass in which opposites are reconciled[7] and the ideal forms of the past meet with the promise of the future in an eternal present. Earlier in the scene, when Alfons, pressing the laurel garland on Tasso, tried to persuade him of the hero's need of the poet, Tasso instinctively rejected garland and principle together. Alfons's words are evidently the groundwork for the later vision, but here Tasso has with complete consistency transposed the principle to the only realm where it applies: that of the imagination.

The mirror appears once more, in the last speech of the play, where it is the surface of a sea. The pool of the Elysian vision was surrounded by rocks and trees, but these had no essential part in the image. Here there is a double contrast: between the water and the rock, representing Tasso and Antonio, and between the water itself when it is calm and when it is stirred up by a storm. The contrast between water and rock is related to other such antitheses in the play's imagery.

> . . . On life's inconstant wave
> You keep a steady heart,   [II.iii.1255–56]

Tasso has already said to Antonio. Earlier he has seen in the princess one of those divine figures who are set apart from the fate of ordinary men:

> Much that seems to us
> The crash of wave hurled forcefully on wave,
>   To them is gentle wavelets rippling past,
> Murmuring round their feet; they do not hear
>   The storm that roars around and casts us down. . . .   [II.i.1074–78]

These lines reflect the impossibly idealizing quality of Tasso's passion, as do those in V.iv.3246–48, where the princess appears to him as a holy angel bending towards his bewildered mortality; there the division between ideal and real worlds is clearly too absolute for him to overcome, whatever bold step he may take. His passion is also, of course, directed as it were necessarily towards an impossible object. In these closing lines of the play the complementary figures, the storm-tossed and the unmoved, are parts of the same scene and derived from the same source:

> Nature's mighty power
> That laid these rocks' foundation, gave as well
> Its lightly-fleeting movement to the wave   [V.v.3437–39]

"Nature" also establishes the other contrast: that between the water when still and when troubled:

> She sends her storm: the wave is driven on
> And rolls and swells and breaks again in foam.
> In this same wave the sun beheld its face

> Shining reflected, and the stars reposed
> In calm upon this gently-stirring breast.
> The gleam has vanished, and the calm is fled   [3440–45]

In tranquillity the poetic spirit is able to mirror and reconcile in its surface sun and stars, day and night, as Tasso claimed before in his words to Alfons: but, it seems, only in tranquillity. The man is subject to natural passions by which the calmly reflecting surface is broken.

Here the metaphor changes again:

> The helm is shattered: now on every side
> The ship is breaking up. Beneath my feet
> The deck splits, and the timbers rush apart!
> I grasp you with both arms! as, even so,
> The sailor, cast away, at length must cling
> Fast to the rock on which his ship went down.   [3448–54]

Precisely what is the transition? The figure of the rock for Antonio remains the same, but instead of being the watery surface that is now calm and now troubled, Tasso is the seaman standing in a vessel that the storm has split, himself threatened with death by dashing against the rock. The storm, then, the wild upheaval of Tasso's own emotional forces, is also carried over from the earlier part of the metaphor, but here he has detached himself from it. The safety provided by the ship (before the wreck) replaces the calm state of the water, and the subject of the metaphor is not the water itself, which has become merely the element in which the storm is active, but the threatened seaman. Thus the crisis at this point involves not only Tasso's poetic faculty but something recognized as more personal still: his sanity, or perhaps his life. From total submersion, so to speak, Tasso comes up a man; and it is as a man that he reaches out towards his opposite and complement Antonio and, we are to understand, for the present is saved.

Tasso's turning at last to Antonio is not the only moment of resolution at the end of the play; it is immediately preceded by Tasso's statement about the power of poetry itself to alleviate suffering. In connection with this we may cite the princess's lines about her singing:

> There was one thing
> Which in my solitude could give me pleasure,
> The joy of song: I entertained myself
> With that, and through soft notes sorrow and longing
> And all desires I gently lulled to sleep.
> So suffering would become a source of pleasure,
> And even sadness turned to harmony.   [III.ii.1806–12]

Tasso's words are as follows:

> One thing remains:
> Nature has given us tears, has given too
> The cry of pain, when at long last the man
> Can bear no longer—And to me beside
> She left in sorrow melody and speech,
> To tell the heavy fullness of my grief:
> And while in deepest torment man is dumb,
> A god gave me to tell out what I suffer.   [V.v.3426–33]

Like the princess, Tasso, when it seems that nothing else is left, can still find relief in self-expression, here the outburst of grief that is released when the individual is driven past the limits of endurance. In the princess this is already carried into the realm of art, and exemplifies the power to bring beauty out of suffering; but her gift is not itself a creative one. Tasso is able to reshape his experience by giving voice to it: it is this power which, though based on natural faculties, is so far above the natural order as to seem a divine gift. These lines, then, sharply constrasting with earlier statements by Antonio and Leonore that make of poetry merely a refreshment for the tired mind, convey Tasso's reconciliation as poet to his tragic situation, and at the same time clearly state the sense in which the poet is more than the man.

At the very end of the play, with the crisis centering on the implied opposition between man and poet, we may recall expressions of it from other characters earlier in the play:

> A talent best can shape itself in stillness,
> A character, best in the world's main stream.

> First by mankind man learns to know himself,
> And life alone can teach us what we are.

> The man will gain all that the poet lost.

The first and obvious opposition in the play is that between Tasso's way of life and that of the practical men with whom he is contrasted, supported by that between Belriguardo and the outside world. This opposition Tasso strives to overcome by claiming that as a poet he is able to reconcile in his own sensibility all oppositions—day and night, action and contemplation, outwardness and inwardness. However, there is something wrong either with the claim or with the way in which it is stated. Tasso's declaration to the princess that the art that strengthens the healthy spirit can only ruin him is borne out elsewhere in the play. The "healthy spirit" is not the man without poetry—neither Alfons nor Antonio is that—but he is the man for whom, as for Ariosto and Virgil, poetry does not take the form of a madness or a disease but is a part of life and seen in fitting proportion. Antonio's praise of Ariosto compares the poet's labor to that of Nature:

> As Nature decks her richly fruitful breast
> With a broad garment green and gaily-colored,
> So in a flowery dress of fable he
> Shows all that makes man worth both love and honor.   [I.iv.711–15]

The analogy with nature saves this from being a view of poetry merely as ornamented truth, and it is something of a corrective; for insofar as it dictates his unbalanced way of living and responding to experience, Tasso's art does indeed come very close to "ruining" him. However, when at the time of his greatest suffering poetry becomes for him not an alternative to life but its complement and completion, it comes at last to "strengthen and refresh." It is this reconciliation that is established in the second last speech of the play. But Tasso's passion carries him past even that moment; and it is in his turning as a man to reach out for human companionship that the play is finally resolved.

Tasso's important relationships in the play are with the princess and with Antonio. For each of these Goethe provides a balancing figure of the same rank and opposite sex, this diagrammatic balance suggesting that perhaps the relationships themselves will be in some sense symmetrical. [8]

Recognizing in the princess a poetic nature like his own, Tasso sees in her the ideal soulmate, the center of his love and inspiration: he goes farther, and tries to seize and attach to himself by a physical gesture the treasure that emotionally and spiritually is clearly already his. When in a moment of frenzy immediately following he flies to the other extreme, he denounces her as "Sirene," the fair but fatal water fairy. Her earlier symbols have similarly suggested remoteness, though in a more ideal sense: the "pearl" hidden in its shell among the sands of the seashore (II.i.885–87), and the "moon" that gives a little light to the traveler but no warmth (III.iii.1956–59). The morbidity of Tasso's attempt to "bind to himself [his] Joy" is emphasized by the delirious quality both of his raptures and of his despondencies, complemented by the princess's passivity, retiring temperament, and consequent dependence on her poet's tact and understanding.

Tasso's relation to Antonio is at first the precise reverse of that to the princess. He resents the reminder in Antonio's presence of the outside world of practical affairs and of rational and objective standards of judgment, so that Antonio appears as a threat to his subjective and contemplative paradise. Tasso's salvation as a man, however, takes place when, having by his rashness lost all that Belriguardo represents to him, and especially his soulmate in the princess, he recognizes and loves in Antonio not his double but his necessary complement. This development is pointed up by the two climactic embraces at the end of the play.

The opening setting of *Tasso,* the garden with its flowering walks and its busts of the poets all surrounding a pleasure-castle, to say nothing of "the rare and festive garments of the fair ones," is from the outset suspiciously elegant, artificial, and remote from reality. At any rate, however gracious a part of life it seems, it cannot be the whole—it is too much built upon exclusion.[9] For the princess, a woman of withdrawn interests and uncertain health, it is perhaps enough; for the men of the world it is a place of refreshment and repose: for the poet, what? Evidently a paradise not too secure, or the arrival of Antonio could not threaten it. Tasso as man, and even as poet, must learn to include, not exclude: not to shun the world of action and practical concerns but to wed it to his imaginative world and incorporate both with the other pairs of opposites in his breast—day and night, life and death.

Tasso's rôle at the beginning of the play, both physically and imaginatively, is that of the poet–genius of a pastoral–poetic scene, in harmony with its powers and rejoicing in his love and his inspiration. As the play progresses, a split appears between the physical and the imaginative setting. While the pastoral scene remains unchanged, that supplied by the imagery becomes increasingly dark, wild, barren, desolate, and sinister as Tasso feels both his love and his inspiration threatened. To the contrast between garden and wilderness corresponds that between safe shore and rushing river; then with garden and shore both lost in the past, river and wilderness give place in turn to the open sea.

As the world of the garden scenes begins to retreat, we become more aware of the palace the garden surrounds, appearing as a shrine of honor and merit. However, Tasso's vision is gradually darkening, and with it our own: the palace becomes a place of detention, and instead of continuing to see in the circle of his friends a full, rich, and self-complete sphere, the poet is forced to turn inward and protest the integrity of his inner world. Before the end of the play this too is shattered: the self-spun web is replaced by the mirror, the image of a humanly receptive sensibility founded on the community of nature and in itself not the sufficient basis of a way of life.

The reconciliation of opposites at the end of the play comes about through Tasso's final understanding of "Nature." The opening setting has a quality of Armida's-bower artificiality and "unnaturalness," and the real world of nature intrudes mainly through the imagery. Tasso does not talk about "Nature" as such in the course of the play, and until the end he seems to have no single conception of it. His experience is divided: on the one hand is his subjective imaginative world, associated with the artificial-pastoral scene of Belriguardo, on the other the world of action, outward concerns and the practical reason, which he sees as intrusive, threatening, full of hate, envy, and malice. The two forces seem to him irreconcilable. Further, the inward force, the creative impulse in his own bosom, is divided like a microcosm of his world into beneficent and de-structive powers; and moreover, he feels that the poetic art, healing and refreshing to the sound in spirit, will end by destroying him, having already made him a wild-eyed exile and a disturbing apparition to the children of the peaceful, natural countryside. The solution comes with the discovery that the alien or hostile is the excluded: that Nature, rather than the poet, is the creative Titan able to embrace all opposites as comple-ments, and that imitation of her is not only the poet's task, but man's escape from solitude and madness.

Three *Elegy and the Elegiac*

Adam saw it in a brighter sunshine, but never knew the shade of pensive beauty which Eden won from his expulsion.
—*Nathaniel Hawthorne*

Completed in 1789, Goethe's *Tasso* is the first full-length treatment of the Romantic artistic temperament. With his dreaminess, his love-melancholy, his love of solitude, his capacity for brookside visions, Tasso is a kinsman of the poetical characters who figure in the elegiac poetry of the age of sensibility in England. Whatever symbolic patterns we find in *Tasso*, Goethe is of course using them, and in large measure creating them, to portray and expose his hero's Romantic subjectivity. Throughout most of the play the balance of Tasso's sanity is precarious; in this he is another Werther. It is in his account of the genesis and reception of *Werther* (*Dichtung und Wahrheit* [Poetry and Truth] xiii.) that Goethe discusses at greatest length contemporary English poetry, and his remarks there are equally relevant to *Tasso*. The tone he takes is in the main respectful, but certainly not free from irony.

Goethe speaks first of the sources of ennui, which he sees as the offspring of solitude. Moreover, pleasure in life is founded on the regular recurrence of outward conditions—of day and night, the seasons, flowers and fruit—but the same cyclical pattern can become a hell:

> The more open we are to these enjoyments, the happier we feel ourselves to be; but if these phenomena in all their diversity revolve before us without our feeling any interest in them, if we are unreceptive to the delights they offer us, then sets in the greatest evil, the most oppressive sickness—we regard life as a loathsome burden. It is said that a certain Englishman hanged himself rather than go on every day dressing and undressing.

These and other melancholy feelings were diffused among German youth by English literature, especially poetry, which always combined with its admirable features a solemn gloom. With this Goethe associates the striking frequency among English poets of calamitous personal fates. This was often noted at the time: we can illustrate from Burns's "To a Mountain Daisy," published in 1786, where a generalized stanza on the betrayal of the village maid, "Sweet flow'ret of the rural shade," is followed by:

> Such is the fate of simple bard
> On life's rough ocean, luckless starr'd!
> Unskilful he to note the card
>   Of prudent lore
> Till billows rage, and gales blow hard,
>   And whelm him o'er!

English poems, continues Goethe, even when tender in intention are full of sad objects, like deserted maidens and lovers drowned or eaten by sharks:

> ... and if a poet like Gray settles down in a village churchyard and takes up once more the familiar melodies, he will be sure to gather around him a number of friends of melancholy. Milton's "Allegro" has to chase gloom away in vigorous verse before he can achieve even a moderate mirth....

Other authors he mentions are Young, Goldsmith, the creator of Hamlet, and Ossian.

Young, Gray, and Ossian all make the figure of the Poet central to their elegiac themes. Young in *The Complaint, or Night Thoughts,* 1742–44,[1] presents himself as a much-bereaved man brooding on the fates of his dead. At the end of Gray's *Elegy,* the poet appears as elegiac subject and object. He is a child of Melancholy (105–08)—

> Hard by yon wood, now smiling as in scorn,
> Mutt'ring his wayward fancies he would rove,
> Now drooping, woeful wan, like one forlorn,
> Or craz'd with care, or cross'd in hopeless love

—and his epitaph concludes the poem.

Still on the subject of the melancholy of English poetry, Goethe introduces James Macpherson's Ossian.

> That all this gloom might not lack its ideally suited setting, Ossian had enticed us all the way to Ultima Thule, where on a grey unending heath, wandering among rigid moss-covered gravestones, we saw the grass around us stirred by a chilly wind and above us a darkly-clouded sky. Not till the moon appeared did this Caledonian night become day: departed heroes, faded maidens, floated around us....

Ossian, son of Fingal, is the last survivor of a glorious race, singing in the midst of desolation. The substance of Ossian's song is the deaths of the heroes whose ghosts press round him, mingled with lamentations for his own present state. The peculiar pastoral–elegiac feature of these poems is their "ideally suited setting," the mutual mirroring of mood and scene, outward desolation and inner.

The important literary sources of eighteenth-century poetic melancholy are Milton and, whether directly or transmitted through Milton, Burton. Burton distinguishes between pleasurable and acute forms of melancholy, and so does Milton, in the contrast between the lady dismissed in "L'Allegro" and the one called up in "Il Penseroso." In later writers, mild forms of melancholy are evoked with the help of the scenes in "Il Penseroso," with their stress on the visionary and imaginative and culminating in the Gothic pile and the hermitage, and of the more somber atmosphere of *Comus:*

> . . . their way
> Lies through the perplex't paths of this drear Wood,
> The nodding horror of whose shady brows
> Threats the forlorn and wandring Passinger.   [36–39]

For the intenser varieties they draw on the gloomiest pictures in *Paradise Lost,* such as the "scath'd" oak or pine[2] "on the blasted Heath" (I.612–15), and

> many a Frozen, many a fierie Alpe,
> Rocks, Caves, Lakes, Fens, Bogs, Dens, and shades of death.   [II.620–21]

"Il Penseroso" taken by itself is a mood piece, but Milton's later work adds to that mood's force by fitting it into a moral and psychological cosmos; it is thus for Milton's successors implicitly connected with the central elegiac themes of the loss of Paradise and all the resulting limitations of man's happiness, powers, and understanding. Where, as often in the mid–eighteenth century, the high seriousness of Milton's great context is left aside in favor of the comparative aestheticism of "Il Penseroso," it may still seem to be invoked between the lines to add to the humorless portentousness of the atmosphere.

The self-fancying and "picturesque" trait of il Penseroso becomes more prominent in the eighteenth century; it appears for example at the end of Gray's *Elegy,* and in another medium in the Tischbein portrait of Goethe in the Campagna, 1786–88, dressed as a traveler and with his eyes fixed on the horizon. Some romantic enthusiasts, like Macpherson's Ossian and Goldsmith's Traveller, while converting Milton's assertion of universal fall into a plaint of personal malaise, are very close to invoking his theme to lend dignity to their own plight. Solitude is never the same again once Adam has invoked it in *Paradise Lost* Book Nine (1084–85); and by the end of the next century the solitary is usually found to be either the passive man of sensibility to whom some sorrow has opened the whole prospect of human wretchedness, or the man of action who has come to know it through guilt. These meet in the titanic egoism of the Byronic wanderer that expands as if to bear alone the full burden of human destiny.

What Goethe sees in Goldsmith is of particular interest for us:

> . . . even the cheerful Goldsmith loses himself in elegiac sensations, when his *Deserted Village* charmingly but sadly brings before us a lost paradise which his "Traveller" searches the whole earth to recover. . . .

The Vicar of Wakefield was one of the books Goethe read with most affection and most liked to connect with his own life, and so late as March 11, 1828, he was to put forward to Eckermann the peculiar vitality and originality of Goldsmith's works. Possibly Goethe is making Goldsmith the vessel of an originality more truly his own. The shaping spirit is anyway at work in our quotation; the metaphor of a lost paradise is Goethe's, and so is the order of the poems, *The Traveller,* 1764, being the earlier by five years: he is arranging them in terms less of their actual themes than of the elegiac pattern.

Earlier in *Dichtung und Wahrheit* (xii), Goethe speaks of *The Deserted Village:*

> All that one rejoiced to look upon, that one loved, prized, passionately sought in the present in order to share in it with youthful enjoyment, is there described, not as living and viable, but as a departed, vanished way of life.

In the village preacher is recreated the Vicar of Wakefield,

> yet no longer in his living, bodily form, but as a shade called back by the soft, mournful notes of the elegiac poet.

The gathering round of ghosts from the past is one of the elegiac devices of Ossian, and Goethe himself uses it with immeasurable effect in the "Dedication" of *Faust:*

> Once more you venture near, you wavering phantoms
> That early dawned upon my troubled eyes. . . .

The Vicar of Wakefield suggests nostalgia for an old-world simplicity and innocence and primitive Christian values, for example in the opening of chapter 4:

> Remote from the polite, [our neighbors] still retained a primaeval simplicity of manners, and frugal by long habit, scarce knew that temperance was a virtue. . . . They kept up the Christmas carol, sent true love-knots on Valentine morning, eat pancakes on Shrovetide, shewed their wit on the first of April, and religiously cracked nuts on Michaelmas eve. Being apprized of our approach, the whole neighbourhood came out to meet their minister, drest in their finest cloaths, and preceded by a pipe and tabor: also a feast was provided for our reception, at which we sat chearfully down. . . .

Goethe in *Dichtung und Wahrheit* recalls the novel in order to cast a similar idyllic glow over the Sesenheim episode. For Goethe as for Goldsmith's wandering Burchell, his sweetheart's father's house and the patriarchal manners that rule it offer a slightly unreal pastoral retreat from the circumstances of ordinary social life. Remoteness from city and court in both narratives stands in a way for remoteness in time, nostalgia for a happier, simpler past.

In connection with Goldsmith's Traveller's quest for happiness, whether past or future, we might notice two passages, from the beginning and the end of the poem, where the symbolism is very close to that of the quest in *Tasso:*

> But me, not destin'd such delights to share,
> My prime of life in wand'ring spent and care:
> Impell'd with steps unceasing to pursue
> Some fleeting good, that mocks me with the view;
> That, like the circle bounding earth and skies,
> Allures from far, yet, as I follow, flies . . .   [23–28]

> Vain, very vain, my weary search to find
> That bliss which only centres in the mind. . . .   [423–24][3]

A more sinister version of the "fleeting good" is found in *The Vicar of Wakefield* (chap. 8, "A Ballad," st. 3):

> "Forbear, my son," the hermit cries,
> "To tempt the dangerous gloom;
> For yonder phantom only flies
> To lure thee to thy doom."

The delusive pursuit is a favorite topic of eighteenth-century poetry, and we are pausing over it briefly here because of some Romantic developments we shall shortly be encountering. Further, the quotations from Goldsmith very modestly illustrate a point that becomes important: the way in which certain key images function both as figures of speech and as narrative features, often side by side in the same work. Such images in this chapter and the next include the blasted tree, the broken dream, the precipice, the abyss, the storm, the torrent, the flood. Storm and flood showed the same double function in the *paysage moralisé* of *Paradise Lost.*

Already in the earlier eighteenth century the delusive pursuit can sometimes be presented as a physical situation, for example in Thomson's "Spring," where the swain vainly pursues the rainbow (212–17), or in Collins's "Ode on the Popular Superstitions of the Highlands of Scotland," where another swain meets death by drowning through following a goblin "faithless light." James Beattie is particularly fond of sinister lights in metaphors. A stormy night in a horrific wilderness is haunted by "many a fire-eyed visage"; Hope, Fancy, and Fame are likened to the fleeing and "illusive" rainbow; moments of happiness belong to "life's deceitful gleam"; Fancy, Reason, and "False science" are all represented as meteoric "blaze," "rays," or "glare" that light up the dreadful scene and afflict the wanderer worse than the darkness. The night-wanderer, usually busy being led astray, is also a favorite ornament of poems of the period. Thomson introduces him at length in "Autumn" (I can find no earlier considerable eighteenth-century passage):[4] night has just fallen:

> Drear is the state of the benighted wretch,
> Who then, bewilder'd, wanders thro' the dark,
> Full of pale fancies, and chimera's huge;
> Nor visited by one directive ray,
> From cottage streaming, or from airy hall.
> Perhaps impatient as he stumbles on,
> Struck from the root of slimy rushes, blue,
> The wild fire scatters round, or gathered trails
> A length of flame deceitful o'er the moss:
> Whither decoy'd by the fantastic blaze,
> Now lost and now renew'd, he sinks absorpt,
> Rider and horse, amid the miry gulf: . . .
> While still, from day to day, his pining wife,
> And plaintive children his return await,
> In wild conjecture lost. At other times,
> Sent by the better genius of the night,
> Innoxious, gleaming on the horse's mane,
> The meteor sits; and shows the narrow path,
> That winding leads thro' pits of death, or else
> Instructs him how to take the dangerous ford.   [1147–66]

The source for this is in *Paradise Lost,* where Satan beguiling Eve is compared to a will-o'-the-wisp:[5]

> . . . as when a wandring Fire,
> Compact of unctuous vapor, which the Night
> Condenses, and the cold invirons round,
> Kindl'd through agitation to a Flame
> Which oft, they say, some evil Spirit attends,
> Hovering and blazing with delusive Light,
> Misleads th'amazed Night-wanderer from his way
> To Boggs and Mires, and oft through Pond or Poole,
> There swallow'd up and lost, from succour farr.
> So glister'd the dire Snake. . . .   [IX.634–43]

Milton probably has in mind the activities of Puck in *A Midsummer Night's Dream,*[6] but equally important are some remarks in Burton's *Anatomy:*

> Fiery spirits or devils are such as commonly work by blazing Stars, Fire-drakes, or *Ignes fatui;* which lead men often *in flumina, aut praecipitia.* . . .

"Terrestriall devils" include

> those which Mizaldus calls *Ambulones,* that walk about midnight on great Heaths and desart places, which (saith Lavater) *draw men out of the way, and lead them all night a by-way, or quite bar them of their way;* these have several names in several places; we commonly call them *Pucks.*   [I.ii.1.2]

We can trace ultimately to Burton the eighteenth-century tendency to use the night-wanderer as a figure for mental bewilderment and to make of his wanderings a "labyrinth" or "maze":

> Voluntary solitariness is that which is familiar with Melancholy, and gently brings on like a Siren, a shoeing-horn, or some Sphinx to this irrevocable gulf . . .; most pleasant it is at first, to such as are melancholy given, to lie in bed whole days, and keep their chambers, to walk alone in some solitary Grove, betwixt Wood and Water, by a Brook side, to meditate upon some delightsome and pleasant Subject, which shall affect them most; *amabilis insania*, and *mentis gratissimus error*. A most incomparable delight it is so to melancholize, and build castles in the air. . . . So delightsom these toyes are at first, . . . they cannot I say go about their more necessary business, stave off or extricate themselves, but are ever musing, melancholizing, and carried along; as he (they say) that is lead round about an Heath with a *Puck* in the night, they run earnestly on in this labarinth of anxious and solicitous melancholy meditations, and cannot well or willingly refrain, or easily leave off, . . . until at last the Scene is turned upon a sudden, by some bad object, and they, being now habituated to such vain meditations and solitary places, can endure no company, can ruminate of nothing but harsh and distastfull subjects. [I.ii.2.6]

This last passage, dealing as it does with "the spirit of solitude," contains several images very central to our concerns: apart from the wanderer, the Puck, and the labyrinth[7] (often hereafter found juxtaposed), we shall be reminded later of the siren luring to the gulf, the daydream by the brookside, castles in the air, and the sudden turning of the whole scene for the worse.

Three other kinds of delusion that the traveler encounters in a wilderness-world can briefly be connected: we shall meet them again in later chapters. First, the echo or deceiving voice:

> A thousand fantasies
> Begin to throng into my memory,
> Of calling shapes, and beckning shadows dire,
> And airy tongues that syllable mens names
> On Sands, and Shoars, and desert Wildernesses. [*Comus* 205–09]

Ariel operates somewhat in this manner, but more to the point is Burton:

> In the desarts of *Lop* in *Asia*, such illusions of walking spirits are often perceived, as you may read in *M. Paulus* [i.e., Marco Polo] the *Venetian* his travels; If one lose his company by chance, these devils will call him by his name, and counterfeit voyces of his companions to seduce him. [I.ii.1.2]

Second, the mirage or enchantment:

> For Happiness was never to be found;
> But vanish'd from 'em [the ancient philosophers] like
> Enchanted ground. [Dryden, *Religio Laici*, 1682, 27–28][8]

God beautifies Nature to man's eyes "By kind illusions of the wondering sense":[9]

> So fables tell
> The adventurous heroe, bound on hard exploits,
> Beholds with glad surprise, by secret spells
> Of some kind sage, the patron of his toils,
> A visionary paradise disclos'd
> Amid the dubious wild; with streams, and shades,
> And airy songs, the enchanted landscape smiles,
> Cheers his long labours and renews his frame.
> [Akenside, *The Pleasures of Imagination*, 1744, III.491, 507–14]

The enthusiast in December hugs his fire:

> Then let my thought contemplative explore
> This fleeting state of things, the vain delights,
> The fruitless toils, that still our search elude,
> As through the wilderness of life we rove.
> This sober hour of silence will unmask
> False Folly's smile, that like the dazzling spells
> Of wily Comus cheat th'unweeting eye
> With blear illusion. . . .
> [T. Warton, *The Pleasures of Melancholy*, 1747, 80–87]

A variation, pointing to Prospero as the enchanter, occurs in Young's *Night Thoughts:*

> Who builds on less than an immortal base,
> Fond as he seems, condemns his joys to death.
> Mine dy'd with thee, Philander! thy last sigh
> Dissolv'd the charm; the disinchanted earth
> Lost all her lustre. Where her glittering towers?
> Her golden mountains, where? all darken'd down
> To naked waste; a dreary vale of tears;
> The great magician's dead! Thou poor, pale piece
> Of out-cast earth, in darkness! . . .   [I.342–50]

A poem in Mrs. Radcliffe's *Romance of the Forest*, 1791, called "Morning, on the Sea-Shore," based mainly on *A Midsummer Night's Dream*, recalls at its close, besides "Il Penseroso," Milton's juxtaposition at the end of *Paradise Lost* Book One of magical building and fairy vision (chap. xviii):

> O fairy forms! so coy to mortal ken,
> Your mystic steps to poets only shewn:
> O! lead me to the brook, or hallow'd glen,
> Retiring far, with winding woods o'ergrown. . . .
> E'en now your scenes enchanted meet my sight!
> I see the earth unclose, the palace rise,
> The high dome swell, and long arcades of light

Glitter among the deep embow'ring woods,
And glance reflecting from the trembling floods!
While to soft lutes the portals wide unfold,
And fairy forms, of fine aetherial dyes,
Advance with frolic step and laughing eyes. . . .
Thus your light visions to my eyes unveil,
Ye sportive pleasures, sweet illusions, hail!
But ah! at morn's first blush again ye fade!
So from youth's ardent gaze life's landscape gay,
And forms in fancy's summer hues array'd,
Dissolve at once in air at truth's resplendent day!

The third category of delusions is what Milton calls the "beckning shadow," or the phantom luring to destruction,[10] a wilderness version of Burton's siren with gulf. The phantom pursuit, usually minus gulf, is a long-lived poetic commonplace,[11] as a few passages will show:

Distance presents the object fair
With Charming Features and a graceful Air,
But when we come to seize th'inviting prey,
Like a Shy Ghost, it vanishes away.
                    [John Norris of Bemerton, "The Infidel," before 1687]

. . . watch the busy scenes of crowded life;
Then say how hope and fear, desire and hate,
O'erspread with snares the clouded maze of fate,
Where wav'ring man, betray'd by vent'rous pride
To tread the dreary paths without a guide,
As treach'rous phantoms in the mist delude,
Shuns fancied ills, or chases airy good.
                    [Johnson, *The Vanity of Human Wishes*, 1749, 4–10]

That motley drama!—oh, be sure
It shall not be forgot!
With its Phantom chased for evermore,
By a crowd that seize it not,
Through a circle that ever returneth in
To the self-same spot. . . .
                    [Poe, "The Conqueror Worm," 1843]

The same image[12] is at work in Arnold's "The Buried Life," 1852:

And there arrives a lull in the hot race
Wherein he doth for ever chase
That flying and elusive shadow, rest.

The best verse example of the phantom chase leading to destruction is that from Goldsmith already cited: we can compare some lines from Prévost's novel *Cléveland*, 1731–39, a work much influenced by its author's English reading[13] and in turn widely read in England:

> Les homes sçavent ils ce qu'ils desirent, lorsqu'ils se proposent des contentemens de leur choix! Ce qui leur paroit le plus propre à faire leur bonheur, se change pour eux en une source d'infortunes et de miséres. Ils abandonnent un repos assuré, dont ils se lassent par inconstance; & l'ombre après laquelle ils courent, les conduit à leur perte.   [I,67]

Another prose example is to be found in *Tristram Shandy*, 1759, referring to Uncle Toby's researches into the science of projectiles:

> —stop! my dear Uncle Toby—stop!—go not one foot further into this thorny and bewilder'd track,—intricate are the steps! intricate are the mazes of this labyrinth! intricate are the troubles which the pursuit of this bewitching phantom Knowledge will bring upon thee. —O my uncle!—fly—fly—fly from it as from a serpent.   [II,iii]

Let us now consider a less harrowing experience of the traveler in dim light. The commonsense traveler uses the darkening sky as his clock:

> The west yet glimmers with some streaks of day:
> Now spurs the lated traveller apace
> To gain the timely inn.   [*Macbeth* III.iii.4–6]

The more romantic night-wanderer looks for guiding lights, notably in *Comus:* "the Stars . . . give due light / To the misled and lonely Traveller" (197, 199–200), and the Elder Brother addresses the "fair Moon / That wontst to love the travellers benizon" (330–31).[14] In "Il Penseroso" the moon herself is "wandring,"

> Like one that had bin led astray
> Through the Heav'ns wide pathles way.   [67, 69–70]

The figure of the traveler whose path is lit by the uncertain light of the moon appears in *Tasso:* the passions of the princess

> . . . gleam, as the moonlight's silent rays
> Touch charily the traveler's path by night.   [III.iii.1956–57]

We can compare Arimant's speech to Indamora in *Aureng-Zebe:*

> Think you . . .
> So weak your Charms, that, like a Winter's night,
> Twinkling with Stars, they freez me while they light?   [II.i.86–89]

A more familiar passage from Dryden is the opening of *Religio Laici:*

> Dim, as the borrow'd beams of Moon and Stars
> To lonely, weary, wandring Travellers
> Is Reason to the Soul.

To this discouraging light[15] we can perhaps link Aeneas's famous glimpse of Dido in the underworld, recalled by Milton at the end of *Paradise Lost* Book One:

> Among them Phoenician Dido . . . was wandering in a great wood; the Trojan hero, when he came near and recognized her dim figure through the gloom—as at the beginning of the month one sees, or thinks he sees, the moon rising through the clouds—wept, and spoke. . . .　　[*Aen.* vi.450–55]

To conclude this group of images—it is not a historical line but perhaps a cluster—here is Ossian ("Carthon"):

> Age is dark and unlovely; it is like the glimmering light of the moon, when it shines through broken clouds, and the mist is on the hills; the blast of the north is on the plain, the traveller shrinks in the midst of his journey.

Via Blake's echoing line, "The Lost Traveller's Dream under the Hill," from the end of *The Gates of Paradise,* we can move to another favorite trope, and one related to the two foregoing: the broken or disappearing vision or dream. Usually this is connected with love, as in Handel's *Semele:*

> O sleep, why dost thou leave me?
> Why thy visionary joys remove?
> O sleep, again deceive me:
> To my arms restore my wand'ring love.　　　　　　　　　[II.ii]

The words were written by Congreve in 1707.[16] Such pictures are very familiar by the time Ambrosio in *The Monk* dreams of Matilda (chap. ii): ". . . he clasped her passionately to his bosom, and—the vision was dissolved."[17] Beattie is fond of the dissolving dream metaphor, using it frequently, like the delusive light, to illustrate the nature of Fancy or Hope:

> O, who shall then to Fancy's darkening eyes
> Recall th'Elysian dreams of joy and light?
> Dim through the gloom the formless visions rise,
> Snatch'd instantaneous down the gulf of night.
> 　　　　　　　　　　　["The Judgment of Paris," 165–68]

The important earlier associations are with Milton's sonnet "On His Deceased Wife"[18]—"I wak'd, she fled, and day brought back my night"— and his account of Adam's dream in *Paradise Lost:*

> Shee disappeerd, and left me dark, I wak'd
> To find her, or for ever to deplore
> Her loss, and other pleasures all abjure.　　　　　　　[VIII.478–80]

These descriptions recall Aeneas's meeting with the ghost of his wife
Creüsa:

> Three times I tried to embrace her: three times I grasped in vain at a phantom
> that fled from my hands like the light winds, and most like a fleeting
> dream.   [ii.792–94][19]

In Virgil and Milton the visions cited reveal a higher reality: in
eighteenth-century poetry, not unlike the Old English "Seafarer," the
stress is usually on the pleasurable illusion that then gives place to sad
reality. The remarks on the broken dream in *The Minstrel* are typical:
Edwin has dreamed beside a "haunted stream" of the fairies:

> The dream is fled. Proud harbinger of day,
> Who scar'dst the vision with thy clarion shrill,
> Fell chanticleer! who oft hast reft away
> My fancied good, and brought substantial ill!   [I.xxxvi]

Certainly "day brought back my night" is usually applicable. The
broken-dream trope (used three times in *Tasso*)[20] is in line with the favorite eighteenth- and nineteenth-century theme of emergence from the
idyllic illusions of youth to the necessities of real life, and is frequently
pressed into its service.[21] In Romantic use the dream—I am not speaking
here of dreams associated with prophecy and inspiration—may take on
again the representation of higher truth, perhaps an image of the world as
it should be even if confuted at every turn by what Coleridge in "Dejection" calls "Reality's dark dream"; the title of Coleridge's lyric "The
Visionary Hope" implies this, and so does the famous couplet in
Wordsworth's "Ode: Intimations":

> Whither is fled the visionary gleam?
> Where is it now, the glory and the dream?

In passages of eighteenth-century poetry that seem to draw on Burton,
it is likely Burton Miltonized that we are encountering. In Armstrong's
Art of Preserving Health, 1744, when the "restless mind" is given over to
solitude,

> . . . the dim-ey'd Fiend,
> Sour Melancholy, night and day provokes
> Her own eternal wound. The sun grows pale;
> A mournful, visionary light o'erspreads
> The chearful face of nature: earth becomes
> A dreary desart, and heaven frowns above.   [IV.92–97]

In Thomson's account of love-melancholy in "Spring,"

> 'Tis naught but gloom around. The darken'd sun
> Loses his light. The rosy-bosom'd Spring

To weeping Fancy pines; and yon bright arch,
Contracted, bends into a dusky vault.
All Nature fades extinct. . . .   [1006–10]

Often the fall from a joyful world to a bleak one is epitomized in a dream.
Here is Pope's Eloisa, 1717:

I hear thee, view thee, gaze o'er all thy charms,
And round thy phantom glue my clasping arms.
I wake—no more I hear, no more I view,
The phantom flies me, as unkind as you.
I call aloud; it hears not what I say:
I stretch my empty arms; it glides away:
To dream once more I close my willing eyes;
Ye soft illusions, dear deceits, arise!
Alas, no more!—methinks we wandring go
Thro' dreary wastes, and weep each other's woe,
Where round some mould'ring tow'r pale ivy creeps,
And low-brow'd rocks hang nodding o'er the deeps.
Sudden you mount! you beckon from the skies;
Clouds interpose, waves roar, and winds arise.
I shriek, start up, the same sad prospect find,
And wake to all the griefs I left behind.   [233–48]

And here is Thomson again:

Exhausted Nature sinks a while to rest,
Still interrupted by distracted dreams. . . .
Oft with th'enchantress of soul he talks;
Sometimes in crouds distress'd; or, if retir'd
To secret-winding flower-enwoven bowers,
Far from the dull impertinence of Man,
Just as he, credulous, his endless cares
Begins to lose in blind oblivious love,
Snatch'd from her yielded hand, he knows not how,
Thro' forests huge, and long untravel'd heaths
With desolation brown, he wanders waste,
In night and tempest wrapp'd; or shrinks aghast,
Back, from the bending precipice; or wades
The turbid stream below, and strives to reach
The farther shore; where, succourless and sad,
She with extended arms his aid implores;
But strives in vain: borne by th'outrageous flood
To distance down, he rides the ridgy wave,
Or whelm'd beneath the boiling eddy sinks.
                              ["Spring," 1050–51, 1054–70]

That passage[22] recalls perhaps both, in Virgil, Orpheus's parting from
Eurydice as she is carried away from him, stretching her hands in vain,

and Clarence's dream of drowning in *Richard III* (I.iv.9–10). Another passage that associates dream with perilous flood occurs in Young's *Night Thoughts:*

> From short (as usual) and disturb'd repose,
> I wake: how happy they who wake no more!
> I wake, emerging from a sea of dreams
> Tumultuous; where my wreck'd, desponding thought
> From wave to wave of fancy'd misery,
> At random drove, her helm of reason lost. . . .   [I.6–11]

What is most conspicuously recalled here is the love-melancholy of Petrarch's sonnet 189, translated by Wyatt as "My galy chargèd with forgetfulnes."

Sometimes the contrast between idyllic and terrific scenes is one between two different kinds of dream. In *The Castle of Indolence,* 1748, Thomson notes two kinds. One is represented by "guileful angel-seeming sprites," otherwise "fair illusions" and "artful phantoms," who dispense a "fairyland" and pour "all th' Arabian Heaven upon our nights":

> But for those fiends, whom blood and broils delight;
> Who hurl the wretch, as if to hell outright,
> Down down black gulphs, where sullen waters sleep,
> Or hold him clambering all the fearful night
> On beetling cliffs, or pent in ruins deep:
> They, till due time should serve, were bid far hence to keep. [I, sts. 44–46]

"Due time" presumably is the revelation of the hell that is the cellar of the castle's heaven, briefly depicted by Thomson and his friend Dr. Armstrong at the end of canto I. Young too categorizes dreams:

> While o'er my limbs sleeps soft dominion spread,
> What though my soul phantastic measures trod
> O'er fairy fields; or mourn'd along the gloom
> Of pathless woods; or down the craggy steep
> Hurl'd headlong, swam with pain the mantled pool;
> Or scal'd the cliff; or danc'd on hollow winds,
> With antic shapes, wild natives of the brain?   [I.91–97]

The first kind mentioned, quickly snatched away, would seem to be the regular idyllic fairy vision, "Such sights as youthful Poets dream / On Summer eeves by haunted stream." The second kind is mildly melancholic or Penseroso, while the last group is luridly horrific, recalling Claudio's fearful imaginings on death in *Measure for Measure.*

Eighteenth-century poetry whether sleeping or waking loves to depict sharply contrasting natural scenes, evocative of mild and of acute melancholy, the gentle and the awesome, the "beautiful" and the "sublime." Sometimes the opposites are reconciled in a Shaftesburian view of the harmony of nature to the innocent and faithful spirit:[23] they are nature's companion pieces, as "L'Allegro" and "Il Penseroso" are Milton's. Elsewhere, as in some of the dream passages just cited, it is their opposition that is stressed, with overtones suggesting the Miltonic fall of nature.

Near the end of the first chapter we noted in English Romantic poetry a pastoral–elegiac mode divorced from both the form and the situation of pastoral elegy proper, with the mourner bewailing his own state rather than the loss of a friend and often calling himself wanderer or exile. Such poems have for their background the eighteenth-century poetry of melancholy, or what we could call the elegy of Sensibility, of which we have noted several examples in passing. In Beattie's *Minstrel,* written over 1766–73, nature under Providence remains the stable and all-embracing in spite of the entrance of three elegiac themes: mortality, called up by the sight of a storm; the disillusioning course of human history—"For virtue lost, and ruin'd man, I mourn" (II.xix); and inability to continue the poem due to the loss of a friend. In the elegy of Sensibility, as later in Romantic elegy and what we shall call "elegiac romance," such facts as death, guilt, and loss of inspiration regularly are associated with the presence of sinister elements in the *locus amoenus* or the transition from one kind of landscape to the other.

During the course of the eighteenth century, we can see the substance and feeling of such poems being gradually carried over into prose fiction. Or, more accurately, to some extent this is happening, and at the same time to some extent the poetic models of eighteenth-century poetry are also directly influencing eighteenth-century prose and producing parallel effects there. The consequence in fiction is the appearance of certain striking types of characters and settings and a peculiar relation between them, as well as of some particular kinds of situation. As an example we can take the symbolic or significant dream,[24] already briefly illustrated. The context in which we noted it would suggest that such dreams might be a Burtonian theme: actually the subject hardly comes into the *Anatomy* at all. The important seventeenth-century passage is Eve's dream of flying in *Paradise Lost* (V.30–93); and still more directly influential is that we quoted from Pope's "Eloisa to Abelard," a poem singled out for admiration from Prévost and Rousseau to Goethe and Byron.[25]

In Pope and the other poets who describe such dreams, the dream has a partly psychological and realistic function, but at the same time is a rhetorical, almost figurative, way of heightening intensity and conveying the tyranny of passion: it is an imaginative device, not really a realistic or documentary one. It is perhaps because the motif derives from poetry, where readers have become accustomed to it, that it can be inserted into much less obviously stylized prose contexts. Fairly early in the course of eighteenth-century fiction, elaborate emblematic dreams visit Clarissa and Lovelace. In Clarissa's (II, letter 39, p. 283), Lovelace stabs her to the heart and throws her among half-rotted corpses in a grave: in his (VII, 48,

p. 159), the spiritual form of Clarissa eludes his grasp and rises to heaven, while he falls into the bottomless pit. Both dreams in their detail and in their prophetic quality look towards the dreams later to be featured in the Gothic novel.[26] A closely connected emotional detail that again seems to emanate from "Eloisa" into prose fiction is that of being pursued day and night by the image of the lost beloved.[27]

The suiting of place or weather to state of mind is another poetic feature that establishes itself in prose. This is of course something more completely carried out in *Paradise Lost* than anywhere else in literature, and numerous variations occur before the appearance of the new spirit in which Shelley without irony addresses the West Wind and Byron the sea.[28] Pope, remembering Ovid's Sappho, matches scene to the mood of his Eloisa. A more directly Miltonic version appears in the best-known scene of George Lillo, a playwright admired particularly by a pioneer of Sensibility in fiction, Prévost, and later by Rousseau. The hero of *George Barnwell, or The London Merchant,* 1731, is about to murder his rich uncle:

> A Dismal Gloom obscures the Face of Day; either the Sun has slipped behind a Cloud, or journeys down the West of Heaven, with more than common Speed to avoid the Sight of what I am doom'd to act. Since I set forth on this accurs'd Design, where'er I tread, methinks, the solid Earth trembles beneath my Feet. Yonder limpid Stream, whose hoary Fall had made a natural Cascade, as I pass'd by, in doleful Accents seem'd to murmur,—Murder. The Earth, the Air, and Water, seem'd concern'd; but that's not strange, the World is punish'd, and Nature feels a Shock, when Providence permits a good Man's Fall!   [III, iii][29]

Richardson in *Pamela*, 1740, almost never shows this kind of imaginative sensibility. The one passage I can recall where he does, Pamela's first view of Mr. B's country house, seems to echo phrases from *Comus* and "Eloisa."[30] The considerable extension of sensibility in *Clarissa* is gained very substantially by quotation from and allusion to the poets. A passion for quotation, mainly from the dramatic poets and especially from Dryden, is a main element in Lovelace's makeup, as a person and as a creation, and one of the features that makes him seem a complete being where Mr. B does not. The whole book is "literary," unlike *Pamela*, and both main characters occasionally take up book-learned poses: note Lovelace in the "Ivy-Cavern"—"Gloomy is my Soul! and all Nature round me partakes of my gloom!" (II, letter 19, p. 131)—and Clarissa speaking of solitude and contemplation (II, 24, p. 160). The novel is full of submerged allusions to Milton, especially his Hell and the prince of it: Lovelace in V, letter 8, page 88 describes one of his bad actions with the words "like the devil in Milton (an odd comparison tho'!)," but only a dense reader by then will agree it is odd.[31]

The accord between character or state of mind and setting is everywhere between the lines in *The Castle of Otranto*, 1764, and henceforward down the Gothic tradition. It settles perhaps rather late into the novel of sensibility. In Charlotte Smith's *Celestina*, 1790, when the lovers are parted Celestina in the Isle of Skye pursues "wild solitude" (III, ii, 21) and "images of horror" (40) and gazes on scenes formed by a "strange concussion" (27) or "tremendous convulsion" (III,71) of nature, while Willoughby diverts himself among the Pyrenees:

> Dashing down amongst these immense piles of stone, the cataracts, formed by the melting of the snows, and the ice of the Glaciers, in the bosom of the mountains, fell roaring into dark and abyss-like chasms, whither the eye feared to follow them—yet, frequently, amidst the wildest horrors of these great objects, was seen some little green recess, shaded by immense pines, cedars, or mountain-ash. . . . Never did such a spot offer itself to the eyes of Willoughby, but the figure of Celestina was instantly present to his imagination—he saw her sitting by him, enjoying the beautiful and romantic scenery; he . . . remembered a charming description given by Rousseau, in his Julie, of a spot of this sort among the rocks of Meillerie.—"Il sembloit que ce lieu désert, dût être l'asyle de deux amants; échappés seuls au bouleversement de la nature".
>
> For a moment or two he indulged such a delicious reverie, till the sudden recollection of the truth cruelly destroyed it.—Celestina was not, never could be his. . . . At that idea he started up, and hardly conscious of the rugged precipices beneath him, renewed his wandering researches; and sought, by activity of body, to chase the fearful phantoms of lost happiness that haunted his mind.   [IV, viii, 192-94][32]

Among Mrs Smith's numerous poetic quotations are two apt ones from *Paradise Lost* Willoughby is about to travel:

> Having thus loosened almost every tie that connected him with England, from which he did not wish even to hear, lest the information of Celestina's marriage should reach him, "The World was all before him where to chuse".
>   [IV, viii, 188]

Celestina leaving home is more pathetically affected:

> As she passed along the avenue, the bench under one of the great elms, where she had so often sat with Willoughby in their childhood . . . struck her most: it looked like a monument to the memory of lost happiness! As the great gate of the park shut after the carriage, she felt exiled for ever from the only spot in the world that contained any object interesting to her; and though little disposed to think of poetry, almost involuntarily repeated
>
> > "O unexpected stroke, worse than of death,
> > Must I then leave thee paradise? thus leave
> > Thee native soil, these happy walks and shades!"   [II, i, 12]

The development that we have been illustrating, the assimilation of eighteenth-century poetic effects and motifs into prose fiction, culminates in the novels of Ann Radcliffe in the 1790s. Mrs. Radcliffe deals mainly in landscape and mood: her main use for plot is to account for feeling. "The feeling . . . gives importance to the action and situation, and not the action and the situation to the feeling," as Wordsworth said of *Lyrical Ballads*. Her prospects are generally of two kinds: those appropriate to her delicate heroines, L'Allegro scenes of domestic joy, spots of sunny greenery enlivened with peasant dance and song; and those befitting the somber characters of her villains, portentous landscapes ranging in mood from Penseroso to horrific, "Sands, and Shoars, and desert Wildernesses," pervaded with groans, echoes, and funereal strains. To the former, distance lends charm and pathos and refinement, and their music is borne faintly to the ear; while the dreariness of the latter is intensified by the contrast with happier scenes now lost. These descriptions are built up from three sources: from travel books and paintings, but no less from the poets. Within paragraphs of description, and especially in epigraphs, Mrs. Radcliffe draws heavily on Thomson, Gray, Mason, Beattie, Ossian, and the romantic Shakespeare and Milton, frequently quoting more than suits her ostensible purpose. Moreover, her heroes and heroines all have fits of "the poet's rapture," brought on by landscape combined with emotional stress: their poems are dependent on the same models as their author's prose. The next generation of poets, including Scott, Shelley, and Byron, in their turn draw notably on Mrs. Radcliffe, as of course do numerous writers of prose.

The point here is that landscape, hitherto of very small relevance in fiction, from now on can be as vital to it as character; moreover, that its function will usually be symbolic and in some way to be related to Milton's theme of the loss of Eden. With landscape there comes into fiction, if not precisely the mourner or "lone enthusiast" (Beattie) of eighteenth-century elegiac poetry, then certainly his offspring, the romantic solitary. Childe Harold and the hero of *Alastor* are attached to scenes blasted or autumnal or full of ruins, while the poets of "Ode: Intimations" and "Kubla Khan" lament lost happy landscapes: these are matched in fiction by heroes of "sensibility" like Chateaubriand's René, fleeing with his grief and nostalgia into the forests of the New World, and by a whole line of later tragic exiles to forest, flood, or jungle, like Major John Richardson's Wacousta, Verne's Captain Nemo, and Hudson's Mr. Abel.

Perhaps we were unfair in accusing Mrs. Radcliffe of extravagance in her quotations. Let us look at a couple of examples. In *The Mysteries of Udolpho,* when the mysterious voice is heard in the castle, the chapter (II, vii; xx) is epigraphed:

Of aery tongues, that syllable men's names
On sands and shores and desert wildernesses.

The "aery tongues" are appropriate, and so is the *Comus* context of the virtuous lady's captivity by forces of disorder and riot, but why the indication of landscape? She quotes in *The Italian*, 1797, to head II, v (xvi), which describes the interrupted marriage of Ellena and Vivaldi in the lakeshore chapel,

> The lonely mountains o'er,
> And the resounding shore,
> A voice of weeping heard, and loud lament!
> From haunted spring, and dale,
> Edg'd with poplar pale,
> The parting genius is with sighing sent;
> With flower-inwoven tresses torn
> The nymphs in twilight shade of tangled thicket mourn.

Here the landscape is appropriate, but why bring in genius and nymph? Because in their imaginative origin the figures of these romances are essentially *genii loci*. The ventriloquist's voice in the castle has the rôle of conscience sounding in the villain's gloomy inner world; Ellena and her lover in joy and in grief are projections of the moods of particular kinds of landscape. Mrs. Radcliffe's young heroes and heroines keep their aspects as spirits of place[33] through the fineness with which their sensibilities are attuned to nature, while her villains suggest the destructive side of nature personified. In poetry, Ossian is an earlier figure with the same air of being the spokesman for the mood of a certain landscape; later, such beings abound in Wordsworth, from Lucy and Lucy Gray to the Leech-Gatherer and Michael. Some consciousness of this process of the engendering of persons from scenery can be read into two sentences of Charlotte Dacre's *Zofloya; or The Moor*, 1806, a very good product of the Radcliffe school, and one freely pillaged by Shelley for *Zastrozzi* and *St. Irvyne* (1810, 1811) and by Hogg for *Confessions of a Justified Sinner* (1824). The demoness Victoria is pursuing the fragile, fairylike Lilla with a dagger through a mountainous landscape:

> Again the fell poignard was uplifted for surer aim—when springing from her knees, on which she had cast herself, to implore mercy, she forgot at once her wounds and her weakness, and endeavoured by speed to escape her barbarous enemy; seeming, as she wildly flew, the beauteous and timid spirit of the solitude. [218–19]

Again:

> They now entered the cave; in the midst of a few straggling bandit ⟨sic⟩ sat the chief, still masked, with his bold companion by his side, showily habited, and looking the wild genius of the terrible abode. [241][34]

It is time we looked briefly at some conceptions of solitude, that two-sided state. In *Paradise Lost* the two accounts of solitary states most relevant to us are that of the fallen Adam looking through changed eyes at Eden (IX.1084–85) and that of the poet's nocturnal wanderings like "the wakeful Bird," at the opening of Book Three. There is, then, a blessed solitude of self-forgetfulness and communing with solemn powers, and a haunted solitude of egoism and remorse.

Prévost's Cléveland, "le philosophe anglais" brought up as a deist, has a good deal to say about solitude, most of it negative. He and his mother early seek it in a cavern, being convinced of the malignity of mankind; to the young boy it is a happy condition on the whole, except that he begins to long for a friend to share it. Later he blames some of his unhappiness in life on his eccentric education, as man is after all made for society. When at different times he particularly seeks solitude and even dreams of the grave, this is a result of the disabling melancholy to which the events of his life and, it seems, his nationality make him prone: "Oh! my dear!" as Clarissa exclaimed to Miss Howe, "the finer Sensibilities . . . make not happy!"[35]

A book widely read until well into the nineteenth century, in England as well as in Germany, was Dr. J. G. Zimmermann's *Ueber die Einsamkeit* (On Solitude), 1785.[36] The English preface of 1798 assures the reader:

> No writer appears more completely convinced than M. Zimmerman ⟨sic⟩, that man is born for society, or feels its duties with more refined sensibility.

Summarizing Zimmermann's main points, it continues:

> It is under the peaceful shades of Solitude that the mind regenerates and acquires fresh force; it is there alone that the happy can enjoy the fulness of felicity, or the miserable forget their woe; it is there that the bosom of sensibility experiences its most delicious emotions; it is there that creative Genius frees itself from the thraldom of society, and surrenders itself to the impetuous rays of an ardent imagination.   [vi, ix–x]

Favorite exemplars of the appreciation of retirement are Rousseau and, particularly, Petrarch; among emblems of the state are the Druids, and also Numa conversing with the nymph Egeria. Zimmermann wrote at length of the dangers of a solitude long unmixed with social converse or dominated by indolence or religious melancholy, but on the whole in this version his picture of the state is idyllic, and full of such touches as this:

> The mind of Petrarch was always gloomy and dejected, except when he was reading, writing, or resigned to the agreeable illusions of poetry, upon the banks of some inspiring stream, among the romantic rocks and mountains, or the flower-enamelled vallies of the Alps.
> ["Influence of Solitude upon the Mind," 47]

Figure 1. *Engravings from title pages of J. G. Zimmermann's* Solitude, or The Effect of Occasional Retirement. *London, 1798.*

In the English version of 1798, titled *Solitude,* the two title pages are adorned with two little engravings showing, first, a hermit meditating under a tree with book in hand and, second, a young man sitting beside a brook in the typical attitude of pensiveness or melancholy.[37] Other illustrations are titled, "Observe the Shepherd..." and "Rousseau contemplating the wild Beauties of Switzerland."

Our two quotations from *Zofloya* described two contrasted embodiments of the mood of solitary places: one beautiful and fragile, the other fierce and fear-inspiring. They correspond to the two contrasted kinds of picturesque scenery we discussed above in connection with eighteenth-century poetry and with Ann Radcliffe.[38] We mentioned also Wordsworth's human figures embodying qualities of landscape. These too fall into contrasting groups, with idealized beauty or innocence on the one hand (Lucy, Lucy Gray, the Idiot Boy, the Danish Boy) and guilt and sorrow on the other (the mother of "The Thorn," Oswald and Marmaduke in *The Borderers* as their more extravagant speeches depict them, the Wandering Jew). Between these two groups falls a third, including Michael, the Leech-Gatherer, and the shepherd figure of *The Prelude* Book Eight, whose special qualities are patience and endurance, reaching a kind of transcendence in the tasks of daily life. This middle ground is Wordworth's own; but the other two connect fairly readily with the conventions we have noted. The fragile, pathetic, or faintly macabre tinge of all the Wordsworthian "idyllic" figures, and of *Zofloya*'s Lilla, suggests that the ideal aspect of solitude is fading into the background in favor of the demonic one. When such childlike, virginal nature-sprites appear in nineteenth-century fiction, we shall usually discover them to be fatal or impossible loves. The demonic solitary, on the other hand, through the intensity of his passions will sometimes come (like Manfred, or Wacousta, or Heathcliff, or Captain Nemo) to take on a special quality, almost a purity, that eludes the morally simpler endings of the ordinary Gothic line that runs from Walpole and Clara Reeve (*The Old English Baron,* 1777) to Maturin and Hogg. We shall meet this type later as the Avenger.

If, as I have tried to demonstrate, the work of Mrs. Radcliffe and her successors represents the assimilation of some features of English poetry into prose fiction, comparable adaptations are to be found elsewhere. In France, Rousseau (see Appendix to this chapter), Saint-Pierre,[39] and Chateaubriand are the responsible authors: in Germany, to some extent Schiller[40] but principally Goethe. In both France and Germany it is specifically English literature that is drawn on. Several of the elegiac motifs we have noted—the loss of a pastoral Eden, the attendant nostalgia of the exile or wanderer, the barren waste with its delusions, the phantom quest through external scenes for a good realizable only in the mind, the sad waking from a happy dream, the poet as elegiac subject—are carried over into *Werther* before being fully unified and developed in *Tasso.*

Appendix: *Julie, ou la Nouvelle Héloïse*

We shall briefly note some points in Rousseau's *Julie, ou la Nouvelle Héloïse,* 1760, that reflect motifs we have been, or shortly shall be, discussing.

The work is epigraphed from Petrarch ("Non la conobbe il mondo, mentre l'ebbe / Conobbil'io, ch'a pianger qui rimasi"—in effect Wordsworth's "She lived unknown, and few could know . . ."). Part I, letter 23, p. 84, St-Preux in the mountains complains that his happy fancies have taken flight; 26, pp. 90–92, he compares the bleak, wintry scene around him with the state of his heart, then, after tormenting himself with a "fantôme" of his lost Julie, in an access of frenzy rushes from cavern to cavern. II, 14, p. 236, the world is a desert and a frightful solitude, and he goes about grasping at apparitions that vanish before they can be seized; 15, p. 236, to his claim that he dreams of her nightly, Julie replies that she sees him everywhere by day; 16, p. 244, her presence is so real to him that he tries to grasp it—"elle s'échappe, et je n'embrasse qu'une ombre"—"tes charmes triomphent de l'absence, ils me poursuivent par tout, ils me font craindre la solitude." III, 18, pp. 353, 357, Julie says that a moment's wandering from "la droite route" has led her imperceptibly to the abyss—"On tombe enfin dans le gouffre, & l'on se réveille épouvanté"—and later, "je suivois pour toute lumiere la fausse lueur des feux-errans qui me guidoient pour me perdre"; 20, p. 376, she speaks of having too long pursued "un vain fantôme," a false idea of virtue; 26, p. 396, St-Preux setting off on his travels declares, "Je vais errer dans l'univers sans trouver un lieu pour y reposer mon coeur." IV, 3, p. 412, St-Preux says that he tried in vain to flee Julie's image, being pursued by it to the ends of the earth; 17, pp. 518–19, contains the sentence quoted by Charlotte Smith above (p. 53)—here at Meillerie St-Preux shows Julie the rock from which he used to gaze towards her home—he has improved it with several inscriptions from Petrarch and Tasso "relatifs à la situation où j'étois en les traçant." V, 7, p. 603, Julie's estate suggests the Golden Age and the era of the patriarchs; 9, p. 616, St-Preux dreams emblematically of Julie veiled. Many of these expressions travel from Pope and Richardson via Rousseau into *Werther,* as will become evident.

The idyllic description of the Wolmar estate, recalling set pieces praising the Golden Age like the famous passage in Tasso's *Aminta,* suggests two possible fictional models: the presentation in Prévost's *Cléveland* (VI, 54) of the island of Madeira as a golden-age paradise to the heroine by the deceiving villain; and, more to the point, the elaborate lectures on the running of an estate that help fill out the second half of *Pamela.* However, Rousseau has incorporated this dead matter as a vital part of his design, as the ideal order and serenity of the later part of the lovers' career balances the wild prospects in the earlier part that convey the devastation wrought by their unrestrained passions.

A Richardsonian feature, but clearer in Rousseau, is the one described in Hans Wolpe's article "Psychological Ambiguity in *La Nouvelle Héloïse*" (*University of Toronto Quarterly* 28 [1959]: 279–90): the rivalry, worked out with parallels and variations, between love and friendship. The dying Clarissa gazes at a picture of Miss Howe: "Sweet and ever-amiable *Friend—Companion—Sister—Lover!* said she" (VII, letter 107, p. 461: cf. VI, 90, p. 404; 91, p. 405). This will appear later as a pastoral motif.

Four   Werther: *Elegiac Romance*

> . . . *shall I say my Mistress Melancholy, my Egeria, or my Evil*
> *Genius?*
>
> —*Robert Burton*

> . . . *these confused masses of Eulogy and Elegy, with their mad*
> *Petrarchan and Werterean ware.* . . .
>
> —*Thomas Carlyle*

The obvious differences between *Torquato Tasso,* 1789, and *Die Leiden des jungen Werthers* (The Sorrows of Young Werther), 1774,[1] are that Tasso's story has a happier outcome, and that its characters embodying the practical world and rational judgment are fully and sympathetically developed and allowed to speak for themselves. Werther also is more isolated than Tasso in that his Charlotte, for all her understanding and affection, is a normal if passive young woman adequate to and happy in her domestic ties and duties, whereas the princess and Tasso are two of a kind. Werther and Tasso are both artists; with both the nature of their sensibility raises questions as to the basis of their inspiration; each pursues and loses a soulmate and is convinced of the hostility of everyone else about him, showing an excessive (though oddly blind) sympathy in one quarter and very little elsewhere. In each an unbalanced emotional life results from an unbalanced sensibility, so that the love-tragedy is not central but symptomatic.

Tasso, as a drama, concentrates on relations among persons; though these relations carry themes supported by symbols, it is they that are the substance of the play. *Werther* is quite undramatic: it centers on a single person, and in form and expression is almost lyrical. We can call it an elegiac romance, considering both its tone and the shape of its central event. *Werther's* matter is its hero's sensibility and its contents, in which Nature, both form and spirit, bulks almost as large as personalities and happenings. The natural world, which in *Tasso* is metaphor and symbol, in *Werther* is subject matter, and plays as such a critical part.

At the opening of the book that describes his sorrows, Werther, seeking to forget an unhappy love affair, finds himself in the springtime in "paradisal" country surroundings, rejoicing in solitude amid the beauties of nature, in fact passively possessed by them. Earth and sky repose in his soul like the image of a beloved woman (May 10, 1771). Though too absorbed in his tranquil existence to draw a line, he feels himself a greater artist than ever before. Detached from the world of men, he is wholly open to impressions from nature.

> Every tree, every hedge is a bouquet of flowers, and one could wish to become a cockchafer, so as to be able to swim about in a sea of pleasant scents.   [May 4]

The scenes where he wanders, conversing with peasants and children, are pervaded by a classical or "patriarchal" (May 12) calm. Nature is benign, idyllic, harmonious, sympathetic to man and to life at large. Above all, perhaps, it is vital, crammed with multifarious life. Werther's mood for the most part has in it little of calm, rather an intoxication, first of rapture, later of despondency. It is characterized less by serenity than by ecstatic "soaring" and "swimming," and there are moments when he loses the sense either of himself or of his surroundings. Perceiving the world of nature, his soul becomes "the mirror of the infinite God":

> But I am overpowered by it, I sink under the force of the splendor of these visions.   [May 10]

Werther's complete contentment does not last. On May 17 he complains of the lack of companionship. On May 22 he describes

> the limitations within which the active and exploring powers of man are confined.

The inner life is as unsatisfactory as the outer:

> I return into myself, and find a world, one more of inklings and dim desires than of clear conception and active power. And then everything swims before my senses, and I go on smiling dreamily at the world.

The symbolic theme of *Tasso* concerns the equilibrium of inner and outer worlds. In *Werther* the central opposition seems to be between the confined and the limitless, and the writer continually plays with and varies the theme of their confrontation. The ordinary condition of man is bounded and hemmed in: when the bounds are lost, the effect ranges from a moment's delirium to the individual's destruction. So at least the next few letters appear to suggest.

In the letter of May 26, Nature is described as the artist's one inexhaustible instructor. To apply rule and regulation destroys art as it would destroy love; genius, itself destructive, is a rushing torrent which the prudent souls settled along the bank strive to restrain, for fear it should overflow their kitchen gardens. On June 21 Werther discusses contrary or successive human urges, that sending men out to wander and discover and that drawing them back to a confined existence. A distant prospect allures like the future; one longs to be "there," only to find it another "here": the goal has cheated us; so the restless traveler finds at home at last the happiness that through the wide world he sought in vain. July 24:

> I have never been happier, my feeling for nature down to the smallest stone or blade of grass has never been more complete and profound, and yet—I do not know how I am to express myself, my conceptual power is so feeble: everything swims and sways so in my mind that I can grasp no clear outline. . . .

On August 12 he talks with Albert about suicide:

> Observe a man in his circumscribed state, how impressions affect him and ideas become established in his mind, till at length an increasing passion robs him of all powers of calm reflection and ends by destroying him.

Continuing, he tells the story of a young girl betrayed by her lover. He stresses the "narrow circle of household pursuits" in which she grew up and the limited nature of her wishes and desires before new ones were aroused by her betrayer:

> Her longing, uncorrupted by the empty amusements of a fickle vanity, makes directly for its aim: she wants to be his, to enjoy in an eternal union all those pleasures she has long desired. Repeated promises, sealing to her the certainty of all her hopes, bold caresses that increase her desires, surround her whole soul; she floats in a vague consciousness, an anticipation of every joy; her feelings are at the highest pitch of excitement, finally she stretches out her arms to embrace all she has longed for—and her lover leaves her. Stunned, almost senseless, she stands on the edge of an abyss. . . .

Before describing the culmination of this theme[2] in the letter of August 18, we shall note three relevant passages in Book Two. The letter of October 20, 1771, speaks of the danger of solitude: our imagination, compelled by its nature to expand itself, figures forth a range of beings of which we ourselves are the lowest and everyone outside us appears more perfect; that ideal happiness and splendor with which we compare our own state so painfully is our own creation. On November 3, 1772, speaking of his past and present state, Werther says his heart is dead, his tears are dried up; the outward scene whose infinities he once longed to embrace now is empty for him, and his own creative power, which once produced worlds around him, now has left him. Again, on December 6:

> What is man, the demigod we extol! . . . if he soars upwards in joy, or sinks down in sorrow, is he not checked in both, brought back to dull, cold consciousness, just at the moment when he longed to lose himself in the depths of infinity?

The contrast is not between joy and sorrow, notably, but between the infinity to which they both lead and the narrowed consciousness to which man's weakness too soon returns him.

If there is a single crucial event in *Werther,* it is the pastoral catastrophe described in the letter of August 18, 1771, the change in his vision of Nature.

> The warm, full feeling of my heart for living Nature that flooded me with such bliss and made the world around me a paradise, has now become an intolerable vexation, a tormenting spirit that pursues me wherever I turn.

The life of the valley, the river, the groves, the animation of all Nature, exalted him to feel "in this overflowing fullness as if ⟨he⟩ had become a god, and the glorious figures of the infinite world stirred animatingly in ⟨his⟩ soul." A panorama unfolded before him of vast mountains and abysses, cataracts, rivers, all teeming with life:

> All, all peopled with thousandfold beings; while men crowd together for safety in their petty houses, and build their narrow nests, and in their minds lord it over the wide world!

In all things breathes "the spirit of the Eternally-creating." Werther has often longed to be carried to the margin of the boundless sea, there to drink of the bliss of life from the foaming cup of the infinite,

> and for one moment only, with the confined powers of my breast, to feel a single drop of all the blessedness of that Being who brings forth all things in and through himself.

This quest of the absolute in Nature, resembling the Faustian passion to embrace all of experience, has now given place to a different vision.

> It is as if before my soul a curtain had been drawn back, and the prospect of eternal life changed before me into the abyss of the eternally open grave.

Time in its course is overwhelmingly swift; everything is carried away in its torrent, submerged, and dashed against the rocks. Everyone at every moment is consumed and also consumes; at every step we destroy countless living beings and the fragile structures raised by the insects. He is less disturbed by floods and earthquakes than by "the devouring power that lies concealed everywhere in Nature," the universal mutual preying.

> Heaven and earth and the active powers about me! I can see nothing but an endlessly devouring, endlessly ruminating monster.

The shift is from an infinitely creative Nature to an infinitely destructive one; and yet it is the same process. Only the imagery and feeling have changed. The "creative" scene opens with a wholeness and harmony of rocky mountain and green valley, widening to mountain ranges, abysses, cataracts and rivers and the infinite sea, with their numberless contrasts and immense variety of life; and all this is set against the confined, as it were barricaded, existence that men in their blindness choose. Werther, who has already clearly indicated (from the first two letters on) that his is a soul especially open to the wonders of Nature, dreams of an instant of the life without barriers, the merging of his spirit with the infinite life. In the "destructive" scene, torrent, "grave," and "abyss" dominate: immensity breeds not rapture but horror. What is without bounds is the indifferent, the mindlessly devouring capacity of a Nature no longer beneficent and quasi-divine but a "monster." The "limited" here is the fragile structure raised by life, from the anthill to (we infer) human individuality or sanity, liable at any moment to be broken into and crushed from outside.

When in August of the following year Werther returns (as "a wanderer, a pilgrim on the earth"—June 16) to Wahlheim, his disillusionment progresses to a farther stage. All is changed: Charlotte is married, the youngest child of the kindly peasant woman is dead. He compares himself to a ghost returning to the splendid castle left by the living man to his son and finding it burnt out and in ruins (August 21). "As Nature declines towards autumn, so it becomes autumn in and around me. My leaves are turning yellow..." (September 4). Ossian has replaced Homer in his heart (October 12). The landscape of Ossian, with its caverns, graves, cold grasses, and lonely northern sea, represents not a "destructive" Nature but a Nature dead and haunted, full of memories of a happier past and the sighs of forlorn ghosts. On October 19 Werther complains of "the dreadful emptiness that I feel in my breast!" On October 27, "I have so much, but without her it all means nothing." It is a haunted emptiness that characterizes his inner world like the outward scene. The letter of November 3 already cited describes as "a little varnished picture" a Nature whose beauty and animation he no longer feels. On November 30 he meets a madman searching in vain in this season for flowers for his mistress, and compares this man's state with his own. The madman blames the States-General for his condition: happy he who can ascribe his unhappiness to an outward cause rather than to its true source within! And happy are they who, however vainly, undertake with trust long pilgrimages in search of health or peace of conscience.

The climactic "natural" scene near the end of *Werther* is that of the flood, described on December 12, 1772. Werther says his state is like that of those unfortunates who used to be believed possessed by an evil spirit. A mysterious rage drives him outside to wander in this inclement season. The previous night, seized by such an impulse, he had hastened out and encountered a flood: the river had risen and overflowed in a sudden thaw, and the whole valley appeared "a raging sea in the howling of the wind." Seeing the moon reflected in the wild waters, he was filled with fear and longing together.

> With outspread arms I stood facing the abyss and gasped, "Down, down!" and lost myself in the ecstatic idea of dashing down there my torments and sorrows, to rage there with the waves! . . . how gladly would I have abandoned my humanity to tear apart the clouds with that storm-wind, to clasp the floods! Yes! and will not this rapture one day perhaps be imparted to my imprisoned spirit?

This ecstasy of destruction recalls the ecstasy of total participation described in the letter of August 18, 1771; but here it is death, not life, that he longs to embrace entire. Following this moment, he notes with sadness that landmarks sacred to himself and Charlotte have been swept away:

> And the sunbeam of the happy past touched me, as to a prisoner might come a dream of flocks, meadows, and honors!

The infinite of sunshine, activity, and life is lost in the past, to be recalled only as a moment's delusive dream; the boundless world from which the "imprisoned" man is still held back is the "abyss" of annihilation. The former boundless world has become the latter, as the idyllic valley has become a chaos of raging waters.

We first encountered the raging torrent in the letter of May 26, 1771, where it is a metaphor for the power of genius, here closely associated with the creative power of Nature, that the prudent seek to confine as a destructive force. In the letter of August 18, the sea is the symbol of the creative infinity of life, while in the "destructive" vision that follows time is the rushing river that carries everything away. In the scene of the flood, the water represents an infinite power of destruction. The shift in the symbol from the absolutely "creative" to the absolutely "destructive" is prepared for by its use in the May 26 letter, suggesting that the vision of an idyllic and vital Nature already contains within it that of a world of threatening and disrupting powers. For a warning indication we might point back to the words of May 10: "But I am overpowered by it, I sink under the force of the splendor of these visions." The glorious is also the overpowering and crushing to the artist's sensibility; elsewhere he remarks on the lassitude and swimming vision that accompany his closest attunement to Nature.

Another threatening phrase immediately follows, opening the letter of May 12:

> I know not whether deceiving spirits haunt this neighborhood, or whether the warm and blissful fancy that makes everything around me seem so paradisal comes from my own heart. In front of the house there is a well, to which I am bound by a spell like Melusina and her sisters.

On May 22 he feels that "the life of man is only a dream." In the flood scene much later he compares himself to one possessed by an evil spirit. References to delusions of one kind and another are frequent; a few, like the madman's explanation of his unhappiness, are briefly consoling, but most are exclusively destructive. After Charlotte's marriage, Werther still mentally calls up possibilities that could yet enable him to be happy with her, such as Albert's death:

> . . . and then I pursue the phantom, till it leads me to abysses from which I start back in terror.   [August 21, 1772]

The association of delusive desire with the "abyss" is cumulatively built up. The deceived girl who drowned herself "stretches out her arms to embrace all she has longed for—and her lover leaves her. Stunned, almost senseless, she stands on the edge of an abyss. . ." (August 12, 1771). On August 21:

> In vain I stretch out my arms toward her when I wake in the morning after oppressive dreams; in vain I seek her at night in my bed when a happy, innocent dream has deceived me. . . .

There is no abyss in this letter, but Werther when he wakes pours forth "a torrent of tears" and weeps "comfortless at the prospect of the dark future." "Future" itself was linked with "distance" as delusive on June 21, but this is its sad reality. On August 30 he describes a faintness that often overtakes him in Charlotte's company, culminating in a weakening of his hold on reality: "I often do not know whether I really exist!" This feeling drives him out to wander among precipitous cliffs and trackless woods until he lies down exhausted to sleep in the moonlight. On September 10 he sees Charlotte for what he expects will be the last time:

> They went away down the avenue: I stood there, looked after them in the moonlight, threw myself on the earth and wept: then I sprang up and ran out onto the terrace, from which I could still see, down there in the shadow of the high lindens, her white dress faintly gleaming. I stretched out my arms, and it vanished.

On October 30 of the next year, he says how close he has often come to embracing Charlotte, and how hard it is "to see so much loveliness moving about before one and not be permitted to grasp it." On November 24 she sings to him,[3] and he swears inwardly never to kiss those lips "about which heavenly spirits hover." On December 6 Werther complains that her image pursues him; when he closes his eyes he sees hers before him, "like an ocean, like an abyss." It is in this letter that he complains that man cannot lose himself in either joy or sorrow.

Charlotte through the progression of these passages takes on in Werther's mind a delusive, phantasmal quality, along with an aura of magical taboo. As a person she does not at all resemble the princess of *Tasso*; but as a vanishing moonlit figure, inaccessible, untouchable, to whom one stretches one's arms in vain, and in consequence a form of delusion perhaps leading to destruction (Tasso's "Siren"), she is handled very similarly. Each begins as the ideal, the personification of all that is highest in the lover's surroundings and in his own nature; but necessarily the ideal becomes more and more a fleeing one, leading the protagonist to the brink of the abyss. The necessity is different in the two works, but in both it develops from the protagonists' excesses of sensibility. Tasso proceeds from extravagant triumph to extravagant overture towards Antonio to extravagant concentration on the world of his own feelings, and thence to catastrophe; the feeling passivity towards experience, and especially towards Nature and the growth of love, robs him of his creative power, unfits him for dealings with his fellows, and makes him helpless to spare himself or those he loves.

Leaving aside resemblances of detail like the relation of the Bauernbursch and maniac incidents in *Werther* to events in Tasso's career, we can notice in both the rôle of "Nature" and natural landscape. Werther passes over a two-year period from an idyllic spring scene with almost golden-age features to the desolation of fall and winter, haunted with evil spirits and culminating in the scene of the flood, prefigured by the young girl's drowning described earlier (August 12, 1771) and the long reading from Ossian. *Tasso* begins in an idyllic though confined setting; the mental landscape gradually darkens, and the imagery leads through solitudes, night, wilderness, river, to the sea. In both works as the setting becomes less harmonious or self-sufficient the protagonist gradually becomes that special pastoral figure, the wanderer or unsatisfied traveler,[4] shut out from the contentment that familiar scenes once offered. Both pursue a goal elusive or delusive and connected with the memory of lost happiness, the prisoner's dream[5] or the *fata morgana* appearing to the exile. In both, and this is the central point of resemblance I want to stress, the landscape is from the opening elegiac in its feeling, even at its happiest nostalgically imbued with the graces of a lost past. To the scenes of *Tasso* in particular the closest visual equivalent would be the classical landscapes of Poussin or of Claude Lorrain, with their proportion, their planes of distance, their dark woody masses against which glimmer water and marble columns.

In chapter 3 we looked at a number of conventional eighteenth-century expressions, most of which appear again, with special dramatic force, in either *Werther* or *Tasso*. Two more figures particularly relevant to *Tasso* are the shipwreck and the collapsing house. Clarissa writes conventionally enough to Miss Howe (V, letter 5, p. 55), "I have escaped with my

Honour, and nothing but my worldly prospects . . . have suffered in this wreck of my hopefuller fortunes." Prévost frequently uses "naufrage" in the same way.[6] Cowper's "The Castaway," Burns's "To a Mountain Daisy" (quoted p. 38), the last act of *Tasso,* and later *In Memoriam* xvi, all fill out the expression with meaning. More important, for its later development, is the figure of the shattered or dissolving building. Dryden is fond of it as a figure for a person, a scheme, or a state of mind, and his regular word for it, recalling Prospero, is "fabric." At least, if "fabric" does not every time recall Prospero, it is used singularly often for buildings metaphorical, visionary, or tending to dissolution. Here is Dryden:

> I begin
> To stagger; but I'll prop myself within.
> The spacious Tow'r no ruin shall disclose,
> Till down at once the mighty Fabrick goes   [*Aureng-Zebe,* 1676, V.i.425–28]

> The tyrant must not wed Almeyda; no,
> That ruins all the Fabrick I am raising.   [*Don Sebastian,* 1690, II.i.350–51]

Prévost expresses himself similarly: "J'étois trahi par une perfide qui . . . a détruit en un jour tout l'édifice de ma félicité" (*Cléveland,* V,33). Tasso asks:

> Has he not overturned, from roof to base,
> The entire structure of my happiness?   [IV.v.278–83]

In the play's last scene, Tasso's desperation makes him carry the metaphor over to the actual building in which he is:

> Has my sorrow,
> As if the earth had shaken, turned the house
> Into a frightful heap of rubble?

The falling house or splitting ship[7] becomes an elegiac motif when the physical shell is seen, as here, as the vessel of consciousness.

Some other terms may be noted, ones which are usually so flatly employed as hardly to seem metaphors at all. They include floods and torrents, storms and tempests, precipices and abysses, labyrinths, mazes, deserts and wildernesses, and they are linked with such abstractions as "troubles," "passions," and "life." They are not new with our period: witness Burton:

> In a word, the World it self is a maze, a labyrinth of errors, a desert, a wilderness, a den of theeves, cheaters, &c., full of filthy puddles, horrid rocks, precipitiums, an ocean of adversity, an heavy yoke, wherein infirmities and calamities overtake, and follow one another, as the Sea waves. . . .
> [I.ii.3.10]

Most can be abundantly illustrated from Dryden's plays or from any one of *Cléveland, Clarissa, La Nouvelle Héloïse, Die Räuber, Celestina*. Such a use as Goethe's in *Werther*, where they are linked with landscape both real and highly significant, gives them the kind of force, not merely figurative but symbolic, that several of them had a century before in Milton. They are indexes of distance from Eden; and having gained this force, they tend to carry it over into the next period of literature.

Appendix 1: "Trilogie der Leidenschaft"

The work of Goethe's later life that most specifically recalls both *Werther* and *Tasso* is the cycle of three poems making up the "Trilogie der Leidenschaft" (Trilogy of Passion): "An Werther" (To Werther), which Goethe characterized as "exposition"; "Elegie," "catastrophe"; and "Aussöhnung" (Reconciliation), "a reconciling conclusion." The occasion is Goethe's parting from Ulrike von Levetzow. The three poems were written separately and in a different order, and later arranged as we have them. "An Werther" was written for a new edition of *Werthers Leiden*, and "Aussöhnung" is a brief lyric about the reconciling power of music. The famous lines from *Tasso*, "Und wenn der Mensch..." (V.v.3432–33), are adapted to supply the last line of "An Werther" and an epigraph to the "Elegie."

The "Trilogie" in form and symbolism, which is all that here briefly concerns us, is very close to pastoral elegy. The imagery moves between spring and winter, "paradise" and wilderness, and between inner and outer worlds. Another contrast, less explicit, is between youth and age. "An Werther" speaks of the confusions of youth: happiness is near, but we fail to recognize it. Stepping forth in the springtime, the young man in gay freedom thinks he sees it in woman; he gives up his freedom for the confinements and disappointments of love, wandering the "labyrinth" of the passions. (Cf., for example, from *Faust*'s dedicatory poem, "die Klage / Des Lebens labyrinthisch irren Lauf"; Werther's letter of August 12, 1771: "Die Natur findet keinen Ausweg aus dem Labyrinthe der verworrenen und widersprechenden Kräfte, und der Mensch muss sterben.") Werther by his "terrible parting" hasn't missed much, after all. The "Elegie" commences with the paradise of love, but this fails to last; the lover must take leave, and he departs as though driven forth by a flaming cherub (iv). Nevertheless, the world is all before him with its beauty, and the sky with its numerous changing forms. Gazing into the heavens, he thinks he sees the form of the beloved:

> Yet but a moment dost thou boldly dare
> To clasp an airy form instead of hers;
> Back to thine heart! thou'lt find it better there,
> For there in changeful guise her image stirs.... [vii]

There follows a history of his happiness with the beloved, and of how she rescued him from a previous state in which his empty heart was a wilderness peopled with specters; like sunlight and like spring, she melts self-will and egotism. But all that is over; now he is far away:

Yearnings unquenchable still drive me on,
All counsel, save unbounded tears, is gone.   [xix]

Her image is still present to the mind, but wavering and sometimes disappearing, then uncertain, then again bright and distinct:

How could the smallest comfort here be flowing?
The ebb and flood, the coming and the going!   [xxi]

The last two stanzas, set off from the body of the poem, are a little different in imagery. Companions, leave me here, alone among the rocks in the moorland; the world is open to you, go on and probe Nature's secrets:

To me is all, I to myself am lost,
Who the immortals' favourite erst was thought;
They, tempting, sent Pandoras to my cost,
So rich in wealth, with danger far more fraught;
They urged me to those lips, with rapture crowned,
Deserted me, and hurled me to the ground.   [xxiii]

The transition from "paradise" to dreary moorland is the regular pastoral "fall." Associated with it is the motif of the phantom-woman, the cloud image delusively clasped. The image "within" proves equally phantasmal. Both are identified at last as "Pandora," the fatal gift of the gods. The theme of probing Nature's secrets as the task of those not yet disillusioned, we shall note elsewhere in a different context. "Aussöhnung," the final poem, represents the elegiac consolation, here accomplished by the power of music.

(The lines quoted above are from the English translation by John Storer Cobb in Goethe's *Works*, vol. 7, *Poetical Works*, pp. 248–49.)

Appendix 2: The Lieder Cycles

A special and limited development is the way Werther leaves his mark on German lieder cycles. The great cycles are thoroughgoing Romantic phenomena, especially as they deal with love. The earliest of them, Beethoven's "An die ferne Geliebte" (1816), with very undistinguished text, speaks of love in absence and how spring comes everywhere but in the lover's heart. In the separate songs of the Romantic lieder composers, happy landscapes, tragic seascapes, brokenhearted wanderers, sirens, nixies, and phantoms of lost delight are everywhere to be met with. The four cycles expecially relevant are Schubert's "Schöne Müllerin" and "Winterreise," Mahler's "Lieder eines fahrenden Gesellen," which follows the narrative line of the first two rather closely and is really a late re-creation of this particular Romantic mode, and, a little apart, Schumann's "Dichterliebe." The Schubert cycles are both settings of groups of lyrics by Wilhelm Müller; in each a young man tells how unhappy love makes him an outcast. "Die schöne Müllerin" depicts a landscape from first to last idyllic, with increasing stress on the stream in which at the end the young miller drowns himself and his grief. "Die Winterreise" is wilder and more desolate. The wanderer sets forth in the winter night, with no destination, but in flight from memory and passion; his happiness is lost like the flowers of summer that the snow has hidden. A frozen river he passes reminds him of the state of his own heart. He is led astray by a will-o'-the-wisp; later he dreams of the return of spring and love, but wakes again to the world of chilly reality. Frost falls on his head and he imagines that he has suddenly grown old; a black crow, symbol of doom, hovers over him. A rising storm again seems to express his own state; then he is lured on by another illusion, what appear to be the lights of a house beaming through the ice and snow. Half delirious, he thinks he sees three suns, of which two—her eyes?—disappear. At the end, he encounters the figure of the old organ-grinder, cranking his melancholy tunes through the winter day with no one to listen: should the wanderer go along with him? The Mahler work similarly begins with the young man fleeing from unhappy love; he journeys through smiling pastoral scenes where he once was happy but now sees only dreariness. He is led onwards by the blue eyes of his lost love, moving phantomlike before him. At last he is promised rest, in sleep or death.

"Dichterliebe" is an arrangement of poems from Heine's *Buch der Lieder*. Its hero is not the artless provincial youth but the poet, and its scenes are accordingly the sophisticated ones of garden and city. The poet loves a flowerlike maiden, and his joys blossom with the spring and are shared with the flowers, as later his griefs are. The most solemn of the songs, though it ends in a joke, opens with the tremendous sight of Cologne Cathedral mirrored in the Rhine; and this great union of profound river and aspiring stone centers on an image that is after all that of his love. The maiden then is lost to him; cruel, she is herself preyed on by remorse. Now he is left to grief, solitude, and dream. In dreams she appears, smiling on him and offering a cypress branch, symbol of death; with the morning, all is taken away. His dreams take him also into the fairy world of the old stories, radiant, melodious, and where every stream is full of magical reflections. Could he only return there! but again, morning takes it all away. It is time that the old songs and dreams were buried. Aided by the old folklore powers of the Rhine valley, he has his love and grief carried in a great coffin out to sea and there ritually sunk.

We have already seen a number of the motifs at work in these lyric cycles: the loss of love paralleled by the transition to fall and winter, the lover turned wanderer, the vanishing happy dream, the will-o'-the-wisp, the delusions, the water resembling or overwhelming the passionate heart. Some others—the appearance of sudden aging, the crazy music, the splendid edifice on the water—we shall encounter later. As important as these individual motifs are the emotional tone, the feeling for landscape, and the repetition and interconnection of allusion, that make these works constitute a special line on their own.

Part Two

Five   Narcissus : Echo : Siren

> And all the phantom, Nature, stands —
> With all the music in her tone
> A hollow echo of my own, —
> A hollow form with empty hands.
>
> —Alfred, Lord Tennyson
>
> ... or if there be true happiness amongst us, 'tis but for a time;
> "A handsome maid above, a fish below."
>
> —Robert Burton

In the simplest form of his story, Narcissus is a beautiful youth who either pines away and dies for love of his own image reflected in a spring or river, or drowns trying to grasp it. Very likely the story is to be connected with the superstition, found in ancient Greece as elsewhere, that to catch sight of one's own reflection or dream of one's own image is a sign of approaching death. Frazer more specifically explains the death of Narcissus as due perhaps to one of those water fairies who drag one's reflection under water, leaving one to die without it.[1] This explanation can be supported from the myth of Hylas, the companion of Heracles, who when sent to a spring for water was drawn down by the water nymphs, who were enamored of his beauty. The theme of the "false mermaid," the lady "with a comb and a glass in her hand," and other varieties of water fairy, is very common in European folklore, and in Romantic writers comes into fresh prominence, as in Goethe's poem "Der Fischer" and Heine's "Die Lorelei."

Whatever the reason, the developed Narcissus myth very rarely leaves the beautiful youth alone with his image; there is nearly always a shadowy third. The Renaissance emblem writers Alciati and Whitney use Narcissus as an emblem of self-love, and there in the background is a figure who could be Teiresias trying in vain to warn him of his doom, or perhaps Nemesis pointing him out as an example. In another classical version than the one with Teiresias and Nemesis, the extra figure is the ghost of a young man, Ameinias, whose love Narcissus has fatally spurned, and in another it may stand for the dead twin sister with whom Narcissus was in love and for whose sake he gazes on the reflection of features identical with hers.[2] These two accounts, however it comes about, neatly represent two obvious outward manifestations of morbid narcissism, whether psychological or literary: homosexuality and incest.

The most familiar account of Narcissus is that given by Ovid in Book Three of the *Metamorphoses*. It is he who makes Teiresias utter his warning, and he brings in too the punishing goddess Nemesis, who at the prayer of a rejected lover sees to it that Narcissus shall encounter his reflection. However, his most important addition to the theme of Narcissus is that of Echo, the nymph despised by him who at last fades away to nothing but an answering voice. Just why Ovid's sense of fitness led him to bring the two figures together is not at all certain; but once linked, they seem to belong together. As the mirror image is a visual reflection, so the echo is an aural reflection: "a shadow of all sounds," Shelley calls it in *Adonais*. Thus Echo and the reflection of Narcissus in a way mean the same thing; the calling nymph who in this story replaces the water fairy is metaphorically the same as the deluding image.[3]

The figure of Echo has a place in Renaissance commentary on the myth of Narcissus. Bacon's exposition of the latter in *De Sapientia Veterum* (Of the Wisdom of the Ancients), quoted by Sandys in his commentary on the *Metamorphoses*, derives in the main from Boccaccio, *De Genealogiis Deorum Gentium* VII, who interprets Echo as Fame:

> Fame flies from many who care little about it and who, seeing in water (that is, in insubstantial worldly pleasures) themselves (that is, all their ambition), disdain renown, and presently pass away as if they had never been, leaving behind them names not unlike the flower, which in the morning is purple and fresh but in the evening drooping and faded. . . .
> [Quoted by Lemmi, *The Classic Deities in Bacon*, p. 184.]

However, as I have suggested, it is in Romantic literature that the story of Narcissus and its associations are most elaborately developed. There the water fairy takes many forms, being by no means confined to German ballad imitations or to reshapings of the Melusina and assorted nixie legends. We could see something like her in, for example, Shelley's false Epipsyche and the apparition or apparitions of *Alastor*. Little Pearl, the reflection of her mother's guilt, till the climactic scene of *The Scarlet Letter* is presented as demonic or an elf-child, still to be endowed with a soul, like Fouqué's Undine or the Little Mermaid of Hans Andersen's story. The water fairy's incarnations range from the innocently appealing to the distinctly hellish. In this variety she is true to her origins; the European mermaid is after all derived partly from the sirens of Homer and partly again from Atergatis, the fish-tailed form of the Mediterranean mother-goddess, who has among her progeny the Whore of Babylon, sitting on many waters. Into the latter's orbit gets sucked, in European balladry, the woman of Samaria at the well: in the Middle Ages her five husbands and the sixth who is not her husband are interpreted as the five senses and the devil;[4] and Blake in the *Descriptive Catalogue* quite properly makes a shop-worn Venus of her descendant, the Wife of Bath. It would be Bath.

Some curious things happen also to Narcissus in his transit to the present, the strangest of them being his allegorization in Neoplatonic and Hermetic philosophy.[5] The first tractate of the *Corpus Hermeticum,* the "Poimandres," retells the Narcissus story as part of the history of the Primal Man, itself a mythological explanation of how it was that elements of the spiritual world came to be imprisoned in the lower world of matter. In this account, the Father brings forth a Man in his own image, and love of his own beauty in him causes him to allow the Man to pass down through the hierarchy of the spheres. At the lower limit of the heavenly realm he reaches that ruled by Nature, who sees in him "the beautiful form of God."

> When she saw that he had in himself inexhaustible beauty . . . , Nature smiled with love; for what she saw was the features of that marvellously beautiful form of the Man reflected in the water and in his shadow on the earth. And he, having perceived that form resembling himself as present in Nature, reflected in the water, loved it and wished to dwell there; and at the instant when he wished it, it was done, and he came to inhabit the irrational form. Then Nature, having received into herself the beloved, surrounded him entirely, and they were joined; for they were burning with passion.
>
> And that is why, alone of all beings living on the earth, man is double-natured, mortal in his body, immortal in the essential Man.

The writer then goes on to tell how from the embrace of Nature and the divine Man were born seven androgynes, which God in time separated, giving them the commandment to "increase and multiply," but at the same time informing them that "the cause of death is love."

Out of this very suggestive narrative with its repeated Narcissus motif, let us note here just two points, which will be relevant later on. First, the beautiful reflection is used as a decoy by a (much less attractive?) female power called Nature: in that way, this story seems closer to folklore origins than the sophisticated account of Narcissus in Ovid, who splits the water fairy into Echo and reflection. Second, the mingling of the Man and Nature suggests an androgynous single form, even if we were not told that androgynes spring from the event. The Androgyne or Hermaphrodite as a symbol of unfallen perfection is familiar from the fable told by Aristophanes in the *Symposium* and from later syncretistic speculation on the creation narrative in Genesis, and as a type of ideal beauty it is occasionally found in classical sculpture (and in Shelley's *Epipsychidion* fragments and one poem each of Gautier and Swinburne). However, the obvious classical source here is an appropriately sinister one, Ovid's story of the youth Hermaphroditus and his capture by the hair-combing reflection-gazing fountain nymph Salmacis.[6] Ovid's ornamental details are striking (*Metamorphoses* IV): for example, gazing on his beauty, Salmacis's "eyes flamed with a brilliance like that of the dazzling sun, when his bright disk is reflected in a mirror." Salmacis is the original female clinging vine, and the gods grant her prayer never to be separated from him:

> the nymph and the boy were no longer two but a single form, possessed of a dual nature, which could not be called male or female, but seemed to be at once both and neither.

A prayer of Hermaphroditus then also is granted by the gods: henceforward the pool is cursed, so that anyone who touches its waters will depart weakened and effeminate. It is not hard to see how this story readily gets crossed with that of Narcissus. At any rate, investigation of Narcissus will occasionally throw up figures recalling the Androgyne.

The combined Narcissus–Hermaphroditus occurs again in Blake's *The Four Zoas*, Night the First, following the fall of Tharmas and his separation from his emanation Enion. The Spectre of Tharmas after spending three days in "self admiring raptures" unites with Enion, in a manner recalling the myth of the "Poimandres":[7]

> Mingling his brightness with her tender limbs, then high she soar'd
> Above the ocean: a bright wonder, Nature,
> Half Woman & half Spectre; all his lovely changing colours mix
> With her fair crystal clearness; in her lips & cheeks his poisons rose
> In blushes like the morning, and his scaly armour softening,
> A monster lovely in the heavens or wandering on the earth,
> With spectre voice incessant wailing, in incessant thirst,
> Beauty all blushing with desire, mocking her fell despair.

Enion herself at the end of Night the Third becomes an Echo figure:

> For now no more remain'd of Enion in the dismal air,
> Only a voice eternal wailing in the Elements.

In Night the Third Urizen listens to the vision narrated by Ahania, from which comes this passage:

> "Then Man ascended mourning into the splendors of his palace,
> Above him rose a Shadow from his wearied intellect
> Of living gold, pure, perfect, holy; in white linen pure he hover'd,
> A sweet entrancing self delusion, a wat'ry vision of Man
> Soft exulting in existence, all the Man absorbing.
>
> Man fell upon his face prostrate before the wat'ry shadow . . ."[8]

We shall meet the idea of "all the Man absorbing" again. It seems to have here the associations of Salmacis's enervating fountain, to judge from Urizen's indignant reply to Ahania:

> "Shall the feminine indolent bliss, the indulgent self of weariness,
> The passive idle sleep, the enormous night & darkness of Death
> Set herself up to give her laws to the active masculine virtue?

> ... Once thou wast in my breast
> A sluggish current of dim waters on whose verdant margin
> A cavern shagg'd with horrid shades, dark, cool & deadly, where
> I laid my head in the hot noon after the broken clods
> Had wearied me; there I laid my plow, & there my horses fed:
> And thou has risen with thy moist locks into a wat'ry image
> Reflecting all my indolence, my weakness & my death...."

The Narcissus myth suits Blake's structure particularly well because Narcissus, reflection, and echo readily arrange themselves into subject, Spectre, and Emanation, Blake's eternal triangle. Landino's explanation cited earlier, that Narcissus represents the man who yearns after earthly beauty, the shadow, while his own soul, the reality, fades away within him, gives exactly the configuration of Blake's lyric "My Spectre Around Me."[9] The same pattern applies in Blake's view of the Fall: the watery surface in which Narcissus sees his image corresponds to Adam's sleep in which his emanation Eve is separated from him and becomes the delusive object-world of Nature.

If we call the romantic solitary Narcissus, it is because he does not very long remain satisfied with his solitude. At first, perhaps, the natural scene through which he wanders is enough for him; then, say, he meets a maiden who embodies all the charm of the landscape and with whom he shares an inner, paradisal world of exquisite sympathy: this is the soulmate, to whom he feels himself irrevocably bound by all the ties of a higher world. But their union cannot be permanent—she departs or becomes elusive—and the outward paradise is now devastated by his inner loss. In *Werther* no other adjustment is possible for the hero, while Tasso unites himself not to his counterpart but to his complement, the man at home in a world not paradisal.

Pastoral has its familiar love-and-friendship triangle of shepherd, confidant, and coy mistress; in the works with which we shall be concerned, these may become artist-hero and two supporting figures of opposite sexes. One or other may be linked to the hero by an uncanny physical or spiritual resemblance, or by ties of blood or adoption—be in some specific sense an alter ego. The moral status of one, or both, may appear profoundly ambiguous, and the hero will probably make a choice between them. The group may correspond to Narcissus, the other self, and Echo, or in Blake's convenient terms, the individual with his "spectre" and "emanation." I offer these formulations very tentatively, as innumerable variations are possible.

These triangles are based on possible pairings; and our fictions, being close to romance, deal in figures paired or complementary, suggesting aspects of human nature rather than human individuals. Even the realistic novel may reflect such a design, setting perhaps a fair woman all soul, like Dinah Morris, against a dark one all body, like Hetty Sorrel (*Adam Bede*). Eighteenth- and nineteenth-century fiction in general likes stylized pairs of brothers and sisters and cousins and inseparable friends, very much as Shakespearean comedy does. This has some thematic bearing, which we shall consider.

The mood of an unfallen pastoral scene is "sympathy": between man and landscape, shepherds and nymphs or Muses. The landscape below this is one of "sensibility" and an obscured communion, with the happier world reflected only in memory and desire. Nature on this level has some language, or some meaning bearing on man's state, but though he feels his heart respond, he cannot quite make the message out.[10] Here the soulmate glimmers elusively through the shades, or is borne away on the stream of necessity like Eurydice from Orpheus. In herself she is apt to be also full of sensibility and rather passive, given to twangling responsively like an Aeolian harp; she lives in her lover's light like the moon in the sun's, waning almost to disappearance when they become estranged. Probably it will then be his destiny to turn away and seek a lower landscape still, one ruled by solitude; here nature is hostile or dead, peopled only with mocking echoes, and the exile fleeing through its terrors probably has murdered his object of love and is now preying on himself. This is the locale of the classic horror story, whether set indoors or out, whose evil spirits are the hero's own and whose ghosts are sad phantoms of a happier time.

What makes this complex peculiarly "Narcissistic" is the fact that the hero at every point is dealing primarily with "other selves" of his own, physically or morally. A typically Romantic discovery is the symbolic identity of apparent opposites: "... The Bright One in the highest/Is brother to the Dark One in the lowest," as Tennyson in another context ("Demeter and Persephone") puts it. In the Miltonic universe, while Satan fell from a place close to the Highest, top and bottom of the scale are in absolute opposition. Romanticism likes to bring the extremes as close together as possible, as in the Byronic hero, with his immense and ambivalent powers.[11] The sense of a cyclical historical necessity may add to this, as when the Phantasm of Jupiter is the appropriate enunciator of Prometheus's curse, or, in Blake's words, "The iron hand crushed the Tyrant's head/And became a Tyrant in his stead."[12] Our heroes tend to be faced with images of their own best and worst selves, which morally if not always physically they should recognize, and to be forced into a symbolic choice of one or the other. The bright young hero probably has a dark other self somewhere whose claims he cannot discount; or he may in time become the image of his own worst possibilities, and a final ironic recognition will then make this plain. We shall examine these relationships more fully later on.

One point about the ambiguity of alter egos requires a historical note. Renaissance mirror symbolism tends to be linked with Platonic and Pauline conceptions of the natural world as dimly "shadowing forth" the divine, hence of the mirror image as much inferior to its original. Romantic writers, on the other hand, often suggest that the mirror image is more beautiful than the reality,[13] and thus it becomes a symbol for the ideal. (This is a variation on the Narcissus theme proper, as Narcissus has no ground for comparison.) It seems more natural to think of the mirror image with Paul and Plato (in the days of bronze mirrors) as fainter and duller than the object mirrored; but in Romantic imagery the limitation of the mirror is frequently understood as an editing principle, refining out what is gross or imperfect or too suggestive of physical nature. Perhaps this idea is to be connected with the primitive notion, mentioned at the beginning of this chapter, that the reflecting surface actually catches not just an image of the body but the soul or spiritual being itself. If so, then these two opposed conceptions become incorporated in the developed story of Narcissus's fixation and death, making him the victim simultaneously of an illusion and a soul-snatching. The ambiguity of the pattern in later literature, where the image or double represents sometimes an essence and sometimes a phantom, suggests that the original tension, never resolved, is part of the fascination of the theme.

Let us in the light of all this look at Shelley's *Alastor, or the Spirit of Solitude*, 1815. The hero is an idealized youth who, while not transformed into his own demonic opposite, from a serene and gentle being becomes a wild and obsessed one. His female complement seems either to be double-natured, delightful in her appearance but sinister in her effect, or perhaps to have an evil counterfeit self, an Odile to the real Odette, who beguiles the hero. The poem is elegiac in that the poet Shelley is mourning the decline and death of a brother-Poet, the victim of a delusive pursuit.[14] The Poet at first appears like a god or an elemental, and with his departure, for Shelley the spirit has gone out of external nature and the human world, leaving them empty and meaningless. Within this framework the same theme is repeated in the Poet's own career. He, like the poem's narrator, whom for convenience I am calling Shelley, has been a lover of Nature and seeker into her mysteries;[15] suddenly he is visited by a dream-maiden who embodies something of both his own inner being and the essential reality of Nature that he has been pursuing. When the vision has fled he pursues it through the external world, which now appears bleak and empty, and at last dies wasted to a shadow by his passion. The double structure of the poem is striking: as the maiden to the Poet, one might say, so is the Poet to Shelley[16]—at once object and reflection of subject; and on each the loss has the same effect of draining the life of both himself and his world.

Alastor's immediate literary context is established by allusions to a series of pastoral works: "Kubla Khan," "Tintern Abbey," "Nutting," "Ode: Intimations," and "Lycidas." The Poet's decline—"his scattered hair / Sered by an autumn of strange suffering"—is presented in seasonal terms, and after his death the narrator longs for "Medea's wondrous alchemy"that is able to bring spring flowers out of winter. On this pastoral-elegiac background is elaborated a highly Narcissistic complex. The Poet comes to his death through brooding on a form made up partly of his own image, partly of a female spirit of Nature. Even Echo, in a very curious passage, does her best to lead him on.[17] The Poet in turn is also to some extent a double, and is similarly an object of tragic involvement to his original, Shelley. Further, leaving aside numerous reverberations, shades, shadows, spectral forms, daemons, and phantasms, the poem has seven separate references to reflections in water, one closely modeled on Ovid's description of Narcissus's pool, and all of them thematically important. The four scenes where the vision either appears or is suggested are set beside water, though it must be noted that there are few entirely dry spots in the poem. Finally, the flowers with which the Poet thinks of decking his brow are narcissi,[18] and when he compares himself to a bird it is that coming favorite image of romantic solitude, the swan.

A broader context of *Alastor* is the literature of that mood of youthful longing without a specific object that its Preface describes. As a widely familiar human experience, Shelley is able to characterize it from Augustine's *Confessions;* however, his own age produced several notable descriptions, starting with that in the *Confessions* of Rousseau:[19]

> L'impossibilité d'atteindre aux êtres réels me jetta dans le pays des chimères, et ne voyant rien d'existant qui fut digne de mon délire, je le nourris dans un monde idéal que mon imagination créatrice eut bientôt peuplé d'êtres selon mon coeur.

The poem's essential ambiguity concerns the real nature of the vision. According to the summary in the preface, the Poet is a sublimely gifted young man who, ceasing to be satisfied by the contemplation of nature, imagines an ideal soulmate and dies of disappointment when his wanderings—in singularly unfrequented places—fail to lead him to her human embodiment. The author comments, "The Poet's self-centred seclusion was avenged by the Furies of an irresistible passion pursuing him to speedy ruin." This might seem purely figurative if its sinister suggestion were not carried on by two passages in the poem, the statement that "the spirit of sweet human love has sent / A vision to the sleep of him who spurned / Her choicest gifts," and the lines in which Death seems to offer the maiden, or a phantom of her, as a "lure."[20] Responsibility for the poem's title cannot all be assigned to Peacock's suggestion, as Shelley found it appropriate: "alastor"is an evil genius[21] or an avenger, the Greek word meaning literally "he who does not forget." The avenger motif, making of the maiden a delusive siren, is certainly not primary, but neither is it to be explained away.

Narcissus in Ovid's account was punished by the goddess Nemesis for spurning all offers of love. Classical analogues are Hippolytus, vowed to the service of chaste Artemis and destroyed by her rival Aphrodite, and possibly too Adonis. In one story he is the object of rivalry between Aphrodite and the underworld queen Persephone. Behind the more familiar story of Aphrodite's love for him, his being gored by the boar, and her lamentation lies the obscurer Babylonian tale of Tammuz whom the great goddess Ishtar loved and destroyed—only one in the catalogue of her doomed minions declaimed by Gilgamesh as he fatally taunts her. The first and most influential of formal pastoral elegies, Theocritus's First Idyll, has for its central figure a kind of lesser Adonis, the semidivine shepherd Daphnis. For a reason not made clear—refusal to love? to love her?—Aphrodite visits him with a wasting passion for a rejecting maiden, of which he dies, to her eventual regret even though he has taunted her while dying. (Theocritus's metaphorical language makes Daphnis in death "go down the stream" and the waters close over his head, bringing him into line with our other pastoral archetypes.) Something like the *White Goddess* comprehensive figure who is man's "mother, bride, and layer-out" seems to hover behind the First Idyll's offended Aphrodite. Such a figure is clear in Blake's Tirzah or Vala with their efforts to bind and restrict the immortal Man, the imagination, and perhaps can be dimly made out also in *Alastor*'s triad of Nature–maiden–Fury.

The Poet of *Alastor* begins as a shunner of men and ignorer of substantial maidens, preferring to them the search for the essence of "Nature." Are Nature and "sweet human love" shown as rivals for his attention? Hardly, unless very briefly where the visionary maiden's hinted presence (perhaps only in recollection, if the light of "two starry eyes" is the same as that which "shone within his soul") distracts him from communion with a Spirit of the woods. We can say little more than that the maiden and the Spirit are not one and the same; at the same time, something of the poet's vision of Nature seems to adhere to the maiden. She appears to him first while he is still joyfully if somewhat obsessively absorbed with Nature's secrets, and like Coleridge's Abyssinian maid she appears singing and playing on a stringed instrument; elsewhere both the Poet and Shelley himself are instruments played upon by Nature.

Shelley believed when he wrote *Alastor* that "Mind . . . cannot create, it can only perceive" ("On Life," [1815], *Works* VI, 197). In the poem, the Poet's mind is a mirror surface waiting for meaning to be "flashed" onto it. Nature, not man, is the creator, seizing on a passive sensibility and making it if anything still more passive. As Goethe indicated in *Werther* and Shelley in *Alastor* seems to suspect, such determined passivity is the way to possession and madness: "We receive but what we give, / And in our life alone does Nature live."[21] So far as the name "Alastor" relates to the Poet himself, the Muse of him who is unable to forget will be one of "Dame Memory's Siren daughters" (see below, p. 89), beckoning to reflection on the past as well as on the secrets of nature; this interest the Poet clearly shares with his author. Hence his inability to recognize in the visionary maiden his own creation. In so far as she is a "siren," she is, as the preface says, assembled out of scraps of experience in his memory. To that extent she is "demonic," since I take it that the true demonic is precisely something of oneself that splits off and becomes recognized as "the other"; recognition of the "other" assumes a relation to oneself, so that one sees it as "obsessing," "haunting," or "possessing."[23]

The Poet of *Alastor* becomes a wild-eyed "spectral form" and his vision a beckoning "fair fiend." His pursuit of the maiden through the external world is delusive and life-devouring. To the extent that she represents memory, she is behind him rather than ahead, so that like the Actaeon of *Adonais* the pursuer is also the pursued—"driven / By the bright shadow of that lovely dream," 232–33—going round in circles like any victim of Echo. Hence the suggestion of pursuit by Furies,[24] who usually represent remorse, or the past as devouring: a comparable representation is the "frightful fiend" of "The Ancient Mariner," an image which Shelley takes over in the early lyric "O! there are spirits of the air," where the pursuit of companionship in an imaginatively animated nature and in human society ends by making a haunting "foul fiend" of a man's "own soul." The maiden of *Alastor* is the Poet's "own soul" in reflection projected onto that Nature upon which he reflects; the mystery of Nature which he has been seeking is actually that of his own "soul within our soul" (this phrase from Shelley's essay "On Love" is an English equivalent for his word "Epipsyche"), so that the vision embodies a truth misunderstood. It becomes an obsession with the Poet, first draining the life and beauty out of the natural world around him—an event recorded in words that echo the comparable crisis in "Ode: Intimations"[25]—then becoming so to speak the will-o'-the-wisp of an insane pursuit that drains his own life—"all the Man absorbing," one might say. The vision becomes desolating when it is pursued in the outward world instead of the inward one; so the poet of *Epipsychidion,* ignoring the warning "The phantom is beside thee whom thou seekest," continues the pursuit and immediately falls into the wintry power of the false Epipsyche.

Much of the ambiguity of *Alastor* can be related to, even if not explained by, the various possibilities of Narcissus's relation to the female alter ego. If "Echo" and "reflection" are the same, their rôle is not one but a gamut: the soulmate neglected or dying, the dummy-woman who can only respond, the delusive siren, and the Fury (Ovid's punishing Nemesis) or demon-woman. All four, as we shall see, become important fictional types.

Let us give some attention to the visionary maid. The poet of the age of Sensibility, influenced by sources both Grecian and Celtic, is apt to think of himself as wandering with his lyre or harp in his hand, and metaphorically the instrument comes to represent his inspiration or Muse. So in Blake's poem "To the Muses," which begins "on Ida's shady brow" and ends with the forced sounds of "languid strings." Coleridge's Abyssinian maid is the Muse of a paradisal realm, and Shelley's Poet's visionary maid is at least in part a figure of his own inspiration.[26] Typical Muse-maidens of the works of elegiac fiction to which we shall come are Mme de Staël's Corinne and the guitar-playing Isabel who is the sister of Melville's Pierre. All these damsels but Shelley's (unless the "Arab maiden" influenced the dream) are dark exotics, like Novalis's Zulima and Keats's Indian Maid, beings from a different if not always happier clime.[27]

The eighteenth-century vogue of the Aeolian harp as supplying music for "the pensive, melancholy mind"[28] gives us the symbol for the poet himself as an instrument in the hands of Nature or a mantic inspiration: the Poet of *Alastor* has been "A fragile lute, on whose harmonious strings / The breath of heaven did wander," and *his* poet is "a long-forgotten lyre / Suspended in the solitary dome / Of some mysterious and deserted fane" awaiting Nature's breath.[29] The poet's sensibility as stringed instrument is like the use of "mirror" for the same metaphorical purpose in *Tasso*. A famous formulation is that of Béranger:

> Mon coeur est un luth suspendu,
> Sitôt qu'on le touche, il résonne.

These lines,[30] later to be quoted by Svengali to Trilby, stand as the epigraph to "The Fall of the House of Usher" (1845 version), where they represent a morbidly passive state like that of woman awaiting demon lover.

If Roderick Usher is a musical instrument, he is one that has been too tightly strung and snaps;[31] and this brings us to the cliché-conception of mental derangement as "a rift in the lute" and the figure of the maniac or demon musician. The musical madman of Shelley's "Julian and Maddalo" is a sort of male Ophelia,[32] but usually such figures are more sinister than pathetic. Burton mentions a folklore original: "At Hammel in Saxony, An. 1484. 20. Junii, the Devil in likeness of a pied Piper, carried away 130 Children, that were never after seen" (I.ii.1.2). The beguiling magical musicians of Tieck and Eichendorff are of his family, with the organ-grinder a the end of "Die Winterreise" and the fiddler of Keller's *Romeo und Julia auf dem Dorfe* (A Village Romeo and Juliet) perhaps not too distantly related.[33] The Harper of Goethe's *Wilhelm Meister* has been driven mad by remorse; Coleridge in "Dejection" calls the storm-wind a "mad lutanist"; Rat Krespel in the story of that name and Baron B. in the *Serapionsbrüder* (Serapion Brethren) are Hoffmann's frantic violinists, and in the opera *The Tales of Hoffmann* the Krespel episode acquires a demon fiddler in Dr. Miracle. A real-life one was Paganini, supposed to have sold his soul to the devil, to be assisted in his performance by the devil, to have a Mephistophelean familiar always with him, and to work spells by his playing: all these notions and others are suggested for example in Heine's *Florentinische Nächte* (1835). Demon music-masters, still to come, are John Jasper in *The Mystery of Edwin Drood*, Erik in *The Phantom of the Opera* (see chapter 10 below), and of course Svengali.

Related to the idea of the artist's sensibility as instrument is that of the sympathy existing between the musician's instrument and himself. Bards who break stringed instruments at death are the heroes of "McPherson's Rant" (traditional, reworked by Burns) and Moore's "The Minstrel Boy." A splendid expression of more sentimental desolation is the stanza from Hector Macneill's "The Harp," 1789, adapted by Scott as an epigraph in *The Pirate:*

> Still'd is the tempest's blust'ring roar;
> Hoarse dash the billows of the sea; —
> But who on Kilda's dismal shore
> Cries - "Have I burnt my harp for thee!"

Moore's Harp of Tara seems to be attuned to human sensibility, like the ancient violin belonging to Rat Krespel that cracks apart when his daughter dies. We shall shortly come to another like it in *Zanoni.*

In chapter 1 we briefly indicated a correlation between the unfallen pastoral scene and the element of air. Poems that make some play with this range from Spenser's *Muiopotmos* and the Epilogue in *Comus* to Shelley's "The Sensitive Plant" and Eliot's "Burnt Norton." Air being hard to depict, authors exploit references to, besides Ariel, "airs" both perfumed and musical, like the "aires, vernal aires" in Milton's Eden (*PL* IV.264), which are both at once.

The lost paradisal landscape is usually a hill of the Muses or place of inspiration or spontaneous song; it tends to ring mysteriously with music as Prospero's island and Ann Radcliffe's happy landscapes do. Music in the fallen scene, like Orpheus's lyre among the snows of Thrace, is a reminder of the happy past—something saved from the wreck—but also a lament for it. The musician in a fallen world may appear not as saved from the catastrophe but as reshaped by it, his creative impulse now morbid or destructive.

The playing or singing maiden may represent something a little different: pure responsiveness, which again comes down from the lost world of "sympathy" into the more clouded one of "sensibility." The most explicit accounts of this kind of communion are the one in *Alastor* and a very similar passage in *Rosalind and Helen:*

> Yes, 'twas his soul that did inspire
> Sounds, which my skill could ne'er awaken;

And first, I felt my fingers sweep
The harp, and a long quivering cry
Burst from my lips in symphony. . . .
I paused, but soon his gestures kindled
New power, as by the moving wind
The waves are lifted, and my song
To soft low notes now changed and dwindled. . . .   [1139–63]

"Symphony" might almost be paraphrased "musical intercourse." Rat Krespel's daughter Antonia, the wonderful singer, owes her extraordinary voice, "sometimes like the breathing of an Aeolian harp, sometimes like the warbling of a nightingale," to a morbid chest condition; the influence of her father, to whom she is most dutiful, cannot prevent her from singing duets with her lover, and she dies in consequence with a look of rapture. The responsive maiden's song is often associated with that of the nightingale, as in Emily's in *Epipsychidion,* suggesting beauty in pain or captivity as befits a lower world—"most musical, most Melancholy."[34] Such a maiden is not an inspiring Muse: she is a passive instrument responding to lover's or father's moods, or to his presence or absence. The Radcliffe heroine is of this description, tremulously vibrating. She embodies aspects of the feminine ideal of her age, being usually pious, dutiful, and submissive as well as of an exquisite emotional balance. In fiction, the early models are Richardson's young ladies and Rousseau's Julie; in them, however, responsiveness is matched with good sense and a sprightly wit, lack of which makes later sensibilious damsels seem very supine. These are regularly weak vessels and born victims, easily imposed on and led astray. Sharing the special vulnerability of their male counterparts to delusion and nervous collapse, they may exemplify also mediumism, somnambulism, susceptibility to hypnosis, and a tendency to be subjected to vampirism physical or spiritual. Seen in its most positive light, this type is the echo-woman as soulmate, and it is the desired object of a good many fictional heroes down to Meredith's Sir Willoughby Patterne, in whom the wish is as anachronistic as it is narcissistic. The echo-woman as completely soulless, and again as the ideal of an age almost past, appears in Rosamond Vincy; self-absorbed to the point of being without personality, this star pupil of a deportment school puts up a fair imitation.

> Rosamond played admirably. Her master at Mrs. Lemon's school . . . was one of those excellent musicians here and there to be found in our provinces. . . . Rosamond, with the executant's instinct, had seized his manner of playing, and gave forth his large rendering of noble music with the precision of an echo. It was almost startling, heard for the first time. A hidden soul seemed to be flowing forth from Rosamond's fingers. . . .
> Her singing was less remarkable, but also well trained, and sweet to hear as a chime perfectly in tune. It is true she sang "Meet me by moonlight", and

Figure 2. Portrait of the author, frontispiece of The Missionary, by Lady Sydney Morgan. London, 1811.

"I've been roaming".... But Rosamond could also sing "Black-eyed Susan" with effect, or Haydn's canzonets, or "Voi, che sapete", or "Batti, batti"— she only wanted to know what her audience liked.   [*Middlemarch*, II, xvi]

The contrast with Charlotte's music (see p. 66 and note, above) is instructive; for George Eliot and her age "soul" is unreal if separated from "character." The conventions of realism would be broken if Eliot portrayed Rosamond much more directly; as it is, she provides her with a swan neck and the mermaid's long fair hair.

This demonic extreme of the echo-maiden brings in another classical line of ancestry, that leading down through Homer's Sirens, notorious for their sweet voices and beguiling song. In vase paintings they have lyres in their hands. Originally bird-women, in late classical times they are given the fish-tailed form of Atergatis, and from them descend the medieval mermaids. Classical mythology knows of a contest in which the Sirens challenged the Muses in song and lost; at the same time they could in paintings represent music just as the Muses did, and were said to be the daughters of a Muse. Thus, though there are traditions of "good" Sirens, the more familiar ones not only inhabit a flowery island that hides heaps of dead men's bones, but are evil pretenders to the place of the Muses.[35] Both "good" and "bad" Sirens can be illustrated from Milton. In "At a Solemn Music" and the Genius of the Wood's speech in "Arcades," Sirens are spirits of the harmony of the spheres, a conception taken from the myth of Er in *The Republic*, Book Ten. Those of the invocation to Sabrina in *Comus* (878–82)—

> By ... the Songs of Sirens sweet,
> By dead Parthenope's dear tomb,
> And fair Ligea's golden comb
> Wherewith she sits on diamond rocks
> Sleeking her soft alluring locks—

come via the late classical refined and gentle embodiments of song from Sannazaro, the poet of Naples, where Parthenope's tomb was still shown in his time. However, in *The Reason of Church Government*, preface to Book Two, Milton dismisses as a source of inspiration "Dame Memory" (to the Greeks the mother of the Muses), "and her Siren daughters" in favor of "that eternall Spirit"—in terms even harsher than those of *PL* VII.39, "For thou [Urania] art Heav'nlie, she [Calliope] an empty dreame."

In elegiac fiction we meet about the same range of sirens, except that there are no Romantic ones corresponding with those at the top of Milton's scale. The "celestial" Siren, representing the heavenly harmony, has departed, as a mark of whatever fall it is that takes place in the transition from Renaissance to Romantic myth. Many later settings could be said to derive their elegiac quality from being haunted by her ghost, or sometimes its evil double.

In the area we are discussing, "Siren" is a usual term for the demon woman, whether musical or not. Conventional as the expression may seem, in several of our works the reference to the beguiling water fairy is relevant to the symbolic pattern. Perhaps not in Godwin's *St. Leon*, 1799, where the unhappy lover denounces his betrothed Pandora as "this delusive syren," but certainly so in Tasso's denunciation of the princess, in that scene where he is all at sea and sees her briefly as "Sirene" and the realized Armida of his poem. She has earlier been seen as moon-woman and as "pearl" and briefly identified with the elusive "treasure" of Tasso's quest; to her mode of living as well as to Tasso's perception of her there attaches a faint otherworldly shimmer, ambiguously flickering between spiritual essence and *fata morgana*.

The figure of the Siren, by that name, is most elaborately treated in Bulwer Lytton's *Zanoni*, 1842. The book as a whole belongs in another part of our discussion, that centered on the alchemist or magus, but its heroine, Viola, belongs here. She is the "other child" of a somewhat unbalanced violinist, the "elder," or his "Familiar," being his violin (I, i)—"his soul, his voice, his self of self" (ii). Viola is from childhood a gifted musician, especially as a lutanist and singer, owing in part to her simplicity and innocence; "for the mind that rightly conceives Art is but a mirror, which gives back what is cast on its surface faithfully only—while it is unsullied" (i). Her brain is filled with "phantoms of sound," whose movement and changes dominate her moods and expressions. She is a dreamer, and indulges her visions beside the blue Parthenope, the Siren's sea, in "the . . . grotto of Posilipo—the mighty work of the old Cimmerians—and seated by the haunted Tomb of Virgil." For her operatic début she sings her father's great work—"his other child—his immortal child—, the spirit-infant of his soul; his darling of many years of patient obscurity and pining genius; his masterpiece,—his opera of the 'Siren'!" (ii). Shortly afterwards the musician catches a fever, in the course of which he seizes his instrument and plays it for the last time; then he drops it so that the strings snap, at the same moment "the chords of the human instrument were snapped asunder" (ix), and he falls to the ground beside the laurel wreath his wife had bound for him on the night of his triumph. "Broken instrument, broken heart, withered laurel-wreath!"[36]

All this is meant to indicate as completely as may be that Viola, who represents human instinct in its striving after the Ideal, is "the daughter of music," seeking first through art, before she encounters love, to mirror the Ideal in her soul. Her single great rôle is the Siren; though we learn very little about the opera itself, we can assume that its Sirens are those of gracious Neapolitan memory. At the approach of love, Viola's world of the theater dissolves into a garish tinsel show, and she flees with Zanoni, the ever-living Chaldaean mage, who has been drawn down to earthly life for her sake, "fascinated" by her eyes and voice and even hair as if she

were any fatal lady. As he becomes more closely bound to her, his supernatural powers leave him; he can call up no longer ministering powers,
but only shapes of horror. Viola at length forsakes him, frightened by an
appeal to her superstition; he is forced to wander in search of her, and
finally dies in her place under the guillotine as one of the last victims of the
Reign of Terror. Viola, whose story is modeled somewhat on Psyche's, is
seen throughout as unblemished in purity and intentions, and does not
consciously practice any seductive arts; but only at the end is it apparent
that her influence has not lowered but raised her lover in the spiritual
scale—as the author asserts in the final conclusion that "the Universal
Human Lot is, after all, that of the highest privilege."[37]

Zanoni is an incoherent, theosophical, cliché-ridden work; many of its
best effects come from its clichés, and from its allusions to other literature.
These alone would be enough to set it within our context. Byron's *Heaven
and Earth* and the Faust-Gretchen romance with its transcendent conclusion loom in the background, along with Apuleius's romance of Love and
the Soul. The opening scene is filled largely with the Naples of elegiac
poetry and the Shelleyan halcyon isle of the honeymoon, the story plung-
ing from there to Rome and Venice, places of temptation, and to Paris
under the Terror, the place of disillusionment and death. The world of
Naples is supported by the pervasive presence of Tasso: the greater
number of the epigraphs are taken from the *Gerusalemme* and *Aminta,* and
their poet occasionally emerges into the text, once as himself learned in a
benevolent "Theurgia" (VII.ix). Armida's island and palace is used once
as an image for the entire world of the book (I.x.), and once in the Paris
scene for Viola's lost happiness (VII.iv):

> As when, in the noble verse prefixed to this chapter, Armida herself has
> destroyed her enchanted palace, not a vestige of that bower, raised of old by
> Poetry and Love, remained to say "it had been"!

The dissolving fairy structure is a regular variation on the collapsing-
house metaphor we noted in chapter 4 above.[38]

To recapitulate somewhat. In the unfallen pastoral scene, the heavenly
harmony is reflected in the peculiar songful and even antiphonal quality
of the happy landscape. This is a feature that comes into pastoral with
Virgil, and is familiar in Renaissance poetry.[39] Birdsong is attuned to the
water's fall, and the shepherd has only to lift his voice for the woods to
answer and their echoes to ring—a special feature of the sympathy of
nature in a scene somehow synonymous with the world of poetry. Where
the landscape has darkened, Echo speaks mournfully from the past, reminding of lost happiness:

> O Woods, O Fountains, Hillocks, Dales and Bowrs,
> With other echo late I taught your Shades
> To answer, and resound farr other Song.   [*PL* X.860-62]

On a lower level still, in the landscape of solitude, Echo conveys mockery or horror:

> Hell trembl'd at the hideous Name, and sigh'd
> From all her Caves, and back resounded *Death*.   [II.788–89]

The human embodiment of sympathy or responsiveness expressed in sound, or in metaphors suggestive of it, may be called the Echo-maiden, whose associations usually are either pleasing or sweetly pathetic. When such sympathy or responsiveness is apparent only and has the effect of luring or betraying, the maiden is that other self of Echo, the delusive water fairy, or, for our purposes, Siren—Aeolian Harpy? And as Echo and water fairy can be identified also with Narcissus's own reflection in one medium or the other, so true and false soulmates probably reflect aspects of the hero's nature. In *Zanoni*, Viola incarnates those human feelings that the mage, unlike his preceptor Mejnour, has not entirely put off, and it is by renouncing his supposed "higher" powers for this attachment that he romantically perfects his greatness and becomes a redeemer figure. Bulwer Lytton dwells on the beauty of sacrifice, but keeps his fantasy clear of the evident Christian overtones. Less philosophically developed, we find also cases where the resemblance of Narcissus to his soulmate is of a more strictly physical nature, as we are about to see.

Another example of the involuntary Siren is the heroine of Mary Shelley's prose idyll, *Mathilda*, 1819. This maiden's mother dies at her birth, and the father, leaving his child to be brought up by a relative among the romantic solitudes of the Scottish Highlands, flees to the Continent to forget his loss. When he returns, Mathilda is sixteen, and in her the beauty of her mother lives again. Her father falls in love with her; she forces him to confess the trouble that is preying on him; he leaves suddenly and hastens "towards the sea," pursued through night and storm by Mathilda,[40] who has no clear intention but finds him, as she expected, drowned. She then departs to a cottage on a lonely heath, where she pines until she dies. The pastoral framework is built largely on allusions to Dante's Matilda and to Wordsworth's Lucy, both maidens whom we know less in themselves than as their presence or absence affects their poets. Though the narration is in the first person, Mathilda still manages to give us descriptions of herself as from outside, like her father's first sight of her on Loch Lomond:

> As I came, dressed in white, covered only by my tartan *rachan*, my hair streaming on my shoulders, and shooting across with greater speed than it could be supposed I could give to my boat, my father has often told me that I looked more like a spirit than a human maid.   [p. 14][41]

On the journey towards the sea, her hair again streams wildly as she dashes through the night, this time soaked with rain and shaking with fever. In her most Siren-like mood after the catastrophe, she sets two cups of laudanum for her sympathizing friend Woodville and herself and invites him to drink:

> "What fool on a bleak shore, seeing a flowery isle on the other side with his lost love beckoning to him from it would pause because the wave is dark and turbid?
>
> What if some little payne the passage have
> That makes frayle flesh to fear the bitter wave?
> Is not short payne well borne that brings long ease,
> And lays the soul to sleep in quiet grave?
>
> . . . I am Despair; and a strange being am I, joyous, triumphant Despair. . . . Behold the pleasant potion! Look, I am a spirit of good, and not a human maid that invites thee, and with winning accents (oh, that they would win thee!) says, Come and drink." [p. 68]

Incest in *Mathilda* is by no means a mere device of plot to make impossible the marriage of lovers; it suggests what should be an ideal relation. The father does not love in his daughter merely the image of his lost Diana, for an old servant, speaking of his master's mysterious grief, tells Mathilda,

> " . . . when I heard that he was coming down here with you, my young lady, I thought we should have the happy days over again that we enjoyed during the short life of my lady your mother—But that would be too much happiness for us poor creatures born to tears. . . . You are like her although there is more of my lord in you. . . ." [pp. 23–24]

Mathilda never confesses to a guilty passion—the action that has set the mark of Cain on her brow is extracting her father's secret—but there has never been nor can be another love for her, and she sets out after him with no thought but to force him to live. The only happiness afterwards remaining for her is the thought of meeting him in heaven; she expects that her own guilt will be eradicated then, but speaks as if he had never incurred any.

The book is full of images of pursuit and elusive objects. The ride towards the sea is prefigured by a dream in which Mathilda follows her fleeing father and sees him plunge over a precipice into the sea. During his wanderings after Diana's death,

> "At first . . . I could not bear to think of my poor little girl; but afterwards as grief wore off and hope again revisited me I could only turn to her, and amidst cities and desarts her little fairy form, such as I imagined it, for ever flitted before me." [p. 14]

After her father's death, Mathilda seeks solitude in which to indulge the "shadowy happiness" of communing with her father's spirit; for

> . . never again could I make one of the smiling hunters that go coursing after bubles that break to nothing when caught, and then after a new one with brighter colours; my hope also had proved a buble, but it had been so lovely,

so adorned that I saw none that could attract me after it; besides I was wearied with the pursuit, nearly dead with weariness.   [p. 48][42]

Happiness a number of times is imaged as a fleeting ray, like the smiles of Woodville's lost beloved:

> ... not like a human loveliness ... but as a sunbeam on a lake, now light and now obscure, flitting before as you strove to catch them, and fold them for ever to your heart.   [p. 62]

Mathilda in her father's eyes, before jealousy provokes him to carnal passion, is a spiritual being from higher realms and also something of a nature spirit—"a nymph of the woods," as he calls her. The two realms are not in opposition, as Nature in these early days of their relationship has still something of a transcendent light. To quote her father's last letter:

> "All delightful things, sublime scenery, soft breezes, exquisite music seemed to me associated with you and only through you to be pleasant to me. . . . You appeared as the deity of a lovely region, the ministering Angel of a Paradise to which of all human kind you admitted only me. I dared hardly consider you as my daughter; your beauty, artlessness and untaught wisdom seemed to belong to a higher order of beings; your voice breathed forth only words of love: if there was aught of earthly in you it was only what you derived from the beauty of the world; you seemed to have gained a grace from the mountain breezes—the waterfalls and the lake. . . ."   [p. 38]

References to Beatrice and to the world of Spenser add suggestively to her Matilda-aspects, while the ambiguous Lucy side—or rôle of Nature with regard to Lucy—is borne out perhaps by the allusions to Proserpina, betrayed by her father and by Earth, and to Psyche, who lost an enchanted palace and discovered the two-sided nature of Love.

Mathilda's father figures too somewhat as an elegiac subject. His idyllic marriage to a childhood sweetheart, whose name Diana suggests a moony chastity, is broken by her death, and the loss drives him out to wander the world. Returning to enjoy the promise of restored happiness in his daughter, he discovers the promise is delusive; he cannot enjoy without possession, because in adult life that is the way things are. His paradise is altogether lost in the past—he is by now the inhabitant of another region—and any attempt to continue living in it is mistaken and harmful.

A rather wandering path brought us from *Alastor* to *Mathilda;* now we have her, can we relate her more directly to the subject of Narcissus? "Narcissus" is the name we are giving to the subjective figure who is to Romantic elegy what Adonis or Orpheus is to earlier pastoral elegy. If we place *Alastor* among such poems as "Ode: Intimations," "Dejection," "Kubla Khan," and Goethe's "Elegie," it fits naturally in with them but at the same time is the most mythological, presenting a "genius" figure who resembles Adonis and Orpheus only less than he does Narcissus. This group of poems we can call male-centered elegy. Poems of the corresponding female-centered group are apt to be less subjectively lyrical, more mythological–narrative like *Alastor:* they include Blake's *Book of Thel,* Wordsworth's Lucy poems, perhaps "Christabel," certainly Shelley's "Sensitive Plant." The archetypes here are Persephone- and Eurydice-figures, and not least Echo. It is with these that Mathilda belongs: her idyll is a kind of prose equivalent, if we consider the numerous nature-spirit suggestions attached to her. However, she is less passive than the maidens of the poems; she brings on her own fall through her (in effect) fatal curiosity, breaking a taboo just as Eve and Psyche do. The event is of the same kind as the trespass of Mary's father William Godwin's Caleb Williams, who is more or less a male Psyche. There is an element of broken taboo in the story of the original spring-and-fall maiden, Persephone: not only does she pledge herself to the underworld by eating the pomegranate seeds, but as she is flower-gathering on the field of Enna Earth sends forth to beguile her "for a trick" a wonder never seen before, the bright narcissus, and as she leans to pick it Hades seizes her. "Narcissus," like "narcotic," implies a numbing power, hence the flower's sinister associations. The story of Persephone and the narcissus will be found in the "Homeric Hymn to Demeter."[43]

Besides "pastoral" and "fall" connections, we can note two kinds of "narcissism" in *Mathilda,* the heroine's and her father's. Let us say at once that we do not get far in mapping the associations of the Romantic Narcissus without stumbling into an analogy with what Freud meant by "narcissism" as a psychological term. The narcissism of the young child is natural, innocent, and even charming, a necessary self-centeredness before in adolescence he begins to develop an interest in other people for themselves and a sense of his place among mankind, the latter process being very gradual and never total in its transference of "psychic energy," and its central event being the birth of love. The ego-centered universe is the paradise into which the child is born, and growing up requires learning to move out of it. In literature[44] the positive aspects of this state are often represented by absorption in vision, dream, and noble fancy, or by communion with nature or idyllic human companionship of a virginal or suprasensual kind. Its symbols, regularly ambiguous, tend to suggest a watery or mirror world, with overtones not only of self-love but also of fleetingness, instability. Allusion to Ovid's myth of Narcissus allows Milton to present with great delicacy the state of mind of the newly created Eve:

>   I thither went
> With unexperienc't thought, and laid me downe
> On the green bank, to look into the cleer
> Smooth Lake, that to me seemd another skie.
> As I bent down to look, just opposite,

A Shape within the watry gleam appeerd
Bending to look on me. I started back,
It started back; but pleas'd I soon returnd,
Pleas'd it returnd as soon with answering looks
Of sympathic and love; there I had fixt
Mine eyes till now, and pin'd with vain desire,
Had not a voice thus warnd me, What thou seest,
What there thou seest fair Creature is thy self. . . .   [*PL* IV.456-68]

When she is led to Adam, she finds him

    . . . less faire,
Less winning soft, less amiablie milde,
Then that smooth watry image.   [478-80]

In the manner of a Renaissance emblem this does indeed point the reader forward to the self-love that leads Eve to her fall; but within its immediate context it also leaves with us a persuasive impression of the untouched grace of body and mind in this new being. A quality of "watry gleam" appears again in Blake's introduction of Thel:

Down by the river of Adona her soft voice is heard,
And thus her gentle lamentation falls like morning dew:

"O life of this our spring! why fades the lotus of the water,
Why fade these children of the spring, born but to smile & fall?
Ah! Thel is like a wat'ry bow, and like a parting cloud;
Like a reflection in a glass; like shadows in the water. . . ."

In both cases the message that comes to the pining maiden directs her to sympathy with other beings as a release from a world of shadows.

However, besides a natural and inevitable narcissism of inexperience, Freud recognizes also a morbid narcissism in the person who has failed to move out of immaturity. The usual indications of such a state, in literature as well as in life, include incestuous, homosexual, impossible, and vampiric loves: all are disguises of self-love, and, unlike the imperfect loves of Eve and Psyche, usually there is no cure for them.

Mathilda's father, like the hero of *Alastor,* is subject to a morbid narcissism which he fails to outgrow. However, both are more victims than persecutors, and evoke pathos rather than horror. Pathetic too is the Eve- or Psyche-maiden, like Viola or Mathilda, who readily becomes the involuntary siren. Less involuntary and more sinister, because nothing will ever really change her, is Rosamond Vincy: Henry James, describing her with relish as "this veritably mulish domestic flower," is outdone by her husband, who likes to call her "his basil plant, . . . a plant which had flourished wonderfully on a murdered man's brains."[45] Since at present we are dealing with youthful and only passively harmful figures, let us leave demonic narcissists of both sexes for later treatment. They are usually much older, sometimes by centuries, and very well able to wait.

Six *Nymphs, Swains, and Spirits of Solitude*

> *O Solitude! where are the charms*
> *That sages have seen in thy face?*
> *Better dwell in the midst of alarms,*
> *Than reign in this horrible place.*
>
> — *William Cowper*

Taking as we did Milton's English pastoral as definitive of the Renaissance pastoral cosmos, we were led very largely to omit the important erotic component. While happy love of course keeps the natural world turning, it's the frustrations of desire that make for story and situation. The pursuit of maidens, often nymphs of Diana vowed to chastity, through bushes and briars is a feature of the Ovidian pastoral scene. Nymphs flee or are pursued in pastoral contexts in Horace and Virgil, and again in Petrarch, Politian, Tasso, and Spenser. If as so often in this rather intellectual form the nymph embodies "ideal" qualities, she may owe it to herself and them to keep fleeing: "Wave us away, and keep thy solitude," as Arnold counsels the Scholar-Gipsy.

Other traditions blend with this one to make the nymph figure we have been discussing. One is the "sylph,"[1] a wispy emanation from Renaissance magic. Another is that of "nympholepsy," the state of being nymph-struck, from late classical folklore. Horace Smith prefaces his pastoral drama *Amarynthus, the Nympholept*, 1821, with a very well informed account:[2]

> The [Nympholeptoi] of the Greeks, and the Lymphati or Lymphatici of the Romans, were men supposed to be possessed by the Nymphs, and driven to phrensy, either from having seen one of those mysterious beings, or from the maddening effect of the oracular caves in which they resided. Plutarch particularly mentions that the Nymphs Sphragitides haunted a cave on Mount Cithaeron, in Boeotia, in which there had formerly been an oracle, and where, from the inspiration they diffused, Nympholepsy became an endemic complaint. According to Festus, it was formerly thought that all those who had merely seen the figure of a nymph in a fountain were seized with madness during the remainder of their lives. Ovid himself dreaded this event, as appears in the fourth book of his Fasti....

The term *lympha* in *lymphatici* "is a rendering of 'nymph', but in the sense

Figure 3. *Frontispiece of volume 10 of Anderson's* British Poets. *London, 1795.*

of 'water' '':[3] the nymph of this chapter is very close to the water fairy of the last.

"Nympholepsy" is a favorite nineteenth-century term, occurring in the works or correspondence of Shelley,[4] Peacock, Byron, De Quincey, the Brownings, Bulwer Lytton, and Swinburne. They may use it loosely for any passion for an unattainable object, though usually symbolized by the pursuit of a maiden elusive or insubstantial. If "The Lotos-Eaters" and "The Hesperides" are Tennyson's Siren songs, "The Voyage" has an element of nympholepsy; while other quest images, the "sinking star" of "Ulysses," the "wandering fires" of "The Coming of the Grail," and the Gleam itself, remind us that the fleeing nymph of the nineteenth century to some extent takes over from the delusive lights so well established—if we can put it that way—in the eighteenth. Typical nymphs, apart from those mentioned in the last chapter, are imaginary figures like the "syl-phide" of Chateaubriand and those maidens of Romantic story who are first glimpsed in mirror, painting, or dream before their realized presence either rewards or wrecks their lovers.[5]

"The nympholepsy of some fond despair" is Byron's phrase for the attachment of the virtuous early Roman king Numa to his preceptress, the nymph Egeria, whose "cave-guarded spring" he describes in *Childe Harold* IV.cvi. Theirs is a paradisal relationship, unlike the one of woman and demon lover recalled by the "Kubla Khan" echoes of cviii or those described in Byron's *Heaven and Earth*. [6] It is also unlike love as we know it, which is a desert or a garden of poisons remote from "The unreach'd Paradise of our despair." Like Werther (p. 62 above), this speaker declares that the mind projects its own ideal conception of beauty and value into the outward world, which of itself can show nothing comparable. This conception then leads us in pursuit of "idols" through "the world's wilderness":

> ... still it binds
> The fatal spell, and still it draws us on. ...
> The stubborn heart, its alchymy begun,
> Seems ever near the prize—wealthiest when most undone.   [cxxiii]

Alchemy is here a symbol of delusive pursuit, as in *Aureng-Zebe's* lines (IV.i.43–44), "I'm tir'd with waiting for this chymic gold, / Which fools us young, and beggars us when old." Byron's next stanza speaks of "phantom lures" that prove "meteors" at last.

Another fountain nymph who dispenses hidden wisdom is Scott's White Lady of Avenel in *The Monastery*, 1820; she is modeled on the French legend of Mélusine, and this time is not an object of love. [7] (Such figures may remind us of a further tradition behind the "nymph," namely the fairy lore of postclassical Europe.) An ancestor of Donatello's in *The Marble Faun* loved a fountain nymph until he came to her to wash off a bloodstain and she fled him; her image in stone still stands beside the fountain (xxvii, "Myths"). As it is placed in the novel, this anecdote illustrates how guilt comes between man and the innocent powers of nature. Rima in W. H. Hudson's *Green Mansions*, supposed by the Indians to be the daughter of a water spirit, is first glimpsed across a stream, with whose sounds her song is mingled (v). A youth whose association with fountain nymphs suggests a frequenting of Muses is Sordello, whose favorite spot in boyhood was an inner chamber holding as its "main wonder" a stone font supported by marble maidens: "Constant as eve he came / To sit beside each in her turn" (*Sordello* I.430–31), perhaps recalling Milton's "Nightly I visit." The poetess Corinne poses by moonlight for a glimpse beside a Roman fountain in Mme de Staël's novel of 1807 (IV, vi, to be recalled in *The Marble Faun* xvi):

> Corinne, ... oppressée par la douleur, descendit de sa voiture et se reposa quelques instants près de la fontaine de Trévi, devant cette source abondante qui tombe en cascade au milieu de Rome et semble comme la vie de ce tranquille séjour. ... C'est le bruit des voitures que l'on a besoin d'entendre dans les autres villes; à Rome, c'est le murmure de cette fontaine immense,

qui semble comme l'accompagnement nécessaire à l'existence rêveuse qu'on y mène: l'image de Corinne se peignit dans cette onde, si pure qu'elle porte depuis plusieurs siècles le nom de *l'eau virginale*. Oswald, qui s'était arrêté dans le même lieu peu de moments après, aperçut le charmant visage de son amie qui se répétait dans l'eau. Il fut saisi d'une émotion tellement vive, qu'il ne savait pas d'abord si c'était son imagination qui lui faisait apparaître l'ombre de Corinne . . . ; il se pencha vers la fontaine pour mieux voir, et ses propres traits vinrent alors se réfléchir à côté de ceux de Corinne.

Coleridge's "The Picture: or, The Lover's Resolution," 1802, was designed as "A Poem on the endeavour to emancipate the soul from daydreams" (*Notebooks*, ed. Coburn, vol. 1, entry 1153 and note). The speaker, newly released as he thinks from "passion's dreams" and able to enjoy natural beauty for its own sake, depicts the nymphs and gnomes of the woodland scene as uniting to eject any love-melancholic "wretch" who should stray into it. In his "triumph" he congratulates the breeze on never having toyed with a maiden's hair and the stream on not having mirrored maidenly features in its pools. The latter thought is elaborated at length, and the reader is not surprised when the speaker, having followed the path of the stream till it divides to flow around an island and then joins again, is reminded by all he sees of his own unhappy attachment, and by the end of the poem is invoking etiquette to justify his return to captivity: the maiden has dropped a birchbark sketch on the path, and "fit it is" he should take it back to her. The lengthy mirror passage is as follows:

> And thou too, desert stream! no pool of thine,
> Though clear as lake in latest summer-eve,
> Did e'er reflect the stately virgin's robe,
> The face, the form divine, the downcast look
> Contemplative! Behold! her open palm
> Presses her cheek and brow! her elbow rests
> On the bare branch of half-uprooted tree,
> That leans towards its mirror! Who erewhile
> Had from her countenance turned, or looked by stealth,
> (For fear is true love's cruel nurse), he now
> With steadfast gaze and unoffending eye,
> Worships the watery idol, dreaming hopes
> Delicious to the soul, but fleeting, vain,
> E'en as that phantom-world on which he gazed,
> But not unheeded gazed: for see, ah! see,
> The sportive tyrant with her left hand plucks
> The heads of tall flowers that behind her grow,
> Lychnis, and willow-herb, and fox-glove bells;
> And suddenly, as one that toys with time,
> Scatters them on the pool! Then all the charm

Is broken—all that phantom-world so fair
Vanishes, and a thousand circlets spread,
And each mis-shape the other. Stay awhile,
Poor youth, who scarcely dar'st lift up thine eyes.
The stream will soon renew its smoothness, soon
The visions will return! And lo! he stays:
And soon the fragments dim of lovely forms
Come trembling back, unite, and now once more
The pools becomes a mirror; and behold
Each wild-flower on the marge inverted there,
And there the half-uprooted tree—but where,
O where the virgin's snowy arm, that leaned
On its bare branch? He turns, and she is gone!
Homeward she steals through many a woodland maze
Which he shall seek in vain. Ill-fated youth!
Go, day by day, and waste thy manly prime
In mad love-yearning by the vacant brook,
Till sickly thoughts bewitch thine eyes, and thou
Behold'st her shadow still abiding there,
The Naiad of the mirror!   [72–111]

Here the idea of nympholepsy in a strict sense—that of Festus—is attached to the vision of a purely natural maiden, which becomes a "treacherous image" like that of the earlier "Lewti," 1798. While the poem makes no connection between the pool and poetic inspiration, in 1816 Coleridge in his note on "Kubla Khan" describing his interruption by the "person on business from Porlock" says that he

> on his return to his room, found, to his no small surprise and mortification, that though he still retained some vague and dim recollection of the general purport of the vision, yet, with the exception of some eight or ten scattered lines and images, all the rest had passed away like the images on the surface of a stream into which a stone has been cast, but alas! without the after restoration of the latter!

He goes on to quote from "The Picture" the lines, "Then all the charm . . . The pool becomes a mirror."

In our third chapter we saw in *Tasso* a "broken reflection" figure standing for the loss of a peaceful state of mind. To the passages by Goethe and Coleridge we can add a much earlier one; a troubling thought comes to dispel the inward calm of Parnell's Hermit (1722):

So when a smooth expanse receives imprest
Calm nature's image on its wat'ry breast,
Down bend the banks, the trees depending grow,
And skies beneath with answ'ring colours glow:
But if a stone the gentle scene divide,

Swift ruffling circles curl on ev'ry side,
And glimm'ring fragments of a broken sun,
Banks, trees, and skies, in thick disorder run.   [13–20]

The still reflection in nonmetaphorical use is an idyllic landscape feature expressing the harmony of nature, sometimes even a paradisal quality: so Wordsworth, "The swan on still St. Mary's Lake / Float[s] double, swan and shadow" ("Yarrow Unvisited"), and so the perfect reflections in Poe's paradisal Domain of Arnheim and to be found near Landor's Cottage. Milton's Eden contains

> a Lake,
> That to the fringed Bank with Myrtle crownd,
> Her chrystall mirror holds . . .   [*PL* IV.261–63]

which suggests also the unity of perfect married love[8] ("myrtle"—associated with Venus—and "her"), though perhaps too, taken in conjunction with Eve's first experience shortly to be recalled, a hint of female vanity. Mutual mirroring is a favorite device in *Prometheus Unbound* to convey the state of the liberated cosmos, as in the "Heaven-reflecting sea" of act three.[9] The nymph too embodies an idyllic view of nature, a nature with which man can commune: she is in her best, or Egeria, capacity "the sympathy of Nature" incarnated. That the reflection can be shattered or have sinister import, and the nymph easily becomes either pathetic or enslaving, indicates the fragility and even the dangers of the associated idyllic states.

Among the examples we have given, with the exception of Egeria all these maidens have something elegiac in their nature. In function Scott's White Lady is partly a banshee: moreover she continually laments her own soulless nature, and is last seen prophesying doom to those she loves and expecting momently to fade away for ever. Hawthorne's nymph also fades sadly away, the bloodstain of man's guilt on her brow. Rima is fated to an early death. Sordello's stone nymphs receive his body in their tomb. Corinne relinquishes Oswald and dies of grief. The virgin of "The Picture"—hypothetical—beguiles her hypothetical swain to madness.

While visionary origin renders a girl a recognizable nymph or spirit-maiden, other factors may have the same effect. These are extreme youth, virginity, cloistral habits, or exceptional delicacy of constitution or temperament; or, as in the case of Werther's Charlotte, a quite normal young woman made inaccessible by moral taboo may take on the air of the vanishing dream. The nymph is a being too subtle and elusive for dealings with the ordinary world, and often seems beyond both passion and morality; she may suggest the changeling, or what one might get if one crossed Miranda with Ariel. Hawthorne's "elf-child," Little Pearl, is a "nymph" in our sense. So is Rima, who specializes in birdcalls and pretending to be an echo, and goes off the stage as a death-moth or mournful Psyche. Moreover she is an extraordinarily translucent or perhaps refractive being: her appearance changes with the quality of the light. Besides their affinities with the water fairy, these two are both linked also especially with the element of air.[10] The spirit-maiden's destiny is either, like Pearl, to be humanized by love, suffering, or a long illness and then successfully married, or else like Rima to die while still very young. For this type there is a barrier between girlhood and womanhood, and without an ordeal, even a rite of passage, she can't cross it. Or, the transition may be in the point of view of the beholder: Wordsworth sees first "a Phantom of delight" fitted "to haunt, to startle, and way-lay," then "upon nearer view, / A spirit, yet a Woman too," and last a complete human being, a unity of natural and spiritual whose affinities are more angelic than phantasmal. If the Phantom of delight has achieved it, Wordsworth's Lucy never manages the passage. The failure most explicitly described in poetry is that of Blake's Thel, who gets to the gate and gives up with a shriek.

In fiction the type is more elaborately developed. Hawthorne's Hilda in *The Marble Faun*, the "white bird" of xiv, can respond to love only after great trials. In Bulwer Lytton's *A Strange Story*, 1861–62, the unearthly maiden Lilian is fair, fragile, harp-playing, and mediumistic:

> [a] young creature to whom all the evil of the world is as yet unknown, to whom the ordinary cares and duties of the world are strange and unwelcome; who from the earliest dawn of reason has loved to sit apart and to muse; before whose eyes visions pass unsolicited; who converses with those who are not dwellers on the earth, and beholds in the space landscapes which the earth does not reflect... who is moved to a mysterious degree by all the varying aspects of external nature,—innocently joyous, or unaccountably sad...   [xxvi]

To her is contrasted the womanly child Amy (the names are significant):

> She had no exuberant imagination; she was haunted by no whispers from Afar; she was a creature fitted for the earth,—to accept its duties and to gladden its cares.... [H]ow I wished that Lilian, too, could have seen her, and have compared her own ideal phantasies with those young developments of the natural heavenly Woman!   [xlvi]

Lilian comes under the influence of the evil magician Margrave, through which the passivity and remoteness already characteristic of her are increased to the point of total emotional alienation. She becomes very ill, and the crisis of the illness coincides with the defeat of the enchanter, after which she can become the hero's wife in fact as well as in name, as the saying goes.

The special state of the spirit-maiden may be symbolized by an intense aversion to the shedding of blood, as in the cases of Lilian and Rima and Donatello's ancestor's nymph. This signifies her belonging to a higher, harmonious order of being, ideal as compared to earthly reality, but perhaps too is to be connected in a more direct way with her sexual innocence. This theme is found very explicitly in *The Heart of the Ancient Wood*, 1900, by Sir Charles G. D. Roberts, in which a Canadian Miranda (*sic*), a child of the backwoods, passes two crises in her courtship by a young man: first she shoots her pet bear when it threatens his life, and then she gives up vegetarianism. Until their crisis spirit-maidens are elusive, one might say "unreclaimed"; they need the seal of sympathy—in folklore it would be baptism, or wedlock as in *Undine*—to join them to the human world. A similar instinctive decision for normal life as against a visionary principle is made by the blonde Quakeress in *High Noon* when she seizes a gun and defends her lover.

Here we are dealing no longer with the half-mystic taboo attaching to a nymph, but with something more like a quirk of character in a human personality. The Quaker girl's sisters are the women idealists: Scott's Flora Mac-Ivor and Minna Troil, Tennyson's Princess, and Dorothea of *Middlemarch*. Dorothea's ordeal is not symbolic but realistic in the extreme. Princess Ida, whose name connects her with barren and war-seeding mountaintops as well as with Ideas and the Ideal, nearly causes the death of her lover by her waywardness, but is persuaded in time to come down to the real earth of seedtime and harvest and marry him, thereby I suppose becoming Mother Ida. Her ordeal includes a near-drowning, a battle, and also a sacrifice, in the metaphorical theme of the "lost child," which comes closest to the surface in the lyric "As Thro' the Land at Eve"; the child-self that the Princess puts off before she can grow up includes a range of things, from sexual purity to pure selfishness. [11]

Some maidens too pure for the demands of earth are saved by death, like Little Eva. Others, not rigorously virginal but bestowers of a more idyllic existence than nature can long support, die giving birth to female children, cherished then as tender memorials by their fathers, whether Mathilda's too-fond parent or le grand Meaulnes. The spirit-maiden who can neither marry nor die has the worst fate of all. An extreme case occurs in *Dracula:* she has the standard name of Lucy, has the standard mediumistic capacity in the form of somnambulism, and becomes a vampire, bloodsucking in that novel having all the suggestion of demonic cohabitation. Hans Andersen's Little Mermaid is Lucy's converse: she acquires a soul by suffering, and by refusing to regain her mermaid state through shedding her beloved's blood.

Blake speaks in *Milton* (plate 18) of the female principle "that cannot consume in Man's consummation": Northrop Frye calls this character "the asbestos virgin." A nymph unredeemed by the capacity to die or change becomes sinister or even a demon, an embodiment of the morbid narcissism we remarked on at the end of the last chapter. "Sinister" describes frozen virgins like Dickens's Estella, Flaubert's Salammbô and Mallarmé's Hérodiade, while the demons include numerous fatal women (an elegant selection is available in Praz's *The Romantic Agony*), culminating in the wandering-goddess type exemplified in the durable ladies of Vernon Lee's story "Amour Dure" and Arthur Symons's lyric "Modern Love," and Pater's ghoulish Mona Lisa, all immeasurably old and infatuated with their own mystery.

In some fictions of the group we are interested in, the fatal immaturity is in the hero rather than in his nymph: he is a dreamer whom we do not expect to achieve his quest unless he can transform himself along the way. Shelley's heroes in *Alastor* and (presumably) "Prince Athanase" are of this kind. While the theme of "great expectations," or hopeful youth coming to terms with reality, is prominent in English fiction from *Rasselas* in 1759 to at least *The Ordeal of Richard Feverel* in 1859, among Romantic writers we can expect to find it colored in a special way. It is one of the unifying themes in the novels of Scott, linked with a zealous love on the part of youth or maiden for the values of a real or fanciful heroic past. The heroine of *The Pirate*, 1822, the "high-minded and imaginative" Minna Troil, "gifted with such depth of feeling and enthusiasm, yet doomed to see both blighted in early youth, because, with the inexperience of a disposition equally romantic and ignorant, she had built the fabric of her happiness on a quicksand instead of a rock," renounces her pirate and finds a tempered happiness as a pious maiden aunt. She describes her disillusionment as an awakening from a dream (xxii). Cleveland, her beloved, is (like Geordie Robertson in the earlier *Heart of Midlothian*) an example of the apparently romantic outlaw as really callous, sordid, and unable to deal with real life; in the end he is reformed but not rewarded. Scott's first novel, *Waverley*, has two characters roughly comparable to these two in Flora Mac-Ivor and her brother Fergus; however, the central figure is Edward Waverley, a poetic, dreaming, and at times dangerously indolent youth, to whom the fates of Flora and her brother serve as lessons in the school of life. Near the end of the book Waverley revisits scenes of former happiness, now devastated by the useless warfare that once seemed to him so splendid; as for his inward world:

> Now, how changed! how saddened, yet how elevated was his character, within the course of a very few months! . . . "A sadder and a wiser man", he felt, in internal confidence and mental dignity, a compensation for the gay dreams which, in his case, experience had so rapidly dissolved.
>
> [lxiii, "Desolation"]

All through his boyhood Edward Waverley,

> like a child among his toys, culled and arranged, from the splendid yet useless imagery and emblems with which his imagination was stored, visions as brilliant and as fading as those of an evening sky. [iv]

The next chapter, describing "the effect of this indulgence upon his temper and character," also gives the book's one sample from Waverley's poetic compositions. The poem reflects, in metaphorical form, the displacement of a local maiden in his thoughts by his proposed military career; it has a wider reference too, that becomes apparent later, in Waverley's emergence from youthful dreams and poetic moods into the realities of adult life: that is, it foreshadows the pattern of his development throughout the story.

> Late, when the Autumn evening fell
> On Mirkwood-Mere's romantic dell,
> The lake return'd, in chasten'd gleam,
> The purple cloud, the golden beam:
> Reflected in the crystal pool,
> Headland and bank lay fair and cool;
> The weather-tinted rock and tower,
> Each drooping tree, each fairy flower,
> So true, so soft, the mirror gave,
> As if there lay beneath the wave,
> Secure from trouble, toil, and care,
> A world than earthly world more fair.
>   But distant winds began to wake,
> And roused the Genius of the Lake! . . .
> Then as the whirlwind nearer press'd,
> He 'gan to shake his foamy crest
> O'er furrow'd brow and blacken'd cheek,
> And bade his surge in thunder speak.
> In wild and broken eddies whirl'd
> Flitted that fond ideal world,
> And, to the shore in tumult tost,
> The realms of fairy bliss were lost.
>   Yet, with a stern delight and strange,
> I saw the spirit-stirring change . . .
> [And], joying in the mighty roar,
> I mourn'd that tranquil scene no more.
>   So, on the idle dreams of youth,
> Breaks the loud trumpet-call of truth,
> Bids each fair vision pass away,
> Like landscape on the lake that lay,
> As fair, as flitting, and as frail,
> As that which fled the Autumn gale—

> For ever dead to fancy's eye
> Be each gay form that glided by,
> While dreams of love and lady's charms
> Give place to honour and to arms!

These lines are supposed to convey "the wild and irregular spirit of our hero," but even for a youth of "sixty years since" they are rather unadventurous. They show one more example of the familiar broken-reflection figure, combined with the vanishing fairy vision[12] and the fleeing dream that gives place to truth. Among the objects reflected are the colored sunset clouds that themselves are visionary stuff enough; and, while the storm that shatters the image suggests the passing also of autumnal tranquillity as the season advances, even without it the image would inevitably soon vanish with the coming of night (cf. Wordsworth's "Lines" of 1789, which we shall quote later); thus the elegiac motifs of the passing of the season and of the day contribute to the effect. While the immediately surrounding text supplies the one missing association, the nymph, a later somewhat visionary scene supplies a better one.

Waverley's next attachment, much more serious, is to the Highland Jacobite lady, Flora Mac-Ivor. After his conventional introduction to her in the family house, she makes an outdoor appointment and presents herself in her own way. Scott later added in his note headed "Waterfall":

> The appearance of Flora with the harp, as described, has been justly censured as too theatrical and affected for the ladylike simplicity of her character. But something may be allowed to her French education, in which point and striking effect always make a considerable object.

However, the art is not all Flora's: Scott lays all possible emphasis on the ideality of the scene. Waverley is conducted "like a knight of romance" to a glen that seems "to open into the land of romance"; here Flora and her maid appear on a bridge high in the air, "like inhabitants of another region." A "sylvan amphitheatre" contains a "romantic waterfall" that fills a large and clear natural basin in a scene of "romantic wildness":

> Here, like one of those lovely forms which decorate the landscapes of Poussin, Waverley found Flora gazing on the waterfall. Two paces further back stood Cathleen, holding a small Scottish harp, the use of which had been taught to Flora by Rory Dall, one of the last harpers of the Western Highlands. The sun, now stooping in the west, gave a rich and varied tinge to all the objects which surrounded Waverley, and seemed to add more than human brilliancy to the full expressive darkness of Flora's eye, exalted the richness and purity of her complexion, and enhanced the dignity and grace of her beautiful form. Edward thought he had never, even in his wildest dreams, imagined a figure of such exquisite and interesting loveliness. The wild beauty of the retreat, bursting upon him as if by magic, augmented the

mingled feeling of delight and awe with which he approached her, like a fair enchantress of Boiardo or Ariosto, by whose nod the scenery around seemed to have been created, an Eden in the wilderness.

Flora moreover sings for Waverley in this setting, after introducing her song:

> "To speak in the poetical language of my country, the seat of the Celtic Muse is in the midst of the secret and solitary hill, and her voice in the murmur of the mountain stream. He who woos her must love the barren rock more than the fertile valley, and the solitude of the desert better than the festivity of the hall."

It strikes Waverley that "the muse whom she invoked could never find a more appropriate representative" (xxii). Her lament harmonizes with the sounds of the waterfall and the rustling of the leaves; as she concludes, her brother tells Waverley, "This is Flora's Parnassus, and that fountain her Helicon" (xxiii).

Though Flora does not at all play the part of a siren with regard to Waverly, she is part of the chivalric-romantic enchantment through which he slips into a false position; and as she departs at the end for a French convent, remorse "haunts" her "like a phantom" (lxviii) with the fear that it was her fanatical idealism that brought her brother to his death. For Waverley, parting with the Mac-Ivors is to leave youth and its illusions behind him; he marries a much more earthbound woman and settles down to live in the light of common day. But there is enough of poet-hero about Waverley, though he outgrows poetry too, for the concluding dedication of the book to seem fitting: it is to Henry Mackenzie, whose best-known works include *The Man of Feeling*, 1771, and a pair of brief essays interpreting Hamlet as a victim of excessive sensibility.[13] Henceforward, it may not be unfair to observe, Scott's significantly poetic characters are usually either uncanny or insane.

Like the idyllic dream or the cloud castle, the serenely reflecting mirror surface appears to be a symbol characterizing the mental state of high-minded but unexperienced youth, and its shattering is a version of the pastoral "fall" following which the hero has to find his place in the real world. A parallel to some of what we have been looking at could be made with the later part of *Richard II*, noting particularly the climax of the deposition scene, where Richard smashes the mirror. The young Richard seems close to pastoral myth: the play is full of garden, seasonal and renewal imagery, and its hero is a bit of a Narcissus or maybe Adonis. An Old Vic production of some years back saw him that way, and accordingly tended to dress him in pale green and light him in yellow. An almost ritual pattern of complement pervades the climactic scenes: king and hermit, king and beggar, full and empty scale, full and empty bucket, sun king and snow king (for another "mockery king," cf. "glistering Phaethon" in III.iii), dead king and living king. Too, the balance of some of the lines recalls the formula, "He must increase, but I must decrease" (John 3 : 30):

> God save the king! although I be not he:
> And yet, amen, if heaven do think him me. . . .
> God pardon all oaths that are broke to me!
> God keep all vows unbroke are made to thee!
> Make me, that nothing have, with nothing griev'd,
> And thou with all pleas'd, that has all achiev'd!
> Long mayst thou live in Richard's seat to sit,
> And soon lie Richard in an earthy pit!   [IV.i.174–75, 215–20]

Parting from the queen, Richard says:

>   learn, good soul,
> To think our former state a happy dream;
> From which awak'd, the truth of what we are
> Shows us but this.   [V.i.17–20]

Another mirror shattering that seems "To make a second fall of cursed man" (*Richard II* III.iv.76) occurs in "The Lady of Shalott," resulting from the Lady's breaking a taboo and thereby inviting the working-out of a curse. The fable is extremely ambiguous; but the cracking across of the mirror, combined with rending of the "web," signalizes the passage from a cloistered world of shadows to a direct (and fatal) encounter with reality. It has also a striking pastoral aspect, as the Lady's fateful act takes place precisely at the turn of the year from golden harvest season to squally, blood-freezing late autumn. A comparable fable is that of Cosmo related in George MacDonald's *Phantastes: a faerie romance,* 1858. Cosmo, a poetic-souled youth, acquires a mirror in whose depths from time to time appears a beautiful woman, bound there by evil enchantment. She urges him, " 'Cosmo, if you love me, set me free, even from yourself; break the mirror.' " He stops to consider: "The whole world would be but a prison, if he annihilated the one window that looked into the paradise of love. Not yet pure in love, he hesitated." When he attempts it, he is too late and fails; later he does break the mirror and release the lady, but at the cost of his life. The unearned and incomplete enjoyment of the beloved object represented by possession of the mirror is a childishly selfish dream-state corresponding to the entirely passive nature of Cosmo's sensitivity:

> His mind had never yet been filled with an absorbing passion; but it lay like a still twilight open to any wind, whether the low breath that wafts but odours, or the storm that bows the great trees till they strain and creak. He saw everything as through a rose-coloured glass. . . . He was in fact a poet without words; the more absorbed and endangered, that the springing waters were dammed back into his soul, where, finding no utterance, they grew, and swelled, and undermined.   [xiii]

Cosmo belongs to the same family as the Poet of *Alastor*, Prince Athanase, or Waverley, while his lady, like the one of Shalott, is an Amoret in need of heroic rescue.

The inset story of Cosmo epitomizes much of the theme of *Phantastes*. MacDonald's romance is modeled somewhat on the two-world arrangement of *The Faerie Queene*. Its hero, Anodos (Way Up?), is no knight, but a youth of whom near the end the best that can as yet be said is, "There is something noble in him, but it is a nobleness of thought, and not of deed." The title refers to the genius of Imagination in Fletcher's *Purple Island*, and the whole realm described is rather a "chamber of maiden-thought." Our sense in reading Spenser that none of the adventures or quests is complete in itself but only a preparation, is matched here by certain indications that the book describes a world of dream or childhood or even of the unborn: not life but a preparation for it. In this it resembles *Alice in Wonderland*, published seven years later. Moreover, it has allusions to a looking-glass world, Prospero's realm, Dante's journey up the Mount of Purgatory, Virgil's grove of bleeding trees, and the mirror world of the "Magus Zoroaster" speech in *Prometheus Unbound*. Its first episode recalls Spenser's Wandering Wood and looks towards Alice's garden of talking flowers. Perhaps like Anodos himself, the trees of the wood are all growing up to be human.

Most of the story describes Anodos's quest of a lady whom he first meets in the shape of an alabaster statue, to which she is confined by a spell; the form is that of Pygmalion's creation, and he finds it in a grotto with a spring, a place that seems suggestive of Homer's Cave of the Nymphs.[14] (As the following quotation will suggest, *Phantastes* is strikingly full of literary reminiscences, even for a romance of this period.)

> I thought of the Prince of the Enchanted City, half marble and half a living man; of Ariel; of Niobe; of the Sleeping Beauty in the Wood; of the bleeding trees; and many other histories.   [v]

Inspired by a wild hope that "life might be given to this form also," he tries a kiss; then,

> I bethought me of Orpheus, and the following stones; that trees should follow his music seemed nothing surprising now.

When he sings to the lady, she springs up "like a sudden apparition" and hastens away into the woods. He is later able to release her once more by his songs "from the death-sleep of an evil enchantment" (xix), but her destined rescuer and husband is another man. After her union with the latter, the lady speaks regretfully of Anodos: "He was but the moon of my night; you are the sun of my day."

Carrying on his quest, Anodos meets a form resembling the one he is in search of, and says, "It is my white lady!" A voice replies, "It is your white lady" (vi); but this nymph has the rôle of deluding Echo, and leads him astray. Shortly afterwards Anodos becomes burdened with his Shadow and is told that this usually happens after one has met the false nymph of the forest (viii). In the ninth chapter, epigraphed with most of stanza 4 of "Dejection," the blighting effects of the Shadow are described. The flowers on which Anodos lies will recover:

> Not so those on which my Shadow had lain. The very outline of it could be traced in the withered, lifeless grass, and the scorched and shrivelled flowers which stood there, dead, and hopeless of any resurrection. . . . Rays of gloom issued from the central shadow as from a black sun, lengthening and shortening with continual change. But wherever a ray struck, that part of earth, or sea, or sky, became void, or desert, and sad to my heart.[15]

Henceforward he is more concerned with getting rid of the Shadow than with pursuing the lady. Eventually he is killed in a heroic undertaking, whereupon the lady and her knight bury him with tears and he enters his own world again. The couple are in a somewhat parental relation to Anodos, who achieves little in this rather prenatal realm of Fairyland beyond getting himself born out of it.[16] Back on earth he concludes: "Thus I, who set out to find my Ideal, came back rejoicing that I had lost my Shadow" (xxv): the triangle of the Narcissus myth and of "My Spectre Around Me."[17]

The prenatal overtones of *Phantastes* are numerous and conscious. Anodos is helped on his way by various maternal powers that after his return to earth run together in his memory, adding up to something like the "sweet voice" with a consoling secret—here, "something too good to be told"—at the end of Tennyson's "The Two Voices." In xviii he is carried over a sea of genesis like that of Asia in *Prometheus Unbound*. Perhaps most curiously, he reads about an unknown world where babies are found rather than born, where women have wings and water does not reflect, and this develops into a world of romantic passion like that in *Alastor*:

> The sign or cause of coming death is an indescribable longing for something, they know not what, which seizes them, and drives them into solitude, consuming them within till the body fails. When a youth and maiden look too deep into each other's eyes, this longing seizes and possesses them; but instead of drawing nearer to each other, they wander away, each alone, into solitary places, and die of their desire. But it seems to me that thereafter they are born babes upon our earth; where if, when grown, they find each other, it goes well with them; if not, it will seem to go ill. [xii]

Anodos, whose power of action is almost all in his singing, is a kind of embryo unconscious artist. The most conscious artist in the story is someone he first meets as a young girl with a music-making globe; when he seizes it, the sound increases, the globe throbs violently, and then it shatters. Later, when she is a woman, her singing releases him from imprisonment, and she tells him,

> "I do not need the globe to play to me; for I can sing. I could not sing at all before. Now I go about everywhere through Fairyland, singing till my heart is like to break, just like my globe, for very joy at my own songs. And wherever I go, my songs do good and deliver people." [xxii]

They deliver Anodos in fact even from his Shadow. The woman has become one of the benevolent powers of Fairyland; Anodos cannot begin to compare himself with her. Hers is a song schooled by suffering, like the poetry of earth; his is comparatively unearned and feeble.

Anodos's poetry belongs to the nobility of thought only, and does not help him towards the knighthood he admires. When he translates his impulse into act, he is as likely to have done the wrong thing as the right. Once by his song he is able to make the white lady appear, and then he seizes her: immediately she shudders and springs away, crying reproachfully, "You should not have touched me!" The palace setting disappears, and he finds himself on a wintry hillside among "great stones like tombstones."

> A white figure gleamed past me, wringing her hands, and crying, "Ah! you should have sung to me!", and disappeared behind one of the stones. [xvi]

Following her, he finds only a cold gust of wind and a hole in the earth. The chapter is epigraphed from Schiller's "Das Ideal und das Leben":

> Ev'n the Styx, which ninefold her infoldeth,
> Hems not Ceres' daughter in its flow;
> But she grasps the apple—ever holdeth
> Her, sad Orcus down below.
>
> [MacDonald's translation]

Variations on this scene occur in three other places in the book. We mentioned Cosmo's failure to break the mirror; when he tries the first time, he hears a clap of thunder and falls senseless, and when he wakes the mirror has disappeared. When Anodos grasps the girl's sounding globe, it gives out "a low tempest of harmony" and throbs and vibrates increasingly while she tries to get it back from him;

> ... at last it burst in our hands, and a black vapour broke upwards from out of it; then turned, as if blown sideways, and enveloped the maiden, hiding even the shadow in its blackness. She held fast the fragments which I abandoned, and fled from me into the forest ... , wailing like a child, and crying, "You have broken my globe!" [ix]

Anodos tries to follow to console her, but a storm rises and prevents him. The remaining parallel incident occurs in the ballad that Anodos hears sung. Sir Aglovaile has betrayed a maiden and left her to die with her baby; repentant, he is granted a series of assignations with her ghost, but during one of these he clasps her and finds her a corpse in his arms, after which he never sees her again. The song concludes:

> Only a voice, when winds were wild,
> Sobbed and wailed like a chidden child:—
> "Alas! how easily things go wrong!
> A sigh too much, or a kiss too long,
> And there follows a mist and a weeping rain,
> And life is never the same again".   [xix]

There is more to this series of situations than a parallel with Orpheus's second loss of Eurydice, or even the catastrophe of *Tasso*. Seizure followed by wind, thunderclap, storm, mist, and rain, and someone's suddenly becoming either much older or much younger, recall perhaps the events of the fall in Eden, and much more definitely those of Blake's "The Crystal Cabinet." The youth snatched from the "Wild" and shut up in it by the maiden discovers,

> This Cabinet is form'd of Gold
> And Pearl & Crystal shining bright,
> And within it opens into a World
> And a little lovely Moony Night.

Within is another England and another maiden, this time threefold:

> I bent to Kiss the lovely Maid,
> And found a Threefold Kiss return'd.
>
> I strove to sieze the inmost Form
> With ardor fierce & hands of flame,
> But burst the Crystal Cabinet,
> And like a Weeping Babe became—
>
> A weeping Babe upon the wild,
> And Weeping Woman pale reclin'd,
> And in the outward air again
> I fill'd with Woes the passing Wind.

There is something about a moony, paradisal mirror world, such as many of our fictions have as their vision of bliss, that resists the effort to "sieze the inmost Form" and achieve closer contact; the state is essentially passive, and to exert oneself is for better or worse to leave it. The speaker of Blake's poem seems to have forced on the teasing beloved, instead of the flirtation that she expected, the necessity of giving birth to him, a much rougher process, and thus delivering him helpless to the lower world.

The history of Anodos fits our theme partly because it so clearly demonstrates the Narcissus triangle of self, ideal, and evil other. The two simplest kinds of story embodying this pattern, favorites in ballet and opera plots because of their definite outlines and folkloristic quality, are what we could call, from Spenser, the Amoret and False-Florimell themes: hero's rescue of maiden from enchanter and hero's diversion from true beloved through intervention of false. They are often found combined, for example in "Swan Lake" and *Tales of Hoffmann,* as they are among the numerous incidents of *Phantastes.* In the latter two works, what makes the triangle "narcissistic" is the sense it conveys that what the hero encounters is intimately and mysteriously (more mysteriously than in Spenser) bound up with what he is. The same elements dominate the narrative of Melville's *Mardi,* 1849. In his capture of the tabooed blue-eyed pearl-maiden Yillah, the hero Taji acquires simultaneously an ideal beloved and the ineradicable guilt of murder. Yillah is shortly lost to him; he pursues her through the whole world of the book, and is himself pursued by three "avengers" of the man he has killed and by three "sirens," emissaries of the dark witch-queen Hautia, who tries to distract him from his love.[18] This hero ends as a kind of Satan, having as "the last, last crime" chosen solitude and the "realm of shades": when he has finally lost his phantom bride and cast off his friends, he passes the world-surrounding reef in his boat and flies onward into emptiness with the spectral avengers after him: "And thus, pursuers and pursued fled on, over an endless sea" (cxcv).[19]

Another feature of *Phantastes* is its delineation of the hero as infant. The innocent Narcissus-hero is marked out not necessarily by self-love or self-absorption so much as by a more subtle clinging to his solitude through some childish self-sufficiency. Shelley's Poet neglects love; Zanoni till the last moment regards it as a weakness; Anodos and Mathilda's father, like Blake's speaker and Goethe's Tasso, are impelled to grab and so cheat themselves. Like the dream-vision or the watery reflection (whether in Ovid's tale of Narcissus or Aesop's of dog and bone), the object grabbed at dissolves or disappears.

The fact that Narcissus's failure in adult love is often imputed not to his own will but to some elusiveness or taboo in the maiden should remind us that in our fiction characters are not dramatic individuals but soul-fragments. The immaturity in passion for a narcissistic or nympholeptic object consists partly in unrecognized self-love, partly in the willful and knowing attachment to an impossible soulmate, perhaps by perversion of the memory of an unfallen state. Nineteenth-century writers are apt to regard either wistfully or ironically the association of the world of romance with youth. Often, accordingly, the happy ending will hinge on hero's or heroine's ability to grow up into the realities of a condition mixed but also shared. This requires a recognition of the limitations of an idyllic world, and departure from it onto a lower but more "real" plane of existence.

Let us return briefly to a term used in Chapter 4, "elegiac romance." There we applied it to *Werther*, in consideration both of the book's central event and of its prevailing tone of lyrical lamentation. The same kind of tone pervades, for example, large stretches of *La Nouvelle Héloïse* and the novels of Mrs. Radcliffe, and to those parts the term "elegiac" could reasonably be applied. In what follows, we are distinguishing for purposes of definition among elements often found combined in the same work. Further elegiac romances are, first, narrations clearly conveying a fall from a state at least superficially paradisal or idyllic to a comparatively imperfect one, such as *Tasso, Mathilda*, Tennyson's *The Princess*, Poe's "Eleonora," Melville's *Pierre*. (As appears from some of these examples, imperfection may have much to recommend it.) Second, narrations describing the death or degradation of a central figure embodying such a state: *Paul et Virginie, Alastor, The Marble Faun, Maud, Green Mansions*. Third, and this becomes more complex, narrations suggesting an unfallen state seen from this side of the fall, even though the event itself may not be described. Two books of this kind to which we shall come later are *Trilby*, glowing with nostalgia for a lost past, and *The Deerslayer*, set in unspoiled jewellike scenes in the stainless youth of America and of Natty Bumppo. Another such romance is that published by W. H. Hudson in 1885 under the elegiac title, *The Purple Land That England Lost*. The first chapter not only expresses the hero's bitterness about the circumstances through which the Banda Oriéntal was lost to England, but darkly conveys to the reader that his stay there was followed by a period of imprisonment for him, contrived by his father-in-law, and during it his wife died brokenhearted. At the end of the book the hero and his wife return from the Purple Land to face her angry father, and the last sentences are full of foreboding. The point of this otherwise entirely undeveloped theme seems to be to illuminate the period covered by the story with the rays of an unrecognized peace and happiness. When one has finished reading, the impression is left of a self-contained romantic world whose gate has clanged shut.

One last category of fiction we should look at is, though not exactly elegiac romance, connected with it: those works in which a fall has taken place and a happier state is represented only by memory or monument. The history of Rider Haggard's *She* enacted among the ruins of the great and good civilization of Kôr is an example, along with accounts of beings like Dickens's Miss Havisham shut up in desolate houses that once were cheerful and alive. Again, a demonic figure either having a friend who remembers when things were different—Frankenstein—or bearing in his face the marks of some catastrophe or shattering experience—Byron's Lara—is a subject of this kind. So is the somber Hester Prynne, who carries the mark of her fall in the scarlet "A." The story of the decadent last survivor of a noble family belongs here, like Beckford's *Vathek*, 1786, Roderick Usher, or Huysmans' Des Esseintes, 1884. Each of these three, and especially the last, exhibits some form of the infantilism we expect of Narcissus.

The original title of Huysmans' *A Rebours* was *Seul,* the solipsism of the character having advanced to a point at which other persons are unnecessary provided their functions are filled. Suffering from an absolute ennui in which the world can give him nothing he wants, Des Esseintes dreams of

> une thébaïde raffinée, à un désert confortable, à une arche immobile et tiède où il se réfugierait loin de l'incessant déluge de la sottise humaine.
>
> ["Notice"]

He contrives such a retreat, and there carries on perverse researches in the pleasures of the several senses, delighting to defy "nature," which he regards as monotonous and vulgar. Having cut himself off from real experience, Des Esseintes constructs an inner life mainly out of literary memories and allusions. His dream of visiting wet and foggy London, for instance, comes to him from Dickens:

> La ville du romancier, la maison bien éclairée, bien chauffée, bien servie, bien close, les bouteilles lentement versées par la petite Dorrit, par Dora Copperfield, par la soeur de Tom Pinch, lui apparurent naviguant ainsi qu'une arche tiède, dans un déluge de fange et de suie.   [xi]

At length his doctor orders him to dismantle his house and go back into society, which he does with lamentations. As moving-men trundle his belongings about, he complains:

> . . . tout est bien fini; comme un raz de marée, les vagues de la médiocrité humaine montent jusqu'au ciel et elles vont engloutir le refuge dont j'ouvre, malgré moi, les digues . . .—Seigneur, prenez pitié du chrétien qui doute, de l'incrédule qui voudrait croire, du forçat de la vie qui s'embarque seul, dans la nuit, sous un firmament que n'éclairent plus les consolants fanaux du vieil espoir!   [xvi]

In whatever vessel, Des Esseintes' aloneness is always on a wide sea. As in *Là-Bas,* the catastrophe deplored by the hero is the advent of the common man, along with the passing of a faith that made possible the great saint and the great sinner, perhaps combined,[20] as in the figure of Gilles de Retz, whom *Là-Bas* glorifies. By contrast Des Esseintes is totally enervated and lives in a world of echoes and shadows. His most satisfactory love affair is with a lady ventriloquist, his worst experience is an excessively bad dream about the Pox, and his greatest triumph comes when his doctor tells his servants to feed him by enema: "Quelle décisive insulte jetée à la face de cette vieille nature dont les uniformes exigences seraient pour jamais éteintes!" (xv). Passivity could hardly be carried further. The essence of a palace-of-art situation like this one is that, once it has been set up, no decision on its maker's part should ever be necessary again, were it not that solitude itself then becomes a factor. The spirit of solitude is in practice an avenger, and the being who takes steps to preserve his infant-ego sense of aloneness, whether or not knowingly, usually in the end like Des Esseintes must either reverse them or die.

Part Three

Seven   The Artist: Setting

I would build that dome in air

—S. T. Coleridge

Like wrecks of a dissolving dream.

—P. B. Shelley

An imaginative literature of psychological crisis flourished throughout the Romantic period, ranging chronologically, in verse, from *The Prelude,* "Dejection," and *Alastor* to *Pauline, In Memoriam,* and *Empedocles on Etna;* in prose, from *Werther* to *Sartor Resartus* and *Aurélia.* Much of this literature can be called elegiac, as marked by a sense of the loss of some precious quality in one's world or in oneself, and as drawing remotely on the love complaint, more directly on the literary theme of melancholy, and principally on the pastoral–elegiac tradition and its expansion in *Paradise Lost.*

A figure particularly susceptible to crisis is, as we have seen, the poet or artist, who may suffer from loss of creative powers or of his sense of promise and destiny. In Romantic literature we often meet Narcissus not just as ideal or idealistic youth but as the Artist—or the Artist's Specter, the dilettante. Like the divine Imagination in Blake that falls into a passive doting and ceases to create, this figure suffers from a self-absorption, often disguised as love for an ideal other or for "Nature," that becomes paralysis of will. This is much of the meaning of what is called Wertherism. Werther and Tasso both cultivate their own sensibility until the ordinary barriers of self-containment break down and phantoms crowd in, Werther in particular having opened his soul to Nature to the point of being almost crushed by it. Each of them carries his practice of sensibility to an extreme at which his imaginative life either is threatened or threatens him. This situation is strikingly developed in Poe. Roderick Usher is an obsessed and enervated caricature of the artist: his apartment with its clutter of papers and musical instruments looks like a preliminary study for Dürer's "Melencolia." It seems characteristic too that when the figure is not passive but engaged in creation or some activity symbolic of it, the impulse comes like a fit of insanity and is terrifying to beholders. Since Ophelia, madness arising from excess of sensibility has expressed

121

itself in wild song. The bard at the end of "Kubla Khan" speaks of inspiring "holy dread" by a shamanistic evocation of Kubla's paradise; and at a further extreme, it is when Roderick Usher sings his song of "The Haunted Palace" that the narrator realized he is mad. For both these poets the elegiac event seems already to have taken place, leaving them so to speak stranded in an afterworld, Coleridge's poet as a nostalgic Orpheus and Poe's as an unmistakable Specter.

For Milton and his eighteenth-century following, solitude was the poet's halo, signifying his converse with higher powers. In that spirit Thomson's "Hymn" to it begins

> Hail, mildly pleasing Solitude,
> Companion of the wise and good.

Later, "haunted solitude" darkens in meaning, suggesting rather the fallen Adam's "in solitude live savage." Solitude now indicates loss, deprivation of a better state of being, the torment of happier memory. It may become the scene of the poet's pursuit of, or by, some figment sinister because not more but less than fully human. This progress from a sanctified to a demonic solitude is epitomized in *Alastor,* and underlined by the transition from a goddess-Nature to "Nature's vast frame" left echoing and empty with the departure of the "dream" and "frail exhalation" that the Poet has come to personify. The Artist for our purposes includes, besides the poet, painter, sculptor, and musician, also the aesthete or connoisseur of sensations, and we shall view him as the immediate offspring of the eighteenth-century man of sensibility. His Narcissus-trait of solitude is manifested in his relations with his surroundings and with the soulmate, and in this and the following chapter we shall be concerned with these.

This figure, particularly when more aesthete than producing artist, is notoriously an indoor type. Consequently we are apt to meet him in architectural transpositions of Milton's universe rather than simply adaptations of Milton's natural world. "Kubla Khan" shows the way, to be followed by many houses built on water or on sinister vaults, or palaces of art with a threat built in. Metaphorically, this is what Tasso's Belriguardo is: a pleasure-house balanced on water and potentially a prison. "The Fall of the House of Usher" is the clearest example we could wish for, and its inset lyric, "The Haunted Palace," shows that, just as the order of the Miltonic cosmos corresponds to that of the human faculties, so the palace of art can be something of a house of the soul—Psyche's castle, we might say.

Buildings of this kind almost always have some direct relation to Paradise: usually, that of demonic imitation or parody, as being of our world or worse. A very few nonsinister versions are to be found. Shelley has several significant cave dwellings, notably the "pleasure-house" of *Epipsychidion* lined with plants and formed from that geological figment "the living stone."[1] A later one is the Growing Castle of Strindberg's *Dream Play,* which at the end bursts into flower. Another is hinted at in Douglas Grant's remarkable idyll, "The Great House,"[2] where in a ruined Georgian mansion it seems briefly that all the broken parts, particularly the staircase, can renew themselves and join up again. Another, less mythic in conception, is the tree house of Truman Capote's *The Grass Harp,* where the just society briefly assembles, to scatter again, as from the gate of Eden, in a storm of rain. It will be noted what these places have in common: their materials are not what any January can freeze together but are organic and alive, like those of Tennyson's Camelot, Yeats's Byzantium, or the Kingdom. These places belong to what we shall later characterize as "the summer vision," where the movement of life is idyllically unified with the stability of art.[3]

If the house built on water is a paradigm of the ordered cosmos, the palace of art is a microcosm of it. Its great aim is self-completeness: like aestheticism itself, of which it is regularly a symbol,[4] it wants to render the soul independent of an outside world, even to make it forget that such exists. The builder of Tennyson's Palace of Art carefully includes by representation the four quarters of the earth (symbolized in Eden by the four rivers) and all the resources of outward nature as well as of the human mind. A comparable self-completeness is symbolized in Prince Prospero's abbey in Poe's "Masque of the Red Death"; the building is "the creation of the prince's own eccentric, yet august taste," and the seven rooms of its "imperial suite" are decked in some approximation to the seven colors of the spectrum. A more frivolous encyclopaedic house is that of Des Esseintes at Fontenay, fitted up so that its owner can, for example, enjoy all the sensations of a long sea voyage without ever leaving home. Another encyclopaedic feature found in some such buildings is the separate provision for the delights of all the five senses. Des Esseintes of course takes pleasure in confounding them; but Sir William Jones's *The Palace of the Seven Fountains,* 1767, and the opening of *Vathek* both make a point of such arrangements. While the House of Usher supplies few pleasures of any kind, Roderick's living arrangements have to be adjusted negatively on the same plan:

> He suffered much from a morbid acuteness of the senses; the most insipid food was alone endurable: he could wear only garments of a certain texture; the odours of all flowers were oppressive; his eyes were tortured by even a faint light; and there were but peculiar sounds, and these from stringed instruments, which did not inspire him with horror.

In "The Palace of Art" and "The Masque of the Red Death," there is an implication of spiritual pride in the effort to make a countercreation to God's, and the elements that one has tried to exclude are the ones that successfully invade. In contrast to the organic living structures mentioned above, these buildings do not eternalize life but render it captive, petrified, or dead. The early Gothic correspondence between architectural setting and state of mind later can become almost a semblance of life, the closed room appearing as brain or conscience and the castle bell or clock[5] in Poe a kind of heartbeat; but far from being reassuring, this is a peculiarly ghoulish horror-property.

Many traditions go into the makeup of these symbolical places. The detailed allegory of Poe's Haunted Palace recalls that of Spenser's House of Temperance or the original of all such structures, the house of the body described at the end of Ecclesiastes. Another ancient source is Apuleius: from her enchanted palace built by Love, Psyche is cast out, like Adam and Eve from their paradise, for breaking a taboo. Psyche's castle comes down into fairy tales as on the one hand the house and garden of Beauty's Beast, and on the other Bluebeard's palace with its locked chamber of terrors, this latter linked with Spenser's House of Busyrane.[6] Another fairy-tale *locus amoenus*, reminding us of Psyche's castle but also of the islands of Circe, Calypso, and the Sirens, is the island and palace of Tasso's Armida, which Spenser adapts for his Bower of Bliss.

Apart from any questions about its inhabitants—we shall come to these—Psyche's house of wonders is a place not in itself unequivocally good or evil. To Psyche at first it is a place of respite, far better than what she expected but not for the moment offering final answers. And when she thinks of home and sisters, her palace seems to her nothing but "a fine prison" (*The Golden Ass* v.5, trans. Adlington). Her sisters succeed in persuading her that it is so in fact, and only when she is forced to leave it does she recognize it as the place of perfect happiness. It had a touch of the delusive, in that it was not yet fairly won. In the tale of Beauty and the Beast too there are factors that prevent Beauty from recognizing both her paradise and her lover until they are almost lost. Bluebeard's house is similarly ambiguous and a place of temptation and taboo, but it perhaps tempts the maiden in the other direction: passively to repose in its splendors without looking behind them.

Busyrane's house is the darker aspect of Psyche's, the state of enslavement to false Love. The Bower of Bliss is a false paradise, the place that looks like one's true home but is not; as with the Sirens' rock in the *Odyssey*, "He who tarries there will never look upon his wife and dear babes again." The houses of Keats's Lamia and Peacock's Rhododaphne are Romantic equivalents. Other delusive happy places are Spenser's House of Pride, Thomson's Castle of Indolence, and Jones's Palace of

Seven Fountains, each having a dismal dungeon as an essential part of its design,[7] and Beckford's Hall of Eblis (*Vathek*), a palace only gradually found to be the place of the damned. Armida's palace disappears like a cloud castle "Or like vain dreams" (XVI.lxix.4, trans. Fairfax), and another of that kind is Klingsor's in *Parzifal*. A metaphor in *Melmoth* suggests cloud castle perched on dungeon:

> there are some *criminals of the imagination*, whom if we could plunge into the oubliette of its magnificent but lightly-based fabric, its lord would reign more happy.   [I, xii]

Milton sets against his Eden an oriental delusive paradise:

> ... where Abassin kings their issue guard,
> Mount Amara, though this by some suppos'd
> True Paradise, under the Ethiop line
> By Nilus' head, enclos'd with shining rock,
> A whole day's journey high. ...   [IV.280–84]

This hint from the travel books is developed in the Amhara of *Rasselas* and the Abora of "Kubla Khan." Like Eden, Mount Amara is a pleasure garden high on an unclimbable mountain, and again it is a place jealously guarded by a paternal power. Rasselas's sojourn in the Abyssinian Happy Valley becomes intolerable because it deprives him of both action and choice: it is a way of life built utterly on exclusion. The delusive paradise most relevant to "Kubla Khan" is the realm of the Old Man of the Mountain described by medieval travelers. This demonic figure established cunningly contrived palaces and gardens full of birds and flowers and singing and playing damsels, and with springs of milk and honey bursting from the ground. Here young men were brought drugged with hashish, spirited away again in the same state after a brief taste of its pleasures, and afterwards forced to desperate deeds by the promise that at death they would return to this Paradise; thus was formed the secret society of the Assassins. Eventually the Old Man (historically, it appears, the eighth Old Man) was attacked and killed, and his gardens were razed and his palaces destroyed. Marco Polo places his activities correctly in Persia; Mandeville puts him in the land of Prester John, or Abyssinia.

These two oriental pleasure-gardens represent what we have called "the tyrant's solitude," where a despotic power can shut out anything that might trouble its pleasures. Belriguardo would appear as such, if we did not believe that Alfonso and his adviser joined enlightenment with privilege and deserved their place of repose. Tennyson's Palace of Art is such a place, as the allusions to Herod, Belshazzar, and Nebuchadnezzar (st. 58) imply. A counterpart in prose fiction is F. Scott Fitzgerald's "The Diamond as Big as the Ritz," an adaptation of the folklore theme of the mountain of diamond or alabaster.[8] Its pleasure-house is built on a diamond mountain, visitors are imprisoned or murdered, and the cellars are mined, all under the command of an evil old patriarch. Earlier owners of houses with mined cellars are the pacha of Yanina in *The Count of Monte Cristo*—whose hero owns a hashish paradise—and the Phantom of the Opera; the two latter establishments are also built on water, but the implied presence of a fiery underworld is appropriate to the volcanic energies of all three. The delusive mountain paradise without exit and embodying the will of an Old Man is so familiar that when James Hilton in *Lost Horizon*, 1933, sets one up and tries to persuade us that the truly wise man will wish to stay, the effect is somewhat perverse.

The murmurs in Kubla's cellars bring in another line: the Gothic haunted castle. This for our fiction first becomes prominent in Walpole's *Castle of Otranto*, 1764, where the usurping Duke Manfred's knowledge of his own guilt is matched by a series of apparitions and uncanny happenings in his family, and where moreover the gloomy immensity of his castle and its subterranean labyrinthine intertwinings make it correspond to his moods and his nature. What is behind Walpole in this regard is Shakespeare's castles of Elsinore and Dunsinane, where the dead past will not stay buried; a Romantic re-creation of a castle-specter/tyrant's-conscience scene occurs in Pushkin's *Boris Godunov*, 1825. Centrally Gothic are the scenes in the castle of Udolpho and the regular atmospherics raised and dismissed in *Northanger Abbey*.

One more tyrant's fastness requiring mention by way of background is Pandaemonium in *Paradise Lost* Book One. It is compared to the temples and palaces of Egypt and Babylon, comment enough on the quality and resources of Satan's leadership. It rises to music, like the fabled walls of Troy and Thebes, but with much more sinister implication, and "like an Exhalation," which suggests that its solidity is delusive, counterfeiting what Hamlet calls the "majestical roof fretted with golden fire" of God's cosmos (II.ii). Later comparable palace dwellers will arrange lamps, as Tennyson's Soul does, to "mimic heaven," or, as Poe's heroes often do, altogether replace the natural lights with artificial ones. The horrific features of the House of Usher include, by the way, "the unnatural light of a faintly luminous and distinctly visible gaseous exhalation which hung about and enshrouded the mansion."—As the builder or designer of the palace of art, the artist is very closely linked with the magician, and part of this discussion will fall into a later chapter.

The delusive paradise is sinister not just because it is an attempt by man to emulate the work of God, but because the imitation is of something that we have already lost. Fallen man can only pervert Paradise, or make it an instrument of his own damnation. In Milton, Eden after it falls is shut away from man for his own good; all the gifts it could offer would be curses to his present state. Man's task is now to rebuild it spiritually, within; its material embodiment is a temptation, and so is the effort to live among its ruins. We have already seen Memory as a demon, and the phantom of lost happiness, which the wanderer should put behind him, as a siren that he pursues to his death.

In a realistic and historical sense, the ancient and magnificent building may embody the will of an old order to resist change; hence that special category of sinister buildings, the vampire house. An appropriately Gothic example is Satis House in *Great Expectations,* with the rooms in which Miss Havisham keeps all the decaying memorials of her broken-off marriage exactly as they were on that day all those years ago. The house is not just a spectacle but an instrument of vengeance; the future of the young lives in its shadow is to be shaped in the image of her own past. Beyond Miss Havisham there gradually opens the prospect of a useless and archaic genteel class, unable to fend off decay, and parasitic on the real work done in society.

Another vampire or Gorgon house is Shelley's Tower of Famine, Ugolino's prison in Pisa.[9] In the beholder's eye, the effect of its grim shape amid palaces and temples is

> As if a spectre wrapt in shapeless terror
> Amid a company of ladies fair
>
> Should glide and glow, till it became a mirror
> Of all their beauty, and their hair and hue,
> The life of their sweet eyes, with all its error,
> Should be absorbed, till they to marble grew.

The vampiric touch enters with the craving for form and color of what itself is without them: the tower, or what it stands for, is itself famished. As the Gothic uninvited or spectral guest usually has some claim on the revelers,[10] if only by virtue of their efforts to forget about him, so here the word "error" implies that human weakness, even if only through compliance, has raised and used the tower, and that the solidity and solemnity of the surrounding buildings rest on social institutions of which the house of torture is a necessary correlative. As with the *Four Zoas* Spectre that arises from man's brain and then acquires an independent life at his expense, "all the Man absorbing," the power to appal of any specter worth its sheet comes from within.

Similarly Gothic, and similarly conveying a view at least partly of a social reality, are the Romantic Rome, built on ruins, and the Romantic Venice, built on water. Of the former, Hawthorne's Rome of *The Marble Faun,* with its miasmic gardens, its chasm and precipice, its tombs, catacombs and underground places of penitence, its wealth built on squalors, gives the general idea.[11] Its Plutonian underworld has an acknowledged hold on the dark lady Miriam, and through her gains one on the sunlight-bred Faun himself.

Poe's story "The Assignation," consisting mainly of a suicide scene in the bizarre apartment of an aesthete—"a very young man, with the sound of whose name the greater part of Europe was then ringing"—opens precisely where canto IV of *Childe Harold* does:

> . . . in Venice, on the Bridge of Sighs,
> A palace and a prison on each hand.

The story has a siren in the Marchesa Aphrodite—that Venus often associated with the spirit of Venice—the beautiful, unhappy, lost beloved. The hero has written a poem about her in which their love was a happy green isle now blasted,[12] whose memory makes him dead to all voices but that of the past, unconscious to both present and future:

> Now all my days are trances,
> And all my nightly dreams
> Are where thy dark eye glances,
> And where thy footstep gleams—
> In what ethereal dances,
> By what Italian streams.

The "Italian stream" that we actually see is the Grand Canal, not paradisal but murkily dangerous; funereal gondolas glide over it like portents, and the Marchesa's child has to be snatched from its waters. In the hero's palazzo apartment hangs the Marchesa's portrait, supernaturally beautiful, with a smile of enigmatic melancholy, decked with wings (she is one of Poe's many Psyche figures) and pointing to the poison cup.

The story implies that the hero, originally English, has followed his Aphrodite to Venice, where she is held in captivity by loveless wealth and pride. However, apostrophizing him, the narrator suggests that Venice is his proper home:

> Once more thy form hath risen before me!—not—oh! not as thou art—in the cold valley and shadow—but as thou *shouldst be*—squandering away a life of magnificent meditation in that city of dim visions, thine own Venice. . . .

In his last speech the hero adds to this:

> "To dream", he continued, resuming the tone of his desultory conversation, as he held up to the rich light of a censer one of the magnificent vases—"to dream has been the business of my life. I have therefore framed for myself, as you see, a bower of dreams. In the heart of Venice could I have erected a better? . . . Like these arabesque censers, my spirit is now writhing in fire, and the delirium of this scene is fashioning me for the wilder visions of that land of real dreams whither I am now rapidly departing."

This "business" of dreaming has been glowingly defended in the opening apostrophe:

> Who then shall call thy conduct into question? who blame thee for thy visionary hours, or denounce those occupations as a wasting away of life, which were but the overflowings of thine everlasting energies?

Certainly for Poe his hero typifies all the highest capacities of genius.

In brief digression, we might remark that the tone of passionate admiration for a hero with whom his author seems closely identified, and whose death may allow license for rhapsodic eulogy, is met with again and again in the fiction with which we are concerned, and belongs to the world of Narcissus. We saw it in *Alastor;* Byronic heroes like Lara show it; in Poe it is nowhere stronger than in "The Assignation"; female figures to whom it attaches are Mme de Staël's Corinne and (especially) George Sand's Lélia. Alchemists touched with this trait are Frankenstein and Zanoni, and among the avengers are the Count of Monte Cristo, whose beautiful hair and hands become quite tiresome, and Du Maurier's Peter Ibbetson, whose physical charm is all the more remarkable for breaking through the modesty of first-person narration. Become more maniacal and possessive, this trait perhaps develops into obsessions with the lost maiden's eyes, Trilby's feet, Berenice's teeth—elusive beauty trapped at last in some physical part. (The choice of the name Berenice underlines that hero's quest of a trophy not sentimental but vampiric.)

To speak of Venice as a dream-city is very usual in the nineteenth century, from Byron—"her aspect is like a dream" (preface to *Marino Faliero*)—to Dickens[13]—"I have, many and many a time, thought since, of this strange Dream upon the water: half-wondering if it lie there yet, and if its name be VENICE" (*Pictures from Italy*, "An Italian Dream"). Samuel Rogers offers a possible explanation in *Italy*, 1822–30:

> There is a glorious City in the Sea . . .
> No track of man, no footsteps to and fro,
> Lead to her gates. The path lies o'er the Sea,
> Invisible; and from the land we went,
> As to a floating City—steering in,
> And gliding up her streets as in a dream,
> So smoothly, silently. . . .   ["Venice"]

Venice as a fairyland or creation of magic we owe in part to *Childe Harold*.

> I saw from out the wave her structures rise
> As from the stroke of the enchanter's wand. . . .   [IV.i]

> I loved her from my boyhood; she to me
> Was as a fairy city of the heart,

Rising like water-columns from the sea,
Of joy the sojourn, and of wealth the mart;
And Otway, Radcliffe, Schiller, Shakespeare's art
Had stamp'd her image in me.... [IV.xviii]

Among these names, the most important one for *Childe Harold* is Radcliffe; but we should briefly consider the other three and some of their connections. The setting of *The Merchant of Venice* is the "mart of wealth" that lives by trading and makes use of moneylenders and slaves while despising them, extending its boasted Christian virtues only to fellow citizens while a rigorous law keeps aliens in check. In *Othello*, it is Iago who comments on the Venetians, ascribing "supersubtlety" to their wives (I.iii.363); the delicacy and refinement of these latter is implied, and with it (III.iii.201–04) a certain worldliness or callous sophistication. The romantic devotion to the state expressed in Othello's last speech is matched by Otway's Pierre (*Venice Preserv'd,* 1682), who wants to purge the corruption of the "Adriatic whore," and most conspicuously by the younger Foscari of Byron's play (1821), who, in full knowledge of the intrigues and cruelties on which the power of his native city rests, returns from exile and willingly accepts death rather than leave again. The Venice of Byron's plays is a fatal mistress, a Venus from the ocean but also a new Whore of Babylon, drinking the blood of the great and veiled in mystery.

Schiller's unfinished novel *Der Geisterseher,* 1789, depicts another Venetian enchantment. Its hero, an upright young German prince, becomes enmeshed in a network of seemingly supernatural events along with a love affair with a beautiful unknown, which prevent him from leaving the city; its pleasures rapidly undermine both his character and his fortune. At the heart of the mystery, we gather from Schiller's notes, sits the Inquisition, the whole vast scheme being designed to make the prince turn Catholic. However incomplete, this tale seems to have been widely influential, incidents from it reappearing in, for example, *The Monk,* Coleridge's *Remorse,* Maturin's *Fatal Revenge* and *Melmoth,* a ghost story in Hoffmann's *Serapionsbrüder,* Disraeli's poet-romance *Contarini Fleming,* and *Zanoni.* (See further chap. 6, n. 5; chap. 11, n. 36.)

Contarini Fleming, whose history (1832) once more links Venice and the involuntary siren, is an earlier Tonio Kröger, his artistic temperament springing from the marriage in him of cool and practical North with ardent South. His mother, a Contarini of Venice, died at his birth, and he has been brought up in a Scandinavian capital. His first love is a northern beauty, Christiana; next he loves a woodland nymph, a creation of his fancy, an Egeria remote from Numa's, perhaps, but close to Childe Harold's At length he flees from duty to Venice, where he meets his cousin and fated bride, the last of the Contarini. The meeting is heralded by dreams, portents, and his early passion for a painting of the Magdalen strangely associated with her, as well as for the visionary city of Venice itself, of which she appears to him an embodiment (III, v, "Adrian bride"). She, however, is vowed to a convent, and as he tears her from the cross she clings to—in the pose of the pictured Magdalen—she falls into a deathlike trance, from which she wakes forgetful of her vow. Not only is she called Alceste, she comes to him at last thus almost literally from the grave, and after an idyllic year on a Grecian isle (Crete) she dies in childbirth. Contarini Fleming now devotes himself to the practice of poetry, enriched by his experience; then suffering a nervous collapse, he undertakes some romantic travels. He returns to Europe and is greeted by his father's farewell letter describing his own Venetian passion, which included a romantic plot to restore the lost glory of "that fatal city," "for which I would have perilled my life" (VI, xiv). Father and son have been victims of the same spell, but the ensuing grief that made one a cynic has made the other a poet. Like *Wilhelm Meister*, *Contarini Fleming* blends the history of a poet's making with the "psychological," or mildly occultist, romance, so that it is no surprise that its hero's lifework is in the end not a poem but a palace-paradise cum art museum, with a tower dedicated to the Future: "poet" here means something very like "seer."

To return to Byron's remaining allusion: the unfortunate Emily in *The Mysteries of Udolpho* sees in Venice mainly scenes of ostentation and ambition, but sees too the city's beauty, especially from a distance.

> Nothing could exceed Emily's admiration on her first view of Venice, with its islets, palaces, and towers rising out of the sea, whose clear surface reflected the tremulous picture in all its colours. . . . As they glided on, the grander features of this city appeared more distinctly: its terraces, crowned with airy yet majestic fabrics, touched, as they now were, with the splendour of the setting sun, appeared as if they had been called up from the ocean by the wand of an enchanter, rather than reared by mortal hands.   [II, ii; xv]

> Emily sat, given up to pensive and sweet emotions. The smoothness of the water, over which she glided, its reflected images—a new heaven and trembling stars below the waves, with shadowy outlines of towers and porticos, conspired with the stillness of the hour, interrupted only by the passing wave, or the notes of distant music, to raise these emotions to enthusiasm.   [II, iii; xvi]

> Emily sat alone near the stern of the vessel, and, as it floated slowly on, watched the gay and lofty city lessening from her view, till its palaces seemed to sink in the distant waves, while its loftier towers and domes, illumined by the declining sun, appeared on the horizon, like those far-seen clouds, which, in more northern climes, often linger on the western verge, and catch the last light of a summer's evening.   [II, iii; xvi]

Behind Ann Radcliffe's Venice again is Prospero's power to call up and dismiss a vision (attributed in turn to Radcliffe by Scott):[14]

> ... like the baseless fabric of this vision,[15]
> The cloud-capp'd towers, the gorgeous palaces,
> The solemn temples, the great globe itself,
> Yea all which it inherit, shall dissolve
> And, like this insubstantial pageant faded,
> Leave not a rack behind.

The fairy vision of Venice, recalling both Radcliffe and Prospero, is called up again in Shelley's "Julian and Maddalo":

> ... we stood
> Looking upon the evening, and the flood
> Which lay between the city and the shore
> Paved with the image of the sky...   [64–67]
> and half the sky
> Was roofed with clouds of rich emblazonry
> Dark purple at the zenith, which still grew
> Down the steep West into a wondrous hue
> Brighter than burning gold...   [70–74]
> —as if the Earth and Sea had been
> Dissolved into one lake of fire...   [80–81]
> o'er the lagune
> We glided, and from that funereal bark
> I leaned, and saw the city, and could mark
> How from the many isles in evening's gleam
> Its temples and its palaces did seem
> Like fabrics of enchantment piled to Heaven.   [87–92]

That view is the ideal Venice, seen at sunset, appearing briefly as a triumph of man's sublime powers, uniting in a supreme marriage of the elements not just land and water but water and fire. Immediately afterwards, however, the pessimist Maddalo from "a better station" shows a different view.

> I looked, and saw between us and the sun
> A building on an island; such a one
> As age to age might add, for uses vile—
> A windowless, deformed and dreary pile
> And on the top an open tower, where hung
> A bell, which in the radiance swayed and swung;
> We could just hear its hoarse and iron tongue:
> The broad sun sunk behind it, and it tolled
> In strong and black relief.—"What we behold
> Shall be the madhouse and its belfry tower,"
> Said Maddalo.   [98–108]

In their context, these are conflicting images of human achievement and destiny, as we are reminded when they visit the madhouse:

> Through the black bars in the tempestuous air
> I saw, like weeds on a wrecked palace growing,
> Long tangled locks flung wildly forth. . . .   [213–15]

In "Lines Written among the Euganean Hills" the fire-crowned vision is presented (at sunrise) and immediately snatched away:

> Now is come a darker day. . .
> . . . .
> Those who alone thy towers behold
> Quivering through aërial gold,
> As I now behold them here,
> Would imagine not they were
> Sepulchres, where human forms,
> Like pollution-nourished worms
> To the corpse of greatness cling,
> Murdered, and now mouldering. . . .   [117, 142–49]

The poem emphasizes, like Byron's "Ode to Venice," Rogers's *Italy* and Poe's "The City in the Sea," that Venice's eventual fate must be to sink under the waves, and implies as Poe does that it will remain there as an unpurged source of gloom and terror.

Childe Harold IV deplores the loss of the famous Venetian strains, the alternating chant of the gondoliers:

> In Venice Tasso's echoes are no more,
> And silent rows the songless gondolier.
> Her palaces are crumbling to the shore,
> And music meets not always now the ear. . . .   [iii]

Later comes the claim that the reputation of Tasso alone should have been enough to make the invading tyrant relent (xvii), and soon afterwards five stanzas praise Tasso as transcending the oblivion that has swallowed his despotic patrons and their "petty power" (xxxv–xxxix).

"Julian and Maddalo" more specifically links a shattered artistic personality with Venice, in the person of the maniac. This figure seems to be based partly on the history of Tasso, from whose circle comes the name Maddalo (Maddalo in fact was the gentleman of Ferrara with whom Tasso quarreled). The circumstances of his condition are left vague—it is too intense a tale of passion for "the cold world"—but they involve his "spirit's mate," a proud lady who visits and then leaves him. He lives in the madhouse tower in a room overlooking the sea, fitted up for him (by the cynical but nonetheless practical and generous Maddalo) with books, flowers, and musical instruments. His music is fragmentary but "most touching"; its strains

> ... charm the weight
> From madmen's chains, and make this Hell appear
> A heaven of sacred silence, hushed to hear. [259-61]

His speech similarly is unconnected, but sufficiently impressive for the humanitarian Julian to want to offer friendship and help:

> —And this was all
> Accomplished not. Such dreams of baseless good[16]
> Oft come and go in crowds or solitude,
> And leave no trace. [577-80]

As with Goethe's Tasso, the madman's poetry is connected with his griefs, though not quite in the same way:

> "Most wretched men
> Are cradled into poetry by wrong,
> They learn in suffering what they teach in song." [544-46]

Though Shelley's maniac is not an obvious model for any one of Poe's mad geniuses, these are beings of the same family, especially Roderick Usher. Another fated artist on whom the plight of Tasso throws some light is Mme de Staël's Corinne. In the Ferrara chapter of *Corinne* (XV, vi) we are told that she resembles him in having the kind of genius that is developed through suffering; and at Sorrento she speaks of him:

> "Devant vous est Sorrente: là demeurait la soeur de Tasse, quand il vint en pèlerin demander à cette obscure amie un asile contre l'injustice des princes; ses longues douleurs avaient presque égaré sa raison; il ne lui restait plus que du génie; il ne lui restait que la connaissance des choses divines; toutes les images de la terre étaient troublées. Ainsi le talent, épouvanté du désert qui l'environne, parcourt l'univers sans trouver rien qui lui ressemble. La nature pour lui n'a plus d'écho, et le vulgaire prend pour de la folie ce malaise d'une âme qui ne respire pas dans ce monde assez d'air, assez d'enthousiasme, assez d'esprit. La fatalité, continua Corinne avec une émotion toujours croissante, la fatalité ne poursuit-elle pas les âmes exaltées, les poètes dont l'imagination tient à la puissance d'aimer et de souffrir? Il sont les bannis d'un autre région. ..." [XIII, iv]

Let us return for a moment to the association of Venice with Prospero's cloud palace, definite in Radcliffe and Shelley and probable in Byron. It is definite too in Longfellow, who can usually be relied on to epitomize the extreme of conventionality[17]:

> White phantom city, whose untrodden streets
> Are rivers, and whose pavements are the shifting
> Shadows of palaces and strips of sky;

> I wait to see thee vanish like the fleets
> Seen in mirage, or towers of cloud uplifting
> In air their unsubstantial masonry.

To judge from "Julian and Maddalo," Prospero's phrases in Shelley's mind are related less to the transience of earth and its splendors than to what is conveyed by the phrase, sixteenth-century in origin, "castles in the air," though with the sense more of idealistic vision than of day-dream. We could compare Scott's figure, cited earlier, of young Waverley's imaginings as pictures formed of sunset clouds. The use of "fabric" during the seventeenth and eighteenth centuries for an idyllic state ("fabric of one's happiness") or a scheme in the mind prepares us for this application. With all these senses coming together, then, we can expect Venice to embody not only fading brilliance, but also the possibility of permanent deception or disillusionment.[18]

Another association of Venice should be noted. It is a place of temptation, usually in the form of sexual seduction. Its courtesans were famous in the Renaissance; Ascham hints, and Coryat says plainly, that they possess all the wiles of Circes and Sirens. This reputation continued at least to the end of the Republic: Candide's Paquette goes to Venice to take up the profession (xxiv), and Montoni brings ladies of pleasure from Venice to enliven the glooms of Udolpho. Catharine Smith in 1815 titles a singularly pointless romance *Barozzi: or, The Venetian sorceress*, apparently for mere suggestiveness; and Venetian sirens and enchantments continue to abound for another century. At Venice Charlotte Dacre's Leonardo is beguiled by "the syren Megalena" (*Zofloya* xiv), and it is in the demoness Matilda's Venetian apartment that the climax of Shelley's *Zastrozzi* takes place (xiii–xv). It is presumably because of this kind of association that *The Tales of Hoffmann* moves the events of Hoffmann's story of a lost reflection, which features a courtesan-sorceress and a magic mirror, from Florence to Venice. Théophile Gautier's remarkably kittenish vampire, Clarimonde ("La Morte Amoureuse"), carries her young priest off every night to revel with her in the Venetian palace that in her lifetime was her place of business.

The atmosphere of Venice is evoked in two midcentury seduction scenes. In *The Ordeal of Richard Feverel* (xxxviii, "The Enchantress"), Mrs. Mount exerts all her practiced charms on Richard to make him forget his Lucy, and with effect: "He was a youth, and she an enchantress. He a hero; she a female will-o'-the-wisp." She climaxes the performance with songs:

> The lady wandered to Venice. Thither he followed her at a leap. In Venice she was not happy. He was prepared for the misery of any woman anywhere. But, oh! to be with her! To glide with a phantom-motion through throbbing streets; past houses muffled in shadow and gloomy legends; under storied

bridges; past palaces charged with full life in dead quietness; past grand old towers, colossal squares, gleaming quays, and out, and on with her, on into the silver infinity shaking over seas!

And in *Mardi,* the siren-enchantress-queen Hautia leads the hero Taji to her cave of pearls, where she hopes to displace the memory of his lost Yillah: "All Venice seemed within" (cxciv).

It seems curious that the Sirens and Circes traditionally belonging to Naples are thus continually being assigned to Venice. The associations of Naples in Romantic writing, when not dwelling on volcanoes and ruined palaces, are on the whole ones of cheerfulness and spontaneity; and moreover Sannazaro has attached great charm to the names of the Sirens, such as is called up again in the *Comus* invocation to Sabrina, in Mrs. Piozzi's poem addressed to Parthenope,[19] and also in *Zanoni,* cited earlier. Perhaps the darker aspect of these enchantresses, finding itself homeless in its original territory, betook itself by sympathetic attraction to the city of artifice and fabled corruption.[20] Naples and Venice are both in their different ways celebrated as maritime cities, and with the former are associated the palaces and towers of licentious Baiae, quivering in the water as visionary Venice quivers in the air. To both too belongs that special Romantic motif that Eino Railo (*Haunted Castle,* p. x, in Contents) labels "Songs and boating"; for more elegance we might say, "Music on the water." Notable Neapolitan scenes of this kind occur in *The Italian* (xiii) and *Corinne* (XIII, iv).

Samuel Rogers, who like Longfellow is revealing because he is so very pedestrian, associates Venice with enchantments. After describing the horrors of Venetian prisons, he hastens on:

> Yet who so gay as Venice? Every gale
> Breathed music! and who flocked not . . .
> To wear the mask, and mingle in the crowd . . .
> Pursuing through her [Venice's] thousand labyrinths
> The Enchantress Pleasure. . . .   [*Italy,* "St. Mark's Place"]

A list of famous persons one might hope to see in St. Mark's Place consists of: the six dethroned kings with whom Candide has supper (xxvi), "the Armenian" (the magus of *Der Geisterseher*), "the Cypriot" (an alchemist named Bragadino executed with his two dogs at the end of the sixteenth century), and Gualdi, who in the year 1687 at Venice showed a Venetian gentleman a portrait of himself painted by Titian. Considering the range of Shakespearean and other personages available, the choice here is distinctly biased in favor of the occult. References to magic, prophecy, and alchemy frequently occur in connection with Venice in the seventeenth

and eighteenth centuries, the motif reappearing so late as in Rilke's sonnet about fatal woman and entangled youth, "The Courtesan":

> The sun of Venice works within my hair
> And forms its gold, of all of alchemy
> The illustrious issue. . . .

The Titian gold of Venetian women's hair, mentioned here and in "A
Toccata of Galuppi's," was said to have been achieved by a combination
of bleaches and sunlight.[21] Gold of another kind is a regular Venetian
allurement, from the money-making projects of Sir Politic Would-be in
Volpone to a short story of Balzac.[22]

A different sort of supernaturalism attached to Venice is its frequently
being described as a place of ghosts. In the fourth and last of Gautier's
"Variations sur le Carnaval de Venise" (*Emaux et camées*, 1856), "Clair de
Lune Sentimental," the poet encounters whether dead or alive a being
from the past:

> Au loin, dans la brume sonore,
> Comme un rêve presque effacé,
> J'ai revu, pâle et triste encore,
> Mon vieil amour de l'an passé.

Among Arthur Symons's numerous poems on Venice, one (1908) is called
"Venice—Minuet: the Masque of the Ghosts," and describes the ghosts of
carnival masquers going through their paces unwillingly:

> Venice, the tyrant of the years,
> Compels you to perpetuate,
> With listless feet and weary tears,
> The sunken splendours of her state.

Symons's Venice is in general that of moonlight, trembling water, and
mad but brief love affairs, very much in the spirit of Meredith's paragraph
quoted earlier. One Venetian ghost gets to England: Browning's Galuppi,
"like a ghostly cricket, creaking where a house was burned."

Our quotations from Meredith and Melville illustrate that the world of
the late Romantic Venice and its associations is a detachable solid block
that can be neatly fitted into other kinds of fabric. No other restricted
literary motif that I can think of goes on being used again and again in so
much the same way in a concentrated time span by so many considerable
authors: "I was never out of England— 'tis as if I saw it all."[23] Here is
another example, this time from Wilde. Dorian Gray, having just murdered Basil Hallward in his attic, comes downstairs and listlessly starts
turning over the pages of a luxury edition of *Emaux et camées*. He hastens
with shudders past the poem on the hand of the murderer Lacenaire—

"Vrai meurtrier et faux poète, Il fut le Manfred du ruisseau!"—and arrives with relief at "Sur les Lagunes":

> L'esquif aborde et me dépose,
> Jetant son amarre au pilier,
> Devant une façade rose,
> Sur le marbre d'un escalier.

T. S. Eliot, quoting among others Gautier, demonstrates in "Burbank with a Baedeker," 1919, the convention by which Venice is seen as a palace of art, constituted of echoes, shadows and reflections: Grover Smith says of "Burbank," "This poem contains more quotations and functional allusions than any of comparable length that Eliot has published."[24]

Samuel Rogers in *Italy*, in the section titled "Venice," says that the city "Rose like an exhalation from the deep." Besides recalling the building of Pandaemonium, the term "exhalation" covers in poetic use mists, vapors, meteors, fireballs, and will-o'-the-wisps: it well suits the look of a place whose miasmal air is famous, and where phantasmal visions of happiness are regularly shown gliding over a real underworld of captivity and death. Only one or two connections need to be made for Venice to appear to sum up the whole symbolism we have been discussing, with the one modification that the important characters are not usually inexperienced young persons. We have seen Venice associated with dreams by Byron, Rogers, Poe and Dickens, with sunset clouds and fairy visions by Radcliffe and Shelley, and with phantoms and mirages by Symons and Longfellow, to say nothing of enchantments, siren songs, and delusive pursuits.[25] The identification of Venice as mirror world[26] occurs in two letters of Rilke's:

> this dreamlike city, whose existence is like a picture in a mirror...
>
> [15.viii, 1903]

> Ultimately the whole of Venice is like that: one doesn't receive here as if with vessels and hands, but as if with mirrors; one "grasps" nothing, rather one is taken into the confidence of its elusiveness...   [25–26.vi, 1920]

If a single term could cover all the associations of Venice, we might call it a threshold or intermediary place. It stands between east and west, sky and sea, past and present, as its Bridge of Sighs connects palace and prison. Browning describes it in *Sordello*:

> Venice seems a type
> Of Life—'twixt blue and blue extends, a stripe,
> As Life, the somewhat, hangs 'twixt naught and naught:
> 'Tis Venice, and 'tis Life—as good as you sought
> To spare me the Piazza's slippery stone

Or keep me to the unchoked canals alone,
As hinder Life the evil with the good
Which make up Living, rightly understood.   [III.723–30]

This depiction is unusual in its concreteness and its focus on "Life." More often, as the dream is between sleep and waking, so Venice is between this world and the next; Poe, as we saw, calls it an "Elysium"; it presents not spiritual reality but an otherworld or afterworld, a place of ghosts, fays, mirage. As a point of contact between contrasted realities, it provides a fitting image for the mind of the artist; but so strong are its connotations of dream and illusion that the vision of the artist conveyed by means of it is a rather desperate one. Browning in *Paracelsus*, act II, builds up in "the House of a Greek conjuror" a typical Venetian scene with typical Venetian shattered ghost-seeing artist, Aprile; but though Paracelsus's "attainment" here is illusory, the perspective has a quality of hope and freshness in that the city is named not Venice but Constantinople. Venice as echoing afterworld is presented in James's "The Aspern Papers," 1888, with Miss Tina's thwarted attempt to exchange the dead poet's letters on which her aunt has "lived" for a chance of life, and again in Hemingway's surprisingly allusive and evocative novel of 1950, *Across the River and into the Trees*,[27] describing an old soldier's last love affair and last few days of life.[28]

We can conclude this account of one possible setting for the artist with some remarks on Thomas Mann's *Death in Venice*, 1911. The novella's hero, Gustav Aschenbach, has founded an artistic career on "the union of dry, conscientious officialdom and ardent, obscure impulse" (12).[29] The former has predominated in his writings and in the discipline from which they proceed, counterfeiting somewhat the effect of the latter. Feeling the need of a break in his working routine, Aschenbach goes to Venice, where the first thing that happens is that he is carried in a gondola past his intended destination by a tyrannical boatman whose motives are quite obscure. Lulled by the movement of the boat into a mood of dreamy acquiescence, Aschenbach accepts this, though his tyrant has something of both privateer and underworld ferryman. At his hotel, he is attracted by another visitor, a young Polish boy named Tadzio, beautiful in the Greek sculptural manner but obviously delicate. The attraction becomes a passion, as he pursues his sailor-suited charmer through narrow Venetian byways, consoling himself the while with Socratic precedents. Losing all shame, he becomes a kind of self-parody, the image of the leering old dandy who at an earlier stage disgusted him. The Greek connection is developed by humorous references to the *Odyssey*, with its enchanted islands that beguiled Odysseus, especially Phaeacia, land of fresh-washed linen, heated baths, and magical boats. Aschenbach's last moment of bliss comes as, sitting on the beach, he sees Tadzio moodily separate himself from a friend and, wading in the sea, turn to look at the older man:

> It seemed to him that the pale and lovely Summoner [Ger. "Psychagog"] out there smiled at him and beckoned; as though with the hand he lifted from his hip, he pointed outward as he hovered on before into an immensity of richest expectation.   [83]

But the only immensity waiting for Aschenbach is that of death, which immediately overtakes him.

The original beckoning fair one of the tale, siren and death-angel, is Venice itself, recognized as the goal of his wanderings by Aschenbach almost simultaneously with his noting threatening elements and making plans to escape.[30] The city then becomes revealed as Venice mercatrix, its corrupt officialdom striving not merely to combat the plague that has crept in from the east but to prevent the tourists from learning that there is a plague at all, thus heightening the sense of artificiality and palace-prison captivity that surrounds the life of the great hotels. In this rotten and miasmic atmosphere, Aschenbach's passion becomes vampiric; not only will he not take warning and leave, but he decides against speaking to Tadzio's mother as a well-wisher. Just as the effect of the plague in the city is for lawlessness to break out, so the influence of place and circumstance on Aschenbach overthrows his habitual moral restraint; this is symbolized in his dream of the arrival of the "foreigner god," with his rout of bestialized humanity. The god is Dionysus, "sworn enemy to dignity and self-control" (76), and as is well known[31] he comes from the same mephitic East as the plague; Aschenbach has earlier thought of visiting the place of the tigers, but instead it comes to him, Venice being the gateway from the East as well as to it. Further, the god of the wild dancers is a long-haired, androgynous-seeming youth who can exercise, with the most fascinating charm, all the powers of delusion. His emissaries in the story, the traveler, the boatman, and the clown, are recognizable by their animal faces and especially their strong white teeth. On the other hand, it is from the state of Tadzio's teeth that Aschenbach guesses he will not live long; and Aschenbach's prophetic double on the steamer, the old dandy in makeup, wears an unbroken yellow set that are not his own. This seizing on one staring detail helps give the narrative its obsessive or feverish quality.

The setting of this story is Byron's Venice (23) or von Platen's, in more extreme decay, the dreamful ease of the coffin–gondola already suggesting death. The city is a place of deliquescing grandeur and flourishing corruption, at the edge of an ambiguous infinity of sea:

> His love of the ocean had profound sources: the hard-worked artist's longing for rest, his yearning to seek refuge from the thronging manifold shapes of

his fancy in the bosom of the simple and vast; and another yearning, opposed to his art and perhaps for that very reason a lure, for the unorganized, the immeasurable, the eternal—in short, for nothingness. He whose preoccupation is with excellence longs fervently to find rest in perfection; and is not nothingness a form of perfection?   [36]

The enamored Aschenbach becomes a demonic opposite to his former self, less Socrates than satyr: "His art, his moral sense, what were they in the balance beside the boons that chaos might confer?" (74) He is engaged in the guilty and Spectral pursuit of an unattainable beloved to whose well-being he is in effect an enemy; in the evenings he shamelessly stalks Tadzio through narrow alleyways among which death too is creeping (77). Aschenbach's pursuit of the boy is one of those Romantic quests that inevitably end in death; like comparable heroes, he is "lured on by those eyes" (79). A parallel to the Narcissus situation of *Alastor* is suggested in the comparison of Tadzio's smile at Aschenbach, with its "mingling of coquetry and curiosity and faint unease" (58), to that of Narcissus at his reflection. In addition to the motif of homosexuality, we are told that Aschenbach never had a son, and Tadzio, surrounded by five cherishing females, has no visible father. However, despite such natural grounds for attraction, these are not the ones emphasized. Aschenbach's art and the obsession that is inimical to it arise from the same source:

> Solitude gives birth to the original in us, to beauty unfamiliar and perilous—
> to poetry. But also, it gives birth to the opposite: to the perverse, the illicit,
> the absurd.   [29]

Like the Poet of *Alastor* too, Aschenbach formerly has defied Nature in the sense of human reality: he is the master artist who

> in a style of classic purity renounced bohemianism and all its works, all
> sympathy with the abyss and the troubled depths of the outcast human
> soul.   [80]

This rejection of the abyss is noted at the moment when his disordered reveries develop a mock-Socratic explanation of why "we poets can be neither wise nor worthy citizens." *Death in Venice* can be read as one more account, then, of the fated artist on whom Nature takes a worse than natural revenge.

We have seen Venice before as a place of temptation or seduction:

> this was Venice, this the fair frailty that fawned and that betrayed, half
> fairytale, half snare; the city in whose stagnating air the art of painting once
> put forth so lusty a growth, and where musicians were moved to accords so
> weirdly lulling and lascivious.   [63]

The setting reinforces also the aspect in which this is a palace-of-art story; such narrations, like Tennyson's poem or "The Masque of the Red

Death," center more unequivocally than *Alastor* on Nature's revenge. Exclusive concentration on superrefinement or an ideal beauty seems inevitably to involve the aesthete with a horrific or brutish shadow-side that one would have thought its opposite. Aschenbach's previous way of life, though based on restraint, has been positive because it reconciled the different strengths of his personality; it is when he gives himself over to a single half-recognized impulse that his degradation begins.

Palaces of art by their nature invite invasion. Usually this takes its form from one of three available and related traditions: the uninvited guest, the specter at the feast, and demonic possession of an object or place. A kind of possession accounts for the portentous atmospheres of the Castle of Otranto and Hyperion's palace (Keats, *Hyperion* I.171–263), as well as the appearance of vengeful Uranian Love in the place of the dwarfish statue (of carnal love?) in Peacock's *Rhododaphne* and of the spirit of Poe's Ligeia in the body of Rowena. In addition to spectral guests already mentioned, and related apparitions like Madeline Usher, we should note the association, akin to the late-medieval *danse macabre,* of an embodiment of deadly illness with scenes of festivity.[33] Sue's *Le Juif errant* depicts (III, xix) a street pageant in Paris during the cholera outbreak of 1832 whose main figures represent the Plague and his attendants. Later in the century the French artist Willette depicted in his series "Pauvre Pierrot" a group of clowns madly dancing while "le Choléra" appears in the background in the form of a ghostly skull.[34] Poe's figure of the Red Death and perhaps the corpses "fretted" with corruption in Tennyson's palace belong here. So does the nightmare vision of the Pox in *A Rebours,* foreshadowing the sickness that forces Des Esseintes to give up his retreat.[35] So does the clown in *Death in Venice,* reeking of carbolic, who cringes towards the hotel guests but once at a safe distance sings a song full of mocking laughter and then, after so to speak dropping his buffoon's mask, disappears with an insulting gesture. He belongs inseparably to the shadow-side of Aschenbach's passion, as do the phantoms to Tennyson's "Soul's" self-love. Byron's words in *Childe Harold* (IV.cxxii), following the account of nympholepsy, seem applicable:

> Of its own beauty is the mind diseased,
> And fevers into false creation.

Tadzio, the knowing-unknowing embodiment of the ideal beauty, is enigmatic. His mother is distinguished by the author chiefly through the pearls she wears:

> . . . There was something faintly fabulous . . . in her appearance, though lent it solely by the gems she wore: they were well-nigh priceless, and consisted of ear-rings and a three-stranded necklace, very long, of softly gleaming pearls the size of cherries. [32]

The opulence of these adornments is in contrast with the austerity of her air, and suggests a sea- or moon-goddess.[36] Tadzio usually appears on the edge of the sea, sailor-suited or dressed for bathing. The white of his usual costume suggests a spirit figure; combined with his red breast-knot, it belongs to the colors of Eros. Like Venice's, Tadzio's charm is both morbid and captivating; like Venice he represents a snare, being "the instrument of a mocking deity" (73). Aschenbach associates him with a number of beautiful classical youths; the last one of these mentioned, with whom he is not verbally associated, is Dionysus, whose presence is felt but not seen: Tadzio's long hair, androgynous grace, and romantic "foreignness" perhaps offer links. If Aschenbach is an Orpheus torn apart by Maenads, moreover, the story has a singularly sinister aspect with Tadzio as his Eurydice.

Apart from *Alastor* and "The Palace of Art," parallels suggest themselves with other fictions. In *The Tales of Hoffmann*, to which we shall come, the ideal beloved always proves to be in league with or a pawn of the enemy: there the artist rises above the combination, whereas here he succumbs. Most directly Mann's novella recalls the myth of the "Poimandres," where the bright ideal reflection on the water's face is used by a crudely female Nature lurking behind it to decoy the primal man into captivity. A comparable image comes into *Alastor* in the "lure" which the Poet imagines Death to hold before him in the shadowy form of the maiden. These images are troubling most of all because the hero of such an attachment is first robbed of the dignity that belongs to any personal relationship and then given up as prey to what is most alien and repugnant to him. Aschenbach sees Tadzio through his Platonic daydreams as the young, pure soul capable of inspiring and being inspired to all that is noble and fair. He does not think of the other side of the ambiguity of childish beauty: insensitivity, a grace and *superbia* that is physical only, a mermaiden soullessness that might as well be the instrument of the abyss as anything else. The question about such an airy, otherworldly figure, as about the Romantic Venice, concerns its inmost reality: aërial, ethereal, or thin air? essence, pure spirit? or ghost, mirage, hollow form?

Aschenbach shows certain analogies with characters in much simpler fictions, such as Margrave in Bulwer Lytton's *A Strange Story* and Frank Halton in E. F. Benson's "The Man Who Went Too Far," 1912. Both are given over to their animal natures in a way that seems at first to them, and to their friends, liberating and glorious: both come to dramatic and appropriate ends. Margrave in a bush fire has the elixir of life knocked out of his hands by charging herds, and Nature materializes itself to Frank one stormy night as the Great God Pan and leaves him on the lawn a hoof-marked pulp. Mann's story, as dealing seriously with the artist, is much more sophisticated, its setting being not an English village but the rotting splendors of a decadent society, and the demonic embodiment of natural impulse comes disguised not as hairy masculinity but as a fairer-than-life imaginative ideal. A possible imaginative link for us between *Death in Venice* and the rather crude English genre (besides Benson, other practitioners are Saki, Stephen McKenna, Arthur Machen)[37] might be an earlier document, Swinburne's poem "A Nympholept," where the communer with Nature distinguishes two aspects of that mysterious power: Pan, the source of terror and, as in Theocritus, especially to be dreaded at noon, and the ardently sought-for Nymph, mystic, even Porphyrian. Other forerunners of the Great God Pan tales are Pater's two stories of the return of the gods, or of types of pre-Christian natural man: "Denys l'Auxerrois," 1887, where the reader is reminded that "the Winegod . . . had his contrast, his dark or antipathetic side," this being represented in the story by Denys's murderous and scapegoat aspects; and "Apollo in Picardy," 1893, where the radiant Brother Apollyon is also a criminal and outcast. Contemporary with these, Vernon Lee's "Dionea," depicting against a background of Heine-like legends of the survival of the gods the return of Venus in the body of an Italian peasant girl, ends with Dionea's return to the sea after she has caused the German sculptor Waldemar to sacrifice his pale spiritual wife on an old altar and then destroy himself.

In the eyes of later nineteenth-century aestheticism, shading into for example the humanism of Arnold, the conversion of the classical world to Christianity represents so to speak a historical fall. The birth of soul is the death of perfect beauty, or imposes its own kind of beauty at the expense of that of the body. A favorite field for the generating of elegiac feeling is the late age of classicism, the passing of the gods; and favorite figures of that period are Julian the Apostate and the Emperor Hadrian with his "Animula blandula" and his beautiful slave Antinoüs. A similar confrontation of the values of aestheticism or hedonism with those of Christianity occurs in works of the time that are set in other eras, through legendary figures like Tannhäuser or the mermaid; through characters who have escaped the prevailing influences of their age and thus seem throwbacks, like George Eliot's Tito Melema (*Romola*) or Hawthorne's Donatello and Beatrice Rappaccini; or through contrasts in attitudes within a postclassical period, as in Morris's romance "The Hollow Land" with its transition from a bloodthirsty vengeance ethic to one of reconciliation.

Aesthetic religiosity sometimes tries to relate what are felt to be two distinct realms, by mingling them, as in Rossetti's "The Blessed Damozel," or by placing them in chronological sequence, as in Pater's *Marius the Epicurean* and Wilde's short story "The Young King." Usually in these efforts the spiritual realm gets the worst of it, appearing either shadowy or suspect: Rossetti's sonnets "Body's Beauty" and "Soul's

Beauty" make a case in point. Or, aestheticism may be disguised as a kind of religious feeling, thinly in Wilde's *Salomé,* more ingeniously in D'Annunzio's *St. Sébastien.*[38] Already Browning's "Cleon," 1855, satisfactorily uses the pathos of a dying hedonistic paganism to show the limits of the aesthetic attitude. From Goethe's ballad "Die Braut von Corinth," 1797, on, the classical sensual paganisms evoked in our period cannot accommodate "spirit" but show a striking affinity for ghosts and vampires.

The point we want out of this complicated area concerns the elegiac sense of lost wholeness, of a separation between two kinds of good or of beauty, projected into a historical myth.[39] Analogous to the powers that the magician can acquire at the price of his soul are the advantages that the aesthete can acquire by separating himself from his. In *The Picture of Dorian Gray,* whose sources include Des Esseintes' flight from life and William Wilson's flight from conscience, the hero can preserve his youth and beauty indefinitely because the portrait that he calls "the face of my soul" (xiii) ages in his place. Seeing his own beauty for the first time in the finished canvas—as for Narcissus in Ovid, his dangerous moment is that in which he "comes to know himself"—Dorian realized that "The life that was to make his soul would mar his body," (ii) and declared that "he would give his soul" to have the picture age in his place. Dorian is presented from the beginning as a kind of natural man: the artist Basil Hallward sees in him "'all the passion of the romantic spirit, all the perfection of the spirit that is Greek. The harmony of soul and body—how much that is! We in our madness have separated the two, and have invented a realism that is vulgar, an ideality that is void . . .'" (i). From the moment of the completion of the picture, Dorian falls under the corrupting influence of Lord Henry Wotton,[40] and from having been rather careless and self-indulgent he becomes callous and eventually criminal. The theme of calamitous separation appears again in Wilde's impressive (if wordy) short story "The Fisherman and his Soul": a young fisherman who loves a mermaid sends away his soul in order to live with her untroubled under the sea, and the soul, parted from his heart, becomes entirely evil.

Bulwer Lytton's Margrave is another radiant young man, "an idealized picture of man's youth fresh from the hand of Nature," "youth in the golden age of the poets—the youth of the careless Arcadian," expressing above all "a perfect health" which "cannot be enjoyed by those who overwork the brain, or admit the sure wear and tear of the passions" (xxiii). He is compared to wing-heeled Mercury, to "the young boy-god Iacchus amid his nymphs," and over and over again to Greek sculptures: yet it turns out that he is old in depravity and has gained renewed life by a crime, that the principle of soul is dead in him, leaving only animal life, and that thus he is "an incarnation of the blind powers of Nature—beautiful and joyous, wanton, and terrible, and destroying!" (xxxix)[41]

The artist of E. F. Benson's story abandons himself to a cult of Nature and of joy, being persuaded that the Christian virtues of renunciation, sympathy with suffering, and the like lead man the wrong way, and he practices openness and receptiveness. He rejects the doctrine of a suffering God and awaits the revelation that will make him one with the life principle that already plays panpipes in the shrubbery and has given him the beauty and vigor of a much younger man. Like Margrave, Frank cannot tolerate either the experience or the sight of suffering; he is kindly only to those who share his quest of joy. But as his friend points out,

> "All nature from highest to lowest is full, crammed full of suffering; every living organism in nature preys on another, yet in your aim to get close to, be one with nature, you leave suffering altogether out; you run away from it, you refuse to recognize it. And you are waiting, you say, for the final revelation. . . . Cannot you guess then what the final relevation will be?"

The course of this perverse nature worship runs parallel to the course of Werther's fatal cultivation of his own feelings; moreover, it is a fictional equivalent for the pattern of, for example, Swinburne's "Hymn to Proserpina," which moves inevitably from praise of the life of the senses to praise of death. A twentieth-century equivalent might be found in Lawrence's Mexican writings, particularly "The Woman Who Rode Away."

Like tales we have discussed involving palaces of art, the fiction depicting an artificially restored harmony with Nature is one more parable about man's foredoomed attempt to live among the ruins of Eden after he has been driven out. The works we have cited in this chapter are elegiac, partly because their events carry inexorably to disaster heroes who, as artists, embody however mistakenly much that is best in human nature, but mostly because these heroes are all in their various ways betrayed by impulses that reach out for the conditions of an unfallen world.

Eight   The Artist: Soulmate

La femme est la chimère de l'homme ou son démon, comme vous voudrez.

—Gérard de Nerval

. . . [as necessary] as a blonde and a brunette in any moderately well-run romantic household.

—Søren Kierkegaard

The sense that we noted in *Tasso* that "man" and "artist" though housed in the same skin are not entirely compatible—that one may even be said to live in the death of the other—often dominates the artist's relation with his beloved. If he is a painter, he may become confused between her rôle as his bride and as his model or Ideal. His world however devastated is still a form of pastoral, and if he sacrifices his love to his art, our authors will usually regard him as lost. Such a demonic artist is the frantic devotee of Poe's "The Oval Portrait," painting away in his gloomy tower and failing to notice until the last stroke that it is not just the image of his young bride that he is transferring to the canvas, but her life itself. A brief metaphor indicates a triangle: he is already wedded to a sterner bride in Art, who will tolerate no rival. A later version is the obsessed sculptor in an unpublished novel of F. P. Grove's who resolves to live celibately with his love Barbara (her name should warn him): "You will be the mother, not of my children, but of my Art." In this case nature triumphs and takes a crushing revenge.[1]

The wrong choice between art and love, the representative of real life, or the right choice made too late, leads via spectral pursuit of a phantom Ideal to madness and death. We have already noted mad musicians, and must now consider a few mad painters.[2] First, though, an obsessed dancer: this example is trivial, but useful for its absolute conventionality. In the English film *The Red Shoes*, 1948, the artist is represented by a gifted ballerina torn between her marriage and the stage, whose claims are embodied in the company's director, a celibate aristocrat-aesthete and demon puppet-master whose most telling gesture is in a moment of chagrin to smash his fist into his mirrored reflection. While her troubled musician husband labors at a ballet version of "Die schöne Müllerin" (that must be what is meant by "La belle Meunière"), the ballerina is projecting her quandary in a presentation of Andersen's fable "The Red Shoes," where the slippers tied on her feet by the fiendish Shoemaker dance her away from love and the living world. In real life the dilemma proves unresolvable, and at length she throws herself into the path of a train.

In Hoffmann's tale "Die Jesuiterkirche in G-," the fatal triangle exists in the mind of a deranged painter, in a manner reminiscent of the story in *Alastor*. Berthold, once full of aspiration, has been driven to despair by his failure to capture Nature's inmost soul.

> The whole of Nature, which formerly smiled on him, became for him a threatening monster, and its voice, which once in the murmur of the evening breeze, the rippling of the brook and the rustle of the bushes greeted him with sweet words, now proclaimed to him ruin and destruction.

In the neighborhood of Naples he encounters a beautiful woman whom he takes for supernatural,[3] and she becomes the inspiration of numerous successful religious paintings. He later meets her again, during a revolution in which he saves her life, and it then seems appropriate for them to marry. But after a brief period of delight Berthold finds that he can no longer paint:

> "No—she was not the ideal that appeared to me, but to my irremediable destruction she treacherously borrowed the figure and countenance of that celestial woman."

His discovery that she is an earthly woman, however pure and gentle, has invalidated the inspiration: he tells the narrator:

> "The ideal is a vile deceitful dream, engendered from a fever of the blood."

His wife and child disappear, and the artist thereafter until his death shows all the symptoms of having gone mad through remorse for a crime. Hoffmann's "Die Fermate" treats the same subject—the irreconcilability of the two rôles of woman as inspiration and as mistress or wife—more lightly and in terms of music: the rival of the composer's art is an aging scold who nags about broken plates and the ink-stains on his clothes.

Zola's *L'Oeuvre*, 1886, is on the whole a realistic novel, but nevertheless employs the conventions we have noted. After giving a night's shelter to Christine, whom he finds sheltering from a storm in his doorway, Claude Lantier makes her first his model and then his wife. He comes later to concentrate all his powers on a single painting of a naked woman which his wife, though it is painted largely from her, regards as her rival. The figure is a "Venus arising in triumph from the Seine," Claude's attempt to incarnate in splendid nudity "la chair même de Paris" (p. 236). Christine's thoughts recall "The Oval Portrait":

> Il la tuait à la pose pour embellir l'autre, il ne tenait plus que de l'autre sa joie ou sa tristesse, selon qu'il la voyait vivre ou languir sous son pinceau. N'était-ce donc pas de l'amour, cela? et quelle souffrance de prêter sa chair, pour que l'autre naquît, pour que le cauchemar de cette rivale les hantât, fût toujours entre eux, plus puissant que le réel, dans l'atelier, à table, au lit, partout! [p. 244]

A forceful chapter, in which Claude revisits the countryside where he spent the first idyllic months of his marriage, relates the progressive desolation of the surroundings of Paris with what has become of his own life. At length, when his attachment to his painting has grown to be an obsession, and after a scene in which he has been tempted to drown himself in his beloved Seine, his wife demands that he choose between her and his painted love and thinks she has won: Claude returns from her to the studio and hangs himself in front of the painting. The painted woman—crude, gorgeous, golden, jeweled, several times called an "idole," and suggesting to the reader a sort of Whore of Babylon—is destroyed by Claude's best friend in an act of "vengeance," while Christine collapses with brain fever, "'misérable et finie, écrasée sous la souveraineté farouche de l'art'" (p. 353).

This climax, the murderous triumph of the painted woman and the pathetic martyrdom of Christine, has already been prefigured by an extraordinary scene that takes place on Claude's wedding day in the studio of his impoverished sculptor friend Mahoudeau, who has been laboring for months on a subject much the same as Claude's, "La Baigneuse." Constructed on a cheap frame, in the heat of the studio stove the figure begins to slide apart, taking on for an instant a horrid semblance of life. Mahoudeau, who cherishes it like a lover, rushes forward to save it:

> Et elle sembla lui tomber au cou, il la reçut dans son étreinte, serra les bras sur cette grande nudité vierge, qui s'animait comme sous le premier éveil de la chair. Il y entra, la gorge amoureuse s'aplatit contre son épaule, les cuisses vinrent battre les siennes, tandis que la tête, détachée, roulait par terre.
> [p. 224]

Before Mahoudeau gets up from under the collapsed figure, Claude is convinced it has killed him; once disentangled, Mahoudeau sobs and cries, with "une douleur hurlante d'amant devant le cadavre mutilé de ses tendresses." Leaving it reassembled and lying under a cloth like a real corpse, they depart for Claude's wedding. After the ceremony,

> Mahoudeau... se plaignait d'une courbature, qu'il n'avait pas sentie d'abord: tous ses membres s'endolorissaient, il avait les muscles froissés, la

peau meurtrie, comme au sortir des bras d'une amante de pierre. Et Christine lui lava l'écorchure de sa joue de nouveau saignante, et il lui semblait que cette statue de femme mutilée s'asseyait à la table avec eux, que c'était elle seule qui importait ce jour-là, elle seule qui passionnait Claude, dont le récit, répété à vingt reprises, ne tarissait pas sur son émotion, devant cette gorge et ces hanches d'argile broyées à ses pieds.   [p. 226]

Later, at night, the couple both feel that from now on "un autre corps" is lying between them, imparting to them its deadly cold.

This world of obsession and the Gothic embrace, recalling the fate of Roderick Usher or the bridegroom of Mérimée's "La Vénus d'Ille,"[4] does not have the last word. To Claude is contrasted his friend Sandoz, the sane novelist to whom the claims of real life are a support, not a drain.

Sandoz expliqua ses idées sur le mariage, qu'il considéra bourgeoisement comme la condition même du bon travail, de la besogne réglée et solide, pour les grands producteurs modernes. La femme dévastatrice, la femme qui tue l'artiste, lui broie le coeur et lui mange le cerveau, était une idée romantique, contre laquelle les faits protestaient.   [p. 160]

After Claude's miserable funeral, Sandoz speaks through his grief and concludes the book: "Allons travailler" (p. 363).

The ambivalence of woman, her resemblance to Nature in being both mere dull matter and a power capable of leading man to the heights, comes out in many nineteenth-century treatments of the artist's model, who while imaginatively she is an inspiration is often physically more or less a harlot: Daudet's *Sapho* falls within this area. To Serafina, the lady of James's "Madonna of the Future," two artists attach themselves; one is an idealist and one a coarse cynic, and "this bourgeoise Egeria" can match herself to both. In Du Maurier's *Trilby*, while Little Billee sees in the heroine a grand ideal womanhood before which he can only stammer, his mother sees something less than a lady. But whatever abuse and exploitation the model may suffer in the flesh is nothing to what is done to the spirit by the artist or connoisseur who values in the woman only the aesthetically isolable. To the vampire artists cited earlier we can join the aesthete Dorian Gray and the cold aristocrats of "My Last Duchess" and a short story of Zola's, "La Vierge au cirage." Beauty appreciated apart from the soul of its bearer is apt to die, or itself to become destroying or enslaving. If its bearer was from the beginning without soul, then she is probably of the nature of sirens; examples are Andrea del Sarto's wife Lucrezia and the dark maiden of Gogol's "Nevsky Avenue." The sculptor Jules of *Pippa Passes*, when his fallen Ideal appears to him mere hollow beauty, is tempted to reject her as a siren and take vengeance on those who entangled him with her; but instead he goes away with her to begin again in a new setting, and he thereby both securely founds his own future happiness and hers and in addition renews and reinspirits his art. His resolve to endow this beautiful body with a soul links him to one of the most sublime myths of artistic fulfillment, that of Pygmalion, with a happier conclusion than the incident in Mahoudeau's studio.[5] One assumes a domestic radiance like that of artist and model in Picasso's "Vollard Suite," where nobody uses anybody.

Except in rare happy cases, the relations of the artist with his soulmate tend to the two closely related conditions of nympholepsy and vampirism—pursuing an object that cannot be possessed but whose pursuit may destroy him, the siren, and destroying the one available to him, the real nymph. In this formulation, it is clear why we call him Narcissus, and why Pygmalion is Narcissus's mythological opposite. However, sometimes we cannot distinguish between these two demonic operations, as in the relations of Roderick Usher and his sister Madeline or Marcel's involvement with Albertine, the rôles forced upon both women being completely ambivalent. In the kind of fiction we are looking at, every hero is potentially a Pygmalion, because the women he is involved with are in some measure his own creations, projections, or reflex images. If in the *Alastor* situation the maiden's elusiveness turns the lover into spectral pursuer, conversely the fact of having a Spectre on her heels, spying and jealous and anxious to sequester her away from the normal come and go of life, soon gives any maiden the air of fleeing and betraying nymph. The release from such a vicious circle is through a different kind of love or, as Marcel eventually finds, through art.

The wise man is he who can either teach elusive beauty to submit to love or be content to kiss her as she flies. The hero of Tennyson's "Edwin Morris, or The Lake," an artist forth issuing from populous city to breathe country air, loves Letty Hill, a maiden whom he sees "like Proserpine in Enna, gathering flowers." Rejected by her family, he leaves in Byronic disdain and self-pity:

> I read, and fled by night, and flying turn'd:
> Her taper glimmer'd in the lake below:
> I turn'd once more, close-button'd to the storm.

But years later he can say,

> long ago
> I have pardon'd little Letty; not, indeed,
> It may be, for her own dear sake, but this,
> She seems a part of those fresh days to me;
> For in the dust and drouth of London life
> She moves among my visions of the lake,
> While the prime swallow dips his wing, or then
> While the gold-lily blows, and overhead
> The light cloud smoulders on the summer crag.

It is presumably his artistic trait that gives the young man his detached, aesthetic relation to memory and that saves him from the compulsive emotional turmoil experienced in similar circumstances by the heroes of "Locksley Hall" and *Maud*. A comparable, if intenser case is that of Hawthorne's Artist of the Beautiful, 1844, who first loses his beloved and then sees his love gift to her, his masterpiece, destroyed:

> And as for Owen Warland, he looked placidly at what seemed the ruin of his life's labor, and which was yet no ruin. He had caught a far other butterfly than this. When the artist rose high enough to achieve the beautiful, the symbol by which he made it perceptible to mortal senses became of little value in his eyes, while his spirit possessed itself in the enjoyment of the reality.

In this way it is possible to possess the past, not be possessed by it, and instead of a source of suffering to carry about "a Paradise within."

So far we have considered the artist torn between art and love, or bewildered by the ambivalence of woman as representative of a bifurcated Nature. His perplexity may take the alternative form of having to meet the claims of two different women on him.

The arrangement of heroines into contrasting or complementary pairs is a feature of our fiction, which as romance tends to be schematically arranged. In the nineteenth century we meet it everywhere, from Scott through George Eliot to Hardy. The origins of the convention are widely scattered. In the background lurk, for example, scraps of folklore like the rivalry of Fair Annet and the Brown Bride (Child no. 73), as well as the "two loves" of the *Sonnets* and the two wooing nymphs of Milton's companion pieces. The quasi-Shakespearean scheme of *The Castle of Otranto* sets the passive, self-sacrificing Matilda against the sturdier Isabella; Eino Railo in his useful chapter on "The Young Hero and Heroine" connects with them first Mrs. Radcliffe's two types of heroine, the blond, languishing Emilia's and the darker, bolder Julia's (sisters in her first novel, *The Sicilian Romance*, 1790), then Lewis's fair victim Antonia and his dark demoness Matilda. Victim-woman and demon-woman are featured in *Les Liaisons dangereuses*, 1782, in the Presidente de Tourvel and the Marquise de Merteuil. Sade, parodying both Richardson and his disciple Rousseau, writes companion novels about two sisters, the persecuted blond Justine and the fiendish dark Juliette (1791, 1796): he is thinking (of course from a satiric viewpoint) partly of the contrasted fates of the virtuous Pamela and the more unfortunate Clarissa, and partly perhaps of the two women in *La Nouvelle Héloïse*, Julie and her cousin Claire. These latter two seem to derive from the two girls in *Clarissa*, the steadfast heroine and the much sprightlier Anna Howe. In *La Nouvelle Héloïse*, more explicit than Rousseau's text are his instructions to the illustrator:

La plupart de ces Sujets sont détaillés pour les faire entendre, beaucoup plus qu'ils ne peuvent l'être dans l'exécution: car pour rendre heureusement un dessin, l'Artiste ne doit pas le voir tel qu'il sera sur son papier, mais tel qu'il est dans la nature. Le crayon ne distingue pas une blonde d'une brune, mais l'imagination qui le guide doit les distinguer. . . .

Julie est la Figure principale. Blonde, une physionomie douce, tendre, modeste, enchanteresse. Des grâces naturelles sans la moindre affectation: une élégante simplicité, même un peu de négligence dans son vêtement, mais qui lui sied mieux qu'un air plus arrangé . . .

Claire ou la Cousine. Une brune piquante; l'air plus fin, plus éveillé, plus gai; d'une parure un peu plus ornée, et visant presque à la coquetterie; mais toujours pourtant de la modestie et de la bienséance.   [pp. 761–62]

Rousseau goes on to describe the appearance of four other main characters, but it is only for the two women that he indicates any coloring.

In these notes, and in the engravings resulting from them, appear for the first time for our tradition the contrasted maidens dark and fair, active and passive, the maiden of art and the maiden of nature.[6] For future developments, the point is in the polarity, not in any fixed attribution of qualities to either coloring. As here, the fair one will often be the more angelic and spiritual, and sometimes inclined to die early; the dark one, on the other hand, inclined to be physical, passionate, and exotic, is often a predestined victim or lady of sorrows. Which heroine has what qualities or our sympathy depends on the author's preference; and the criterion of judgment is likely to be, less what is better and what worse than the more basically pastoral one of what is fitted for real life. The consciously elaborated contrast between the two is first made by Mme de Staël in *Corinne*. Subtitled "L'Italie," the book is largely a tour of Italian romantic scenery, with a love story interwoven to add drama and intensity. The heroine is an inspired poetess, who at length gives up her claim to her high-born English suitor and dies brokenhearted; disqualified by her Italian blood and passionate artistic nature, she resigns Oswald in favor of her own half-sister Lucile, blond, English, an acceptable shade-loving flower.[7]

Contrasting pairs of maidens are apt to be closely linked, often as sisters, cousins, or best friends. Examples of sisters are, besides Lucile and Corinne, Scott's Brenda and Minna (*The Pirate*), Cooper's Hetty and Judith (*The Deerslayer*), and Bulwer Lytton's Ellinor and Madeline (*Eugene Aram*). Eliot's Dinah and Hetty (*Adam Bede*) or Lucy and Maggie (*The Mill on the Floss*) are cousins, while *Dracula's* Lucy and Mina are friends. The link may be more mysterious in nature, as in the demonic connection between Poe's dark Siren-named Rhine-maiden Ligeia and his flaxen Saxon Rowena. Or, the link may be in the mind of the hero, for example Melville's Pierre, finding some such expression as "Two loves have I, of comfort and despair." Or, as in Poe's stories "Ligeia," "Morella," and

"Eleonora," each may dominate a separate phase of his life. Or, like Tasso in our reading or Ernest Maltravers with dark Florence and fair Alice, he may be faced with both his complement and his counterpart.

Some consistency may be noted in the matter of names. Sometimes an exotic name will be set against a native English one, Rebecca or Ligeia against Rowena, or Zenobia against Priscilla. More often the contrast is in meaning rather than origin. The fair maiden's name most frequently begins with A, C, or L and is related to Alice (lily), Christine, Clara (brightness), Lily or Lucy (light), while the dark lady prefers Judith, Julia, Margaret (pearl), Madeline (Magdalen), or Minna. Thus Rousseau's fair Julie and dark Claire have changed places. The dark lady as Cora or Corinne[8] seems to echo one of the names of Persephone.

The choice between maidens dark and fair, or otherwise complementary, that is available to numerous nineteenth-century heroes frequently faces the artist as well. However, an unequivocal choice between contrasting maidens will not simplify things much for him, because usually each will correspond to one aspect of his nature. The young enthusiast Scythrop in *Nightmare Abbey* must decide for Allegra or Penserosa, however much his original may have inclined to compound ménages. Milton knew he could not "choose to live" with both: the unfortunate Pierre tried it. Perhaps the happiest fate is marriage to "a Spirit, yet a Woman too"—one of the two after she has been tempered by the sufferings of the other: Ellinor in *Eugene Aram*, Dinah Morris in *Adam Bede*, Hilda in *The Marble Faun*.[9] Only seldom does the Artist find such a solution.

Artist-novels in the tradition inspired by *Wilhelm Meister* tend to show striking divisions among female types. *Contarini Fleming* has a scene (I, xv–xvi) in which the hero is placed between two maidens characterized as "Thalia" and "Melpomene," suggesting his two loves, the northern merry-hearted Christina and the southern tragical Alceste. Bulwer Lytton's poet-hero (*Ernest Maltravers, or The Eleusinia*, 1837) in a youthful idyll loves the guileless, fair-haired Alice, loses her, and becomes engaged to the dark lady Florence Lascelles, whose pride and ambition resemble his own. When Florence dies, the victim of a plot, Ernest departs on a course of romantic wanderings of the kind laid down by Rousseau's St-Preux and Laclos's Danceny. In the sequel, *Alice, or the Mysteries*, 1838, he at length rediscovers and returns to his self-sacrificing earlier love. Both have gained from the apprenticeship to life. Bulwer Lytton says of Ernest:

> No longer despising Man as he is, and no longer exacting from all things the ideal of a visionary standard, he was more fitted to mix in the living World. . . . His sentiments were, perhaps, less lofty, but his actions were infinitely more excellent, and his theories infinitely more wise.   [XI, viii]

Alice's early romance with Ernest draws on the same famous episode[10] as Tennyson's "The Lord of Burleigh" (he is given that title in *Alice* I, iii), but she is spared the fate of the rustic maid, having in the meantime greatly gained in mind, spirit, manners, and fortune, and thus become a very good match.

Ernest Maltravers shows that the Artist as well as the soulmate can be mellowed by the troubles of a counterpart. Ernest first meets Castruccio Cesarini at the close of a poetic "music on the water" scene on Lake Como:

> "This poor Cesarini may warn me against myself!" thought [Ernest]. "Better hew wood and draw water than attach ourselves devotedly to an art in which we have not the capacity to excel. . . . It is to throw away the healthful objects of life for a diseased dream; worse than the Rosicrucians, it is to make a sacrifice of all human beauty for the smile of a sylphid that never visits us but in visions." Maltravers looked over his own compositions, and thrust them into the fire. He slept ill that night. His pride was a little dejected; he was like a beauty who has seen a caricature of herself.　　　　　　　　　　　[III, ii]

The next chapter dwells on Cesarini's melancholy and self-centeredness. Later, when rejected by Lady Florence Lascelles in favor of Ernest, Cesarini is influenced to jealousy by Ernest's Iago-like enemy, Lumley Ferrers, and in effect announces that Ernest is his evil genius; in the next chapter he swears to be avenged on him (VIII, iv). After Florence's death through the machinations of the unsuspected Lumley, Cesarini, about to fight a duel with Ernest, is rendered helpless by a fit of the madness to which his ungoverned sensibility has long been tending; Ernest is the first to assist him, and hands him over to a doctor with the charge, "Tend him as my brother" (IX, viii).

In the sequel, Cesarini has long been confined as an incurable madman. Learning that Lumley is the real villain, he swears to destroy him. Escaping from the asylum, he succeeds in smothering Lumley in Paris, and then drowns himself in the Seine.

In the structure of the two novels, Cesarini is the morbid, oversensitive artist compared to the essentially healthy and positive-spirited Ernest. Two casual references to Tasso placed close to Cesarini's first appearance help define his rôle. As a shadow-self of Ernest's, he embodies Ernest's darker possibilities not only for evil but also for intense suffering; Ernest does suffer considerably himself, but he is one of those artist figures who increase in strength and balance as they consider the calamities of those around them: "learning from life" on the model of Wilhelm Meister is a calmer process than turning one's agony into song like Tasso and those artists whose emblem is the nightingale. Bulwer Lytton is careful to exculpate his hero—not only is he no victimizer, he is much sinned against—but a few steps further along Ernest's way lurks the demon artist. Believing he has proposed marriage to his own daughter, Ernest declares he bears the mark of Cain; the real Cain, besides the villain Lumley, is the avenger Cesarini, to whom Ernest has always behaved with generosity and who now both rids Ernest of his enemy and takes on himself the guilt of the action.

To return to symmetry among maidens, it is strikingly featured in *Der grüne Heinrich*, Gottfried Keller's semiautobiographical novel of 1853. The young painter Heinrich loves simultaneously and in different ways his two cousins, the fair and childlike Anna, who dies young, and the dark and sensuous Judith. Later, having gone abroad to study, he tells with indirect application to himself the story of a man of his native town who was ruined by successive attachments to two women, the gay, worldly Cornelia and the sad, spiritual Afra; later again comes the digressive but elaborate story of blooming Rosalie and shy Agnes and the pageant in which they take part as Venus and Diana. Eventually Heinrich returns home and rejoins his old love Judith, but only after a scene in which she declares that their relation henceforward will be that of friends. This touch recalls the treatment of St-Preux first by Julie and later by Claire;[11] within Keller's book, it suggests that Judith has taken on something of the virginal Anna, or that divided loves have become one. They do at the end of *Corinne*, where the dying poetess advises the pallid Lucile how to make her husband love her: "You must be to him both Lucile and Corinne!"

Melville's struggling artist Pierre breaks off his marriage with the fair Lucy in an effort to do justice to his sister Isabel, a somewhat sibylline and inspirational figure with more than a suggestion of dark underworld forces. She is a model of sisterly affection, with nothing destructive in her conscious nature; but her breasts nurse only a poison-flask, and in the closing tableau, when Pierre and his two ladies are discovered in the grip of death, he is also held as in a web of fatality—"her long hair ran over him, and arbored him in ebon vines."

Gérard de Nerval's Sylvie, in the exquisite prose idyll of 1853 called after her, is a dark and vivacious village girl who shares the narrator's heart (the story is more than half autobiographical) with the actress Aurélia, who, in contrast to the flesh-and-blood Sylvie, is an inaccessible figure of dream, a face glimpsed in the "miroir magique" of theatrical illusion. The narrator's love for Aurélia, moreover, is based partly on a childish memory of another fair girl, Adrienne, whom he saw one moonlit night during a country festival, singing in the garden of her ancestral château. Adrienne has entered a convent before the story opens, and her death there is announced at the end. The narrator remembers her as a moonlit phantom figure that even in those days had power to distract him from Sylvie; now Adrienne-Aurélia exercises "un entraînement fatal où l'inconnu vous attire comme le feu follet fuyant sur les joncs d'une eau morte" (iii), and this "spectre funeste" comes between him and Sylvie with the patriarchal countryside with its round of festivals to which she belongs and which he has long ago left for Paris. "Aimer une religieuse sous la forme d'une actrice!... et si c'était la même!—Il y a de quoi devenir fou!" (iii). As Pierre does about Isabel, he questions whether the tormenting spirit is heavenly or evil (xi).[12]

During most of the story the narrator is revisiting the scenes with which both Sylvie and Adrienne are associated, and renewing his fondness for Sylvie. She herself is much the same, but the countryside is changing and being swallowed up; and while Sylvie used to crochet lace, she now makes gloves on a machine. Too, she has forgotten the old folksongs in favor of operatic arias with deliberate phrasing. The narrator is nevertheless about to propose to her, but is prevented by a walk's ending too soon; then he meets a young man he half understands to be Sylvie's fiancé. Returning to Paris, he has a brief affair with Aurélia, who breaks it off when she realizes that he loves not her but a memory. Sylvie has by now married, and the narrator, returning to the familiar countryside, complains that all is changed:

> Je cherche parfois à retrouver mes bosquets de Clarens[13] perdus au nord de Paris, dans les brumes.... Ermenonville! pays où fleurissait encore l'idylle antique... tu as perdu ta seule étoile, qui chatoyait pour moi d'un double éclat... c'était Adrienne ou Sylvie,—c'étaient les deux moitiés d'un seul amour. L'une était l'idéal sublime, l'autre la douce réalité.   [xiv]

The story ends with a visit to the domestic happiness of Sylvie in a nearby town, and a joking comparison of themselves to Lotte and Werther, "moins les pistolets."

The special quality of this wandering narrative, with its free movement in time, is striking but hard to describe. Proust admired it and cited it in connection with his episode of the madeleine, the quest of memory. The landscape itself is thick with memories: it is the land of the "tour abolie," a lost "vie des châteaux" with its parks "à l'anglaise," artificial mirrorlike ponds, and eighteenth-century classical ruins. In a way perhaps reminiscent of Rousseau—his shade, emanating from Ermenonville, pervades the scene—the natural and carefree is blended with the elegance of artifice, and a rustic festival is organized along lines suggested by Watteau's "L'Embarquement pour Cythère": fittingly, perhaps, as the whole narrative is a nostalgic evocation of a vanishing world, an elegy for youth and its illusions. Its literary connections are backwards with Book Three of Chateaubriand's *Mémoires,* to the woods around Combourg where he wandered with his "sylphide," and forwards with the festivals and landscapes of *Du côté de chez Swann* and *Le grand Meaulnes.*

In Nerval's last work, *Aurélia,* or *Le Rêve et la vie,* 1855, the fair and lost beloved appears again, this time as a compound of Beatrice and Eurydice, separated from the narrator by death and by a marriage with a rival who seems to be his evil genius or his double.[14] In happier visions he sees her as an eternal goddess: Mary, Isis, Venus, his mother and his beloved, leading him through the underworld journey by steps and ordeals to the light. He sees too, and perhaps this is another of her aspects, an immense female form hacked to pieces, and thinks, "Voilà ce qu'a produit la puissance déférée aux hommes. Ils ont peu à peu détruit et tranché en mille morceaux le type éternel de la beauté, si bien que les races perdent de plus en plus en force et perfection..." (II, vi). In the last vision he describes of this many-sided Ewig-Weibliches, he and she ride together through the heavens on a triumphal journey, with Messiah between them. Her figure apparently unites active and passive sides, the sufferer and the savior. In his poems too, diverging female ideals are brought together, though here through the influence not of vision but of art, symbolized in "la lyre d'Orphée" and "le laurier de Virgile." In "El Desdichado" the former unites the laments of heavenly and earthly loves, "Les soupirs de la sainte et les cris de la fée." In "Myrtho" beneath the latter's branches "Le pâle hortensia s'unit au myrte vert"; Geoffrey Wagner, the editor and translator of his *Selected Writings,* notes: "The imagery of the last line unites Octavie [a blond English girl whose name titles a section of *Les Filles du feu*], epitomized by the Christian flower... of the north with the pagan and dark beauty of the 'myrte' of Sylvie."[15] Perhaps a look at Virgil's Eclogue 2 (18, 54–55) bears out this interpretation. The setting of these poems, by the way, and that of "Octavie," is Naples, an inviting Romantic locale which for want not of interest but of space we are bypassing.[16]

The most elaborate gamut of choice among beloveds is offered the artist in Offenbach's opera *The Tales of Hoffmann,* based on the "drame fantastique en cinq actes" of 1851 by Nerval's associates Jules Barbier and Michel Carré. If indeed we can call it choice, where the hero offers himself in turn and without reservation to each of the ladies.[17]

The hero of the *Tales* is the Artist, Hoffmann himself.[18] In the first and last acts, which constitute a frame, he loves the singer Stella, who at the end is taken away from him by his saturnine rival, Counsellor Lindorf. In between, to beguile the time, he tells the stories of his three former loves: Olympia, the dancing and singing automaton, Giulietta, the heartless Venetian courtesan, and Antonia, the consumptive singer. These three rôles, all soprano, are properly all sung by the same person, along with that of Stella, of whose symbolic range each is one aspect. In each of the inset stories Hoffmann is faced by a demonic opposite, the bass, last seen as the triumphant Lindorf. The three opposites, Coppélius, Dapertutto,

and Dr. Miracle, are not mere rivals in love; rather, they effectively demonstrate that whatever the claims of owner, father, favorite, or Hoffmann
as lover, the lady is in fact their creature and in their power for life and
death.[19]

Hoffmann's confidant throughout is his servant Nicklausse, rather
young and cocky, whose warnings are unheeded but who always manages to spirit his master away once the damage has been done. The rôle is
a little ambiguous, being sung by a mezzo-soprano. In the last scene,
Nicklausse gets Hoffmann to declare before the company that his three
loves are finished; immediately thereupon all his drinking companions
leave and the Muse appears, mezzo-soprano and radiantly bright, and
claims Hoffmann as her own by virtue of her continued faithful friendship. Her words are reminiscent of the last scene of *Tasso:*

> Ne suis-je rien? Que la tempête
> Des passions s'apaise en toi!
> L'homme n'est plus; renais poète!
> Je t'aime, Hoffmann! appartiens-moi!
> Des cendres de ton coeur réchauffe ton génie,
> Dans la sérénité souris à tes douleurs,
> La Muse adoucira ta souffrance bénie,
> On est grand par l'amour et plus grand par les pleurs!

After she vanishes, Hoffmann falls into a deep sleep. Stella enters, jealously pursued by Lindorf: it is Nicklausse, reappearing, who persuades
her that his master is dead drunk and gently dismisses her to the waiting
Lindorf as the opera ends.

The ladies of the adventures, Hoffmann's "three enchantresses," as he
calls them, present three faces of the earthly Venus: best in the dying
soulmate Antonia, worst in the demon-woman Giulietta, and indifferent
in the dummy-woman Olympia, who has no word but the responsive
"Oui." Each in turn voluntarily or involuntarily proves a delusive dream
to the Poet, even a puppet of the forces of evil, like the Venus of the
Tannhäuser legend, whose master is Satan. The composite woman,
Stella, shows a momentary kindness towards Hoffmann but is easily
drawn away by Lindorf. Her name makes her the goal of aspiration, but
her profession shows her to be worldly and her world one of illusion.
Earthly love is not for the Poet, but the grief its loss has caused him will
instruct his song.

The association of poetic genius with capacity to suffer is of course
pervasive in nineteenth-century writing. Genius as itself destructive, so
forcefully described by Goethe's Tasso, meets us here again in Antonia.
Like Tasso's princess, she is for medical reasons forbidden to sing; she has
inherited her mother's consumption with her voice, and any exercise of

the latter causes the signs of the former instantly to appear. Her evil doctor presents her with a choice between her art and her love and then compels her to choose song, of which within a few minutes she dies, in a pointed adaptation of Hoffmann's story "Rat Krespel" (see pp. 85–86 above). The Poet's art has no such direct link with death, but as well as consoling him for his sorrows, it is strengthened by his encounter with the dark powers.

Leaving aside Hoffmann's other loves, let us proceed from the ambiguous figure that is Nicklausse–Muse. In this discussion we shall sometimes be speaking of the Artist's attitude, sometimes of that of his author. This is very bad form, critically speaking; but owing to the peculiar cast of subjectivity that almost always attends the artist-romance from *Werther* and *Alastor* on, it is scarcely to be avoided.

In the pastoral tradition—witness *The Shepheardes Calender*—the shepherd unhappy in love usually has a male companion to whom he can make his complaint, and the devotion between them is often expressed in extravagant terms. This is true especially in the pastoral drama, but the germ of the development is already present in classical pastoral poetry. Andrew Lang puts the double motif conveniently: he describes the songs of the herdsmen in Theocritus's Eighth Idyll as "variations on the themes of love and friendship (for Menalcas sings of Milon, Daphnis of Nais). . . ." In Virgil's Tenth Eclogue Gallus says that if he had been an Arcadian (that is, belonged to the idyllic world that is in effect lost in the golden past), he would have loved either Phyllis or the dark Amyntas (a masculine name); and his unfortunate passion for the faithless Lycoris is described in an image varied some lines later to describe Virgil's own love for Gallus (53–54, 73–74). From such precedents it is a short step to making the person who hears the sufferer's complaint his passionately devoted friend. The love celebrated in later pastoral is normally that between the sexes; however, the first and most influential of Italian pastoral dramas, Politian's *Orfeo*, is an exception. Its main theme is naturally the love of Orpheus for Eurydice; but at the end, having finally lost his bride, Orpheus denounces the love of women and praises that of Jove for Ganymede, Phoebus for Hyacinth, and Hercules for Hylas. The source of his speech is Ovid's account of Orpheus as the originator of pederasty. The praise of a love "passing the love of women" need not be *faute de mieux*: Spenser's book of Friendship places the ideal companions higher in its scheme than the familiar pairs of lovers. The consensus of the tradition from Theocritus through Virgil to Spenser seems to be that ideal friendship between men is a feature of the Golden Age, and that any standard by which it is distrusted belongs to a fallen world and corresponds to man's loss of innocence. The same is true of incest, as in the union celebrated in "L'Allegro" "When yet there was no fear of Jove." In biblical pastoral worlds too this is the case: the love of David and Jonathan is to the credit of both, and the lover of the Song addresses "my sister, my bride."[20] The hermit of *Atala* says:

> "Je ne vous parlerai point des mariages des premiers nés des hommes, de ces unions ineffables, alors que la soeur était l'épouse du frère, que l'amour et l'amitié fraternelle se confondaient dans le même coeur et que la pureté de l'une augmentait les délices de l'autre."

What were the ideal relations of an unfallen world, in a fallen one have become the most tainted. The artist susceptible to these kinds of attachment can perhaps claim the privilege of that paradise to which he, more than other men, feels he belongs.

As in the childhood of the race, so in that of the individual. Paradisal or idyllic states left behind with youth are commonly characterized in our literature by conditions we could call in a psychological sense "narcissistic." One is self-absorption or absorption in a dream-life, accompanied with the child's inability to love. The others are all forms of ideal and often presexual companionship: with a child-love, a female near relation, or a boy one's own age. The first is epitomized in *Paul et Virginie*, in *Mathilda*, in the romance at the beginning of *Ernest Maltravers*, in Poe's "Eleonora" and "Annabel Lee," and in the Annabel romance that opens *Lolita*. Attachment between brother and sister prepares the catastrophes of *René* and *Manfred*. When the relationship is between cousins, as in *Eugene Aram*, a happier ending may sometimes be augured. Perhaps the most striking association of the love of two boys with a youthful Eden, and of their estrangement with its loss, is that occurring early in *The Winter's Tale*. Such innocent emotional attachments form conspicuous parts of *Contarini Fleming* and Mann's "Tonio Kröger" and *The Magic Mountain*. Melville's Pierre treats his mother as a sister, rejects his bride for his real sister, and ends by shooting his cousin Glen whom as a boy he once loved with boyish excess. The obsessed figure in these cases is the one who tries in the face of reality to reconstitute the lost relationships of the past, or by some excessive means to set right what has gone wrong.[21]

Nicklausse–Muse as the "higher" soulmate prefigures what we could call the "master-mistress" theme. This enters a novel and a short story by Wilde, *The Picture of Dorian Gray* and "The Portrait of Mr. W. H.," which in a sense are complements. In the latter the idea of a W. H. exerts a fatal influence on two lives, while in the former a modern-day W. H. is fatally influenced by two rival friends.

Cyril Graham of the short story is a beautiful and gifted youth who makes a sensation as Rosalind in a university production. Prevented by his friends from making the stage his career, he elaborates a theory about the composition of the *Sonnets,* creating presumably in his own image Shakespeare's beloved, the Elizabethan boy-actor Will Hughes, and commissioning a pseudoantique portrait to convince his friend Erskine. Erskine discovers and denounces the forgery, and Graham shoots himself, after writing to Erskine that he is "going to offer his life as a sacrifice to the secret of the *Sonnets,*" and that it now lies with his friend to present the theory to the world. Erskine examines and dismisses the theory, and later tells the whole story to the narrator, discouraging him from belief and adding, "I believe there is something fatal about the idea." Fired with the theory, seeing Graham as a glorious martyr, tha narrator shuts himself up with the *Sonnets* until Will Hughes becomes to him "a kind of spiritual presence, an ever-dominant personality," tinged with suggestions of Hadrian's Antinoüs, Plato's Charmides, and Piers Gaveston. He writes a long appeal to Erskine to do as Graham has asked him, reiterating Graham's arguments and adding new; when the letter has gone, he finds his own belief has gone with it—in fact it has been passed on to Erskine, who is now as fanatical as formerly Graham was. Two years later, Erskine leaves the narrator a suicide note—he too will die for the theory—and the portrait. Wilde confuses the ending by having the narrator find out that Erskine's subsequent death was actually due to consumption, but this seems to be merely a piece of whimsy: the same device (of a natural death mistaken for violent) occurs in "Lord Arthur Savile's Crime." The story's main outline shows a fatal idea, expressed in the portrait and ghostly personality of the young actor, that passes from mind to mind like an infection. The tragedy of Cyril Graham repeats Shakespeare's own and may foreshadow Erskine's, the narrator's and more to come. Yet the influence of W. H. has its creative as well as its destructive side, inspiring Cyril Graham's lifework along with Shakespeare's.

Dorian Gray is less slight in construction, but again incompletely worked out. The beautiful Dorian is the object of rivalry between the artist Basil Hallward and the man of pleasure Lord Henry Wotton. To Hallward he is an inspiration, like Will Hughes to Shakespeare, while to Wotton, the aesthete and cold anatomizer of human passions, he is the subject of an experiment. It is Hallward who first makes him aware of his remarkable beauty, while Wotton persuades him that he should live only for aesthetic sensations; this he is the more able to do because whether through his rash wish or through the painter's having somehow imbued the canvas with his soul, from then on not his physical but his painted self becomes altered by time and experience. Thus Dorian's youth and air of perfect purity are supernaturally preserved. The blessing becomes a curse: Dorian comes to loathe the silent testimony of his corruption and shuts it in an attic room, where his horror of it causes him to murder its creator. His friendship with Wotton continues without any such climax.

Hallward and Wotton are contrasted somewhat as good and evil geniuses; both are highly artistic, but while Hallward is loving and productive, Wotton is without feeling and satisfied to produce only wickedly brilliant conversation. Dorian's downfall begins when he allows Wotton to draw him away from Hallward, and finds its climax in the latter's murder; the gift of love from Hallward, which at first played the part of conscience, goads the hardened man to further evil.

Besides having these attachments, Dorian early in the book falls in love with an actress, exquisite, gifted, and very young, who plays Shakespearean heroines. After Dorian's declaration of love, Sibyl gives an atrocious performance; for the first time she sees the world of the theater not as the essence of romance but as hollow and sham; like the Lady of Shalott she declares that she is "sick of shadows."[22] All Dorian's love for her now vanishes: " 'I loved you because you were marvellous, because you had genius and intellect, because you realized the dreams of great poets and gave shape and substance to the shadows of art. . . . Without your art you are nothing' " (vii). When he leaves her, she drinks prussic acid and dies. Lord Henry's immediately persuading Dorian to regard the tragedy only as an aesthetic episode sets him in the path he is to follow to the end.

Dorian devotes himself to a lonely search for sensations. In his magnificently appointed house with its locked and fatal-secret-concealing attic, he pursues exotic researches and gathers collections—musical instruments, perfumes, stones, tapestries, forbidden books—specifically on the Des Esseintes model. On wilder adventures he leaves the house and buries himself in strange dens, opium and other, on London's waterfront, involving various young people who never find their way out again. Following the murder he grows increasingly solitary and haunted, and at last, having tried to rip up the fatal picture, he is found lying dead with the knife through his heart and bearing the features he has earned, while the portrait, untouched, has returned to its original flawless beauty.

The novel is so close to allegory or parable that little remains to be said. We may, however, note the contrast between Hallward's love and Dorian's. While Dorian loves in Sibyl only her relation to the world of poetry, and without it has no use for her, moreover dreaming that he will make her a creature for the world to worship and it will be his name that she bears, Hallward, recognizing in Dorian's portrait his best work, is willing either to destroy it or to withold it from exhibition if his friend wishes. He does not share Dorian's vampiric possessiveness—his affinity with the obsessed artists of Hoffman and Poe.

Definable homosexuality seldom figures in our novel. An emotional ambivalence, however, very frequently does, in the intensity with which the hero longs for or recognizes the unique "friend," for example in Hesse's *Narziss und Goldmund,* a modern parable presenting artist and thinker as complements. The intensity may then be transferred to a more conventional attachment to the friend's sister (John Richardson's *Wacousta*, Browning's *A Blot in the 'Scutcheon*).[23] Our fiction deals, we might say, rather with symbolic than with psychological reality, and the question of the alter ego as such transcends that of gender. Moreover, currents of sympathy and influence, magnetic, repelling, or whatever, are more important than mere physical relations: see, for an extreme case, James's *The Sacred Fount*.[24] However, under the heading of ambivalence we must notice the tendency for the soulmate to be surrounded with an aura of social or sexual taboo. In Goethe, who inclined in life and in literature to making a morbid distinction between physical and spiritual loves, this is a matter of the most delicate art. It is managed in *Werther* largely through the hero's dreams and musings, rather than directly presented. In *Tasso*, with its dramatic necessities, we see the princess, filled with such glowing interest in the mental and artistic world, on the plane of daily reality always cautioning self-command, restraint, renunciation; too, she is not strong, and any rough encounter with existence might prove too much for her. The impression of a sensibility too finely tuned affects the reader more than even the social consideration of rank.

The foundation for the artist-novel is laid by Goethe, largely through *Wilhelm Meister*. To the casual reader, having emerged from what seems a farrago of masonic nonsense and pointless intrigues, what stands out? the mad old Harper, probably, and his daughter Mignon, that curious compound of female Cherubino and infant Sibyl. While the various women life seems to offer to Wilhelm—Philine, Therese, Natalie—represent significantly different types, none of them greatly enlists our sympathies: Mignon is by far the most engaging. Not, though she loves him, that Wilhelm ever sees her as a possible soulmate. For one thing, she is too young, and woman and child are mixed in her from first to last—even something boyish, as her equivocal name and choice of garments suggest. She is a figure of inspiration, with her wildly pathetic songs of exile and loneliness. She is also that rather special apparition, the elegiac child. Goethe is clearly not going to allow her to grow up, largely out of moral scruple, as she was born from incest. Perhaps also there is the same kind of implication that we find in Poe, that inbreeding produces a sensibility too attenuated to survive. We do not think of her as growing up and marrying, because she belongs already to a tragic destiny, rather perhaps as Wordsworth's Lucy belongs to "Nature" rather than to her poet.

The plaintive little figure of Mignon is very far from that of a siren. But in her helplessness and passivity, as in that of Ophelia whom she resembles, there is something that almost accuses, and something alarming in her clear predestination as a victim. The ravisher of such a being would feel like a murderer; but so would the one who passed her by. This aspect of terror[25] recalls Faust's encounter on the Brocken: he meets "a pale, beautiful child" whom he takes for Gretchen, and whose sight fills him with compunction and remorse; Mephisto draws him away, explaining that though she seems to everyone like his own beloved, in reality she is "a magic image, is lifeless, an eidolon," and at the same time she is the Medusa and would turn him to stone.

Shelley translates, "She seems to every man like his first love," the change suggesting both nostalgia for one's own youth and at the same time the unthinking egotism of that stage of life, with the later certainty that one must have given pain. He uses the image himself in the second of the two mysterious stanzas concluding his lyric "The Two Spirits," 1820. The poem consists of a dialogue between so to speak a Julian and a Maddalo spirit, one full of bright visions and the other of dark. The dialogue is broken off unresolved, and two concluding stanzas without clear antecedents are tacked on. The first looks like the realization of what the Maddalo spirit thought would happen to the Julian one—to be pursued endlessly by the embodied darkness:

> Some say there is a precipice
> Where one vast pine is frozen to ruin
> O'er piles of snow and chasms of ice
> 'Mid Alpine mountains;
> And that the languid storm pursuing
> That wingèd shape, for ever flies
> Round those hoar branches, aye renewing
> Its aëry fountains.

This is a place of torment like Prometheus's Caucasus; the mood is reminiscent also of the pursuit of weeping Emanation by furious Spectre in Blake's "My Spectre Around Me"—"Poor pale pitiable form / That I follow in a storm. . . ." The last stanza is harder to connect with what precedes it:

> Some say when nights are dry and clear,
> And the death-dews sleep on the morass,
> Sweet whispers are heard by the traveller,
> Which make night day:
> And a silver shape like his early love doth pass
> Upborne by her wild and glittering hair,
> And when he awakes on the fragrant grass,
> He finds night day.

Is this a vision of bliss or of bale? a lost past restored, or fatally luring? Are we to recognize the earthbound First Spirit in either the traveler or the "silver shape"? And in the return of day at the end, in what has been the optimistic refrain line of the Second Spirit's claims, do we find relief that the night has passed, or regret that the vision has fled, as in *Alastor*? Both stanzas suggest, in different ways, the will-o'-the-wisp figure whose history we traced earlier.[26] We can connect also, perhaps, the celebrated lithograph by Delacroix of Faust on the Brocken, 1828, in which Gretchen–Medusa dangles in the black air like a limp puppet, held up by demons by her long hair.[27] A victim of the mingled self-pity, self-hatred, and remorse involved in this kind of "early love" is the speaker of Heine's lyric "Still ist die Nacht," who returns to the house where an old love once lived, to find that a part of himself has remained fastened to the spot— "Thou Doppelgänger! pale companion!"—and responds in all the bitterness of hatred and shame. The example illustrates the sense in which some of Memory's daughters are Gorgons.

Perhaps the two aspects of the very young and defenceless girl, the pathetic and the enslaving, can be seen as prefigured by Spenser's Florimell. Her name and her half-year's underworld detention relate her to Persephone, also a distressed maiden; when we see her she is usually in terrified flight, and her function seems to be mainly to provoke a mixedly motivated pursuit. Her pathos becomes ensnaring when the witch sends out a wintry image of her—like the false Gretchen, an "Idole."[28]

Figure 4. *Lithograph by Delacroix of Faust on the Brocken, 1828.*

Other authors become entangled with elegiac youths or maidens and are seduced into deathbed scenes, like Dickens, or necrophily, like Poe. A descendant of Annabel Lee, Lolita, does not die immediately but escapes and is briefly married, her ultimate normality having been throughout this odd case the very feature that made her finally unpossessable.[29] Lewis Carroll's relation with his Alice can appear in this light too, not in the two books of her adventures but in the faintly eerie poems addressed to her at the beginning of *Wonderland* and the beginning and end of *Through the Looking-Glass*. Alice, the dreamer of the two stories, is here "the dream-child," though already a sense of sad reality and the changes brought by time is present:

> Alice! A childish story take,
> And, with a gentle hand,
> Lay it where Childhood's dreams are twined
> In Memory's mystic band,
> Like pilgrim's withered wreath of flowers
> Plucked in a far-off land.

In the second poem he deplores the swiftness of time that divides their ages and threatens the moment of communication itself, as well as its memory; there are other barriers still:

> I have not seen thy sunny face,
> Nor heard thy silver laughter....

They must take advantage of the moment:

> Come, hearken then, ere voice of dread,
> With bitter tidings laden,
> Shall summon to unwelcome bed
> A melancholy maiden....

Nurse's voice? Not exclusively; and the poet's apprehension does not distinguish between the bride-bed and the grave. In the autumnal third poem, the Alice figure, lost with July, now belongs entirely to a world of illusion, with less of magic than of pathos:

> Still she haunts me, phantomwise,
> Alice moving under skies
> Never seen by waking eyes.

This mood of a weird forlornness recalls the Alice of Charles Lamb's "Dream-Children," receding mournfully into the limbo of the might-have-been.[30]

In conjunction with Lewis Carroll's Alice we may notice his photographs of little girls. His, if any camera ever, had a Gorgon eye. The long sittings and the elaborate costumes are not enough to account for the crystalline unearthliness of the figures he records or creates; each is a sylph or spirit-child, as if only here their artist was free to create "a thing that could not feel / The touch of earthly years," the basilisk triumph of art hinted at in the Alice poems.

None of this becomes very explicit in connection with Alice, though we may note that in the final poem art assures the continuation—occasional renewal, at any rate—of the dream and of the summer vision in which life appears dream instead of being opposed to it. In two histories of perverse loves and a vampiric passion of possession, art at last supplies the changelessness that the flux of nature refuses: one is Proust's memoir, the other Humbert Humbert's:

> I am thinking of aurochs and angels, the secret of durable pigments, pro-
> phetic sonnets, the refuge of art. And this is the only immortality you and I
> may share, my Lolita.

Nine Summer and Winter: Life, Dream, and Art

> ... *meditation and water are wedded for ever.*
>
> —*Herman Melville*

> *Row, row, row your boat*
> *Gently down the stream:*
> *Merrily, merrily, merrily, merrily,*
> *Life is but a dream.*
>
> —*Eliphalet Oram Lyte*

The passage from an idyllic world to a blank or sinister one—the pastoral fall—can be imaged by, for example, the disappearance of a fairy structure, the change of seasons, the abrupt waking from a happy dream, the departure or unmasking of a beguiling nymph or siren. To these motifs we can add a nonmythological version of what the Siren stands for, the untrustworthiness of water: the deceptive stream. The motto of many an adventurer carried farther than he intended might be, "We didn't mean to go to sea." Or "over the edge," as in Thomson's "Winter":

> The sons of riot flow
> Down the loose stream of false enchanted joy,
> To swift destruction. On the rankled soul
> The gaming fury falls; and in one gulf
> Of total ruin, honour, virtue, peace,
> Friends, families, and fortune, headlong sink. [632–37][1]

The stream to which the Poet of *Alastor* says, "Thou imagest my life," plunges over a precipice into an "immeasurable void."[2] Tasso's princess associates the life she has been living, now about to change, with happy days of drifting:

> Ah, what a twilight falls before my eyes!
> The glorious sun, the cheerful consciousness
> Of shining day, the multifarious world's
> All-brilliant presence now is bleak and veiled,
> Dimmed by the vapours that beset me round.
> Each single day I once thought life enough;
> Then care was silent, stilled was all foreboding,
> The river bore us, happily embarked,

Forward on gentle waves without an oar:
Now stealthily a fear of what's to come
Makes its sad presence known within my breast.   [III.ii.1869–79]

The same ignorance of unhappiness to come[3] is the theme of Wordsworth's early "Lines Written While Sailing in a Boat at Evening," 1789:

How richly glows the water's breast
Before us, tinged with evening hues,
While, facing thus the crimson west,
The boat her silent course pursues!
And see how dark the backward stream!
A little moment past so smiling!
And still, perhaps, with faithless gleam,
Some other loiterers beguiling.

Such views the youthful Bard allure!
But, heedless of the following gloom,
He deems their colours shall endure
Till peace go with him to the tomb.
—And let him nurse his fond deceit,
And what if he must die in sorrow!
Who would not cherish dreams so sweet,
Though grief and pain may come to-morrow?

To be carried unthinkingly along on the water is a familiar symbol for abandonment to dream, or to its fiercer aspect, passion: in *Death in Venice* the incident of the gondola prepares us for Aschenbach's surrender to forces stronger than his habitual discipline. From such lassitude one may glide easily into death, like Ophelia and the Lady of Shalott, or be awakened by a shock, like that with which Lord Jim finds he has chosen his fate and leapt from the *Patna*. *The Mill on the Floss* offers a much more elaborate example, where not only the book's whole physical setting with its traditions natural and supernatural, but also metaphors of the force of the water as passion and destiny, support the two great scenes on the river, that in which Maggie lets herself be carried and is lost, and that in which she struggles and is saved.[4] A comparable ambiguous stream is intertwined with the fates of the protagonists in Keller's elegiac novella *Romeo und Julia auf dem Dorfe*. Evil passions overwhelm both their fathers, who from having been prosperous and friendly farmers become degenerate, mutually hating old wretches, one of them drink-sodden, and take to morosely fishing; the lovers find their happiness briefly on top of a hay barge set adrift on the river, which they leave only to seek their death.

Why, apart from ease in rhyming, is the world of dream and sweet illusion so often set on or beside a stream? We have discussed Venice as a dream-city and the "haunted stream" as a place of inspiration; Blake's "Memory, hither come" invokes Memory beside a stream where the poet will "fish for fancies";[5] other poets are subject to visions beside water. About the mysterious quality of water, still or flowing, two interlinked points stand out: its capacity to reflect images thrown onto it while giving them a certain unfamiliarity, usually in Romantic eyes for the better,[6] and the possibility of an otherworldly realm or a treasure—"pearl," perhaps, or sometimes a city, like Müller's Vineta or Heine's North Sea vision—not imaged on the surface but locked in the depths below. The hero or heroine with whom water or a mirror surface is associated as a symbol of dream, ideal, and desire will usually appear to author and reader as immature: a poetic youth who has not yet encountered real life, or a maiden who has not yet encountered love.[7] The young person's relation with the glassy surface may indicate childish self-containment or self-absorption, as in Hawthorne's Pearl or Blake's Thel, or a virginal passion for an ideal, as in Goethe's Tasso or MacDonald's Cosmo, and perhaps Britomart's vision of Artegall in the "world of glass."

More sinister than the nymphs and sylphs who as we have seen can become involuntary sirens, are frozen virgins like Flaubert's Salammbô, Dickens's Estella, and Mallarmé's Hérodiade, and beyond these again are outright demonesses like Balzac's Foedora (*Peau de Chagrin*) and the Marquise of "La Fille aux yeux d'or." Close to the self-absorbed young women, but doing more damage because less passive, are the too-assured attractive young men who make love to older women and then reject them, deciding they owe it to themselves to acquire a later model. Though the theme is a favorite contemporary one and usually (once past *Adolphe* and *Sapho*) far from Romantic concepts and techniques, these heroes make the same mistakes as Goethe's Tasso, failing to recognize their treasure when it is in their hand and making a decisive gesture on the wrong level. Joe Lambton in *Room at the Top* emerges with some self-knowledge and the reader's respect, despite all; Colette's Chéri never emerges at all. On a more mechanical level this type is the standard hero of the mid-twentieth-century commercial pornographic novel, and it is worth observing that he usually comes to a bad end, the author making it clear that he is not after all a pastoral Noble Savage but a being of demonic will who has sinned in making use of love: his main interest is not sex but power. Needless to say, this gentleman requires a ceaseless and numerous chorus praising his acts and attributes, and if he is ever found alone without so much as a mirror, his author will take over the function directly.

In connection with an older figure the attachment to a reflecting surface is almost invariably obsessive or demonic, as in Blake's greedy lover Theotormon (*Visions of the Daughters of Albion*), who seeks a mirror in his soulmate, and the haunted lover of Rossetti's "Willowwood" sonnets. A good example of the demon self-lover is Meredith's Willoughby Patterne, whose imagery of desired objects includes mirrors and chalices. At one point in his courtship the persecuted Clara, whose imagination is of a Gothic cast enough to give an aura of horror story, sees him as a "spotted old man," despite his youth and bloom. Again and again we find that an obsessive passion, whether turned outward or inward, ages the person gripped by it. When, as in the case of Bulwer Lytton's Margrave or of Dorian Gray, the self-lover retains his physical good looks, the author may go to considerable lengths to stress the horrible decay of the soul. More usually he will follow Shelley, who develops Ovid's account of the sudden aging of Narcissus:

> And now his limbs were lean; his scattered hair,
> Sered by the autumn of strange suffering,
> Sung dirges in the wind; his listless hand
> Hung like dead bone within its withered skin;
> Life, and the lustre that consumed it, shone,
> As in a furnace burning secretly,
> From his dark eyes alone.

We noted this motif from *Alastor*[8] also in "Die Winterreise," and shall meet it again in, for example, *Green Mansions*.

Often the obsessed pursuer is genuinely of an older generation than his victim-beloved, particularly in Gothic sadistic situations. Right at the beginning of the tradition, Walpole's Manfred pursues the maiden who was to have married his son; thus Isabella is a perverse if not quite incestuous object. The supreme egoist, Milton's Satan, naturally is incestuous as a lover. A comparable demonic narcissism is that of Lovelace types, who go through the motions of courtship but whose acts of love are more like acts of war. They are motivated sometimes by an experimental curiosity, more often by an obscure sense of what is owing to themselves, emerging as pride, vengefulness, or mere love of power. Laclos's Valmont and Constant's Adolphe belong to the former category, Lovelace, de Musset's Octave (*Confessions d'un Enfant du siècle*), Kierkegaard's Seducer and the pawnbroker of Dostoevsky's "A Gentle Spirit" to the latter. So far from being ordinary sensualists, all of them excepting the one shown with the least inwardness, Valmont, are compulsive and self-torturing, inflicting even more harm on themselves than on their victims.

A different relation between obsessive older figures and mirror worlds, less psychological than emblematic, can briefly be pointed out. While a mirror dominating a young man's room, like Cosmo's garret in Prague, may suggest dream, poetry, and the ideal, in an older man's, like that of the *Red Shoes* ballet director mentioned in chapter 8, it more likely hints at dandyism or a cult of himself: he looks at its surface, where the young man tried to look beyond. If, as very often, he is a tyrant, his surroundings may suitably suggest house of mirrors or ice palace.[9] Out of doors, obsessive will can show itself in landscape design on the Versailles pattern:

No pleasing Intricacies intervene,
No artful wildness to perplex the scene;
Grove nods at grove, each Alley has a brother,
And half the platform just reflects the other.
The suff'ring eye inverted Nature sees. . . .   [Pope, *Moral Essays* IV.115–19]

The same oppressiveness attends the hotel garden in *Last Year at Marienbad,* and certainly there it conveys the impression of a mind trapped in its own shackles.

Théophile Gautier's story "Le Pavillon sur l'eau" illustrates the association of a mirror world with the idealism of immaturity. Two wealthy Chinese families, living side by side, have built identical summerhouses together on the edge of a pond. When a quarrel divides them, they raise a wall that keeps them from having to look at each other's property. However in certain lights the reflection of each pavilion and its inhabitant is visible to a person standing in the other, and in this way the young son and daughter[10] of the two families catch sight of each other and fall in love, eventually reuniting their families and getting married. The story is a pure and unbroken idyll, the usual point of exit back into our world being represented only by the last lines:

Les noces se firent; la Perle et le Jaspe purent enfin se parler autrement que par l'intermédiaire d'un reflet. —En furent-ils plus heureux, c'est ce que nous n'oserions affirmer; car le bonheur n'est souvent qu'une ombre dans l'eau.

The relation between *Alice in Wonderland* and *Through the Looking-Glass* is somewhat that of summer's tale and winter's tale. The first story, which ends on the phrase "remembering . . . the happy summer days," is represented as being told on a July afternoon to three little girls in a boat drifting down a river. The second, its continuation, is taken up in midwinter:

Without, the frost, the blinding snow,
The storm-wind's moody madness—
Within, the firelight's ruddy glow,
And childhood's nest of gladness.
The magic words shall hold thee fast:
Thou shalt not heed the raving blast.

And though the shadow of a sigh
May tremble through the story,

> For "happy summer days" gone by,
> And vanish'd summer glory—
> It shall not touch, with breath of bale,
> The pleasance of our fairy-tale.

The concluding poem recalls the summer scene:

> A boat, beneath a sunny sky
> Lingering onward dreamily
> In an evening of July . . .
>
> Long has paled that sunny sky:
> Echoes fade, and memories die
> Autumn frosts have slain July.

Future children hearing the story will relive the same experience:

> In a Wonderland they lie,
> Dreaming as the days go by,
> Dreaming as the summers die:
>
> Ever drifting down the stream—
> Lingering in the golden gleam—
> Life, what is it but a dream?

The scene of the opening poem of *Wonderland* is recalled in the middle of *Through the Looking-Glass,* where Alice finds herself rowing a small boat (not very efficiently, like the little girls of the poem) on a river with the old sheep. She tries to gather the pretty rushes that surround her, but there is always a prettier one just out of reach, while the ones she has gathered melt away "almost like snow." The author explains that they are "dream-rushes." This is the only place before the end of the book where Alice is admitted to be dreaming. In this imagery, summer, childhood, and the tale itself are analogous, all associated with drifting and especially with "dream."

The vision beside water belongs to youth and summer; so, in its happiest moods, does the house built on water. Tennyson's "Requiescat," side by side in the *Collected Poems* with a sea-and-siren poem, "The Sailor Boy," and a palace-prison or poisoned-Hesperides poem, "The Islet," runs as follows:

> Fair is her cottage in its place,
> Where yon broad water sweetly slowly glides.
> It sees itself from thatch to base
> Dream in the sliding tides.
>
> And fairer she, but ah how soon to die!
> Her quiet dream of life this hour may cease.
> Her peaceful being slowly passes by
> To some more perfect peace.

This might fairly be called a Lucy-poem: it records an inland, cloistrally ideal existence. It has the essence of the summer vision in its image of the perfect but tremulous harmony of body and soul, of life and dream, but this is produced in the knowledge that the idyllic stillness is, at least in one perspective, illusory. It records the same kind of moment as does Prospero's speech following his spring-to-harvest masque, and as do those prospects of an eternal transfigured Venice granted in particular instants of sunset and cloud. The knowledge of dissolution, the sliding apart of the elements, is built into the vision itself, whose mood is of a kind of solstice.

We can illustrate the summer vision further out of Tennyson. We noted in chapter 8 Edwin Morris's lost summer of happy memory in which Letty "moves among my visions of the lake" in scenes characterized by the dipping swallow, the blowing gold-lily, and the "light cloud smouldering on the summer crag," all suggesting lightness and insubstantiality, or the Ariel-level of pastoral (see chap. 6, n. 1). Introducing *The Princess*, Tennyson says, "Why not a summer's as a winter's tale?", and the suggestion is kept present in our minds by many touches throughout. The narration has some submerged analogies both to *The Winter's Tale* and to the winter solstice theme of Epiphany, with its motif of children lost and found. Ida's dream is the college she has established in "a certain summer-palace." It is not exactly built on water, but the prince and his companions follow a river to reach it; and when Ida is overwhelmed with anger she falls into the river and has to be rescued, her attendants meanwhile shrieking with threefold iteration, lest we should miss the point, "The Head!" The prince elsewhere prophesies,

> ... this your Academe...
> Will topple to the trumpet down, and pass
> With all fair theories only made to gild
> A stormless summer.   [II.212–216]

The princess ironically uses another summer image:

> ... While down the streams that float us each and all
> To the issue, goes, like glittering bergs of ice,
> Throne after throne, and molten on the waste
> Becomes a cloud. ....   [IV.52–55]

In that speech she has just characterized "Tears, idle tears" as a siren song; in the structure of the whole poem, the songs, with their intense emotionality and the contrasting view to Ida's of womanly fulfillment that they put forward, represent the buried life-stream of passion that threatens her work and her mental state so long as its presence is not acknowledged. The last two songs bring reconciliation: she is to imitate the lily (Lilia is the womanly little girl for whom the story is told) that "folds . . . her sweetness up / And slips into the bosom of the lake," and then to follow the "torrent" down to the valley-world of domestic bliss with its "myriads of rivulets hurrying thro' the lawn," contributing to the fruitfulness and purposiveness of the whole picture. The ideal heights from which she is about to climb down are now seen as barren, remote, terrifying. By the end of the poem the overstrained, fanciful elements of the princess's high-summer dream have been resolved into a rich autumnal prospect of maturity and harvest, in which the very renunciation of the dream has become a fertilizing factor.

A theme of later summer with some magical qualities appears in the *In Memoriam* series ix–xvii, beginning "Fair ship, that from the Italian shore." The ship bearing Hallam's body home to England is a "sacred bark" moving through luminous summer nights over something very like the "charmèd wave" of Milton's winter solstice poem. The water is glassy, and the ship glides as if within a magic circle formed by the arcs of sea and sky.[11] In ix, with "Phosphor" and "prosperous floods," the magician of the summer vision with his control over the waters seems to be somewhere in the background; perhaps the same associations are operating in cxxx, "I prosper, circled with thy voice." No. xii brings dove and ark, the former a bird of calm as well as of mourning. "This look of quiet flatters thus / Our home-bred fancies": the calm established in these poems is ambiguous, and moreover cannot last. The preternatural serenity of the Indian-summer season is shattered by the autumnal storm of xv, and while the ship glides on smoothly still, the poet's peace of mind is less and less secure. The dreamlike synthesis of reality and desire that has been symbolized by the ship's calm movement through a harmonious, fostering world of kindly elements begins to fall apart; parting from the illusion, he still clings to the symbol of the ship's journey as though it were indeed the vessel of Hallam's consciousness. If he thought for a moment that the ship was involved in the storm raging in the inland scene,

> The wild unrest that lives in woe
> Would dote and pore on yonder cloud
>
> That rises upward always higher,
> And onward drags a labouring breast,
> And topples round the dreary west,
> A looming bastion fringed with fire.   [xv]

The ship has become by now the image of his own state of mind, calm in the first numbness of loss; for the "wild unrest" beginning to break through, the burning cloud in the last light of sunset, with all its suggestion of laboring agony, is a fitter symbol. Noah's ark contained a raven as well as a dove: "Can calm despair and wild unrest / Be tenants of a single breast?" As he characterizes "despair," the perfect synthesis of movement and stillness in the "reflecting" images has given place to something bleaker: "some dead lake / That holds the shadow of a lark / Hung in the shadow of a heaven." When "unrest" succeeds, it is clear what has happened to the "mortal ark" that is the poet's own peace of mind:

> Or has the shock, so harshly given,
> Confused me like the unhappy bark
>
> That strikes by night a craggy shelf,
> And staggers blindly ere she sink? [xvi]

Following this recognition of his own real state, the poet is able to welcome the ship on its arrival and dismiss it again with his blessing in terms that recall his earlier depiction of it; but now the ship is no longer the vessel of Hallam's being or his own, the separation between reality and desire is complete, and no magic or mystery is involved here but human gratitude and goodwill.

> So may whatever tempest mars
> Mid-ocean, spare thee, sacred bark;
> And balmy drops in summer dark
> Slide from the bosom of the stars. [xvii]

In xviii the body is prepared for burial and the poet, seeing that death is death and that no power is available to reverse it, resigns the body to the ground and composes himself to "die not, but endure with pain."

The winter vision stresses not synthesis but separation: cosmic divorce rather than cosmic marriage. The symbol is hollow, or the ideal is hopelessly sundered from life. In Venice you stand between palace and prison and look at towers rotting into the water and the madhouse out in the bay: not the godlike triumph of man, but his corruption and tyranny. The appropriate mode for conveying themes of separation is the Gothic or horrific: the original Winter's Tale, we remember, begins, "There was a man . . . / Dwelt by a churchyard."

Looking-Glass world, entered on a winter afternoon by the little girl who passes through the mirror surface, is dominated by whites and blacks (or reds) and by a set of abstract laws, the rules of chess. Life and dream are not blended here, as they were in Wonderland, but are distinct, though there is some question about which is which and who is the dreamer. Sleep both maintains things as they are and offers an escape from them:

> "Do you hear the snow against the window-panes, Kitty? How nice and soft it sounds! Just as if someone was kissing the window all over outside. I wonder if the snow loves the trees and fields, that it kisses them so gently? And then it covers them up snug, you know, with a white quilt; and perhaps it says 'Go to sleep, darlings, till the summer comes again'. And when they wake up in the summer, Kitty, they dress themselves all in green, and dance about. . . ." [i]

Besides Alice herself, the most important figure in the book is the sleeping Red King, of whose dream all the other characters are figments. It may not be going too far to connect him with Adam's sleep of "four thousand winters"; certainly Alice takes his wife to be "the cause of all the mischief," just as the Queen of Hearts is the villainess of *Wonderland*. If we are right about Adam, then we may note the context in which the Red King is found sleeping: Alice has just left the wood in which child and fawn, unburdened with identities, can be friends, and just after seeing him she witnesses the fratricidal rage of Tweedledum and Tweedledee, learns about "living backwards," and finds herself unexpectedly on the river. Looking-Glass Land in general has a watery aspect, if we are to take seriously the White Knight's fear of sharks and Alice's repeated complaints that she hears too many poems about fish.

Humpty Dumpty, another "fall" figure, begins his fishy poem with:

> In winter, when the fields are white,
> I sing this song for your delight—

which brings us to another aspect of the winter's tale, what Carroll in the prologue poem to *Through the Looking-Glass* calls, from the real Alice's middle name, the "pleasance."[12] Separation can have a positive aspect: while a rude winter rages outside, love, magic, or art draws its cosy circle indoors and calls up within it a re-creation of the lost world of summer. A comparable island of life in a world of death may sometimes be a single figure, like Lucy Gray at the end of Wordsworth's poem, or a group of two, as in Stifter's *Bergkristall* or Mrs. Gaskell's impressive story "The Half-Brothers." In both these last, the supranatural power is that of family affection.[13] Traditionally the establishment of the indoor pleasance belongs to the pastoral praise of friendship,[14] as in a sense it does in *The Blithedale Romance* (ii): "we made a summer of it, in spite of the wild drifts." It may be dedicated to love, like the upstairs rooms of *Hero and Leander* and "The Eve of St. Agnes" or the farmhouse of Dylan Thomas's "A Winter's Tale." Carroll as affectionate spellbinder says of his winter tale-telling,

> The magic words shall hold thee fast:
> Thou shalt not heed the wintry blast.

The fireside circle that shuts the weather out has here replaced the boat on the summer stream, whose seasonable equivalent would be the ark on the wintry flood. The construction of such a protective chamber or vessel is one of the powers of art.

Before leaving a watery world, let us consider the rôle of the ark in our pastoral. Superficially it resembles the palace of art, in offering a retreat from present harsh reality; actually it is more usually its beneficent opposite, representing the carrying over of existence from one kind of life to the next. It is elegiac in that it is the sign of some overwhelming disaster in the past, but it should look also to a new start, being a cradle of life as well as a coffin. Both connotations are suggested in Nabokov's phrase, "the refuge of art."

The Venetian gondola in literature can have both aspects. Clearly in a quite realistic sense, to judge from the goings-on in Browning's "In A Gondola" and Hemingway's Venetian novel, these vessels offer all sorts of chances of getting either stabbed to death or started on one's way towards birth; from Goethe in 1790 on, references to the gondola as coffin or cradle or both are not far to seek. [15] However, that is not the limit of its possible comprehensiveness. Rogers in *Italy*, not a markedly imaginative work, rather mysteriously describes his arrival in Venice by gondola:

> Thither I came, and in a wondrous Ark,
> That, long before we slipped our cable, rang
> As with the voices of all living things.

This suggests the inclusive or encyclopaedic quality the ark shares with the palace of art, though less in its materials than in its passenger list. Describing Venice's immense antiquity among European states, Rogers imagines another ark, possibly with a thought of the Bucentaur, the much-patched and -renewed vessel of the Doges' annual ceremonial marriage with the sea:

> . . . a tempest shook
> All things most held in honour among men,
> All things the giant with the scythe had spared,
> To their foundations, and at once she fell;
> She who had stood yet longer than the last
> Of the Four Kingdoms—who, as in an Ark,
> Had floated down, amid a thousand wrecks,
> Uninjured, from the Old World to the new,
> From the last glimpse of civilized life—to where
> Light shone again, and with the blaze of noon.   ["Venice"]

In our period it is the elegiac and protective aspects of the ark that dominate in literature. The two-ways-facing Noah who looks sadly back at an old world is very reserved in his glances towards a new, like Des Esseintes in our quotations at the end of chapter 6 above. Nostalgia affects also the method of that book, and helps our identification of it as a version of pastoral. It is a feature of pastoral from Virgil through Milton that it early becomes in the detail of its construction the most allusive and scholarly of forms, and our enquiry has suggested that in Romantic adaptations the allusiveness is not absent but disguised. The echo-chamber quality of *A Rebours* makes it one appropriate dead end for the tradition of

"Lycidas," in its palace-of-art fittings but also in the way in which it is put together out of oddments of reading. A comparable though less extreme Alexandrianism (Venetianism?) is evident already in Poe's way of using allusions to add to atmosphere, and in the eclectic existence of the Soul in Tennyson's palace. Earlier works we have seen, and ones closer to pastoral, that consciously employ other literature as part of their essential resources are *Werther,* the novels of Ann Radcliffe, *Mathilda,* and *Sylvie;* in all of these, and in others we shall come to, including *Frankenstein* and *Trilby,* the relation to other literature helps constitute both the pastoral and the elegiac element. And literary echoes are nowhere more vitally constitutive than in depictions of Venice, from *Childe Harold's* catalogue of authors down to Hemingway's *Across the River.* The technique of constitutive allusion can yield very intense effects, ranging from sublimity to pathos or an extreme of decadence. A mildly decadent example in the area of literary criticism, not too remote from either our subject or our approach to it, is Auden's *The Enchafèd Flood.*

Des Esseintes' arks suggest not only something saved from the shipwreck of the past, but also refuge from the present in a synthetic and self-sufficient world not looking towards any future. A more positive function of arks appears in Lewis Carroll, though still with a feeling less of happy landings than of guardedly keeping going. The tale itself in Carroll is constructed as a vessel that preserves even in winter the alchemical secret of the summer days. It is nothing more. It does not keep the author's tone from being elegiac whenever it touches on himself and his own concerns. But it does have an all but magical preservative value, it is a well-shaped urn and a little more than just that. The writer and his Alice are not saved by it from age and separation, but it keeps their happiness fresh for later generations of children to inherit.[16]

The topic of the pleasance built by or exemplifying a power that verges on the magical brings us to the theme of the next chapter. We noted earlier the relation of the palace of art to Eden, whether as re-creation or as demonic parody. A consistent tradition invites us to read "magician" as metaphor for "artist," "poet," from *The Tempest* and "Il Penseroso" down to Shelley, Browning, and Yeats. The work of the good magician or alchemist tends towards the re-creation of Eden, even if only for instants, as when Prospero brings harmony out of disorder and calls up a pastoral vision, or his ancestor the magister of "The Franklin's Tale" does away with the "rokkes blak." A less transcendent figure, again a re-creation of Chaucer's, is Morris's plaintive poet in the "Apology" to *The Earthly Paradise,* telling the last of our winter's tales:

> Folk say, a wizard to a northern king
> At Christmas-tide such wondrous things did show,
> That through one window men beheld the spring,

And through another saw the summer glow,
And through a third the fruited vines a-row,
While still unheard, but in its wonted way,
Piped the drear wind of that December day.

So with this Earthly Paradise it is,
If ye will read aright, and pardon me,
Who strive to build a shadowy isle of bliss
Midmost the beating of the steely sea,
Where tossed about all hearts of men must be;
Whose ravening monsters mighty men shall slay,
Not the poor singer of an empty day.

Ten   The Alchemist

*If the time should ever come when what is now called science,
thus familiarised to men, shall be ready to put on, as it were, a
form of flesh and blood, the Poet will lend his divine spirit to aid
the transfiguration, and will welcome the Being thus produced,
as a dear and genuine inmate of the household of man.*
                                                    —William Wordsworth

*. . . now that I had finished, the beauty of the dream vanished,
and breathless horror and disgust filled my heart.*
                                                    —Mary Shelley

The Tree of Knowledge is not that of Life.
                                                    —Lord Byron

In *Alastor,* the Poet's fatal pursuit of the dream-maiden is only one aspect
of the theme of the quest that pervades the poem's whole conception. The
narrator speaks at the opening of his lifelong pursuit of Nature. He has
watched "in charnels and on coffins," in the hope of "forcing some lone
ghost . . . to render up the tale / Of what we are"; and even in the inter-
change of love,

> Like an inspired and desperate alchymist
> Staking his very life on some dark hope,

he has pursued his search. In various ways he has enjoyed Nature's favor,
but he has never seen unveiled the "inmost sanctuary." The description
of the Poet takes up this theme:

> Nature's most secret steps
> He like her shadow has pursued. . . .

The lament at the end for the Poet returns to the "alchymist":

> O, for Medea's wondrous alchemy,
> Which wheresoe'er it fell made the earth gleam
> With bright flowers, and the wintry boughs exhale
> From vernal blooms fresh fragrance! O, that God,
> Profuse of poisons, would concede the chalice
> Which but one living man has drained, who now,
> Vessel of deathless wrath, a slave that feels

Figure 5. *Illustration to Byron's* Manfred. *From* The Illustrated Byron. *London,*
1854–55.

No proud exemption in the blighting curse
He bears, over the world wanders for ever,
Lone as incarnate death! O, that the dream
Of dark magician in his visioned cave,
Raking the cinders of a crucible
For life and power, even when his fevered hand
Shakes in its last decay, were the true law
Of this so lovely world!

This account of Medea's power to make the old young again links it with
the elixir-of-life aspect of the alchemical quest, and that in turn, as so
often in the mystique of alchemy, with the springtime world of a Golden
Age or Eden. "God profuse of poisons" is the God who lets man taste the
tree of death; and the next "O that" implies the wish, not only that God
would dispense the gift of immortality, but also that man's state could be
such that this was a blessing and not a curse—that the Fall could be
reversed, in the terms of Christian myth. "Lone as incarnate death" links
the Wandering Jew perhaps with the old man of "The Pardoner's Tale"
and by implication with the treasure he speaks of, two-edged like immortality itself. Medea too is a sinister figure, by no means an unequivocal
scatterer of vernal blessings. Shelley's "dark magician," similarly ambiguous, probably has as his immediate source William Godwin's *St. Leon*,
1799, the first of a line that we shall call "alchemical fiction."[1]

Why do these allusions to alchemy appear in *Alastor*? First, the quest of
both the Poet and the narrator, pursuing Nature in order to penetrate her
inmost shrine or wrest her secret from her, resembles the traditional one
of alchemy. Second, Shelley's alchemist has evidently consumed his life
in the quest for more life, and the delicately strung instrument attuned to
every breath of Nature as Muse is the one soonest to be shattered.
Perhaps there lingers in the background the shade of the impetuous
youth who snatched the veil from the image of Isis at Saïs in Schiller's
poem ("Das verschleierte Bild zu Saïs," 1795). In such contexts, you do
not find out that the mystery is either angelic or demonic at its heart; you
simply record the overpowering effect of the revelation, or, if it never
comes, the devastation brought on by the search.

In connection with the Artist we noticed the search for a "treasure,"
usually happiness, and probably in the form of love. The "treasure" of
alchemical fiction is the secret of life, whether the power to create life, to
prolong it, or to control it in others. Love as treasure[2] springs its surprises:
the hero may find he has looked in the wrong place or made the wrong
choice. Knowledge as treasure is usually ironic, and apt to bring destruction instead of fulfillment.

Alchemical fictions on the whole exemplify a simple black-and-white
morality. They do not float in an equivocal atmosphere like that of *Alastor*

and artist-romances generally; their crises are clearly marked and we know exactly where their heroes go wrong. Usually the highest aspirations lead to the greatest possible calamities, because the limitations of human life that the protagonist tries to overcome prove to be after all there for man's protection; therefore the fulfillment of his dreams is less ambiguous than sharply ironic.

Godwin's St. Leon, a French aristocrat ruined by gambling and now living contentedly as a farmer in a Swiss canton, shelters an aged and feeble stranger, who laments his present situation and his loss of past happiness:

> Hated by mankind, hunted from the face of the earth, pursued by every atrocious calumny, without a country, without a roof, without a friend . . .
> [II, i, 9]

Once he was surrounded by his family:

> Where are they now? How has all this happiness been maliciously undermined, and irrevocably destroyed! To look back on it, it seems like the idle fabric of a dream. I awake, and find myself alone! [II, i, 29]

The stranger dies, bequeathing to St. Leon under the seal of secrecy the double power to provide himself with money and to prolong his own life. Secrecy and suspicion then estrange St. Leon's family, and his wife Marguerite, guessing the secret from which all their calamities are proceeding, reproaches him before she dies:

> When I married you, I supposed myself united to a nobleman, a knight and a soldier, a man who would have revolted with disdain from every thing that was poor-spirited and base. . . . At length you have completely reversed the scene. For a soldier, you present me with a projector and a chymist, a cold-blooded mortal, raking in the ashes of a crucible for a selfish and solitary advantage. Here is an end of all genuine dignity, and the truest generosity of soul. You cannot be ingenuous; for all your dealings are secrecy and darkness. You cannot have a friend; for the mortal lives not that can sympathize with your thoughts and emotions. . . . How unhappy the wretch, the monster rather let me say, that is without an equal; that looks through the world, and in the world cannot find a brother; that is endowed with attributes which no living being participates with him; and that is therefore cut off for ever from all cordiality and confidence, can never unbend himself, but lives the solitary, joyless tenant of a prison whose materials are rubies and emeralds! [II, ix, 233–35]

Older, in extremity, St. Leon does once, with what he fears will be his last strength, prepare and drink the rejuvenating potion; but by the end of the novel he has sounded all the hells of solitude and remorse, and understands that with the wretched stranger's secret he has inherited also his fate. Godwin's wanderer does not, like Chaucer's Death or Shelley's

Ginotti (*St. Irvyne*) or Maturin's Melmoth, seek a substitute to bear his curse,[3] but he is nevertheless a prophetic image of what St. Leon will become. Melmoth and Zanoni too experience the dreadful solitude of Flying Dutchman or Wandering Jew. Dreadful again is the stress of the moment when St. Leon hastily and with trembling hands prepares his potion; this scene is reenacted by Bulwer Lytton's evil magician, Margrave, whose soul is dead and who wants to renew physical life at any cost—however, Margrave is too late.[4]

The most famous, and still the most powerful, of alchemical fables is Mary Shelley's *Frankenstein, or the Modern Prometheus*, 1818, whose pivot is that favorite device of Mary's father Godwin, the ironic recognition.[5] The frame of *Frankenstein* is a long letter written by one Captain Walton on the northern seas to his sister Margaret in England. Walton, young and enthusiastic, has embarked on a polar expedition for the sake of scientific discovery. He confides to his sister his longing for a friend, and shortly afterwards rescues from a sledge on the frozen sea the exhausted Frankenstein, in whom he finds just such a one as he would have chosen. Thunder-scarred and dying, Frankenstein still possesses the charm, eloquence, and sensitivity of idealized genius, and he devotes them during his last hours to a recital of his history intended to deter Walton from throwing himself into the fatal pursuit of knowledge.

Frankenstein's own researches have led him to "pursue nature to her hiding-places" and "spend days and nights in vaults and charnel-houses" (iv), following which he is able to create a living man. But beyond its creation he has had no future intention regarding his creature; already as it struggles into life Frankenstein is horrified and flees in terror, abdicating all further responsibility. He never even gives his creature a name, calling him usually "the Being" or "the daemon." Wandering out into the world in vague search of an identity and an education, the Being is everywhere rejected as a monster. His original benevolence turns under this treatment to rancor, and he avenges his wrongs by destroying members of Frankenstein's family. The smiling Swiss valleys of Frankenstein's youth are now exchanged for horrific Swiss icefields, where Frankenstein encounters the Being and hears his bitter reproaches. Hated and feared by man, he has found himself doomed to solitude. This self-revelation induces remorse and compassion in Frankenstein, who agrees to make him a female counterpart on the understanding that both will leave the haunts of man forever. Frankenstein retires to a remote spot in the Orkney Islands to carry out this project; but having nearly finished, he changes his mind and undoes his work. The Being in a renewed outburst of vengeance then strangles, first Frankenstein's bosom friend Henry Clerval, then Elizabeth, his adoptive sister and his bride. From now on Frankenstein has but one object in life, his creature's destruction, and from now on the author handles him ironically: following Elizabeth's death he undergoes a long illness, and he arises from it as the original demon scientist. He pursues the Being over the face of the earth, and always when his strength is giving out he finds indications of direction and fresh supplies of food left mysteriously in his path. He assumes these are sent by his murdered loved ones to help him in his task of vengeance;[6] but in fact, and more appropriately, they are left by the Being, who watches over him with almost motherly care. The chase continues into the dreary North, where Frankenstein is picked up by Walton. Having concluded his story, he dies; whereupon the Being comes and laments over him, "the select specimen of all that is worthy of love and admiration among men," before departing to put a fiery end to his miserable existence.

We briefly noted the shift of locale in Frankenstein's story, from idyllic scenes to horrific ones; we shall say more later about the place of scenes watery or wintry. While the third edition's frontispiece shows the creation of the Being, a title page vignette shows Frankenstein parting from a dirndl-clad Elizabeth at a flower-surrounded rural door, with the world very evidently all before him.

A single phrase will start us on a brief detour through magicians' houses. Like il Penseroso in his "high lonely tower," Frankenstein carries on his researches "in a solitary chamber . . . at the top of the house" (iv). In the 1931 movie *Frankenstein* this has become a stone tower; the special fittings of the laboratory at its top include a roof hinged to open so that the swathed figure on the operating table can be raised into the heart of an electrical storm, since animation by fire is the filmmakers' not unreasonable understanding of "The Modern Prometheus." Originally in mythology, Prometheus's creation of man and his theft of fire are quite separate stories. They come together in late classical traditions used in turn by Shakespeare and Byron, and presumably supplying the English phrase "spark of life" (cf. *Frankenstein*, opening of iv in 1st ed., v in 3d). However, for Mary Shelley, Victor Frankenstein's Prometheanism consists, first, in his playing the creator-god and, second, in his realization of both sin and punishment. If it was an electrical phenomenon that first led him in the direction of scientific enquiry, that is entirely in line with the contemporary speculations mentioned in the 1831 preface.

In later films, in a way that chronologically telescopes other developments we have mentioned, the attic and what is above it lose prominence to cellar and downward stair. *Frankenstein*'s successor *The Bride of Frankenstein*, 1935, begins with the monster emerging from the cellar; the tower has been burned down, but he has been preserved by a pool of water underneath. Later versions continue to make play with the cellars of the building: they contain pits of sulphur or blocks of ice, or they are connected with caverns running in from the sea (a detail likely borrowed from George Reynolds's *Varney the Vampire,* 1849). The house reappears in the (otherwise dismal) last of the Universal series, *Abbott and Costello Meet Frankenstein,* 1948, with a scene which shows how thoroughly accustomed its public has become to Castle Frankenstein's leading down to a watery underworld. The two comics are searching the house for their friend Count Dracula. The fat one (Costello) opens a door: one horrified glance shows him a dank downward stairway leading to a stone jetty where a boat sits on dark waters: hastily closing the door, he replies to his thin colleague's query, "Broom closet." Other horror movies—*Murders in the Rue Morgue,* 1932; *White Zombie,* 1932; *Evil of Frankenstein,* Hammer, 1964—show cellars with trapdoors over surging waters where the demon experimenter, more hardened than the young idealist in the attic, can dispose of failed experiments. Older moviegoers will remember (who could forget?) the place of underworld waters in *The Phantom of the Opera,* 1925, or *Metropolis,* 1926. Just as with the Romantic Venice that links fire and water, with these structures raised or inhabited by evil magicians we are once more in the presence of a version of the house of life, embodying the order of the elements.

Frankenstein can, undoubtedly, be read as a parable about the fatality of impious aspirations, and *St. Leon* along with it. Alchemical fiction is after all an offshoot of the line that runs from the Faust legend down through *Vathek, The Monk, Zofloya, Melmoth the Wanderer,* and *Confessions of a Justified Sinner,* where extraordinary powers come explicitly from the devil and at the price of one's soul; and the alchemist-hero's decision to receive or use his secret can in itself constitute a temptation and fall. This becomes clearer in his modern embodiments, where the hero is less the adept and occultist student and more the doctor or scientist.

Usually the discoverer of the alchemical secret thinks he is conferring the greatest possible benefit on those close to him and mankind at large, only to find that he has brought down on them a scourge. The ironic fulfillment of his hopes is consistent all the way down the tradition through Hawthorne's "The Birthmark" and Stevenson's *Dr. Jekyll and Mr. Hyde* to Huxley's *After Many a Summer,* 1939, and Siodmak's *Donovan's Brain,* 1942. This last, a straightforward and very standard piece of science fiction, recounts the history of a monomaniac doctor in a super-laboratory in the Mexican desert who manages to keep alive a particularly powerful brain after its owner's decease, and through telepathy to follow its processes. He supposes that with enriched feeding and unlimited time for meditation, it will devote itself to all the great questions of life and perhaps find the answers. Instead, it is completely bound up in the sordid details of its earthly career, and succeeds in forcing the doctor out of his role of Olympian spectator; he becomes its agent in all manner of messy errands, climaxing in murder. He is saved only when his laboratory is wrecked and the brain destroyed.

Though something of an idealist in his belief in science, in everything else the doctor of *Donovan's Brain* is a cynic and skeptic, like the rationalistic young doctor of Bulwer Lytton's *Strange Story*. They both learn that there is such a thing as impiety. The alchemist figure usually either denies God or arrogates to himself powers that are God's alone; where he is not presented as directly in rivalry with God, he may aim at a knowledge of and manipulating control over other lives that is felt to be indecent and unforgivable. Further, the alchemist once he has acquired special powers is in bondage to them, like any old-fashioned magician, and usually can free himself only by a renunciation like Prospero's, burning his books or smashing his instruments. Where the alchemist is a doctor or scientist, he may be enslaved to an elixir that has unpredictable or undesirable side effects, or to the repeated necessity of murder.

More prominent still in *Frankenstein* than the theme of impious desires is that of solitude and the search for love and friendship. Several apparently digressive incidents are brought in to emphasize it, but the narrative structure of tale within tale, more complex than that of *Alastor*, is surely sufficient: to put it briefly, Walton, who seeks a friend and has a sister, finds Frankenstein, who had a friend and a sister-bride but has lost both through the Being, who in turn longs for a friend and demands a sister-bride. Moreover, this theme is brought out early in Walton's references to "The Ancient Mariner"—it is the latter's solitude, not his guilt, that is stressed. Nor is it exactly guilt from which Frankenstein suffers: "I felt as if I had committed some great crime, the consciousness of which haunted me. I was guiltless, but I had indeed drawn down a horrible curse on my head, as mortal as that of crime" (III.ii; xix). The theme of solitude is prominent in alchemical fiction; it is felt at its most acute by the possessor of endless life. St. Leon, Melmoth, and Zanoni all descant on the hopelessness of human love, attaching you to the frail flower, if you happen to be the eternal rock.[7]

Walton, seeking a friend, finds Frankenstein, who appears to him a god among men—and yet Frankenstein has the rôle of the old adept in *St. Leon*, the old gambler in Hoffmann's "Spielerglück,"[8] the old dandy in *Death in Venice*. He is the prophetic double, the Satan to Walton's Adam: this is what Walton may become if he pursues his passion for discovery to the bitter end. This framing theme is not developed, as circumstances in the end force Walton to give up his mission and return home; perhaps vicariously his experience is complete.

Frankenstein has grown up with two inseparable companions, his friend Henry Clerval and Elizabeth, the cousin or adoptive "more than sister" (first and third editions respectively) brought up with him. He allows his researches to keep him away from these and from his family, and when he returns to them he is divided from them by his horrible knowledge. Both then fall victim to the rancor of the Being. A perfect harmony formerly existed among the interests and temperaments of the three. Elizabeth, besides being the ideally sympathetic companion, shares with Frankenstein the same filial ties and affections. Clerval's name has the "happy valley" associations appropriate to a romance hero's youth; and in his ardor and eagerness the altered Frankenstein recognizes "the image of my former self" (III.ii; xix).[9] Elizabeth and Clerval appear to him later, with the Being's other victims, in dreams that strengthen his desire for vengeance.

The Being too finds his greatest calamity in being alone. He considers his creator as his natural protector:

> I am thy creature, and I will be even mild and docile to my natural lord and king, if thou wilt also perform thy part, the which thou owest me. Oh, Frankenstein, be not equitable to every other, and trample upon me alone, to whom thy justice, and even thy clemency and affection, is most due. Remember that I am thy creature. I ought to be thy Adam, but I am rather the fallen angel whom thou drivest from joy for no misdeed. Everywhere I see bliss, from which I alone am irrevocably excluded. I was benevolent and good; misery made me a fiend. Make me happy and I shall again be virtuous.
> [II.ii; x]

His appeal is that Frankenstein should at least imitate the creator-God and make him a companion: "My evil passions will have fled, for I shall meet with sympathy!" (II.ix; xvii). It is when Frankenstein finally refuses that the Being destroys Clerval and Elizabeth, the latter on her wedding night.

Behind the action of *Frankenstein* loom the outlines of *Paradise Lost*, far from indistinct. Both Frankenstein and the Being continually compare themselves in its phrases to Adam and to Satan, in respect of infinite happiness lost and endless misery gained. On the sea of ice, Frankenstein is reproached by the Being somewhat in the terms in which Milton's Adam accuses his creator (X.743–45), as quoted on *Frankenstein*'s title page:

> Did I request thee, Maker, from my clay
> To mould me man? Did I solicit thee
> From darkness to promote me?—

The alternation of settings suggests the same model: from enclosing pastoral scenes to tremendous perspectives of icefields, North Sea, and the desolate regions approaching the Pole. Storms mark points of crisis, and calamity is imaged consistently as storm, torrent, flood. Two Romantic versions of the Fall also play their part—besides "The Ancient Mariner," there is *Werther*, to whose attentive readers the Being belongs. The world of *Werther* is suggested in the alteration of the Being's character and outlook from benevolence to savagery,[10] and more particularly in the scenes near the end where Frankenstein pursuing through the desert peoples it in his dreams with phantoms of memory and desire.

The use of water is consistent with what we have seen elsewhere. Following an idyllic boat ride down the Rhine, Clerval is murdered on or beside the northern sea, close to the bleak spot in the Orkneys where Frankenstein has been working, and it is after being almost swallowed down by the sea himself that Frankenstein is led to his body. After his wedding, Frankenstein spends his last happy hours with Elizabeth being rowed along on the Lake of Geneva to Evian, which is to be their first stopping place. As they arrive a storm arises, and during the night the monster appears, strangles Elizabeth, and swims away in the lake.

The original tragic separation of the book is that between the Being and his creator. Frankenstein has in fact produced a creature as humane and idealistic as himself. Each is embittered by his experience and becomes a lonely destroyer, but the monster both suffers more and seems to retain more real magnanimity, so that by the end of the book he has almost become the hero, with the author's permission though not her full cooperation.[11] Frankenstein and the Being should have been friends, like the unfallen Adam and his creator in *Paradise Lost;* they are inseparably connected, for better or for worse. In the words of Shelley's poem recalled in the monster's speech above:

> Thine own soul still is true to thee,
> But changed to a foul fiend through misery.[12]

In the encounter on the sea of ice, the Being declares to Frankenstein that they are bound together "by ties only dissoluble by the annihilation of one of us"; and it becomes clearer as the action proceeds that the plot will require the practically simultaneous annihilation of both.

Together they constitute one of those Gothic fatal pairs between whom the potentiality of love has turned to mutual hate and who can no more pursue separate and independent destinies than Siamese twins—who necessarily suggest a man and his own darker side, shadow or Specter. The relations of such a pair are not always fully worked out in the plots where they appear, but still we know them by their desperate utterances or reflections; Maturin gives a fair specimen of the rhetoric:[13]

> "Our situation has happened to unite very opposite characters in the same adventure, but it is an union inevitable and *inseparable.* Your destiny is now bound to mine by a tie which no human force can break,—we part no more for ever.... We must pass life in each watching every breath the other draws, every glance the other gives,—in dreading sleep as an involuntary betrayer, and watching the broken murmurs of each other's restless dreams. We may hate each other, torment each other,—worst of all, we may be weary of each other, (for hatred itself would be a relief, compared to the tedium of our inseparability), but separate we must never."

That is the parricide monk's address to Monçada in *Melmoth the Wanderer* (viii), and immediately thereafter follows the account of lovers imprisoned together whose relations deteriorate to the point of cannibalism. We shall encounter other such fatal relations with shadow-selves in dealing with the Avenger. For *Frankenstein,* the point is that the hero fails to recognize in his creation, because of its outward ugliness,[14] his own image, with his best potentialities as well as his worst, and that the consequences of his failure develop until the Being has become a fiend and his creator if anything a worse one, whatever outward charm he may retain. If this is not completely explicit in the book, it is the feature seized on and developed all the way down the line of its progeny.

Frankenstein's equivocal creation, combining fearsomeness and pathos, belongs to a type we may call, borrowing a phrase from Archibald Lampman, "the animal man." Its historical connections are with the homunculus, or artificial man, of alchemy and the Golem of Jewish legend. A scholar of great sanctity could animate a man made of clay by placing in its mouth an amulet bearing the Name of God; it would then obey its master's orders until the Sabbath, when the amulet would be taken from its mouth and it would rest according to the commandment like any other servant. Once the Great Rabbi Loew of Prague, who had made a Golem, forgot to release it on the Sabbath, whereupon it went berserk and tore up everything it could reach.

The word *Golem* is found anciently only in Psalms 139:16, where it appears to mean the "unformed substance" of a man before God shapes him into an individual. Thus the creation of such a being, like the alchemical *opus,* is specifically an imitation of one of the acts of God; hence, as with alchemy, the stress on the purity of the operator. The tale of the Golem may be behind the type of the magician's clod-servant in drama, Wagner or Miles (*Dr. Faustus, Friar Bacon and Friar Bungay*).

With this tradition we can associate also tales of artificial innocents, from Kaspar Hauser to modern feral children like Mowgli and Tarzan (and perhaps Herbert Read's Green Child), and some recent novels featuring the simian as pastoral swain.[15] Also, of course, there is Caliban. Caliban adapts himself especially easily to the Romantic compounding of creative and destructive, divine and demonic, in one skin. In *The Tempest,* after *Paradise Lost, Werther,* and "The Ancient Mariner" the fourth of the works whose shadows noticeably fall on *Frankenstein,* Ariel is the higher being, but by virtue of his perfections the less humanly complete one: he is all but sexless, doesn't dream, and could never by any stretch of the imagination "seek for grace."[16] The animal man is in our context to the rule of moral order what the romantically dizzying abyss or stormy sea is to a landscape of pastoral calm. However, the fascination of the type, and of its counterpart to which we shall come, the animal woman, rests in the pathos and melancholy that are inseparable from it; and this is an inheritance, partly from the poetic speech of Caliban, with its monosyllabic moonstruck directness, and partly from the sense of glory lost with which Milton invests his savages in the context of Adam's fall (X.1116).

The question about the unsocialized being is what "nature" in him will prove to be, an influence for harmony or for disorder. In our tradition, the type inspires terror by his appearance but has a pronounced streak of benevolence, thus in his primary endowment resembling less Shakespeare's and Milton's "natural man" than Rousseau's.

Alchemists and scientists with bestial attendants include Frollo and his monster, the Hunchback of Notre-Dame; Hawthorne's Aylmer and Aminadab in "The Birthmark"; the hero of *Donovan's Brain* and his assistant, an older doctor brutalized by alcohol, despised for his sodden idealism through the first part of the book but proving victim-savior at the end; and we can add the comic book characters Mandrake the Magician and Lothar. Together the couple represent a paradigm of intellect and instinct, where even the highest human powers rest on the submissiveness of a thing of darkness. We can recall too the relation of Caligari and his somnambulist Cesare, and the baiting of heart by head in Mann's "Mario und der Zauberer" (Mario and the Magician). Sadistic doctor and beast-man appear together in *Woyzeck*. The pair may suggest the opposition of soul and body, but only if both are allowed to be ambiguous quantities with the powers to seduce and save equally apportioned; if anything the balance is in favor of the lower, darker element as the more "human."

The animal man, in a full-length account like *The Hunchback of Notre-Dame* or *The Marble Faun*, tends to languish or die self-immolated: his death is a triumph, because by it he proves himself after all human. From Caliban on, animal men recommend themselves by a love of music. So does Sir Oran Haut-ton, Peacock's gentlemanly orangutan in *Melincourt*. The "Phantom of the Opera," Erik, like Quasimodo was born a monster, but is also himself the magician, his palace of wonders being the Paris Opera-House. Like his original Eros, or Apuleius's Cupid—one more element in our tradition—Erik is both beast and god, his divine trait being his musical genius. He is something also of a Pluto, to whose underworld the bright maiden Christine has pledged herself to return.[17] At length Erik renounces his powers and the maiden, and dies like Beauty's Beast of a broken heart. Magician and animal man are combined differently in Dracula, who can take bestial forms and has kept himself alive for centuries on human blood, and differently again in the showman of Fellini's film *La Strada*, whose female companion is his unrecognized soulmate, abused and dying.

The Alchemist's soulmate, with those of Artist and Avenger, is apt to fade away like Echo from neglect. This is true in comparatively realistic accounts, like *St. Leon* and Balzac's *La Recherche de l'absolu*, where beloved wives fall victim to the scandal or poverty brought on by their spouses' arts. In *Donovan's Brain* the hero's love-life matches the surrounding desert in bleakness. He married his wife for her money, on which he has equipped his laboratory and is continuing his researches; at the opening of the story she is wasting away; the effect of the climate on her is "withering," "desiccating," she is thin, her eyes are dull, she drugs herself in order to sleep, about the house she leads an unnoticed "shadowy" existence, and her husband has "not talked to her for weeks": all this on page 7. When he is released from his obsession and his laboratory burned down, they start life anew elsewhere and she is saved. Other demon scientists bring their wives under the knife; the most notable example is Hawthorne's Aylmer, the idealistic scientist and aesthete who successfully removes his wife's birthmark but at the cost of her life.[18] The point here is the same as that of the eternal-life novels: since the fall, imperfection is the mark of human life, and to try to eradicate it is impious and even destructive.[19]

The alchemist figure, beginning historically with magic, soon becomes the mad or demonic scientist. Other figures not on the same line of development can be related to it. First, the real magus, Bulwer Lytton's Zanoni or the Lindhorst of Hoffmann's "Der goldene Topf" (The Golden Pot); then the benevolent mystifiers of *Wilhelm Meister*, Jarno and the Abbé. Then the Cagliostro-type trickster, lighthearted in Raffles or the Scarlet Pimpernel, more somber in Schiller's Armenian, Brockden Brown's Carwin (*Wieland*), and the Phantom of the Opera. This type's devices include all the legerdemain of rigged séances, especially ventriloquism, and his passion for mystification is second only to his love of power. He is a juggler or Comus, and something of his makeup goes into Goethe's Mephistopheles and the Devil of the Faustian romances mentioned earlier. Superficially resembling the magus is the cold observer of human life or experimenter with it, like Wilde's Lord Henry Wotton, whose pupil, Dorian Gray, imitates Des Esseintes in turning a young man deliberately into a criminal; all three parody the attitudes of aesthetic appreciation in savoring the painful thrills of other people's nerves. Hawthorne has a large range of such characters, from the harmless but contemptible Coverdale to the sinister Rappaccini and diabolical Chillingworth. At his worst, this type becomes a figure closely resembling the Devil: the abominable showman (Frye's term), in Westermarck (*Blithedale Romance*), Svengali, and Thomas Mann's hypnotist-magician Cipolla (cf. the hypnotist in Fellini's *Nights of Cabiria*). This figure blends science with art; one part of his operation is carried out in the glittering world of illusion, in theater, opera, or circus, the other somewhere in the surrounding darkness.

As hypnotist or showman, the alchemist may have with him, rather than the dying wife shut out of the laboratory, a figure so to speak shut in—the dummy-woman who speaks or sings to order, like Gelsomina in *La Strada*. Du Maurier's Trilby and Hawthorne's Priscilla are the most familiar dummy-women; Hoffmann's Olympia ("Der Sandmann"), Gogol's Katherine ("The Terrible Vengeance"), and Wagner's Kundry (attached to Klingsor in *Parzifal*) belong at least partly with them. These are all recognizable variations on the soulmate as Echo.

The thing everybody knows about *Trilby*, 1894, the heroine's relation with Svengali, takes up very little space in the book, whose connections are less obviously with melodramatic romance than with prose idylls like *Werther* and *Sylvie*, which are more lyrical than narrative. Mostly it dwells with nostalgic affection on the life of art students in Paris in the 1850s, and the atmosphere it effectively builds up is largely created out of allusions to French poetry, folksongs, and student songs. The most oft-repeated of all its quotations, however, is in English: "Oh don't you remember sweet Alice, Ben Bolt?" which as Trilby's one song in the early days has a thematic place in the book. "Sweet Alice" is a kind of poor man's Lucy, a passive virgin dying young, and Du Maurier exploits its vulgarity together with its pathos. Trilby is the book's elegiac maiden; she does not die till the end, when everyone is somewhat older than at the opening, but in the later part of her career she is both not herself and separated from her friends and early lover. She was the embodiment of the spirit of those youthful days in Paris, and regret for her blends with regret for a mood, a setting, a way of life, all lost. She dies actually not by drowning but in a comfortable room and of a kind of exhaustion; but the chapter describing her last days is epigraphed with Shelley's lines:

> The moon made thy lips pale, beloved,
> The wind made thy bosom chill;
> The night did shed
> On thy dear head
> Its frozen dew, and thou didst lie
> Where the bitter breath of the naked sky
> Might visit thee at will.

Svengali earlier teases Trilby by saying that she will be found dead (presumably in the Seine) and laid out in the Morgue:

> "And over the middle of you will be a little leather apron, and over your head a little brass tap, and all day long and all night the cold water shall trickle, trickle, trickle all the way down your beautiful white feet till they turn green, and your poor, damp, draggled, muddy rags will hang above you from the ceiling for your friends to know you by; drip, drip, drip! But you will have no friends. . . ."   [ii, 86]

Svengali, the sadistic and sordid genius-musician, is an artist of the most sinister kind. He discovers his power over Trilby when he finds he can cure her headaches by hypnotism. She has a marvellous voice but is absolutely tone-deaf; Svengali, after marrying her, trains her voice and makes her a superb singer, though only under hypnosis. Trilby falls under his spell when in flight from her lover, Little Billee, a painter also with genius, whose mother has made Trilby promise to give him up, seeing that, though Trilby like Tess is "a pure woman," she too lacks of all the virtues just "virtue."[20]

Little Billee seems an odd choice of hero for his author, who loves forthright titans like Trilby and Little Billee's friend Taffy Wynne. He is small, frail, girlishly beautiful, and a trifle self-absorbed; like Trilby he will die young. He is the boyish fourth Musketeer whom his friends at once protect and treat as a mascot, or the youngest crew member of the Thackeray ballad he is named from. Svengali is perhaps not only his opposite and rival, the dark artist (with hints of Paganini) to his bright one, but his alter ego. Svengali is a Jew, and Little Billee has Jewish blood. Little Billee when Trilby leaves is attacked by brain fever and recovers to find his heart is cold, and his affections return only years later, shortly before the end; thus the period of his self-estrangement coincides roughly with that of Svengali's ascendancy over Trilby. Little Billee has "for the singing woman an absolute worship" (ii, 47), while Svengali creates one. The obvious relation is that of contrast: while Svengali is practicing "playing on" Trilby like a musical instrument, Little Billee has become a sort of fashionable Platonic ladies' man compared by his author to a collector of fiddles who never plays them:

> He may have a whole gallery of fiddles in this innocent way—a harem!—and yet not know a single note of music, or even care to hear one. He will dust them and stroke them and take them down and try to put them in tune— pizzicato!—and put them back again, and call them ever such sweet little pet exotic names: viol, viola, viola d'amore, viol di gamba, violino mio! and breathe his little troubles into them, and they will give back inaudible little murmurs in sympathetic response, like a damp Aeolian harp; but he will never draw a bow across the strings, nor wake a single chord—or discord!
> [v, 180]

Trilby is thus an Aeolian-harp woman, a dummy-woman,[21] and the lost soulmate of a catastrophic first love; she is also a siren, of the involuntary kind.

> Tuneless and insane,[22] she was more of a siren than ever—a quite unconscious siren—without any guile, who appealed to the heart all the more directly and irresistibly that she could no longer stir the passions. [vii, 310]

She is not the "wanton and perilous siren" (viii, 323: cf. ii, 47; vii, 285) that Little Billee's mother chooses to think her. This may be some of the point of the otherwise obsessive insistence on the beauty, strength, and size of

Figure 6. *Author's illustration from Du Maurier's* Trilby, *1894: "Platonic Love."*
Photo courtesy Metropolitan Toronto Library Board.

her nonpareil feet—we are not to forget that she has them. Her origins, however, are distinctly damp. Her great-grandfather was a boatman on Loch Ness,[23] her father was a drunkard, and her mother a barmaid "in the Rue du Paradis Poissonière (a very fishy paradise indeed)," and Trilby herself before becoming an artists' model was a washerwoman.

Trilby as wife–victim–creation of the demon Svengali constitutes a genuinely "popular" image, with an air of having emerged full-blown from the storehouse of folk memory. So indeed it may be. Blended with the lamented maiden-spirit of a lost happy landscape familiar from pastoral elegy and forms descended from it, we recognize a type whose origins are different, though no less remote from "real life." The magician's dummy is apt to have the look of Spenser's martyred Amoret in the clutches of Busyrane—"like a dreary Spright / Cald by strong charms out of eternall night"; and her relation to the magician is usually more daughterly than wifely.

For in fact the magician and the passive maiden are originally father and daughter. They appear under their proper names in Flaubert's *La Tentation de Saint-Antoine,* as the showman Simon Magus and his companion Ennoia-Helena. The core of his legend is the same Simon whom the apostle Philip met in Samaria, working wonders and claiming divinity (Acts 9 : 11). According to the Church Fathers who regarded him as the first of the Gnostic heretics, Simon claimed to be

> a power of God greater than the Creator, that stands, stood and shall stand androgynous and perfect in the heavens. From it came forth a female power called Ennoia or Thought [in one source, Sophia], the universal mother through whom he generated the angels and archangels. These in turn created the world, and out of envy they detained her and dragged her down from the highest heavens into the cosmos. She suffered all manner of abuse from them to keep her from returning to her Father, and she was even enclosed in human flesh and migrated for centuries as from vessel to vessel into different female bodies. And since all the cosmic Powers contended for her possession, strife and warfare raged among the nations wherever she appeared. Thus she was also that Helena for whom the Trojan War was fought, and thus the Greeks and Trojans contending for her beheld a phantasm of the truth; but of herself as she is, the dweller with the first and only God, they were wholly ignorant. Migrating from body to body and suffering abuse in each, she at length became a whore in a brothel; and this is the "lost sheep" whom Simon had descended to redeem. He said further that he was that man who was said to have suffered in Judaea, but he did not suffer; and that whoever believed in him and his Helena should be saved.

This remarkable story,[24] earlier than that of the Primal Man quoted in chapter 5 above, is like it an account of how soul, this time a female principle, first got mixed up with matter; both belong to the Gnostic mythology of descent and separation, alienation and exile, that grew up in the same cultural milieu, headily syncretistic, as early Christianity and Greek and Latin romance. Such myths could be, and were, formed around the life of Christ or the story of the Prodigal Son; this one, like that of the "Poimandres," has a classical core, in the Helen of extra-Homeric tradition—the Epic Cycle Helena who is a Pandora-like fatal beauty begotten by Zeus on an unwilling Nemesis expressly to help reduce the numbers of men who crowd the broad-bosomed Earth, and the story reported by Herodotus and made the basis of his *Helena* by Euripides, that Helen never went to Troy at all, her place being taken by an airy phantom. Plato (*Republic* ix.586c) paves the way for Simon by comparing the pursuit by the ignorant of false and deluding pleasures to the fighting for the phantom Helena (*eidolon*—cf. "Idole" above, pp. 165 and 166) at Troy. While the classical phantom Helena joins with other such shadowy figures, the phantom Eurydice with whom Orpheus was beguiled (Plato, *Symposium* 179d), Ixion's cloud-woman Nephele, and later Spenser's false Florimell, to help form the fleeing nymph of Romantic nympholepsy, Simon Magus becomes Faust,[25] whether or not attended by Helen, and the Ennoia becomes that fatal lady of the late nineteenth century who has usually been Helen of Troy, Mary Queen of Scots, and perhaps another Mary as well, and who troubles men's souls wherever she appears: goddess, victim, and lure.[26]

In his relation with his female companion, the magician's temptation may be to appear as a rival to her lovers, or at least like Prospero to make things hard for them: to forget that she belongs to a younger generation. Rappaccini and Chillingworth can be regarded in this light, like Hugo's Frollo; and Trilby becomes attached to Svengali only in default of Little Billee. The Phantom of the Opera tries to keep Christine from her lover. There is a comparable triangle in Dostoevsky's story "The Landlady." In most such cases we sense an aura, not merely of the violation of youth by age, but of something like the crossing of the incest barrier. This is suggested by, for example, the way in which Erik takes over from Christine's relation with her father before offering himself as a lover, and is explicit in Gogol's "The Terrible Vengeance," whose old magician murders his son-in-law and eventually also his daughter when she refuses intimacies with him. In the original story, of course, the Ennoia is both Simon's daughter and his wife, a privilege allowed the gods; but to Christendom Simon is an evil figure, parodying (like Milton's Satan with Sin) the relation of Christ with his Church, and in his nineteenth-century revival he is not the rescuer of the lady of sorrows but her tormentor and the instigator of her degradation. However, the creator relation is often preserved, in figures like Svengali and Erik and Dickens's Mr. Jasper, where the older man is teacher (usually music teacher) as well as perse-

Figure 7. *Title engraving by Doré for Balzac's* Les Contes drolatiques, *1855.*

cutor. In one such novel I recall, of about the 1930s, the gloomy, misanthropic trainer and ex-lover of a famous young actress conducts with her a farewell dialogue in words borrowed from Prospero's exposition of the past to Miranda. A more distinctly Gothic configuration is that of *Sunset Boulevard*, where the ex-director, ex-husband (Erich von Stroheim) of a narcissistic-vampiric ex-star (Gloria Swanson) after she has committed murder "directs" her from the foot of the grand staircase as she somnambulistically descends to face newsmen and police.[27]

The magician's female dummy regularly represents not, like the animal man, the force and warmth of instinct, but something more subtle and harder to describe, a sensitivity or intuition. She is a kind of human divining rod; as his instrument, she can be dispatched to record impressions to which he is impervious. Or, she may be an unconscious decoy, her charm used to ensnare for his dark purposes, like Olympia in *Tales of Hoffmann*. She is his complement, necessary if his powers are to be complete; but their relation is a demonic one in that she is exploited and abused, as in a rape by the flesh on the spirit. In the idyllic relationships of *The Tempest*, Miranda is in no sense exploited by her father and at last marries with his blessing; on a more exalted level, the father she reveres and the young man she can freely marry would be different aspects of the same figure: that figure belongs to none of our romances but to pure myth, and is the unfallen Simon.

The evil magician regularly has his victim, whether male or female. Conversely the good magician regularly shows a capacity for self-denial or self-sacrifice clearly intended by his author to verge on the Christlike, as at the end of *Zanoni*. In the evil magician, this may be parodied in his claim that he suffers while exercising his magic (Mann's Cipolla), or takes another's pain on himself (Svengali curing Trilby's headaches). However, one of his victims may develop the contrasting power of conscious self-sacrifice and thereby both cancel out the effects of his wickedness and help place him in his proper light as a fiend. Most likely the willing victim will be the animal man. Frankenstein's Being develops a certain air of conscious scapegoat, while the debased and despised older doctor of *Donovan's Brain*, Schramm,[28] gives his life to destroy the malignant brain and save his obsessed friend.

The love triangle involving magician, maiden, and rival is obvious in *Trilby*, as in "The Terrible Vengeance," *Parzifal*, and *The Phantom of the Opera*. It belongs to the structure of *The Hunchback of Notre-Dame* in Frollo's passion for La Esmeralda, who loves only her handsome Phoebus. The latter's name recalls the convenient terms of Eino Railo in his discussion of the Gothic novel: "bright young hero," "bright young heroine," as opposed to the darker, older single figures who are apt to dominate the action. We have noted several heroines whose names indicate brightness;

and the relation of magician-showman to the brooding owners of Gothic castles is obviously close. One link is the atmosphere in both kinds of story: even where Gothic villain or magician does not present himself as a lover, we catch strong erotic overtones. Ann Radcliffe's persecuted heroines are not threatened with rape, but that is the circumstance to which their shrinking and tingling sensibilities continually point. Pamela is after all a bourgeois Psyche or Amoret; *The Mysteries of Udolpho* brings the theme back from Richardson's domestic context, and one of *Udolpho*'s direct descendants, Sheridan Le Fanu's *Uncle Silas,* has been produced as a film (with James Mason and Jean Simmons) in which the heroine not only clears Uncle Silas's reputation but sends her young man and would-be rescuer packing and settles down with Uncle. This is a drastic alteration of the novel, but not out of keeping with the sadomasochistic overtones of its entire line. For evidence that the situation of the young woman on her own in a large unfamiliar house belonging to a man not decrepit and of powerful social position is regularly understood as an erotic one, consider *Jane Eyre,* modern readings of *The Turn of the Screw,* and Margaret Atwood's knowledgeable parody of the "modern Gothics" in *Lady Oracle,* 1976.

Apart from Shelley's bringing them together in *Alastor,* what are the connections between Alchemist and Artist? Certain elements appear in common with both: the artist is apt to live in a recognizable palace of art, the magician to have built one, or to make use of a reasonable substitute like stage or circus tent. The artist is apt to be fascinated by a singing woman or siren as Muse, source of inspiration; for the magician, a similarly mantic figure may represent a source of knowledge or power. Artist or aesthete is combined with magician or man of science in many figures: Frankenstein (in Walton's description), Hawthorne's Aylmer, Svengali, the "Phantom" Erik, Cipolla. Several well-known detectives combine the rôles of magician and artist or aesthete. Poe's Dupin is as much a cloistered dreamer as any other Poe hero;[29] Sherlock Holmes in many ways resembles him[30] and is moreover an accomplished violinist; Wilkie Collins's Cuff is a passionate rose-grower (less the aesthete accordingly than Nero Wolfe, who grows orchids); Peter Wimsey among other displays of talent sings and pulls bell-ropes; and Philip Trent is a successful painter. The contrast between Cuff's official and unofficial pursuits amounts to a double-life theme,[31] balanced by the double life of *The Moonstone*'s villain, the equivocal Mr. Ablewhite. Perhaps it is owing to the pressure of a magical background that "The Purloined Letter," *The Moonstone, Trent's Last Case,* and numerous others all involve Amorets, women in mental bondage. Holmes and Dupin are both close to Gothic in having doubles. Holmes has two—one benevolent, his brother Mycroft who is like him but with less physical activity and even greater penetration, and his evil opposite Professor Moriarty, with powers equal to his own and absolutely without moral sense, an artist in crime. Dupin has an evil double in "the Minister D—," a poet and mathematician[32] whose powers precisely match those of Dupin, and moreover "that *monstrum horrendum*, an unprincipled man of genius": Dupin's message to him— "un dessein si funeste, / S'il n'est digne d'Atrée, est digne de Thyeste"—is not the first hint that the two are in one or another sense brothers.[33] It is interesting that with all its heightened realism of detail and supposed challenge to our capacity for observation, the early detective story is often so close to sheer romance.[34]

Another combination of artistic and alchemistic powers is as follows: while in our scheme the artist's concern is with beauty and the magician-scientist's with truth, in some contexts the artist's operations too yield a "truth" hidden from all but him, as in Hawthorne's story "The Prophetic Pictures" and the incident of Piero di Cosimo's oil sketch of Tito and his foster father in *Romola* (xxviii).[35] A still more positive version of this figure is the poet of Browning's "How It Strikes a Contemporary"—"spy," "recording chief-inquisitor," and "Corregidor," who writes his reports to God. The narrator of *The Blithedale Romance,* Miles Coverdale, is a poet, as certain images he uses remind us: fish in a saloon tank "went gleaming about, now turning up the sheen of a golden side, and now vanishing into the shadows of the water, like the fanciful thoughts that coquet with a poet in his dream" (xxi). At this stage he is still rather idly probing: three chapters later events are becoming ominous, and lurking about the edges of a masquerade festivity he is discovered and pursued, "so that I was like a mad poet hunted by chimeras" (xxiv). Poetic melancholy has given way to poetic madness. Early in the book the heroine Zenobia praised Coverdale's poems and promised to sing them to him; in their last interview she asks him derisively if he has a ballad ready yet on her sad fate. He has become steadily less the poet and steadily more the spy; he does not even as Zenobia implied distill others' sufferings into art, nor does he live his own life fully and independently. Probably it is his artistic trait that made him idealist enough to join the community and gave him what limited insight he has; but without knowing it he is wantonly defective in sympathy, and Hawthorne seems to intend him as a transitional figure between artistic apprehension and the coldly analytical.

Sometimes artist and alchemist face each other as rivals: the configuration of *Trilby* in this chapter is very like that of *The Tales of Hoffmann* in chapter 8. In three stories that occur to me the rivalry or opposition is particularly clearly marked, where the artist figure comes into possession of a talisman embodying in certain ways the supreme powers of art that he longs to exercise, and finds that their real exerciser is an evil older man whose plaything or victim he becomes: Gogol's "The Portrait," Balzac's *Peau de chagrin,* and the story inset in George MacDonald's *Phantastes.* The hero of this latter, Cosmo von Wehrstahl, is a "student of Prague"; hence we hardly need to be told that in his rooms at the top of the highest building available he pores over Cornelius Agrippa and his fellows. Cosmo is a visionary and idealist who sees all womanhood as divine but has never yet loved. He buys a mirror from an old dealer; cleaning it, he thinks:

> "What a strange thing a mirror is! and what a wondrous affinity exists between it and a man's imagination! For this room of mine, as I behold it in the glass, is the same, and yet not the same. . . . All its commonness has disappeared. The mirror has lifted it out of the region of fact into the realm of art. . . . But is it not rather that art rescues nature from the weary and sated regard of our senses, and the degrading injustice of our anxious every-day life, and, appealing to the imagination which dwells apart, reveals nature in some degree as she really is . . .?"   [xiii]

As Cosmo gazes at the mirror, a woman in white walks into the reflected room, "turning towards him a face of unutterable weariness, in which suffering, and dislike, and a sense of compulsion, strangely mingled with the beauty." Night after night she returns, and at last explains to him that she is "the slave of the mirror" and that if he loves her he must break it and release her. It is taken away from him before he can do this; after recovering from a six weeks' bout of brain fever and then undertaking the usual romantic search, and growing pale and haggard in the process, he succeeds in breaking it, but is killed by the courtier to whom the evil dealer last sold it. The story forcefully contrasts the power of love to release with the power of demonic magic that keeps and binds for its own enjoyment and thereby destroys: Cosmo's one fault is in hesitating to break the mirror and set the lady free, as he is asked to, "even from [him] self."

From the magician as the artist's older evil opposite, let us go on to the demon artist or scientist. This figure, whose passion for his work places him outside ordinary morality, has a number of traditional originals. The earliest, though hardly exploited till Joyce, is the Athenian artist-craftsman Daedalus, who among other crimes killed a fellow artist out of jealousy. More familiar to the eighteenth and nineteenth centuries, and often cited, is the legend that Michelangelo, or sometimes Leonardo, calmly painted, or even brought about, the death-agonies of a man for his Crucifixion.[36] An early reference occurs in Sade's *Justine,* where Dr. Rodin is justifying a surgical experiment he plans to perform on his daughter. The legend is reworked in George MacDonald's story "The Cruel Painter," in which a mad artist makes a soulless dummy of his daughter Lilith and torments her lover, rather in the manner of Chillingworth, in order to use both as the kind of models his perverted art requires. MacDonald characterizes him as "the spider painter," just as Du Maurier depicts that other demon artist, Svengali, as a spider in the midst of his web.

We began our discussion of the Artist with Goethe's *Tasso;* and Tasso makes a distinction between two kinds of artist. One is the healthy spirit whose art nourishes and refreshes him, corresponding in the play to

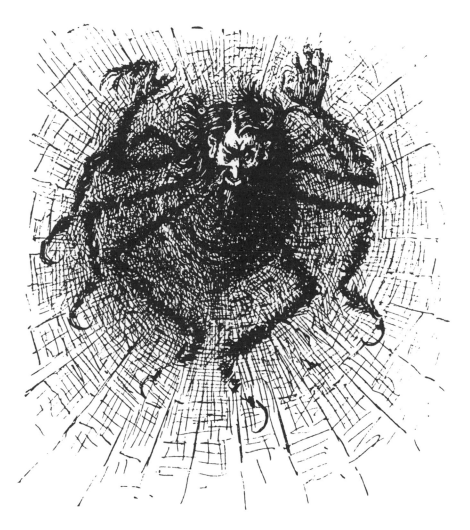

Figure 8. *Author's illustration from Du Maurier's* Trilby, *1894: "An Incubus." Photo courtesy Metropolitan Toronto Library Board.*

Ariosto, whose bust stands in the garden decked with flowers; the other is Tasso's own type, who spins out of his own inner world and thereby brings himself nearer to death. Goethe's image here combines silkworm and spider. Had Goethe wished to bring this in, the corresponding "healthy" art, creating in sunlight from the forms of an outward world, would find an appropriate, and traditional, image in the bee.

The Renaissance symbolism of the spider and the bee, discussed in the Appendix to this chapter, reappears in various forms down to the late nineteenth century. The spider, who as the more lurid is the more memorable, is as familiar in Gothic as its vegetable counterpart, the Upas-tree. At mildest the spider, like the one in Job,[37] is the creator of light, unsubstantial works, for example Sordello spinning his youthful fancies:

> He o'er-festooning every interval,
> As the adventurous spider, making light
> Of distance, shoots her threads from depth to height,
> From barbican to battlement: so flung
> Fantasies forth and in their centre swung
> Our architect,—the breezy morning fresh
> Above, and merry,—all his waving mesh
> Laughing with lucid dew-drops rainbow edged.
>   This world of ours by tacit pact is pledged
> To laying such a spangled fabric low
> Whether by gradual brush or gallant blow.   [I.665–75]

Perhaps we can appropriately compare the lines about the bee near the end of the poem, immediately following Sordello's death:

> By this, the hermit-bee has stopped
> His day's toil at Goito: the new-cropped
> Dead vine-leaf answers, now 'tis eve, he bit,
> Twirled so, and filed all day: the mansion's fit,
> God counselled for.   [VI.621–25]

This artist at least finishes what he set out to do, purposefully creating from the materials at hand.

Usually the spider is more sinister, standing for a rapacious egotism. He lurks in his web like the tyrant in his dungeon-based castle, and as artist is the creator of a world of delusion that is also a trap, like the Old Man's false paradise. His relation to his victims is vampiric: he does not so much eat them as suck them dry.

Closely related to the spider-artist is the spider as mastermind or plot-spinner. Lovelace has an elaborate spider image, which becomes more and more appropriate to his own entangling devices:

> For well thou knowest, that the tame Spirits which value themselves upon
> Reputation, and are held within the skirts of the Law by political considera-

tions only, may be compared to an infectious Spider; which will run into his hole the moment one of his threads is touched by a finger that can crush him, leaving all his toils defenceless, and to be brushed down at the will of the potent invader. While a silly Fly, that has neither courage nor strength to resist, no sooner gives notice, by its buz and its struggles, of its being intangled, but out steps the self-circumscribed tyrant, winds round and round the poor insect, till he covers it with his bowel-spun toils; and when so fully secured, that it can neither move leg nor wing, suspends it, as if for a spectacle to be exulted over: Then stalking to the door of his cell, turns about, glotes over it at a distance; and, sometimes advancing, sometimes retiring, preys at leisure upon its vitals.

But now I think of it, will not this comparison do as well for the entangled girls, as for the tame spirits?—Better o' my conscience!—'Tis but comparing the Spider to us brave fellows; and it quadrates.　　　[III, letter 10, p. 67][38]

Other spider-plotters are Scott's Waldemar Fitzurse, Eugène Sue's Jesuit Rodin, and Bulwer Lytton's Lumley Ferrers, also Hugo's Frollo; and the Master of Ballantrae plays spider to his brother's fly.[39] Here is Sherlock Holmes's account of Moriarty:

"He is the Napoleon of crime, Watson. He is the organizer of half that is evil and of nearly all that is undetected in this great city. He is a genius, a philosopher, an abstract thinker. He has a brain of the first order. He sits motionless, like a spider at the centre of its web, but that web has a thousand radiations, and he knows well every quiver of each of them. He does little himself. He only plans. But his agents are numerous and splendidly organized. . . ."　　　["The Final Problem"]

To return to the comparison of Artist and Alchemist: while the frantic artist pursues an unattainable ideal, the evil magician probably attains his ideal, but in a way that inevitably makes or requires a victim, whether etiolated dummy-woman, suffering animal man, or vampire's walking bloodbank whose physical life-sources are literally being drained.[40] The two figures, both symbolizing demonic kinds of creation, are so closely related that the artist or aesthete may have his victim like Poe's painter or Dorian Gray, and the magician may grasp at a phantom, like Manfred with his Astarte. Browning's Paracelsus, who like his brother magicians is a wrestler with God and has allowed the pursuit of a theoretical good to weaken his humanity, at moments recalls the Spectral career of the Ancient Mariner or the Poet of *Alastor*:

For some one thought would dimly beacon me
From mountains rough with pines, and flit and wink
O'er dazzling wastes of frozen snow, and tremble
Into assured light in some branching mine
Where ripens, swathed in fire, the liquid gold—
And all the beauty, all the wonder, fell
On either side the truth, as its mere robe;

I see the robe now—then I saw the form.
So far, then, I have voyaged with success,
So much is good, then, in this working sea
Which parts me from the happy strip of land:
But o'er that happy strip a sun shone, too!
And fainter gleams it as the waves grow rough,
And still more faint as the sea widens; last
I sicken on a dead gulf streaked with light
From its own putrefying depths alone.   [II.161–76]

On Paracelsus's deathbed, the name of Michal recalls to him one part of
what he has missed:

Cruel! I seek her now—I kneel—I shriek—
I clasp her vesture—But she fades, still fades;
And she is gone; sweet human love is gone!   [V.214–16][41]

The aesthete is quite regularly destroyed by misplaced passion—in our
examples, usually by a quest for fulfillment of whatever kind that wears
him out. The magician, following Prospero's example, is sometimes
drawn by an entirely unforeseen—indeed, to him previously
unimaginable—impulse of love or affection to burn his books and return
to common humanity, and usually in this renunciation we are to see his
salvation.[42] Unless he is saved in this way, his fate probably will be
destruction through a revolt from below, in an uprush of the passions he
has denied, or through the unexpected determination of a being he has
despised. His victim, his creature, his child, or some bit of "mere nature"
like flood or enraged animal,[43] will restore the balance upset by his career;
at least, this is the case with mages not crudely carried off or dropped from
a height by devils.[44] Margrave, the wicked magician in *A Strange Story*, is
trampled by charging herds in the Australian wilderness at the moment of
compounding his elixir. Melville's Bannadonna, the murder-stained
modern-Promethean builder of a belltower Babel, is struck down as if by a
conspiracy between two of his creations, the bronze nymph Una and the
mechanical subman Talus. Dr. Moreau in Wells's novel is killed by an
animal he has tortured in his experiments.[45] The evil eternal-life doctor in
The Man Who Could Cheat Death, a recent sensational paperback, is burned
together with his disfigured ex-mistress Margo when she sets fire to his
hideaway.[46] A similar incident concludes the film *The Bride of Frankenstein*, where the monster blows up mad scientist and tower-laboratory and
monster-woman and himself, only letting a pair of lovers escape. Sue's
Rodin, Frollo, Caligari, and Cipolla all have the tables turned on them by
men they treated as mere instruments; so too the apparently supernaturally endowed Master of Ballantrae, by his despised brother. On the other
hand the obsessed scientist of *Donovan's Brain*, helpless to extricate him-

self from his necromantic entanglement, is saved by the unexpected self-sacrifice of his alcoholic assistant.

The magician is related to our central myth of Narcissus primarily through the way in which stories about him tend to be organized along lines of opposition or complementation. Both are exemplified in *Trilby*, where Svengali, besides being the artist's rival, seems also his older, darker, Spectral other self. The simplest of Romantic alchemist stories, *Dr. Jekyll and Mr. Hyde*, involves not even magician and devil, but a single personality that becomes split. Other stories we have mentioned oppose active and passive, intellect and instinct, ardor and disillusionment, skepticism and faith. The balanced figures of young doctor and old doctor occur in several eternal-life novels: *A Strange Story, Dracula, Donovan's Brain, The Man Who Could Cheat Death;* and we have earlier noted complementary types of women in the first two. Such groupings lend themselves particularly well to the novel with "occult" interests; two such novels are Gautier's *Avatar,* 1856, and the anonymous *Âtman* (U.S., 1890s?). In the former a dark and a fair man, one scheming and the other virtuous, have their souls switched so that the bad one can enjoy the other's wife; but the heavenly Prascovie misses the spirituality that should inhabit her husband's body, and locks her bedroom door. *Âtman* is more complicated: besides the evil doctor Perdicaris, there is George Wolff, the middle-aged, muscularly rugged, intelligent artist, and the young friend to whom he is devoted, Arthur Lawrence, handsome and unthoughtful; Lawrence is engaged to the overspiritual Margaret Haviland, but loves the "superb animal" Félise de Montlhéry, not knowing that, first, she is the puppet and lure of Perdicaris, and second, she has no soul. Perdicaris, eager to make Félise love him, causes the death of Margaret and transfers her soul to Félise; but Félise then shrinks from Perdicaris and discovers she loves Wolff. Perdicaris kills himself, while Félise becomes a nun and dies years later rescuing Wolff from a fire, purified by her sacrifice from the sins of her former life.

These patterns of complementation are to be found again in two books of rather more merit, Rider Haggard's *She,* 1887, and its sequel *Ayesha,* 1905.[47] In the background is a tale of the third century B.C. concerning an Egyptian princess, Amenartas, who fled with her husband Kallikrates, a renegade priest of Isis, into the interior of the African continent, reaching a place ruled over by a mysterious white woman, "a magician having a knowledge of all things, and life and loveliness that does not die" (iii). This being offered to share her immortality with Kallikrates, if he would kill his wife; when he refused, he died by her magic, and Amenartas found her way back to the outside world, where she recorded the adventure in a letter to her infant son. This letter, carrying a message of vengeance, is passed down the line of her descendants, eventually reaching the family's latest representative, Leo Vincey, whose name (from Tisis-thenes via Vindex) means Avenger. Leo is the embodiment of what is conveyed by Kallikrates's name, "Beautiful Strength," being extremely handsome and athletic, but rather simpleminded and apparently shal-low; it turns out that he is the absolute likeness, as "She" takes him to be the reincarnation, of his remote ancestor.

Leo's inseparable friend is the narrator, his guardian Horace Holly, in all ways very unlike him. The introduction presents the pair under the nicknames of "the Greek god" and "Charon"; considering the romantic nature of their friendship, "Socrates and Alcibiades" would be quite as good. Later the savages call them Lion and Baboon. Holly's appearance is insisted on in both books. He is about twenty years older than Leo, and

> just as ugly as his companion [is] handsome. . . . He reminds [the narrator of the introduction] forcibly of a gorilla, and yet there [is] something very pleas-ing and genial about the man's eye.

Just before Holly's death at an advanced age, his doctor records:

> Were I an artist who wished to portray a wise and benevolent but rather grotesque spirit, I should take the countenance as a model. [*Ayesha*, preface]

It is mainly his love for Leo that has made Holly a benevolent human being. He begins his narration with himself at twenty-two, just before he is charged with the child's guardianship:

> Like Cain, I was branded—branded by Nature with the stamp of abnormal ugliness, as I was gifted by Nature with iron and abnormal strength and considerable intellectual powers. . . . Was it wonderful that I was misan-thropic and sullen? . . . I was set apart by Nature to live alone, and draw comfort from her breast, and hers only. Women hated the sight of me. . . .   [*She*, i]

One woman has called Holly in his hearing a "monster," and another has led him to a mirror and asked, "Now, if I am Beauty, who are you?"

Once Leo is of age and has perused the family papers, he and Holly set off into darkest Africa in quest of the ever-living She. When they meet her, She recognizes in Leo her dead lover, and offers him and Holly her own gift of immortality. Holly refuses, but Leo accepts. She leads them both to a cave deep in the earth where stands a column or fountain of fire, the source of her eternal youth. To encourage Leo, she steps into it now once more, but steps out of it again with her two thousand years of age on her; she withers and shrinks before their eyes, and dies, murmuring that she will come again. Holly and Leo with difficulty make their way out, eventually returning home to England.

She is full of threshold symbols[48] and symbols of quest. Two of the latter that stand out are the marshlights suggesting delusion,[49] and the veiled image suggesting mystery. Ayesha, or She, when first seen (xii) is a "swathed, mummy-like form";[50] her subjects have never seen her unveiled, but she shows herself early to Holly, with warnings about rash Actaeon and the power of beauty to blast. In the moonlit ruined city of Kôr she shows Holly and Leo a statue raised by the departed race: a veiled winged woman, the inscription stating that though all men desire to draw back the virgin veil of Truth, only Death is able to. When first met in *Ayesha*, after her return to life, she is again veiled, and this time what is concealed is not perfect beauty but the disfigurement of extreme old age. The suggestion in both books of the veiled statue of Isis at Saïs, embodying the mystery of Nature, can be connected with Ayesha's claims about her own identity; apparently she has been and is both a representative of the goddess Isis to whom the priest Kallikrates broke his vows for Amenartas, and an object of the goddess's vengeance. While much in the two books is allegorical and parabolic, part of Ayesha's mystery may be her author's indecision about her; another version offered is that she is an immortal who loved a mortal man and sinned for his sake. Despite geographical remoteness, her history and relation to the real gods is much like Brünnhilde's in Wagner's *Ring*. The triangle of the Egyptian tale is kept before us, as each book has a representative or reincarnation of Amenartas in a rival for Leo's love. The narrator, Holly, is said to be the reincarnation of an old Merlin-like hermit, Noot, who discovered the source of immortality but would not partake of it himself.

She is in outline fairly close to the standard alchemical theme of impious desires. Ayesha's death seems a proper retribution, less for her offending Isis, which is stressed more in *Ayesha*, than for her murder of a rival, who curses her in dying. Her beloved Leo is less in love himself than fascinated and passive; Holly loves Ayesha, mainly for her physical beauty; both are rather repelled by her cruelty, and there is an element of relief at her death. The friendship of Leo and Holly survives the adventure, seeming at the end more important than the love theme.

Ayesha shows us Leo with his nature deepened and spiritualized and his love for Ayesha the strongest power in him, Holly the self-forgetful loyal friend of both, and Ayesha appearing considerably more human, and less given to the tantrums that in *She* rather queer the picture of this representative of the wisdom of the ages. A further dimension enters this book, in the hints that Ayesha somehow made a Faustian bond with the powers of darkenss and that Leo, purified by love and suffering, has in a series of folktalelike ordeals discharged it for her: the term "redeem" is used twice (xviii, xix). Before the end this theme is dropped; Ayesha rashly promises Leo whatever he will ask, and he demands that she marry him before they undertake the long journey from Tibet, the locale of her reappearance, to the fiery fountain that will make him immortal, with the result that he dies in her embrace, "withered in Ayesha's kiss, slain by the fire of her love" (xxiii). This fulfills the prophecy of a vanquished rival, that "man and spirit cannot mate" (xvi). However, Ayesha claims that the marriage vow has now joined her again with the soul that left her on account of her sin, and thus truly regenerated her. Before she vanishes at last in fire with Leo's body, she communicates to Holly that now Leo's soul and hers are again, as "in the beginning," "*one*," suggesting a gnostical fable like that of Simon, whose emanation fell from him. Though none of Ayesha's myths of origin has any real place for Holly, the necessary third in her relationship with Leo, we are assured that the ultimate consummation includes all three, an apotheosis of love and friendship together, the Beast as well as Prince Charming.[51] The beauty and wisdom of Ayesha cannot be joined to Leo, we gather from the relation of the two books, until he has become more like Holly; and, Leo's sacrifice for Ayesha seems to require also the self-sacrifice of his friend. Behind these features of romance we can perhaps discern the mythical and alchemical marriage of perfect man and perfect woman—the union of Simon and Ennoia in heaven, of Helen and Achilles in the fabulous island of Leuke, of Faustus and his Helena.

The Tibetan magic mountain of *Ayesha* reappears with some other features in James Hilton's *Lost Horizon*, 1933. We may briefly note the arklike conception of this palace-prison of longevity: its walls contain infinite treasures of art and thought stored against the future when the deluge threatening human civilization will have passed. Not only the "rather sentimental headmaster" who christened him "Glory" Conway idolizes the hero, but also his author: he is the nearly perfect man, who seemed destined to fulfill himself in cherishing and guiding the little world of Shangri-La; instead, his fatherly fondness for the foolish youth Mallinson and his love for the flowerlike Manchu beauty Lo-Tsen make him decide to leave Shangri-La in order to help them to escape, though at the sacrifice of his own happiness. Mallinson and Lo-Tsen both die on the outward journey, and Conway is last seen desperately attempting to return. More clearly than Rider Haggard's Holly, Conway knows that his protégé is an unworthy creature compared to himself; still, he and his author seem to believe that he has made the humanly right choice as against an impersonal and detached benevolence and wisdom. His is a decision comparable to that made by Zanoni a century earlier in Bulwer Lytton's romance; but changing fashions in endings prevent a concluding vision of heaven opening to receive a Conway redeemed by self-sacrifice, and the moral status of Shangri-La is left notably equivocal.[52]

The true superman, our novels imply, is he who imitates not so much the divine power as the divine capacity for sacrifice of self or renunciation of power. Conway's greatness, the reader is expected to see, is in his refusal for his friends' sake to assume the powers offered him. If the evil magus can usually be recognized by his association with a victim-figure, we know the white magician, like Prospero and the Franklin's magister, by his Christlike willingness to bear the burdens of those weaker than himself. Halfway between is Ayesha (and cf. the doctor of *Donovan's Brain*), whose great sins in the acquisition and use of her powers are somehow atoned for by her friends' love.

Like the Artist, the Alchemist is in his way attempting to live in a fallen world by the law of an unfallen one. The Artist's way is definable in terms of physical surroundings and of the closest personal relationships, and he comes to grief usually through his failure to keep the worlds of reality and dream in balance; they slide into fatal separation, and an emotional or mental collapse results. The Alchemist, on the other hand, in what looks like the pursuit of wisdom is apt to regard humanity, his own and others', in material or mechanical terms, ignoring feeling or soul and the strength in weakness itself, which may in the end either destroy or save him. Alchemical fable is especially close to religious parable, its message being essentially: To reverse the outward conditions of the fall, by magic or science or a Utopian social order,[53] without transforming one's inner nature first, is to challenge God and invite retribution. The real secret of life if found would enable the finder to purify himself and raise Eden within; thus all merely outward achievements prove ironic, and the Medea, Wandering Jew, and Alchemist of *Alastor* are images of the darker possibilities of the Poet's search.

Something still remains to be said about the magician's typical surroundings. The magic mountains and happy valleys of Rider Haggard and James Hilton can readily be connected with the delusive paradises we looked at earlier (chapter 7); they invite the same question, "Happar, or Typee?" The laboratory is sometimes as well a recognizable palace of art, like Aylmer's in "The Birthmark." The evil doctor of *The Man Who Could Cheat Death* is also a sculptor; besides his laboratory he has a secret storehouse containing his statues of all his mistresses, a sort of Bluebeard's cabinet containing also one living victim, and it is here and through her that he is destroyed.[54] In relation to outdoor scenery, we can use Frankenstein as a kind of link between artist and scientist, because his career includes an early happy stage as the idealistic and sensitive young man, before the devastating event that determines his future course, and seasons and scenery play their part in the depiction. More typically the magician's "fall," like that of Roderick Usher and other shattered artists, has taken place long ago, and he is habituated to a thoroughly blasted scene; Manfred's Alps and Donovan's doctor's desert come to mind. Often, rather than being tied to one setting, he is by temperament or necessity a wanderer, a trait he shares with imaginative seekers like the

Poet of *Alastor* and the narrator of Poe's "Ms. Found in a Bottle."[55] In that case, it is remarkable how often his death comes, like Frankenstein's, as the climax of a horrendous wilderness journey.

Essentially there are two kinds of romantic wandering, oriented to past or to future: St-Preux, René, Childe Harold, Contarini Fleming, Ernest Maltravers, and the man of sensibility in general travel to forget; more alchemical types, like Shelley's Poet, Browning's Paracelsus, Poe's Arctic voyagers, and assorted magisters, travel to discover. On a smaller scale we can often recognize in our novel either the Terrible Journey In or the Terrible Journey Out, either of which incidentally may be combined or replaced[56] with a shattering illness ("brainfever") from which the hero arises a wreck and sometimes a Specter. Frankenstein, Margrave, the Master of Ballantrae, and Dracula all meet their ends after dramatic voyages into the heart of nowhere, in all cases but Margrave's a wintry wilderness. (*The Master of Ballantrae* is fittingly subtitled "A Winter's Tale.") Another Bulwer Lytton romance does display the magician's closing scene in the bleak north: the snake-eyed, eternal-life magus of "The Haunted and the Haunters; or, The House and the Brain"[57] is the last survivor on a corpse-filled ship ringed with polar ice. Having made his way to the top of an iceberg he is last glimpsed (by a narrator in mediumistic trance) surrounded by the stealthy "griesly shapes" of polar bears, under a pitchy sky apocalyptically decked with two moons. An interest in polar exploration may contribute to such gooseflesh-raising scenes, but so assuredly does "The Rime of the Ancient Mariner," with its hallucinated outward settings reflecting the states of the guilty soul. In the opening chapter of *Le Juif errant*, we encounter the title figure standing at the Bering Strait. However, the remorse that can raise the waste wilderness in Eden itself is part of our subject in the next chapter.

Appendix: The Spider and the Bee

The respective attributes for literature of spider and bee are first established in classical fable. The spider is the transformed Arachne, driven by envy and presumption to try to rival Athene in weaving, a figure not unlike the Luciferic artist. On the other hand bees are revered and associated with the Muses: several legends tell of poets shut up in chests and kept alive by bees who bring them honey, incidentally sweetening their song. Plato, playing on the resemblance between the Greek words for "honey" and "song," says that the poets "bring song from honeyed fountains, culling them out of the gardens and dells of the Muses; they, like the bees, winging their way from flower to flower. . . . For the poet is a light and winged and holy thing" (*Ion* 534b, trans. Jowett). More prosaically, Plutarch in "How a Young Man should Read Poetry" cites the bee's capacity to extract honey from pungent flowers among sharp thorns—thus the young can learn to draw wholesome doctrine even from dubious passages (32 E-F); St. Basil, following him, says in his "Address to Youth," Sermon **22,** that the Christian must select like the honeybee from the beauties of pagan literature.

Plutarch effectively launches into the language of criticism not only the bee but also the spider: " . . . the loose fictions and frivolous fabrications which poets and writers of prose produce from themselves, after the manner of spiders, weaving together and stretching abroad their unfounded notions . . ." (*De Iside* xx).

Early in the sixteenth century, Wyatt contrasts spider and bee in his epigram, "Nature that gave the bee"; his editor A. K. Foxwell says that he is handling a saying already common: "A reference to the bee who gathers honey and the spider, poison, from the same place, is to be found in Latimer's Sermons" (*Poems of Sir Thomas Wiat,* vol. 2, p. 66). Whitney's *A Choice of Emblemes,* 1586, shows spider and bee feeding on a rosebush (no. 51, taken from a Dutch source of 1565:

Vitæ, aut morti.

W I T H I N one flower, two contraries remaine,
    For proofe behoulde, the fpider, and the bee,
One poifon fuckes, the bee doth honie draine :
The Scripture foe, hath two effectes we fee :
    Vnto the bad, it is a fworde that flaies,
    Vnto the good, a fhielde in ghoftlie fraies.

Figure 9. Emblem from Geoffrey Whitney, A Choice of Emblemes, *1586.*

see A. Henkel and A. Schöne, *Emblemata,* cols. 302–03). The verses explain that the one takes honey from the same source from which the other takes poison and gall; behind this is a classical tradition that certain insects hate the smell of roses (cf. Plutarch, *Quaestiones Conviviales* vii.7), and a marginal note quotes St. Paul on the letter and spirit of Scripture killing and giving life. A little earlier Golding uses the same image in relation to poetry, in his "Preface too the Reader" (. . . *Ovidius, Metamorphosis,* 1567: cf. Gascoigne, *Epistle to the Reverend Divines,* 1574, *Works,* vol. 1, p. 6):

> Then take theis woorkes as fragrant flowers most full of pleasant juce
> The which the Bee conveying home may put too wholesome use:
> And which the spyder sucking on too poyson may convert,
> Through venym spred in all her limbes and native in hir hart.
> For too the pure and Godly mynd, are all things pure and cleane,
> And untoo such as are corrupt the best corrupted beene.

Nashe (*General Censure,* 1589: ed., G. Smith *Elizabethan Critical Essays,* vol. 1, pp. 332–33) similarly uses spider and bee for contrasted types of readers:

> I commend [the poets'] witte, not their wantonnes, their learning, not their lust: yet even as the Bee out of the bitterest flowers and sharpest thistles gathers honey, so out of the filthiest Fables may profitable knowledge be sucked and selected. . . . [Evil-minded] readers be the Spyders which sucke poyson out of the hony comb and corruption out of the holiest things.

Cf. also Spenser's dedicatory epistle in *Fowre Hymnes,* 1596, and numerous Elizabethan-Jacobean passages; H. Oxenden's use of it in his first commendatory epigram on Alexander Ross's *Mystagogus Poeticus,* 2d ed., 1648, shows him to be like his friend a man belated in the world. Such images and expressions are the background to Bacon's familiar remarks in the *Advancement of Learning,* 1605 (cf. spiderwebs as vain works in Job 8:14, vain and mischievous in Isaiah 59:5–6; "*Aranearum telas texere*" and comment in Erasmus's *Adagia*):

> . . . the Schoole men . . . did out of no great quantitie of matter, and infinite agitation of wit, spin out unto us those laborious webbes of Learning which are extant in their Bookes. For the wit and minde of man, if it worke upon matter, which is the contēplation of the creatures of God worketh according to the stuffe, and is limited thereby; but if it worke upon it selfe, as the Spider worketh his webbe, then it is endlesse, and brings forth indeed Copwebs of learning, admirable for the finesse of thread and worke, but of no substance or profite.   [1605 ed., pp. 19–20; *Works,* vol. 3, pp. 285–86]

While Bacon does not here mention the bee (who, however, in *Redargutio Philosophiarum,* c. 1606–07, unites the virtues of ant and spider, collecting and digesting, as an image for the best kind of study—*Works,* vol. 3, p. 583), there is clearly a place for him as busied among "the creatures of God"; he appears in that rôle in Browne (*Religio Medici* I, 13), in Marvell ("The Garden," st. 9), and in Watts ("Against Idleness"—"How doth the little busy bee," no. 20 in *Divine Songs for Children*).

The contrast is taken up again in *The Battle of the Books* (Swift adds a phrase from *All's Well*—"I . . . wish . . . / Since I nor wax nor honey can bring home, / I quickly were dissolved from my hive / To give some labourers room"—I.ii.64–67):

> You boast, indeed, of being obliged to no other Creature, but of drawing, and spinning out all from your self; That is to say, if we may judge of the Liquor in the Vessel by what issues out, you possess a good plentiful store of Dirt and Poison in your Breast. . . . So that in short, the Question comes all to this; Whether is the nobler Being of the two, That which by . . . an overweening Pride, which feeding and engendering on it self, turns all into Excrement and Venom; producing nothing at last, but Fly-bane and a Cobweb; Or That, which, by an universal Range, with long Search, much Study, true Judgment, and Distinction of Things, brings home Honey and Wax.

The same associations are behind such expressions as the following: Donne, "Twicknam Garden":

> The spider Love, which transsubstantiates all,
> And can convert Manna to gall.

Godwin, *St. Leon*, IV, viii. 183 (the words are addressed to Bethlem Gabor, the misanthrope: in the next chapter we shall see the same symbolism elaborated on in Godwin's later novel, *Mandeville*):

> I weep to think how many high and heroic qualities in your breast are now converted into malignity and venom.

Keats, "Ode on Melancholy":

> Turning to Poison while the bee-mouth sips.

Maturin, *Melmoth*, II, xii. 135:

> He was Jew *innate*, an imposter,—a wretch, who, drawing sustenance from the bosom of our holy mother the church, had turned her nutriment to poison, and attempted to infuse that poison into the lips of his son.

For this last, cf. st. 6 of the first of Spenser's "Cantos of Mutabilitie":

> O pittious work of Mutabilitie!
> By which, we all are subject to that curse,
> And death in stead of life have sucked from our Nurse.

The spider as constructing from his own entrails appears further as follows: Butler, *Hudibras* III.i.1461 (1678): "Those Spider-Saints, that hang by Threads / Spun out o' the Entrals of their Heads"; Swift, *Battle of the Books*, 1697, in *Prose Works*, vol. 1, pp. 148–49: " . . . the Spider's Cittadel . . . 'This large Castle . . . is all built with my own Hands, and the Materials extracted altogether out of my own Person' "; Southey, "To a Spider," 1798, compares it in turn to Satan, the law, human schemers and dreamers, and the poet—"Thy bowels thou dost spin, / I spin my brains"; Keats's letter to Reynolds of February 19, 1818: " . . . almost any

Man may like the spider spin from his own inwards his own airy Citadel"—he moves on to the bee "hurrying about and collecting," and rejects its activity in favor of the "passive and receptive" flower; Shelley, "Letter to Maria Gisborne," moves from the spider web-spinning "in poet's tower, cellar, or barn, or tree" to himself as "worm" "spinning still round this decaying form / From the fine threads of rare and subtle thought" a "soft cell"—poet as *Tasso*-like silkworm.

Besides being entangling, or an image of a kind of creation, the spider's web can be an index of sensibility: Davies, *Nosce Teipsum*, 1599 (ed. Robert Krueger):

> Much like a subtill Spider which doth sit,
> In middle of her Web which spreadeth wide;
> If aught do touch the utmost threed of it
> She [Sense] feeles it instantly on every side.   [1061–64]

Dryden, *Marriage-à-la-Mode*, 1673, II.i: "Our souls sit close, and silently within, / And their own web from their own entrails spin; / And when eyes meet far off, our sense is such, / That spider-like, we feel the tenderest touch" (compare Pope's spider—and bee—in *Essay on Man*, 1734, I.217–20). This symbolism links with that of the musical instrument that vibrates when a single wire is touched, as in Lovelace's letter (V, 8) quoted here, chapter 5, note 30. In later literature— compare Holmes's account of Moriarty, p. 207 above, or Ken Kesey's narrator's of Big Nurse sitting at the center of her "web of wires" (*One Flew Over the Cuckoo's Nest*, pp. 26–27)—sensibility becomes demonic in the vibrating intelligence-network that is only mechanically or electronically "tender."

Eleven   The Avenger

> *. . . Revenge, at first though sweet,*
> *Bitter ere long back on itself recoils.*
>
> —*John Milton*

> *Oui, je suis de ceux-là qu'inspire le Vengeur,*
> *Il m'a marqué le front de sa lèvre irritée,*
> *Sous la pâleur d'Abel, hélas! ensanglantée,*
> *J'ai parfois de Caïn l'implacable rougeur!*
>
> —*Gérard de Nerval*

> *Moderation in the pursuit of justice is no virtue.*
> —*Senator Barry Goldwater*

The magician's fatal knowledge often seems at first a key to a brighter future for mankind; another kind of knowledge concerns the past—the *alastor*, or avenger, we saw, is "he who is unable to forget." The loss or blasting of the pastoral scene may come about through the discovery of a shameful secret or the inheritance of family guilt or feud: circumstances forcing on the hero a knowledge of evil comparable to Adam's. Thus is born, in a mood not elegiac but violent, the Avenger, who may go on to justify himself from what he now sees as the mutual ravin of nature.

Many nineteenth-century fictions are largely taken up with the working out of an elaborate vengeance. *Wuthering Heights*, *The Scarlet Letter*, and *The Count of Monte Cristo* are conspicuous examples; another is the history of Miss Havisham in *Great Expectations*. Intimacies broken off between the children of feuding families, recalling *Romeo and Juliet*, abound from Scott to *Maud* and *The Mill on the Floss*, and these belong to the same theme.

The hero as avenger may live a dedicated life, almost a sanctified one; like Melville's Indian-hater in *The Confidence-Man*, he renounces rest, comfort, and human companionship for the duration of his task. But the avenger proper is an unholy being. The justice that he executes is fallible: going astray or outrunning his intention, it may carry off his dearest friend, his nearest kin, or the man who through marriage or by temperamental affinity should have been his brother. The best-known ironic vengeance is that of *Hamlet*, dubiously inspired and destroying the innocent with the guilty; similar mechanics operate in *Eugene Aram* or *Maud*. Story after story shows how the killer of Cain takes Cain's curse upon himself; and Cain's mark too is in evidence, from Mandeville's scar in Godwin's novel near the beginning of the century to the brand on the heroine's brow in *Dracula* at the end of it.

The misanthrope or hater of mankind at large[1] is a related figure, and his landscape is like the avenger's; he lurks in the forest, among Druid stones, or generally among the tombs. We can class also with the avenger someone who at first glance looks most unlike him—the real Cain, the man devoured with remorse for a crime in the past, or in some other way still ruled by its effects; Byronic heroes from Childe Harold to Lara and Manfred belong here, with, besides Eugene Aram (Hood's and Bulwer Lytton's), Wordsworth's Oswald and Crabbe's Peter Grimes. As Cain hears the blood of Abel crying from the ground, and Orestes has the Furies after him, so these inhabit a landscape eerie with echoes and crowded with phantoms of conscience. For the man whose vision of the world is dominated by guilt, it makes no great difference whether the guilt is his own or someone else's: criminal and avenger when they turn their heads show the same hunted look.

The types of avenger and alchemist are often found associated or combined. Frankenstein like Prospero is both; Roger Chillingworth is a man of science, and Monte Cristo dabbles in elixirs. Dracula, who possesses a version of the secret of eternal life, is the villain hunted down by a group of avengers. Bulwer Lytton's Eugene Aram, tracked by Walter Lester, is presented by his author so as to resemble as closely as possible a student of the occult. Wieland and the Justified Sinner, the murdering righteous, are each led on by a deluding magician, respectively the trickster Carwin and Satan himself. Where the avenger is neither a magician nor associated with one, he may—like Heathcliff or Wacousta or Woyzeck—in some way resemble a Caliban or animal man.

Avenger and alchemist have certain features in common. God set the mark on Cain's brow to reserve him for himself, so that though every man's hand was against him no man might slay him. Justice in this case was expressly the Lord's. Human justice in romantic fiction, from Ann Radcliffe's Inquisition through the legal operations in *Frankenstein* and *Alice in Wonderland*, is usually blindly mechanical, arbitrary, or a savage mockery: part and parcel of the dirty devices of a fallen world. The position of the avenger, taking its execution on himself, is extremely equivocal; like the alchemist, he is playing God. Further, as the alchemist is in bondage to his powers, so is the avenger to his mission, unless like the magus Prospero he can let the dead past go. While the artist pursues an ideal of beauty and the alchemist one of knowledge, the avenger pursues an ideal justice: their Beautiful, True, and Good are at best phantasmal, at worst, fiendish. Their authors seem to agree that they would all do better to seek love; like the others, the avenger usually leaves his soulmate to die broken hearted.

Bulwer Lytton's *Eugene Aram* (1831, slightly revised 1848) illustrates many of the traits of our fiction. First of all, its framework is pastoral in conception. The novel opens with an idyllic village scene, epigraphed as follows:

> "Protected by the divinity they adored, supported by the earth which they cultivated, and at peace with themselves, they enjoyed the sweets of life without dreading or desiring dissolution."
>
> —Numa Pompilius.

Bulwer Lytton explains in the preface of 1848 that

> the time occupied by the events of the story is conveyed through the medium of [natural] descriptions. Each description is introduced, not for its own sake, but to serve as a calendar marking the gradual changes of the seasons as they bear on to his doom the guilty worshipper of Nature.

The action begins in early summer; the main catastrophe falls on the hero's autumnal wedding day, heralded by the bride's shivering remark, "It is a gloomy morning . . . the winter seems about to begin at last" (V, i). The hero languishes in prison through the winter and spring, and dies in August during harvest. It is in May, some years later, that grief and remorse are put aside and life begins again for the survivors. The crime whose discovery destroys Eugene was committed in an earlier winter:

> I wandered from the town, and paused by the winding and shagged banks of the river. It was a gloomy winter's day; the waters rolled on black and sullen, and the dry leaves rustled desolately beneath my feet. Who shall tell us that outward Nature has no effect upon our mood?   [V, vii]

Two literary strains go to make up the presentation of Eugene as we first meet him. He is a "wizard" and "magician," to whom the author applies the lines of il Penseroso:

> Or let my lamp at midnight hour
> Be seen in some high lonely tower,
> Where I may oft outwatch the Bear,
> Or thrice great Hermes, and unsphere
> The spirit of Plato.   [I, iv]

Bulwer Lytton sees Eugene's passion for knowledge as "morbid" and as the source of his crime:

> "For suddenly as I pored over my scanty books, a gigantic discovery in science gleamed across me. I saw the means of effecting a vast benefit to truth and to man. . . . And in this discovery I was stopped by the total inadequacy

of my means. The books and implements I required were not within my reach; a handful of gold would buy them,—I had not wherewithal to buy bread for the morrow's meal! In my solitude and misery this discovery haunted me like a visible form,—it smiled upon me; a fiend that took the aspect of beauty, it wooed me to its charms that it might lure my soul into its fangs. I heard it murmur, 'One bold deed, and I am thine!... For the ill of an hour thou shalt give a blessing to ages!' So spoke to me the tempter." [V, vii]

Needless to say, his aspirations are never fulfilled, as remorse and solitude distract him from them: "The Past destroyed my old heritage in the Future," the "higher" motivation for which, like a lesser Raskolnikov, he has stained his soul.

Besides being something of a Faust, or student of the occult, Eugene embodies another aspect of the heritage of "Il Penseroso," the idealized solitary attuned to Nature, the "genius" who at the same time is almost a *genius loci:*[2]

> Meanwhile, the student continued his path along the water side, and as, with his gliding step and musing air, he roamed onward, it was impossible to imagine a form more suited to the deep tranquillity of the scene. Even the wild birds seemed to feel, by a sort of instinct, that in him there was no cause for fear; and did not stir from the turf that neighboured, or the spray that overhung, his path.   [I, vi]

Elsewhere he recalls the Poet of Gray's *Elegy:*

> The peasant threw kindly pity into his respectful greeting as in his homeward walk he encountered the pale and thoughtful student, with the folded arms and downcast eyes which characterized the abstraction of his mood; and the village maiden as she courtesied by him, stole a glance at his handsome but melancholy countenance, and told her sweetheart she was certain the poor scholar had been crossed in love!   [I,iv]

Twelve pages later (I, vi) Eugene is observed stretched under a tree beside the brook wildly muttering to himself; and in a moment of crisis we see him

> hurrying, with unabated speed, though with no purposed bourn or object, over the chain of mountains that backed the green and lovely valleys among which his home was cast.

Here he arrives at a decision:

> He seemed to breathe more freely, and the haggard wanness of his brow relaxed at least from the workings that, but the moment before, distorted its wonted serenity into a maniac wildness.   [III, vi]

Eugene's normal aspect is serene, and he is continually being compared to waters quiet or still (I, x; II, iii; III, vii), the comparison being not always complimentary:

"Free to confess, Squire Walter, that I don't quite like this larned man as much as the rest of 'em; something queer about him; can't see to the bottom of him; don't think he's quite so meek and lamblike as he seems. Once saw a calm dead pool in foreign parts; peered down into it; by little and little, my eye got used to it; saw something dark at the bottom; stared and stared—by Jupiter! a great big alligator! Walked off immediately; never liked quiet pools since—augh, no!"   [I, ix][3]

The climactic meeting of Aram with Houseman, his partner in the long-ago murder, occurs on a night of storm in a scene reminiscent of the haunts of the villains of Scott, to whom the first edition of the novel was dedicated, and featuring a precipice, a cavern, and the very stream that has lent itself to some of the comparisons mentioned above:

> The same stream which lent so soft an attraction to the valleys of Grassdale here assumed a different character: broad, black, and rushing, it whirled along a course overhung by shagged and abrupt banks.... The stunning noise of the cataract in the place where they met, forbade any attempt to converse; and they walked on by the course of the stream, to gain a spot less in reach of the deafening shout of the mountain giant as he rushed with his banded waters upon the valley like a foe.   [III, vii]

Aram later seeks out Houseman in London, where he lives beside the Thames; lingering on the bridge, he ponders on "the dark river that rushed below."

> A solemn dejection crept over him, a warning voice sounded on his ear, the fearful genius within him was aroused; and even at the moment when his triumph seemed complete and his safety secured, he felt it only as—
> "The torrent's smoothness ere it dash below."   [IV, vi][4]

This symbolism is completed, linking the two men, in the sullen river Nid at the northern town of Knaresboro', beside which Aram brooded on his fate, the murder was committed, and Houseman at last reveals the victim's bones in the cave where they have lain.

Aram in his confession compares himself to Cain (V, vii). The symbol of the crime that has cut him off from mankind is not a visible mark, but his refusal to give his right hand in friendship; he always offers the left, which is early remarked on as an omen (I, xii).[5] To Houseman, however, he gives his right (III, vii). This is appropriate, because Houseman embodies the memory of Aram's crime, of which he was the inciter. We meet him just before we meet Aram (I, ii), his shadow falls continually across Aram's romance with Madeline, his fairer self (I, vii; IV, viii), and it is he who finally exposes Aram. He is not only Aram's "distant relation" (V, vii), he is his shadow-self. Aram has been afraid to admit even a beloved wife to his solitude (I, vi): the darker companion cannot be divorced from him.

"Friends we are not; but while we live there is a tie between us stronger than that of friendship. . . . Is not the world wide enough for us both? Why haunt each other? What have you to gain from me? . . . When you are near me, I feel as if I were with the dead: it is a spectre that I would exorcise in ridding me of your presence." . . .

"I will not stir from the vicinity of your home till my designs be fulfilled; I enjoy, I hug myself in your torments."   [III, ii]

The avenger in the novel is a further character, Walter Lester, the cousin of Madeline, and he accuses Aram of taking his beloved from him:

"Have you not traversed my views, blighted my hopes, charmed away from me the affections which were more to me than the world, and driven me to wander from my home with a crushed spirit and a cheerless heart?"   [I, x]

Setting out from the house where he has lived from childhood with his uncle and cousins, Walter resolves to seek his lost father, and soon finds the thread of his father's past leading into that of Eugene Aram's: Aram, it turns out, was at least an accomplice in Walter's father's murder. The last section of the book (V) is epigraphed from Hesiod:

Surely the man that plotteth ill against his neighbor perpetrateth ill against himself, and the evil design is most evil to him that deviseth it.

On Eugene's wedding day, Walter appears as the accuser and reveals to all, not only that Eugene has committed murder, but that the victim was "the brother of him whose daughter, had I not come to-day, [Eugene] would have called [his] wife!" (V, ii). Faced with the despair of his family, and especially of Madeline and her sister, Walter does not triumph long:

"Justice, and blood for blood!" said Walter, sternly; but his heart felt as if it were broken. His venerable uncle's tears, Madeline's look of horror as she turned from him, Ellinor all lifeless, and he not daring to approach her—this was *his* work!

The estrangement that earlier drove him from home was only a foretaste of what he now feels:

"A voluntary exile and a life that may lead to forgetfulness are all that I covet. I now find in my own person", he added, with a faint smile, "how deeply Shakespeare had read the mysteries of men's conduct. Hamlet, we are told, was naturally full of fire and action. One dark discovery quells his spirit, unstrings his heart, and stales to him for ever the uses of the world. . . ."
                                                                        [V, iii]

After the execution Walter leaves the country, returning after some years to marry Ellinor, Madeline's younger sister and now his only surviving relative.

Walter's cousins are contrasted in temperament and coloring. Madeline is a sensitive and spiritual soul, somewhat unfitted for earthly life. As

Aram's ideal and mirroring companion, she declines during his imprisonment, reporting idyllic hallucinations in the most pathetic tones, and dies when his sentence is pronounced, the chapter being epigraphed with the lines on Ophelia:

> Lay her i' the earth:
> And from her fair and unpolluted flesh
> May violets spring! [V, vi]

The dying Madeline tells Ellinor:

> "You are formed for love and home, and for those ties you once thought would be mine. God grant that *I* may have suffered for us both, and that when we meet hereafter you may tell me *you* have been happy here!" [V, v]

Thus Madeline is something of a conscious martyr, and also bequeaths to Ellinor her first lover, Walter. The author hints that the tragic fates of Madeline and Eugene have not been in vain. When we last meet Walter and Ellinor, the former has become a man, deepened and made more compassionate by the lessons Eugene's history has taught him, while the once merry Ellinor has been tempered and chastened by grief into a perfect and thoughtful womanhood (V, viii). Having the name and destiny of the lady of sorrows, Madeline perhaps surprises us by being fair rather than dark. The buoyant Ellinor has hazel eyes and "raven" hair, while Madeline is blue-eyed and fairer. However, instead of making her angelically blonde to suggest her poetic otherworldliness, Bulwer Lytton several times insists her coloring is "rich," implying—it seems intended—a nature more deeply passionate than her sister's. Certainly she is in conception closer to the "dark lady," like Scott's Minna Troil, than to the usual fair one.

The conscious aura of sacrifice attending the ends of Madeline and Eugene brings us back to the conventions of pastoral. In the original pastoral-elegiac situation, the death that is lamented also has a magical efficacy in making things grow. A comparable ritualism marks our fictions as pastoral: sacrifice always produces some valuable effect. The death of a scapegoat—Bulwer Lytton's idealized criminal certainly has something of that—leaves everyone free for a fresh start, and what is more, the deceased's relationships may even be bequeathed intact. Pastoral demigods leave their vigor to the earth, to come up as harvest; lamented shepherds leave their poetic powers to their chief mourners; inconsolable heroes of elegiac fiction transfer their affections undisturbed from female martyr to her sister or best friend, and this holds from Theodore in *The Castle of Otranto* to *Tess*'s Angel Clare, who is urged by Tess to marry 'Liza-Lu.[6] This feature may arise partly from the lack of differentiation among romance heroines; they can look as distinct as Cynthia and the Indian Maid, but really they are different aspects of the same thing—so to speak, the upper- and lower-world faces of Persephone. There may be some sense also of the virginal "little sister" of the bride in the Song of Songs, whose fate is not to be married but to be built on—taken literally, this would fit our topic of sacrifice. When Lucy in *Dracula* dies, her four adoring men (as well as her vampire lover) without a moment's hesitation substitute her friend Mina in their hearts (or domestic economy). Moreover, when the devoted band at last catch up with Dracula and make an end of him, at the same instant they lose one of their number by way of purification.[7] The astute reader has long ago picked Mr. Quincy P. Morris as a sacrifice, because he is a great-souled, large-bodied, simple nature from the American wilds, with even more and redder blood than the rest of them, plainly the dying lamb atoning for the massacre of the wolf. The simpler a being, the more innocently pastoral, the more clearly marked for sacrifice he may appear—unless he is marked rather by the trait that Eugene[8] and Madeline share with the Poet of *Alastor,* his openness and responsiveness to every impulse of Nature—his "sensibility."

Eugene Aram, because the criminal rather than the avenger is its hero, is perhaps not the clearest example with which to start. However, its insistence on portraying Cain (very much) as Abel and Abel (somewhat) as Cain defines an important ironic theme which we shall encounter again, and in addition the story illustrates most of the features in which we are interested.

In *Eugene Aram* happiness and forgetfulness of the past are associated with the valley of Grassdale and its murmuring stream, misery and guilt with savage or dreary scenes and rushing waters. Impending catastrophe is continually imaged as storm or flood (e.g., IV, viii).[9] His crime estranges Aram from humanity, from science, and even from nature, so that he continually sees

> "a spectre that walked by my side, that slept in my bed, that rose from my books, that glided between me and the stars of heaven, that stole along the flowers, and withered their sweet breath. . . . "   [V, vii]

Reminded of the past and given cause to dread the future, he roams over the mountains like a madman, as we have seen. In part his frenzy springs from the irresistible power of remorse; it is also a heritage from the demonic endowment of the poet as conceived by Sensibility and Romanticism. Even without the remorse that links him to, say, Frankenstein or the mad old Harper of *Wilhelm Meister,* Eugene Aram is an idealized genius in the manner of Torquato Tasso, the Poets of *Alastor* and "Kubla Khan," or Roderick Usher.

Eugene's rage on the mountaintops, with some other traits, probably descends to him from Ferdinando Falkland in Godwin's *Caleb Williams,* 1794. Falkland's young secretary, Caleb, has uncovered the secret that accounts for his master's gloom and fits of seeming madness: Falkland once killed a man who slighted his honor, and let two innocent neighbors be hanged for the crime. Promising never to betray him, Caleb leaves Falkland's service, only to find that Falkland, while still relying on his promise, hunts and persecutes him and will not let him settle anywhere. At length, having been visited and tormented with fiendish malignancy right to the end of a three-volume novel, Caleb resolves to meet and denounce his persecutor. Godwin succeeds in conveying a remarkable shock in their confrontation, where Caleb at last sees clearly that Falkland, even though guilty, was after all the most godlike of men, and that he has destroyed him. Innocent and villain have a way of changing places in our novel, and nowhere more strikingly than on the last page of *Caleb Williams*. Abel is the innocent shepherd of a happy pastoral scene: Cain, the fleeing exile of a blasted one. The ambiguously named Caleb thought he knew which was which. Shelley was fully justified in calling this scene of ironic recognition "terrific," and in comparing with it the confrontation of Frankenstein and the Being on their Alpine sea of ice.[10]

A later Godwin novel, *Mandeville: A Tale of the Seventeenth Century*, 1817, deals at length with the making and destiny of the misanthrope, commencing with an epigraph from Exodus 15:

> And the waters of that fountain were bitter: and they said,
> Let the name of it be called Marah.

Charles Mandeville when very young loses his parents in an Irish massacre of English Protestants, and is brought up in the gloomy mansion of his melancholy, love-bereaved uncle Audley, under the tutelage of a stern and rigorous chaplain who makes him read Foxe's *Martyrs* and trains him above all to hate the Roman church. Mandeville is an apt pupil, pride and solitariness being from the beginning the mainsprings of his character. Before he is twelve, he is thus characterized:

> I loved to listen to the pattering of the rain, the roaring of the waves, and the pelting of the storm. There was I know not what in the sight of a bare and sullen heath, that afforded me a much more cherished pleasure, than I could ever find in the view of the most exuberant fertility, or the richest and most vivid parterre. Perhaps all this proves me to be a monster, not formed with the feelings of human nature, and unworthy to live. I cannot help it....
> [I, 112–13]

> I had hardly a notion of any more than two species of creatures on the earth,—the persecutor and his victim, the Papist and the Protestant; and they were to my thoughts like two great classes of animal nature, the one, the law of whose being it was to devour, while it was the unfortunate destiny of the other to be mangled and torn to pieces by him. [115]

This conception of the classes of mankind remains with Mandeville throughout his career, though the labels change.

The one happy impulse of Mandeville's youth is his love for his sister Henrietta, brought up in another part of the country. The idyllic name of her abode is Beaulieu in the New Forest, whose delights show him "nature's wealth . . . not bought with tears, and groans, and blood" (201), visiting him with "the sensations that might have been habitual to all mankind, if Adam had never fallen" (203), and surrounding him with a cheerful society that makes him reflect bitterly on how different he might have been if brought up here. The associations of his sister throughout the book are "Elysian," "Arcadian," "paradisal":

> And the innocence and simplicity of our affection, which was all soul, and had no alloy of grossness, turned it into a purer, a brighter, and a more heavenly flame. We loved, as the angels may be supposed to love above the cerulean sky.   [177]

At Winchester School Mandeville finds himself in a very different little society, characterized by distinctions among the boys as of master and servant, "the despot and the subject" (219). Here he meets Clifford, the universal favorite, whose charm and naturalness and "airy figure" are characterized much as those of Henrietta were earlier; Mandeville, receiving nothing but generosity at his hands, becomes hopelessly jealous of him. Another boy, the ill-natured and suitably named Mallison, though dark, sallow, and in no way like him, is "perpetually found in [Clifford's] train" (235).

> Mallison possessed the art to turn the careless and good-humoured effusions of Clifford into lampoons, and the devilish chymistry, from honey itself to extract a poison.   [236]

Clifford on the other hand in his discourse possesses all the power of an Orpheus in refining the rude natures around him (252–53). Mandeville, feeling his own worth impaired, chooses to regard Clifford as an evil enchanter (255, 258).

Mandeville, who like most of the boys is a royalist, is falsely accused of possessing a slanderous antimonarchical document and is solemnly tried by his schoolmates, set on mainly by Mallison out of pure malignity. His pride prevents him from clearing his reputation, and the memory of the incident ever afterwards rankles in him, all the resentment arising from it being directed, not against the villainous Mallison, but against Clifford, who has acted honorably throughout. Mandeville falls ill for some weeks, arising again like a "meagre unlaid ghost" (300; *Comus* 434) and with his nature somewhat soured:

> I was a disappointed and discontented soul; and all the wholesome juices and circulations of my frame converted themselves into bitterness and gall.   [303][11]

Everywhere before him he sees Clifford's charm, resembling

> the benignity of the Deity, that diffuses life and enjoyment
> everywhere. . . . What then was I? A dark and malignant planet, that no eye
> remarked, that fain would shine, but that, as long as the sun of Clifford was
> above the horizon, was cut off from every hope of gratification.   [304]

Clifford is now "my only obstacle . . . my evil genius . . . the poison-tree
of Java; the sight of him was death" (305).

After entering Oxford, Mandeville becomes involved in a royalist plot
against Cromwell, but withdraws when a place he has been offered with
the royalist forces proves to have been earlier claimed by a higher author-
ity for Clifford. Returning to the university, where he unexpectedly meets
Mallison, he finds that he is an outcast from society; the story has got
about that he was dismissed from his place as a parliamentary spy, and to
this has been connected the old incident of the antiroyalist book. Denounced by a friend, convinced that his reputation is lost, his life blasted,
and his forehead branded like Cain's (II, 102), he turns all his hatred once
more upon Clifford. [12]

> I was confident, that Clifford and I were linked together for good or for evil
> (no, for evil only!), and that only death could dissolve the chain that bound
> us. . . . It was my destiny for ever to shun, and for ever to meet him. I could
> no more avoid the one, than the other. I was eternally to engage in the flight,
> and eternally to meet the encounter.   [51–52]

> Fate, I was fully persuaded, had bound Clifford and me together, with a
> chain, the links of which could never dissolved. "Marriages", it is said, "are
> made in heaven". The power that moulds us all according to his pleasure,
> divided the human species into male and female, and decreed that it was not
> good for man to remain without his mate. In his Providence he has fitted to
> every variety of the masculine character a female adapted to afford him
> satisfaction and felicity; and happy the man, to whose encounter fortune
> shall present the fair, that by the eternal decree was designated to become his
> partner. In the same manner as, in the world of human creatures, there exist
> certain mysterious sympathies and analogies, drawing and attracting each to
> each, and fitting them to be respectively sources of mutual happiness, so, I
> was firmly persuaded, there are antipathies, and properties interchangeably
> irreconcilable and destructive to each other, that fit one human being to be
> the source of another's misery. Beyond doubt I had found this true opposi-
> tion and inter-destructiveness in Clifford. Mezentius, the famous tyrant of
> antiquity, tied a living body to a dead one, and caused the one to take in, and
> gradually to become a partner of, the putrescence of the other. I have read of
> twin children, whose bodies were so united in their birth, that they could
> never after be separated, while one carried with him, wherever he went, an
> intolerable load, and of whom, when one died, it involved the necessary
> destruction of the other. Something similar to this, was the connection that

an eternal decree had made between Clifford and me. . . . He had made me
the outcast of mankind.   [102–06][13]

Convinced that life is over for him, Mandeville falls into temporary insanity and is nursed by Henrietta, his "guardian genius." His happiness in her and her friends' society is shattered by the introduction to their circle of Clifford. Mandeville's imagery dwells more and more on desert, storm, and flood; he has become a "demon" (203); "I lived but for one purpose, the extinction of Clifford" (240–41).

Meanwhile Mallison's scheming uncle, Holloway, has wound himself into the confidence of Mandeville's melancholy relative Audley, who "like all other sentient beings, wanted something to love" (265). At Audley's death, Holloway becomes his trustee and the guardian of Mandeville and Henrietta. Holloway and Mallison move in on Mandeville, who, while despising them, soon becomes entirely dependent on Mallison's company. Mallison in everything strives to please by flattering, and speaks Mandeville's own thoughts to him in a way resembling "the song of the Sirens" (III, 110). ". . . The sentiments of our fellows concerning us, are an unfailing mirror, refracting the beams of pleasure, and awakening in our hearts self-respect and self-reverence" (113). Recovering from the effects of an accident through which Mallison has tended him, Mandeville considers him for the moment as "my better angel" (115). In flattery and mimicry, Mallison counsels revenge:

"Yes, God assigned to you a high destiny, and to leave a trail of glory behind; but a malignant demon has passed over your intended orbit, and has driven you infinite leagues away from the path in which you ought to have moved, into the desert waste of space. Nothing therefore remains for you, but solemnly to revolve what you might have been, and to retaliate largely and with interest upon the enemy that has destroyed you."   [122–23]

Mandeville confesses his increasing dependence upon Holloway and Mallison:

What was most strange, was, that the more these wretched beings tormented me, the more in a certain sense grew my attachment to them. They were like some loathsome deformity, or envenomed excrescence on the human body, which the infatuated man to whose lot it has fallen, cherishes with obstinacy, and would rather part with his life than be delivered from it. The effect was such as is related of the bird and the rattle snake; the defenceless victim is bewitched by the eye of his adversary, and is necessitated to fly into his mouth, though by so doing he rushes on certain destruction. Holloway and Mallison became in some degree a part of myself. I felt that day maimed and incomplete, in which I did not sup my allotted dose of the nauseous draught they administered. I must have their company. . . .
                                                                       [147–48]

At about this time Clifford is reported drowned, and Henrietta, hitherto unconscious that she loved him, involuntarily reveals it to others as she discovers it herself. Earlier Mandeville, speaking of his attachment to Henrietta, has quoted from "Lycidas" the lines beginning, "Together both . . . "; now Henrietta's meditations recall another part of the poem:

> "No shroud shall cover, and no hearse receive thee. The whelming waters shall roll over thy frame, and the restless tides shall float thee from shore to shore. . . . "   [235]

Clifford survives and returns, and Henrietta, resolved to sacrifice her happiness to that of her sick brother, sees him in order to renounce him for ever.[14] But her friends intervene:

> . . . No justice could require, and no justice permit, that Clifford and Henrietta, framed to be the ornaments of the world, the boast of the present age, and the wonder of posterity, beings, the occupation of every day of whose existence, would be, to be happy, and to make happy, should be consigned to perpetual disappointment, for the sake of one who could never become useful to society, and whose existence would be a burden to his fellow-creatures.   [273]

Holloway, whose schemes require Henrietta to marry Mallison, does his best to work upon both Henrietta and Mandeville, whose love for his sister has by now become a fiendish passion of sole possession, and whose hatred of Clifford has been increased by the one factor that was missing: in kindness to a forlorn old relative, another solitary soul needing something to love, Clifford has become a Catholic.

> I had never loved but one thing, and that was Henrietta. . . . She was the whole world to me; and nature without her was one blank, one universal desert. She was the sun that illuminated all; and, when that sun was once extinguished in the heavens, I wandered for ever in darkness, and on the edge of precipices, where every step threatened to shiver me to atoms, or sink me in a fathomless abyss. Henrietta was a charm that I hung about my neck, and wore next to my heart . . . ; and fierce and gloomy and dismal as was my nature, I had only to think of her, and I became . . . as cheerful, as sea and sky and air, when the halcyon sits brooding on her nest. . . . It was my delight to believe, that she loved as I loved, that she would sacrifice herself as I would, that for all the world she would not be persuaded to an act that would give me pain, and that she was the sister of my soul.   [310–11]

Rather than see Clifford, "this loathsome spider," take from him his "one little ewe-lamb" (319), he would[15]

> sooner have seen her spotted with the plague; . . . sooner have seen her barked and crusted over with the foulest leprosy; sooner, ten thousand times sooner, . . . have followed her to the grave—than that she should touch this man.   [320]

In a frenzy of hatred, but calm in manner, Mandeville appears before Henrietta, adjuring her by their murdered parents, and accusing her of "this crime, this abhorred mixture, this unnatural pollution, this worse than incest," destruction of a brother (330). Henrietta is moved by what appears to be evidence of his love and his sanity, and is about to renounce Clifford and swear to devote herself forever to Mandeville.

> Her heart was mine. . . . Henrietta was saved, saved from pollution, from blasphemy, from the most execrable of crimes, saved for her sex, for her country, for her age, and for me.   [334]

> Yes, I have no doubt, that Providence itself took me by the hand, and placed me there, in answer to her prayer. . . . Oh, that the gracious purpose of a beneficent Providence, that the finger of God stretched out to point the path of rectitude, should have been so wofully defeated!   [341]

For, in his triumph, Mandeville falls into a fit that proves him undeniably a maniac, to Henrietta and to her friends who have come up. In Mandeville's eyes Henrietta now falls and is "lost" (345), her marriage with Clifford being decided upon. Mandeville, having "loved, as never man loved," pronounces a curse on the couple. Under the influence of Holloway and Mallison, he gathers an ambush to carry off Henrietta on the eve of her marriage. The plan is foiled, and Mandeville receives from Clifford a facial wound that will mark him for life.[16]

> The reader may recollect the descriptions I have occasionally been obliged to give, of the beauty of my person and countenance, particularly in my equestrian exercise, when, mounted on my favourite horse, I was the admiration of every one that beheld me. What was I now? When I first looked in my glass, and saw my face, once more stripped of its tedious dressings, I thought I never saw any thing so monstrous. . . . The sword of my enemy had given a perpetual grimace, a sort of preternatural and unvarying distorted smile, or deadly grin, to my countenance. . . . It ate into my soul. . . . Before, to think of Clifford was an act of the mind, and an exercise of the imagination; he was not there, but my thoughts went on their destined errand, and fetched him; now I bore Clifford and his injuries perpetually about with me. Even as certain tyrannical planters in the West Indies have set a brand with a red-hot iron upon the negroes they have purchased, to denote that they are irremediably a property, so Clifford had set his mark upon me, as a token that I was his for ever.   [365–67]

Though following upon an awkward and often tedious narrative, this is not the least powerful of Godwin's ironic conclusions. Until shortly before the end, the deranged Mandeville has maintained some awareness of the true relations of things, and his extravagances are rather involuntary than willful. But before the end Clifford has replaced Mallison as "the spider," Mallison has replaced Henrietta as "the good genius," and Mandeville's characterization, bearing out some of the suggestions of his name,[17] resembles that of Milton's Satan addressing the sun. Like *Caleb Williams, St. Leon,* and *Frankenstein, Mandeville* explores the terrors of isolation from human society; the hero's unfortunate upbringing and the constant fatality that prevents him from having friends has made of him a wasteland demon. And like Satan again, he embodies the essence of tyranny,[18] with his despotic will and his vulnerability to the flattery even of those he knows to be sycophants.

Besides Milton, the novel is full of echoes of *Othello,* which have thematic relevance. Earlier, Mandeville resembles an Iago, or conscious evil-thinker, faced with the "daily beauty" of Clifford's existence; by the end, when even his understanding has been infected by his own self-poison, he resembles Othello, the deluded sacrificer of innocence. The theme of "reputation," or wounded honor, is another link. Mandeville embraces a career of hate because he thinks his loss of reputation has cut him off forever from mankind like a mark of Cain (II, 102), a pursuing blight like Caleb Williams's fatal knowledge; but it is his hatred of Abel that has made him Cain at the end. Like Satan once more, he ends by becoming outwardly what he already was within: it is not, as he supposes, to Clifford that he now belongs, or Clifford's mark that he bears.

The impulse to demand a sacrifice to an angry God conceived in one's own image, suggested especially in the opening chapters of *Mandeville,* is fully developed in the religious bigot of our fiction: Brockden Brown's Wieland, Hogg's Justified Sinner, and Dickens's Mrs. Clennam (*Little Dorrit*), whose motto is Do Not Forget. Each follows the letter of the law, which is death. The type suggests comparison with the Gothic double-natured monk or priest, in Lewis and Hoffmann and elsewhere, and looking back to Shakespeare's Angelo.[19] *Wieland, or The Transformation,* is cited in the preface to *Mandeville* (p. x) as having supplied "the impression, that first led [Godwin] to look with an eye of favour upon the subject here treated." It tells the history of an upright man who, worked upon by inherited predisposition but especially by a master of illusion, Carwin, falls into a religious melancholia in which he kills his wife and children and attempts the life of his sister, the narrator, before being brought to his senses; he then, like Othello, kills himself. Carwin's motive is never really explained: he is not essentially malignant, it seems, but above all a reckless experimenter. The story owes something to the explained supernatural of Ann Radcliffe—effects are all-important, explanations secondary—and presumably also to Schiller's *Geisterseher* and its conspiratorial progeny.

More satisfactory as a novel, and closer to *Mandeville* as a study of morbid psychology, is James Hogg's *Private Memoirs and Confessions of a Justified Sinner,* 1824. It too is concerned with the destruction of a conscience or a better self and identification of hero with evil genius. Two sons of the same mother are brought up separately by their fathers, the elder, George Colwan, as a carefree young laird, the younger, Robert Wringhim, as an adherent of a particularly narrow Calvinist sect. The elder Wringhim, a bigoted pastor, persuades Robert that he is

> now a justified person, adopted among the number of God's children—[his] name written in the Lamb's book of life, and that no by-past transgression, nor any future act of [his] own, or of other men, could be instrumental in altering the decree.   [115][20]

Exalted by this declaration of election, Wringhim goes out and immediately meets a person unknown to him.

> What was my astonishment on perceiving that he was the same being as myself! The clothes were the same to the smallest item. The form was the same; the apparent age; the colour of the hair; the eyes; and, as far as recollection could serve me from viewing my own features in a glass, the features too were the very same. I conceived at first that I saw a vision, and that my guardian angel had appeared to me at this important era of my life. . . .
> "You think I am your brother", said he, "or that I am your second self. I am indeed your brother, not according to the flesh, but in my belief of the same truths, and my assurance in the same mode of redemption, than which I hold nothing so great or so glorious on earth."   [116–17]

Wringhim becomes entirely devoted to this person, whom he takes to be a foreign prince, perhaps from Russia, and who is known to him by the name of Gil-Martin. The stranger persuades him that his task is to cut off the enemies of God, those being always people whom Wringhim already hates in his thoughts. The chief object of his hatred is his brother George, whom he follows about like a "fiend," "shadow," or "demon" (35–37), and at length he kills him, thus inheriting the family estate. After a rape and two more murders that Wringhim can't remember committing, he tries in hate and fear to detach himself from the stranger, who replies:

> "Sooner shall you make the mother abandon the child of her bosom; nay, sooner cause the shadow to relinquish the substance, then separate me from your side. Our beings are amalgamated, as it were, and consociated in one, and never shall I depart from this country, until I can carry you in triumph with me. . . . I am . . . drawn towards you by an affection that has neither bounds nor interest; an affection for which I receive not even the poor return of gratitude, and which seems to have its radical sources in fascination. . . . "
> [189–90]

Later, the stranger, whom Wringhim now calls "tormentor," "my persecutor," rather than, as before, "the prince," "my patron," "my illustrious friend and great adviser," says:

> "I am wedded to you so closely that I feel as if I were the same person. Our essences are one, our bodies and spirits being united, so that I am drawn

towards you as by magnetism and, wherever you are, there must my presence be with you." [229]

The stranger at length denounces Wringhim to the magistrates for his crimes, and persecutes him while pretending to help him escape: he ends by proposing that they commit suicide together, then helps string Wringhim up and departs, having thus ensured Wringhim's soul to himself forever: by the end it has been clear for some time that "his fallen and decayed majesty," "this ruined and debased potentate," is the devil himself, his activities answering exactly to Wringhim's own dreams and wishes. As his domination progresses, Wringhim comes to feel that he has "two souls, which take possession of my bodily frame by turns, the one being all unconscious of what the other performs" (191–92). Gil-Martin replies to this:

> "We are all subjected to two distinct natures in the same person. I myself have suffered grievously in that way. The spirit that now directs my energies is not that with which I was endowed at my creation. It is changed within me, and so is my whole nature. My former days were those of grandeur and felicity. . . . "

This great change, recalling Satan's in *Paradise Lost,* is repeated within the book. Recovered from his period of possession by what seems an alien spirit, Wringhim meets Gil-Martin again and finds him now wearing "the figure, air, and features" of George:

> Yet in all these there were traits so forbidding, so mixed with an appearance of misery, chagrin and despair, that I still shrunk from the view. . . . But, when the being spoke . . . it was the voice of the great personage I had so long denominated my friend . . . but so altered . . . I can scarce conceive it possible that any earthly sounds could be so discordant, so repulsive to every feeling of a human soul, as the tones of the voice that grated on my ear at that moment. They were the sounds of the pit, wheezed through a grated cranny. . . . [188]

During Wringhim's flight from justice, Gil-Martin accosts him again:

> He regarded me with a sad, solemn look. How changed was now that majestic countenance to one of haggard despair—changed in all save the extraordinary likeness to my late brother, a resemblance which misfortune and despair tended only to heighten. [228]

The theme of doubles and alter egos here makes a rather complex pattern. First Wringhim is his brother's evil shadow, then Gil-Martin is Wringhim's, having previously been his more glorious image. As Wringhim's feared and hated other self, he bears no longer Wringhim's appearance but that of Wringhim's victim, formerly detested by Wringhim particularly for his innocence and generosity. The temporary occupation of Wringhim's body by an evil self over whose doings he has no control looks forward to *Dr. Jekyll and Mr. Hyde* and suggests themes of possession and vampirism. Gil-Martin's last metamorphosis, cited above, suggests *Dorian Gray*. Just before meeting him, Wringhim reports,

> I not only looked around me with terror at every one that approached, but I was become a terror to myself; or, rather my body and soul were become terrors to each other; and, had it been possible, I felt as if they would have gone to war. I dared not look at my face in a glass, for I shuddered at my own image and likeness.   [227]

Gil-Martin begins to persuade Wringhim to consider suicide:

> . . . he said his word and honour were engaged on my behalf, and these, in such a case, were not to be violated. "If you will not pity yourself, have pity on me", added he. "Turn your eyes on me, and behold to what I am reduced."
>   Involuntarily did I turn at the request, and caught a half glance of his features. May no eye destined to reflect the beauties of the New Jerusalem inward upon the beatific soul behold such a sight as mine then beheld! My immortal spirit, blood and bones, were all withered at the blasting sight; and I arose and withdrew, with groanings which the pangs of death shall never wring from me.   [234–35]

We can connect these passages, not only with the external image of the soul's condition in Dorian's portrait, but also with the parody of the atonement that in the last chapter we noted as characteristic of the deceiving magician.

A rather different symbolism meets us in two striking parallel passages. On an earlier occasion than that of George's murder, Wringhim follows George in the early morning out of Edinburgh up to Arthur's Seat, intending to kill him. He has a moment of doubt as to whether Gil-Martin's promptings are after all sent from God; and out of the mist emerges "a lady robed in white" (158) who vigorously rebukes him for his evil purposes before vanishing "over the rocks above the holy well." As Wringhim turns homeward, he is stopped by Gil-Martin, whom not long before he has mistaken for his "guardian angel" (117), and who revives his murderous determination. George meanwhile, walking "by the back of St. Anthony's gardens," has "found his way into that little romantic glade adjoining to the saint's chapel and well," where he moves carefully in order not to disturb the dew. He shortly sees "a bright halo in the cloud of haze, that rose in a semicircle over his head like a pale rainbow," a "terrestrial glory." Walking on, he then sits down to "converse with nature without disturbance," and especially without the gloomy and haunting presence of his brother.

The idea of his brother's dark and malevolent looks coming at that moment across his mind, he turned his eyes instinctively to the right, to the point where that unwelcome guest was wont to make his appearance. Gracious Heaven! What an apparition was there presented to his view! He saw, delineated in the cloud, the shoulders, arms, and features of a human being of the most dreadful aspect. The face was the face of his brother, but dilated to twenty times the natural size. Its dark eyes gleamed on his through the mist, while every furrow of its hideous brow frowned deep as the ravines on the brow of the hill. . . . Its eyes were fixed on him, in the same manner as those of some carnivorous animal fixed on its prey. . . .   [41]

In flight from this image, George runs into the flesh-and-blood form of his brother, who has been creeping up from the opposite direction in order to dash George down on the rocks. After a short exchange they separate, and George henceforward "could not get quit of a conviction that he was haunted by some evil genius in the shape of his brother, as well as by that dark and mysterious wretch himself" (45). A friend explains to him the natural phenomenon involved, but does not entirely dispel his doubts. This contrast of Brocken-like "glory" and "spectre" provides an apt image for the opposition of angelic and demonic "other selves." It is used once comparably by Coleridge:[21]

> . . . it is sufficient to say that Pindar's remark on sweet Music holds equally true of Genius: as many as are not delighted by it are disturbed, perplexed, irritated. The Beholder either recognizes it as a projected form of his own Being, that moves before him with a Glory round its head, or recoils from it as from a Spectre.

Apart from the specifically Romantic traits of fiction centering on the avenger, there are other features more or less consistent. In the most important literary archetypes, the *Oresteia* and *Hamlet,* vengeance is exacted for the murder of a father. A destroying past embodied in the angry or injured father is behind the action also of, for example, *Eugene Aram, Maud, The Mill on the Floss,* Nerval's "Emilie," and *Romeo and Julia auf dem Dorfe,* in some of which the heroine's brother becomes the father's representative; and the injured father is suggested also in the relations of certain childless men, such as Falkland and Monte Cristo, with the younger generation. He reappears in the hero of Bergman's *Virgin Spring.*[22] The man of excessive principle appears as the hero's rigorous father in *Corinne,* in *Contarini Fleming,*[23] and in *The Ordeal of Richard Feverel;* each at moments suggests a child-eating Herod, but always from the most exalted motives. With the vengeance situation, then, we can connect the man of rigorous honor or principle, who makes an idealistic decision and thereby sacrifices somebody, himself, his child, or the woman who loves him, like Lord Jim or Angel Clare, or that second-rate *Alastor*-Poet the hero of Longfellow's "Excelsior"; or, who fatally makes a law of his principle and demands a sacrifice to it, like Falkland, the demonic man of honor. Such a figure is close to the sacrificer as religious bigot.[24]

If the man of principle as destroyer is a pastoral type, this is partly because of his association with a scapegoat or sacrifice. Traditional pastoral literature has a well-known limitation in the languidness of its atmosphere and the passivity of its characters. Man in a happy landscape rejoices, in an unhappy one he laments, but he can't be said to *do* much. The central figures of pastoral myth are rather inert: Adonis dies, Persephone is snatched away, Orpheus mourns and is martyred. The devoted figures of biblical pastoral, like Abel, Isaac, Jephthah's daughter, Jonathan, and the seven sons of Saul, tend to be young victims doomed through no sin of their own, either by a stern father or through a father's fault—an offended God or an offending Adam. When we identify the pastoral world of, say, Wordsworth's "Michael" as "patriarchal," we are recalling that the Old Testament is the book of fathers and of the Father, as the New is the book of the Son. The grief and concern of fathers from Adam to David is a powerful emotional element in the Old Testament narrative, but enters the New only in the parable of the Prodigal Son, which in effect brings together the themes of the two testaments. However, when in the New Testament the Good Shepherd lays down his life for the sheep, he does so in order to satisfy the Father's justice, and his crown of thorns is perhaps cut from the bush where Abraham found the ram entangled. If there is a typical pastoral act, apart from acts of love and poetry, it would seem to be in sacrifice or passive death.

Perhaps because of this passivity of pastoral action, the pastoral theme of sacrifice is often attached to a young girl, innocent or helplessly abused, and clearly atoning for the sins of others. These may be represented by what the author regards as a bad heredity: Kleist's half-breed girl Toni in "Die Verlobung [The Betrothal] in Santo Domingo" is the daughter of, besides an unknown white, a murderous old Negress; and Stevenson's saintly heroine in "Olalla" is the child of a viciously degenerate Spanish noble family, of which she is resolved to be the last.[25] This "last of a great race" theme is distinctly elegiac, marking hero or heroine out for a tragic fate from Chateaubriand's "Le Dernier des Abencérages"[26] to *Green Mansions* and later. Like the decadent last descendants we saw earlier, Roderick Usher and Des Esseintes, whose whole life-force was concentrated in their nervous systems, or like the child of incest in Goethe and Thomas Mann, whose endowment is somehow too concentrated to allow him to pass it on, the young person who knows himself to be a last descendant will probably die early or consciously sacrifice himself, and the old man has probably, like Ossian, outlived children or child.

Closer to religious context are the fates of Chateaubriand's Atala and

O. W. Holmes's Elsie Venner, in the works named after them. Atala sacrifices herself to a religious principle improperly understood: her mother has vowed her to chastity, and she poisons herself when no longer able to hold off her despairing lover. The fact that her natural mother made the Jephthah-like vow, and that a spiritual "father" endeavors to temper its Old Testament rigor with Christian mercy, seems to reflect the contrast of carnal law and spiritual gospel. Elsie Venner, the double-natured child of a mother bitten during pregnancy by a poisonous snake, was invented by her author, according to the preface of 1883,[27] "to test the doctrine of 'original sin'"; her case certainly tests the local godly, this being a romance with very practical applications: ". . . if, while the will lies sealed in its fountain, it may be poisoned at its very source, so that it shall flow dark and deadly through its whole course, who are we that we should judge our fellow-creatures by ourselves?" (chap. 28). Elsie dies, not unwillingly, from two combined causes, a broken heart and the presence in her room of some flowers inimical to snakes; but while they destroy her, both work in such a way that the reptilian strain in her dies first and her humanity is fully restored to her.[28] Besides the serpent, another element pointing to biblical myth is Elsie's mysterious birthmark, which fades out before she dies, her variation on the mark of Cain: it looks like a snakebite. Holmes asks in the last of his three prefaces (1891), "May not the serpent have bitten Eve before the birth of Cain, her first-born?"

The pastoral "fall" or infection by evil, then, may be worked out in terms of atonement and expiation and feature a scapegoat along with, or instead of, the avenger. For each of Ophelia, Tess of the d'Urbervilles, and Rima, in their different ways, we could use Blake's phrase "the Female Martyr." Ophelia is the soulmate brushed aside by the avenger, Tess the victim-avenger, Rima the victim for whom vengeance is taken.[29] George Eliot's Maggie Tulliver, like Tess, destroys herself in trying to set right an old wrong: Maggie is particularly conscious of her role as sacrifice, linking it with the fates of other dark maidens, Flora Mac-Ivor, Minna Troil, and Corinne. A male scapegoat is Melville's Pierre, endeavoring by sacrifice to atone for his father's guilt and then finding he has chosen destructively. Pierre, Maggie, and Tess all make pastoral descents, from dewy countryside to city, flood, or the blasted heath of Salisbury Plain, this last not for the first time witnessing guilt and sorrow. Pierre's downward passage leads under a rock (perhaps he is named for it?) that both is an elegiac monument and threatens like Bunyan's Mount Sinai, reminding us that after innocence comes law, which can discover sin but not remove, and that the wilderness of Esau, Ishmael, and Cain is also that of Moses.

The Deerslayer, 1841, the last of Fenimore Cooper's Leatherstocking Tales, is set the farthest back in time, introducing Natty Bumppo at the age of twenty-three. The setting is the unspoiled wilderness heaven-reflecting Lake Glimmerglass, Natty's "first lake," in which he is jokingly urged to look at himself reflected; it becomes too the scene of his first human kill, in a kind of rite of initiation in which his Indian antagonist knowingly participates. Probably too it is the first time he is loved, by Judith Hutter, the daughter of the old ex-pirate whose "castle" and "ark" are the only structures on the lake. Contrasted with her frail, blonde, tender, devout, slightly feebleminded sister Hetty, clearly not long for a wicked world, Judith is dark, passionate, and "light-minded," the term indicating both her superficial vanity and some faint clouds on her reputation. Natty, whose talk of "truth" and "law" has already in the first chapter drawn him the reproach of being a Moravian, rejects an offer of love from Judith that is really an appeal for rescue from the life she sees before her. In her last words she asks Natty if anything said about her before they met by Hurry Harry, whom the reader knows to be frivolous, conceited, and unperceptive, has influenced his feelings; "truth" being "the Deerslayer's polestar," he is silent, and Judith disappears into the woods. She is last heard of as the kept mistress of an ex-officer in England. The reader may find it hard to avoid concluding that Natty's vanity is of a more sinister kind than poor Judith's, just as Angel Clare does more real harm than Tess.

The Deerslayer, the most idyllic and poetic of the books about Natty, is an American *Waverley*, beginning with the ideal mirrorworld of high-minded youth, having a scapegoat dark woman from whose mistakes the hero does or at least might learn something, and ending with a return after absence to scenes of former happiness, to find them desolated and empty. However, the striking difference is just as interesting. Waverley serves an apprenticeship to life, learning to put indolence and dreaming behind him and emerging as a man from his own sufferings and the greater ones of his friends. The Deerslayer when we first meet him has his ideas fully formed, to his author's entire approval. All that can happen is further definition to the reader of what he is, hence the rather ritualistic quality of the incidents. He defines in the course of the book what for him are the important moral points—the sanctity of an obligation, for example, and the occasions when it is rightful to shed animal or human blood; but the occasions do not really develop him or add to his self-knowledge. Moreover, his response to Judith's question tells us that any suspense we felt regarding his interest in her was misguided: he had made up his mind before he met her that his concern for her could never involve him deeply. And apart from the particular case of Judith, the reader will probably gather that his celibacy belongs to his peculiar integrity, and that he will always find himself in friendship more than in love. He is wedded to his vanishing solitudes, and no woman is their fitting embodiment.

Perhaps instead of complaining that Cooper lacks a Hawthorne's awareness of the ironies in moralism, one should regard *The Deerslayer* as what we earlier called an "unbroken idyll," a work depicting in its protagonist an innocence in which "Nature," purity, and the moral law are all in effect the same thing; it is then ironic only in its contrast with the world that the rest of us, and our fellows within the book, live in, and we judge ourselves if we regard as a prude an Adam who refuses to fall. It is in the light of a lower "nature" that we see Judith as more "natural," with her warmth, her moral confusions, her splendid artifice, and her experience of life as inner struggle. As a pastoral figure, she belongs to a type we can call "the animal woman," opposed by her tragic sensuality to the Hettys and Rimas and Ophelias, but enormously appealing by virtue of it. She is a special type of the dark lady of sorrows, lacking the soul-element by which Tess or Minna or Maggie or Hawthorne's Miriam purifies herself; and she is juxtaposed to the moralist rather as the animal man is to the magician. Beside Judith we can set Hawthorne's Zenobia, rejected by the high-minded Hollingsworth much as Judith is by Natty,[30] with the difference that after her suicide he recognizes himself as her murderer, perhaps recognizing too the justice of her reproach that his philanthropy was "nothing but self, self, self!" Hardy's Eustacia Vye in *The Return of the Native*, who is compared to the classical Zenobia and who, like Hawthorne's Zenobia, drowns herself, is another of the type. Florid names and exotic traits are in keeping, as the archetypes are Cleopatra, somewhat, and Dido, very much so: Zenobia's threat to "haunt" Hollingsworth recalls both the peculiarly earthbound nature of the type and the unforgiving mood of Dido in hell; and Elsie Venner, one of whose aspects is the animal woman in all her barbaric magnificence, recalls both exotic queens to her author: in vii she wears with other antique decorations a bracelet "that looked as if it might have been Cleopatra's asp," and at the end of xii and in xxvi Elsie identifies herself with "the forlorn queen of the *Aeneid*."

In *Mandeville* and the *Justified Sinner*, we noted a condition worse than solitude, or an intensification of it: the fatal bond between the hero and the alter ego. Eugene Aram longs in vain to link his fate with that of the lovely Madeline; he is already shackled by the knowledge of evil to his partner in an old crime, and the chain will drag him down in the end, the brotherhood of guilt being as strong as the bond of love. Evidently scapegoats too can have their shadow-selves, or secret sharers. A number of Hawthorne's dark victim-women—Hester, Miriam, Zenobia, Beatrice Rappaccini—are already linked by a mysterious bond to a sinister older man, and thus cannot be united with their lovers; the shadow of the past rests on them, just as it does on Pierre or Tess. Strange partnerships and unwilling complicities loom in Conrad's fiction, like the one that forces Marlow to lie to Kurtz's betrothed. Lord Jim, having chosen to atone for what is less a personal crime than a psychological equivalent of original sin, is touched at his weak point and capitulates to Gentleman Brown's "sickening suggestion of common guilt that was like a bond of their minds and of their hearts" (xlii); thereby he kills his true brother and abandons the wife he calls "Jewel" for an obscure marriage with the shades.

A pastoral idyll that becomes the history of a vengeance and exemplifies some strange companionships is W. H. Hudson's *Green Mansions*, 1904. The prologue, describing Mr. Abel's later life, stresses friendship: he and its narrator—"the nervous olive-skinned Hispano-American of the tropics and the phlegmatic blue-eyed Saxon of the cold north"—are "one in spirit and more than brothers." In his idealistic youth Mr. Abel was involved in a revolution in his native Venezuela, and when it failed he fled into the interior of the country; there after losing a manuscript that had promised him literary fame, he embarked on a search for gold, of which he kept hearing rumors. The search proves fruitless: "all my beautiful dreams . . . had vanished like a mere mirage on the savannah at noon" (i). Later, baffled in the woods by the laughter of the invisible Rima, he compares himself to what he has just been looking at, "the spider that chased the shadow" (v). Like the Poet of *Alastor*, Mr. Abel clearly has been prepared by his habitual questing after delusive objects for the encounter with the visionary maiden. Among the squalid local savages, Abel makes a particular companion of one called Kua-kó, who offers him his squalid sister if he will destroy Rima; Abel is of course revolted by this project of brotherhood. His first face-to-face encounter with Rima is full of threshold symbols: deadly snakebite, storm, vanishing phantom-maiden,[31] leap over precipice, and unconsciousness. Rima is following a mirage of her own, her dream of finding her mother's people; when it is disappointed she falls into a deathlike trance, and she recovers with her elusiveness removed and a more appropriately bridal disposition.[32] She has given up her dream—"I had chased the false water on the savannah" (xvii)—and is ready for reality; but it is immediately after this that the superstitious savages kill her.

Abel's first act after the discovery is to kill Kua-kó (actually in self-defence); then, after cursing God, in a state of "moral insanity" he joins forces with the hereditary enemies of Kua-kó's tribe and sees the village wiped out. In his wrath against God he resolves, "I would hate Him, and show my hatred by being like Him, as he appears to us reflected in that mirror of Nature" (xx): the idyllic, poetic, spiritual Nature that he saw earlier has disappeared.

Abel then returns to Rima's forest, where he builds a hut. His solitude is shared by ghostly memories of Rima, and by an enormous, hideous, poisonous hermit spider that he tolerates, remembering how she sought to protect everything in the wood. He sees himself in her mirror-pool, a gaunt, ragged man with a tangled mass of black hair falling over his shoulders, the bones of his face showing through the dead-looking, sun-parched skin, the sunken eyes with a gleam in them that was like insanity.

The torturing voice of despair tells him he is going mad:

> "It is not the tangled condition of your hair, . . . but your eyes, so wild and strange in their expression, that show the approach of madness. Make your locks as smooth as you like, and add a garland of . . . blossoms, . . . but the crazed look will remain just the same."

In desperation he shatters the image with a stone. After discovering Rima's bones, he ornaments the jar he keeps them in with a pattern of a creeping vine and a serpent, with a motto expressing his desolation: "Sin vos y sin dios y mi." He becomes improvidently absorbed in this task, "like the sorrowful man that broods on his sorrow and the artist who thinks only of his art" (xxi).

After killing an ugly and dangerous snake, Abel begins to feel remorse: "For were we not alone together in this dreadful solitude, I and the serpent, eaters of the dust, singled out and cursed above all cattle?" Like the Ancient Mariner with the water snakes, he even sees some beauty in it, and he fears that Rima would condemn his action: the voice of his despair tells him that Rima would flee from him if she saw him now. His dreams of her that used to make him reluctant to wake are replaced by sad, reproachful ones:

> This, too, was a phantom, a Rima of the mind, one of the shapes the ever-changing black vapours of remorse and insanity would take; and all her mournful sentences were woven out of my own brain. I was not so crazed as not to know it; only a phantom, an illusion, yet more real than reality—real as my crime and vain remorse and death to come.

Later he calls her "my mournful spirit-bride."

At length Abel resolves to make his way out of the wild interior. On the journey he becomes very ill, and as he travels on, his surroundings seem haunted by phantom savages, folklore monsters, and worst, "serpent fancies." His account of delirious wandering and strange places passed recalls less *Pilgrims Progress,* to which he refers, than the *Opium-Eater;* he calls himself "a new Ahasuerus, cursed by inexpiable crime" (xxii). Eventually, long convinced that he is already dead, he reaches a coastal city, where gradually he comes to believe that he has atoned for his crime and earned Rima's forgiveness: "I know that her divine eyes would no longer refuse to look into mine, since the sorrow which seemed eternal and would have slain me to see would not now be in them." He has carried out of the wilderness, and now keeps enshrined in his house, Rima's "sacred ashes," thus inviting comparison with Chateaubriand's René, who never made his peace so completely with the past:

> Indiens infortunés que j'ai vus errer dans les déserts du Nouveau Monde avec les cendres de vos aïeux! vous qui m'aviez donné l'hospitalité malgré votre misère! je ne pourrais vous la rendre aujourd'hui, car j'erre, ainsi que vous, à la merci des hommes, et moins heureux dans mon exil, je n'ai point emporté les os de mes pères! [conclusion of *Atala*]

The hero of *Green Mansions* is an Abel who becomes a Cain and then returns to his proper self. The name of Abel is used with intention in other romances: Abel Magwitch in *Great Expectations* works off the Cain in his nature and dies as pure Abel, unlike his enemy Compeyson, who is pure Cain; and the double-life villain of *The Moonstone* has the hypocritical name of Mr. Ablewhite. Whiteness befits the first shepherd,[33] while dark Cain is the founder of cities; but like other opposites we have seen, Cain and Abel are often hard to distinguish correctly, even when not combined within one person.

Two other tales by Wilkie Collins will furnish examples. *The Legacy of Cain*, 1888, describes the contrasting personalities and histories of two young girls brought up as sisters, Helena, the real daughter of the upright minister and his wife, and Eunice, unknown to almost everyone the child of a condemned murderess who asked the minister to adopt her. Contrary to the expectations and warnings of those who are in the secret, and contrary too to the appearance that the wicked sister endeavors to give to things, it is Helena who grows up capable of murder, while Eunice is in all respects admirable. Not that heredity plays no part: Eunice is tempted in visions by her dead mother, but resists, while in Helena the socially acceptable callousness and meanness of her own mother develop unhindered and make her recognizably diabolical. The author's conclusion is like that of Holmes[34] on the case of Elsie Venner, but emphasizing the character who fails to struggle against inherited evil:

> It was weak indeed to compare the mean vices of Mrs. Gracedieu with the diabolical depravity of her daughter. Here, the doctrine of hereditary transmission of moral qualities must own that it has overlooked the fertility (for growth of good and for growth of evil equally) which is inherent in human nature. There are virtues that exalt us, and vices that degrade us, whose mysterious origin is, not in our parents, but in ourselves. When I think of Helena, I ask myself, where is the trace which reveals that the first murder in the world was the product of inherited crime? ["Postscript," 479-80][35]

Without the nineteenth-century interest in heredity,[36] a similar mechanism operates in the 1962 Robert Aldrich film *Whatever Happened to Baby Jane?* There, Cain and Abel sisters, one of whom has irreparably injured the other, turn out to be, not respectively the maniac blonde and the calmly suffering brunette, but the other way round.[37]

The other Collins tale that varies this Cain-and-Abel theme is *The Frozen Deep*, 1874. Its heroine, Clara, is an orphan who always wears white, a ghostly maiden who has clairvoyant trances. Her two suitors, one accepted and one rejected, are away on the same Arctic expedition, each ignorant of the other's relation to her: it is the rejected one, Richard Wardour, who discovers that Clara's betrothed is Frank Aldersley. Richard, who is known as the Bear for his immense strength and surly disposition, and who is burning with hatred for his unsuspecting rival, drops behind the expedition to stay with Frank when the latter's endurance gives out; much later Clara, from her English garden, sees in a vision how he prepares to abandon Frank in order to save himself, suspense being greatly heightened by this glimpse. Eventually, after incredible travails, Richard staggers crazy and starving into his friends' encampment, with Frank in his arms—"Saved—saved for *her!*" His task finished and the lovers happy, Richard dies of exhaustion. This story of the self-sacrifice of an animal man to save a petted youth for a woman's sake recalls, besides the folklore model of the death of the Beast that brings forth Prince Charming (cf. Erik and Quasimodo in the last chapter), Mrs. Gaskell's story "The Half-Brothers," where the uncouth and unloved shepherd, Gregory, gives his life for the younger brother his mother has made him promise to protect. The couple reappear again, not as brothers or opposed types but as doubles, in *A Tale of Two Cities*[38]—Sydney Carton and Charles Darnay.

A late appearance of the mark of Cain in serious literature (though earlier than Hesse's quasi-gnostic *Demian*, 1919) is in Mann's "Tonio Kröger," 1903, where the artist is distinguished from other men by the "sign on his brow." It indicates not real guilt, but the solitude of a man in whom the love of "life" and of art are so intertwined that he cannot fulfill himself in either apart from the other: his art thus remains humane, nondaemonic, but its practitioner is condemned to wandering between two worlds. This opposition is dramatized at the end in symbols we have met before:

> "My father, you know, had the temperament of the north: reflective, solid, puritanically correct, with a tendency to melancholy. My mother, of indeterminate foreign blood, was beautiful, sensuous, naïve, careless and passionate at once, and with disorderly impulses. It was certainly a combination that bore with it both extraordinary possibilities and extraordinary dangers. It issued in—a bourgeois who strayed off into art, a bohemian with a nostalgia for respectability, an artist with a bad conscience."

Also, while he loves the fair and practical-minded Hans Hansen and Ingeborg Holm, no one loves him but dark, sad, dreaming, clumsy Magdalena Vermehren. He finds companionship at length in a fellow artist, Lisaveta Ivanovna, who as a sturdy Russian combines in her own way the practical and the visionary; this is a friendship, and does not free him from his state of gazing longingly on "life" as it were from outside. The undefined "sign" may relate more to the man of sorrows' crown of thorns than to the mark of Cain, but the two are not unconnected.[39]

Before looking at our last work, Tennyson's *Maud*, let us attempt some preliminary conclusions. A main link between Alchemist and Avenger, or protagonist of a plot concerned in some way with vengeance or retribution or the restoration of moral order, is that each has given himself over to an inexorable law of cause and effect: this element of "law" is the potentially tragic or ironic fact in their stories. The magician signs a bond or receives a terrible secret, refusing to take warning from the prophetic example of the prior fall of the other signatory or secret-bequeather, who clearly has entered on a course that binds him to victimize others. The avenger binds himself by a vow, or feels himself bound by inherited knowledge. To be bound in such a manner is to set moving a plot that can only be tragic unless something occurs either to change its course or to jam the works of the infernal machine: renunciation, self-sacrifice, or an event representing the forgiveness of sin. Law can cancel itself out by showing sin or liability in the accuser, so that the accusation has to be withdrawn and the conclusion is a sort of compromise; this happens in the case of the woman taken in adultery and in that of the Merchant of Venice, both implying that there are some people who can understand no sentence more liberating than, In Adam *all* die. However, gospel or "the quality of mercy" can redeem law, and so turn potential tragedy into comedy, though sometimes of a somber kind. Forgiveness of sin or some analogy of it can be observed in Prospero's renouncing his vengeance, in the chain of magnanimous actions in "The Franklin's Tale" that ends with the magister's taking the whole burden on himself and dismissing Aurelius as if he were newly sprung out of the ground, and in romances that conclude, like *Wuthering Heights*, with families being joined by love that were parted by hate.

One pastoral connection of the theme of vengeance is that the world of wrath inhabited by criminal and punisher alike is always a recognizable wilderness. Another is the possibility of redemption by substitution, which, though widespread in folklore, belongs especially to the history of Israel. The sacrifice of animals is prominent in the ceremonial laws relating to expiation and purification, and the story of Abraham and Isaac combined with dark sayings elsewhere suggests that originally the animal is substituted for a human victim and thus "redeems" the man. St. Paul comments on Moses' sprinkling the people with blood, "Almost all things are by the law purged with blood; and without shedding of blood is no remission" (Hebrews 9 : 22), and then explains that such ceremonies prefigure the effective sacrifice of Christ.[40] This symbolism combined with the comparison of the suffering servant to a lamb led to slaughter in

Isaiah 53 : 7 accounts for John the Baptist's saluting Christ as "the Lamb of God that taketh away the sins of the world" (John 1 : 29). Hence the special force of the animal man as sacrifice or victim in contexts even remotely Christian.[41] Where the overtones are not Christian, they are likely to relate to the emergence of Eros from the dragon, as in those numerous folktales like "The Golden Bird" in Grimm where the last act of the helpful animal is to die. A sacrificial beast whose beneficences recall a cruder paganism, that of the Land of Cockayne, is Al Capp's Shmoo.

In a plot whose main course is tragic or ironic, "law" may be represented by some decree—adulterers, or disobedient daughters, or strangers landing on these shores, are to be put to death. It may be a contract—at the end of twenty-four years the devil can have my soul. It may be a rash saying or promise—Stone Guest, come to my house for dinner; you may claim me when you have made those black rocks disappear; the first living thing that meets me when I return, I will send to the Beast or sacrifice to the Lord. And, very commonly in the nineteenth century, from Scott and *Wacousta* to "Ruddigore," it may be the working out of prophecy, oath, or curse. An early example is Young's tragedy *The Brothers*, in which the king, who sees one of his sons destroy the other, too late recalls his own murder of the Thracian queen and her two sons, and concludes that the princes have suffered for their father's act.[42] In *A Tale of Two Cities*, the innocent Darnay is to suffer for the crimes of his family, as prescribed in the curse of one of their victims. In the book's world of wrath, nemesis cannot be averted, but one victim can take the place of another. And the avenging woman who has chosen to represent Nemesis, Madame Defarge, dies all but simultaneously with Carton's execution. Miss Pross, in a way her destroyer, takes on no burden of guilt for the action, her author being careful to provide her with three distinct loopholes: the gun was the enemy's and deflected by Miss Pross, Miss Pross was acting less in hatred than in defence of herself and her beloved family, and Miss Pross sacrificed something in the encounter, being left without hearing for the rest of her days.

We looked earlier at *The Princess*, Tennyson's "summer's tale" of love and idealism, told in turn by seven friends in an idyllic setting completed by an atmosphere of family affection. *Maud*, his winter's tale,[43] is a history of vengeance and remorse, not medley but monodrama (in effect solitary complaint), and without any frame, thus without that surrounding continuum of natural and human life that is so essential to the Tennysonian "idyllic." Tennyson called it "a little *Hamlet*"; he might just as well have said a little *Werther* or *Tasso*, both those heroes fitting as well to his further description of "a morbid poetic soul."[44]

Under the blight of his father's ruin and suicide, for which he thinks Maud's family responsible, the speaker from his first lines on sees the

world of nature as luridly desolate, with Echo, that reliable guide, reply-
ing precisely as she does in Milton's Hell:

> I hate the dreadful hollow behind the little wood,
> Its lips in the field above are dabbled with blood-red heath,
> The red-ribb'd ledges drip with a silent horror of blood,
> And Echo there, whatever is ask'd her, answers "Death".

The mutual exploitation that is the law of society is the law of nature also:

> For nature is one with rapine, a harm no preacher can heal;
> The Mayfly is torn by the swallow, the sparrow spear'd by the shrike,
> And the whole little wood where I sit is a world of plunder and prey. [I.iv.4]

Against this imagery is balanced the world of Maud's sheltering garden,
with suggestions both of Solomon's garden and that (modeled on it) of
Marvell's Nymph. Her identification as the "milkwhite fawn" looks forward to her rôle as sacrifice, as her appearance to the speaker ghostlike in
a dream near the beginning does to his future haunting by her phantom.
At the climax of the poem, just as it seems that the love of Maud and the
hero will wipe out the family feud, he challenges her brother, "that huge
scapegoat of the race" (I.xiii.3), to a duel in the little hollow, and the
brother falls. Maud apparently dies of the shock, and the hero goes
through a long course of hallucinated depression—"A shadow flits before
me, Not thou, but like to thee" (II.iv.3)—and a period of madness, in
which the paradisal garden becomes a nightmare vision. The period of
mental wandering is the poem's equivalent of the Terrible Journey Out:
his return to the light and the disappearance of the phantom are marked
by his decision to join actively the life of the nation—specifically, to go to
war.

Tennyson's speaker is a typical hero of sensibility, with his mind disordered from brooding on private and social injustice. Typically for this
kind of story—like Hamlet, Faust, Melmoth, Mr. Abel, and the hero of *A
Blot in the 'Scutcheon*—he kills the man who should (or might) have become his brother, thus repeating the primal act of murder. One of the
poem's connections with *Hamlet* is in its view of bloodshed: as in the
play's juxtaposition of Hamlet with Fortinbras, here too one must distinguish so to speak dirty violence from violence clean or purging. The hero
recognizes too late that the act of private vengeance is not an answer to
"lust of gain in the spirit of Cain" (I.i.6) but a continuation of it: Maud's
brother dies by "the Christless code that must have life for a blow," and
thenceforward the speaker continues to hear "a cry for a brother's blood"
(II.i.1). By contrast to both economic exploitation masking the morality of
the jungle, and the duelling code allowing private violence,[45] open war in
the name of a whole people appears a chivalric struggle to cast out evil and

an opportunity of self-purgation: it brings out the Abel-virtues of nobility, unselfishness, and self-sacrifice. These values early in the poem were expressed in Maud's song of chivalry and manliness. During the hero's sufferings it represents all he has lost:

> An old song vexes my ear;
> But that of Lamech is mine.   [II.ii.6]

Lamech came in from the field and said to his wives Adah and Zillah,

> I have slain a man to my wounding, and a young man to my hurt. If Cain
> shall be avenged sevenfold, truly Lamech seventy and sevenfold.
> [Genesis 4 : 23–24]

The hero has persuaded himself that in some indirect way Maud's brother bore the guilt for his father's death, and in the hero's eyes moreover he represents the social extortion and privileged injustice that is the human equivalent of the bloody reign of nature. However, Cain though guilty was driven to the wilderness,[46] with the mark of God set on his forehead "lest any finding him should kill him." The traditional explanation of Lamech's words is that he unknowingly killed his ancestor Cain.[47] But, because the primal act of hate is not to be overcome by hate, the guilt of the avenger is proportionately greater than that of the original murderer. Or, by killing Cain one at very least becomes Cain. No one is righteous enough personally to execute justice; whoever tries to do so is like the impious magician challenging God: only the impersonal institutions of society or nation can venture on such a task, and most of our authors are much more doubtful even of those than Tennyson in *Maud.*[48]

A last connection with the themes we have been talking about is the relation of "the old man" to the action, as it is summed up in the hero's madhouse soliloquy. The poem's essential idyllic scene has become a garden of sterile plants and bloody roses, presided over by the brother, a demon who—Mezentius again?   "linkt a dead man there to a spectral bride." His titles "the keeper" and "Sultan of brutes" suggest the tyrant's exclusiveness. Behind him looms his father, a creature of the wilderness, who "laid a cruel snare in a pit." However, like the avenger's, his act had unforeseen consequences and destroyed those he loved along with his intended victims:

> For what will the old man say
> When he comes to the second corpse in the pit?   [II.v.9]

So we are back to the sorrow of fathers, and of the original "old man" who started it all.

Twelve Epilogue: This Swan Neck of the Woods

Although the literary treasures of "the old world" are ever open to us, and our American neighbours . . . continue to inundate the country with reading matter, intended to meet all wants and suit all tastes and sympathies, at prices which enable everyone to partake of this ever-varying feast; yet Canadians should not be discouraged from endeavouring to form and foster a literature of their own. More than one successful effort towards the attainment of this object has been made within the last few years, and more than one valuable work, Canadian in origin, subject, and sympathies, has been produced and published among us.
—Rosanna Leprohon, 1864

Canada—I am writing in this chapter as a Canadian—is without the decaying traditions of art, magic, religion, aristocracy, and so forth, that are the usual materials of Gothic fiction, and it has not proved very accommodating to ghosts; but still, its landscape does present more horrific possibilities than are exhausted by stories about being lost in the bush with two matches. The general imaginative picture offered by this half of the continent is that of wilderness or flood, or the dragon down whose St-Lawrentian throat all travelers arriving here before the age of flight had to plunge. Most settlers came as fugitives from a bad old world, rather than pilgrims to a new: that sense of visionary America, of world renewed or the country itself as treasure, that sheds an aura about the south from Donne and Marvell on—the America of spice and mine or the prepared refuge of the Ark of God—has never attached easily or obviously to Canada. The scene here is not merely cold-pastoral, it is antipastoral. Something is unsatisfactory or elusive about Canadian reality, with its seasons and its spaces unaccommodated to human needs or to the imaginative and visual conventions of the old world: the identity, the destiny, the secret, the treasure, is perhaps "waiting around the bend."[1] Hence a sense of quest that pervades our literature, with a great deal of uncertainty about what direction the quest should take. Often the direction suggested is less "into" or "to" than "through," a piercing through appearances and outward conditions into a new dimension concealed under the skin, as in that quasi-Canadian romance of John Buchan's, *Sick Heart*

Figure 10. *Pen drawing of Iroquois dancing with serpent who is the god of fire. From* Les Raretés des Indes, ou Codex Canadiensis, Album manuscrit de la fin du XVIIe siècle. *Paris, 1930. Photo courtesy of Metropolitan Toronto Library Board.*

River (described in chapter 10, note 52), where the story of adventure gives place to one of mental struggle and discovery.

The Artist, as we have met him earlier, has very little place in the Canadian literary landscape, despite Charles Sangster's early effort to domesticate on the shores of the St. Lawrence "the lounging student [with] his book."[2] Self-portraiture of the romantic artist has been most solemnly carried out by F. P. Grove, in his novels autobiographical and otherwise. His artist is the man with the wound, though of the thigh and not brow variety, and while seeing himself as a victim, he is still a born victimizer. Perhaps, accordingly, our earlier fictions are well advised in the distrust they show towards the artist. An attractive one is Lefroy in Charles Mair's tragedy *Tecumseh*, 1886; nevertheless, his life is saved by the sacrifice of the Indian girl Iena, who springs before him and intercepts a shot—thus, while in no sense a demon, Lefroy may, like Ernest Maltravers (see chapter 8 above), need others to suffer for him before he can become what he is destined to. Other artists are more or less casual seducers, like Miranda's unscrupulous parent in Roberts's *The Heart of the Ancient Wood* and the very improbable poet of *Jalna*, 1927, Eden Whiteoaks.

The main theme we looked at in connection with the Alchemist, the emptiness of any power over nature or the human mind that is exercised apart from wisdom and virtue, meets us in this landscape frequently and with peculiar force. We could describe in those terms Archibald Lampman's "The City of the End of Things" (before 1899) and F. P. Grove's *The Master of the Mill*, 1944, a poem and a novel linked by their strain of industrial fantasy; A. M. Klein's "*In re* Solomon Warshawer" and Earle Birney's "Vancouver Lights," poems about Nazism and war; and much of the work of E. J. Pratt. Two short stories will also illustrate: D. C. Scott's "Paul Farlotte," 1896, a summer idyll, and Joyce Marshall's "The Old Woman," about 1950, a winter horror tale.[3]

Of our three groups of romance themes, the one most productive for Canadian literature has been that of the Avenger, in versions emphasizing wildernesses, sacrifices, and victims. Poems about the early days in Canada tend to revolve around victims and martyrs, like what must be the third most famous Canadian poem, namely *Evangeline*.[4] The Indian massacre scene in Joseph Howe's *Acadia* (likely written in the 1830s), Lampman's "At the Long Sault," and Pratt's *Brébeuf and his Brethren*, 1940, all relate past episodes in the struggle of civilization, physical and spiritual, to impose its own patterns on the landscape; all are tragic, because the hostile forces of the continent, embodied in the Indians, at least outwardly win. Then comes a stage in Canadian history when the balance turns the other way: poets of the early nineteenth century celebrate in complacent couplets the driving back of Indians and wild animals and the establishment of a stable rural society, congratulating the human community on having conquered the hostile aspects of nature and thereby released the benevolent ones.

Writers of the later nineteenth century who read or think at all find their view of nature and man's place in it becoming more brooding and complicated: it has both more romance and more irony. Their sense of the rising glory of a new nation, child of the True North Strong and Free,[5] is balanced by a sense of the precariousness of human achievement, the certainty of the decadence and decline of all civilizations in their turn, and the ultimate cruelty of an evolutionary nature red in tooth and claw in which one order lives in the death of another. Questions arise about the spiritual cost of material progress, and writers seem to be asking themselves, for example, whether Indian and even wolf didn't have something after all: works featuring these items take on an elegiac tone. The mournful eye that European sensibility turns on ruins, in North America is turned on romantic last survivors. A generation after *The Last of the Mohicans,* Mair writes *Tecumseh* and "The Last Bison," with their panoramas of the lost grandeur and simplicity of a vanishing race. In Canada's National Museum, Ottawa, hangs a painting called *The Last Mastodon,* showing the creature up to its knees at the edge of the sea gazing into the sunset. Again, in Grey Owl's *The Tree* the last Indian and the last grizzly bear and the last pine tree on a particular stretch of prairie get together for a communal fade-out. Whatever we think of the sentimentality that often attends it, unfortunately there is nothing very remote about this theme.

A certain depth is given to such nineteenth-century subjects by a sense of the white man's guilt towards the Indian, and beyond that, of man's guilt towards, or failure to deal justly with, the whole order of nature on this continent which the Indian represents. Man's dealings with the animals belong to this larger theme, and the animal will figure prominently in the remainder of this chapter as a central pastoral symbol.

Canadian Nature, we might say, is ambiguous from the beginning. On one hand it has been the force resisting man's struggle to establish himself here, and on the other it is the thing that the country really has got, in quantities immense and formidable. The trackless white of the winter northland may suggest a terrifying world of death, or an inviting *tabula rasa* of primal purity and innocence: the possibilities put so memorably in "Excelsior." And nature is so much what man makes of it, physically as well as imaginatively, that with every advance in civilization it becomes more and more man's other half or mirror image, necessarily reflecting both the best and the worst in his way of life.

Man's duality, moreover, is such that what is hard on him in one way may in another be good for him. Along with questions about all that mankind obliterates in its advance come questions as to whether we have not moved dangerously far from the hard-pastoral conditions of pioneer life. These underlie Dorothy Roberts's poem "Cold":[6]

My grandparents lived to a great age in the cold—
O cruel preservative, the hard day beginning
With night and zero and the firewood
Numbing the fingers. God could have been in the flame
Responsive among the birch sticks, roaring
Up through the comforting pipes, and served all day
From the frosted woodpile, the continuing flame
As the sun almost let go of the bitter world.

But for them He stayed in the cold,
In the outer absolutes of cold among the fiery orbits,
And gave them the white breath and the blood pumping
Through hard activity stringing out the muscles
Into great age. They lived in cold
And were seasoned by it and preached it
And knew that it blazed
In the burning bush of antiquity
With starry flowers.

The cold is the appropriate manifestation of a God of law, and Moses the harsh shepherd of the wilderness is its fitting visionary. But the poet is talking here about a state already lost in the past, as pastoral innocence or even moral virtue unhappily mostly is. In other words, the poem is a closed idyll standing in ironic relation to our own world. When contemporary Canadian writers describe such innocence or virtue as existing in the present, these qualities are apt to be two-faced, resting either on ignorance or on a jealous puritanism of the kind that automatically demands a sacrifice.

Themes of victimization occur all over modern Canadian poetry and fiction. In *Canadian Short Stories*, 1952, only five out of twenty-four stories are out of our area altogether. In ten of them children are sacrificed to the adult world, are cruelly disillusioned by it, or make some decisive gesture and enter it, often killing an animal by way of initiatory rite. Nine stories (there is some overlapping, naturally) portray animals threatened, suffering, or dying, and the abuse and miseries of Indians or half-breeds. In the *Canadian Short Stories* of 1960, which repeats only a few, there is more variety in types of victim—fewer children, more helpless adults, use of animals more symbolic than direct—but no noticeable change of emphasis.

Most works of this kind are pastoral—significantly rural in setting, primitive in characterization. They tend also to be elegiac in tone, and their subject, the sacrifice of the animal or childlike, is cast in terms of the loss of innocence. What underlies them is the sense of the cost of progress, the split between material and spiritual advancement: to put it more psychologically, the acceptance of guilt, compromise, and willingness to exploit that in our world inseparably belongs to the maturity of individual or nation. Two themes one might expect to turn up in this connection do, but with twists in them. One is the defacement of the land by man's cities and machinery; here a usual approach, especially in poems, is to show the land either swallowing up the intrusive element or forcing its own shape on it—the shopwindow on the city street is a cavern, the bulldozer a primeval monster, the prairie railroad station is set "on the evening and on the sea."[7] The other theme is the rape of female innocence, which tends nowadays to be highly ambiguous. The country maiden seduced by the smart fellow (or fellows) is apt to have all the suffering docility of a beartrap, or James Reaney's highly agricultural Muse of Satire:

> Eyes bright as the critical light upon the white snow;
> With arms of gallows wood beneath the bark
> And torso made of a million hooked unhooking things,
> And legs of stainless steel, knives and scythes bunched together,
> And feet with harrows, and with disks for shoes. . . . [8]

These themes, and especially the deaths of animals, of course are at home in literature elsewhere. Marvell's "The Nymph Complaining," Coleridge's "Ancient Mariner," and Wordsworth's "Hart Leap Well," while all linked to the subjects of our last chapter, do not have the same social and geographical bearing as the comparable Canadian works: they describe more distinct and individual incidents, and their reference is too purely human. Even in Wordsworth, the persecuted animal seems to be called forth from the nature of the persecutor, rather than to be part of an independent natural order. In Canadian writing as a whole, the ambiguity of the animal and of our relation to it, its passivity in suffering, its inability to speak, balanced by the occasional power to make itself felt in destruction, make it embody the imaginative essence of life in this setting. Perhaps for European archetypes we should look less at actual animals like the stricken deer[9] than at the Calibans or animal men, like Frankenstein's Being, who with the world as it is are compelled to act in keeping with their brutish exteriors rather than with their original hidden hearts of gold. Moreover, while compared to Europe's our visual scene is unhumanized, too often among human qualities our civilization values those that link us downwards to "mere" nature.

Animal deaths have different levels and functions. We can borrow a distinction continually implied by Canada's senior modern poet, E. J. Pratt, to whose major themes all this is close: the highest human virtue is self-sacrifice, and the blindest, crudest evil is the urge to sacrifice others.

In Reaney's *A Suit of Nettles*, the hero is a typical pastoral sacrifice, a martyr of love; but the hero is also, at least in his outward, nettle-covered shape, a Stratford, Ontario, goose, and all the geese go to the block in December to contribute to man's Christmas cheer. Or, we can say: the sacrifice proper is the significant death by which something is achieved; the death purposelessly inflicted is waste or murder.

The wasteful or purposeless animal death in fiction is usually the most realistic one. We all know stories about a child's first experience of death in the sad end of a wild animal or a pet. It is a favorite college-magazine genre: while I was pondering this chapter, an example in the magazine of my own college[10] took a little boy on his first gopher hunt and concluded with "snow that would some day be white again, but never young," which conveys the general idea. That kind of death doesn't achieve anything, but simply shows you (in the words of the memorable subtitle of *Caleb Williams*) "things as they are," the facts of a hard world: in a poem by John Glassco,[11] the farmer sees "his calves and chickens and children / Destined for slaughter in the course of things." Sometimes the child learns at the same time about the callousness or perfidy of the adult world, and then the perspective shifts downward to show a realm not just of the haphazard, but of active evil. In Colleen Thibaudeau's story "The City Underground,"[12] a father whose manliness consists in the ability to handle a gun, a car, and a wife takes his little boy for a bracing day in the bush, and in the course of it shoots a poor family's cow in the vindictive pursuit of an abstract right. The puritanical lawgiving father runs from Colonel de Haldimar in Richardson's *Wacousta*, 1832, our first still-readable native novel, via Heavysege's Jephthah (*Jephthah*, 1865) to Avrom in Adele Wiseman's *The Sacrifice*, 1956, and they all incline to murder.[13]

Besides these events, there is the occasional real sacrifice, the death that achieves something; usually here the narration is on a recognizably romantic plane. The animal stories of Ernest Thompson Seton, Sir Charles G. D. Roberts, and their follower Grey Owl, are for the most— and worse—part highly romantic or sentimental. Seton in particular likes to introduce a human love story and to permit his elegiac bears and so forth various human extravagances including suicide. Many of their beasts are proud, kingly, loyal—noble savages on four legs; and in their deaths they are at least holding high the torch of romance, as in Roberts's short story "Strayed," adorned with a quest-imagery comparable to that of *Sick Heart River*. The title of Roberts's novel *The Heart of the Ancient Wood* warns us to expect something rather artificial: Canadian realistic woods are as heartless as the sea, having only a "deeper into," while pointing out the antiquity of a particular Canadian wood means in human terms precisely nothing. The heroine's name, Miranda, suggests in this late age of nature-romanticism that in her forest, like Rima's or the clifftop paradise of *Wacousta's* Clara Beverley, we enter a realm whose idyllic quality is directly connected with the heroine's virginity, or reasonable symbolic equivalent. Miranda, living with her mother in a glade, is a friend of all the animals and a vegetarian. She is wooed by one Dave, a woodsman and a realist. The issue of bloodshed looms large in their courtship, for example when Dave, having ignorantly shot the parents, destroys a family of lynx kittens to prevent their starving or getting eaten. The climax of the book comes when Miranda's pet she-bear, maddened by the loss of a cub, revengefully pursues Dave, who killed it, up a tree. Miranda, after a brief mental struggle, seizes Dave's gun and shoots the bear, proving that her instincts are sounder than her fancy notions—"Come down, O maid" would have made a suitable epigraph. The death of the bear is almost a sacrificial rite of passage, by which Miranda sheds those ideal but childlike traits that have prevented her from entering the world of real life. Once she has taken the remaining step of giving up vegetarianism, she doesn't stay a Nymph Complaining very long. I recapitulate this history because the same theme appears in a male version and modern dress in one of the best-known of Canadian pastoral works:

> That day returning we found a robin gyrating
> In grass, wing-broken. I caught it to tame, but David
> Took it and killed it, and said, "Could you teach it to fly?"

That David is Earle Birney's, in the poem called after him, and the principle is crucial to the poem, which is about a young boy's forced passage to maturity under grimmer conditions than the familiar one of the hunt. The departure from an idyllic state is epitomized in the last line:

> That day, the last of my youth, on the last of our mountains.

The mountain suggests, if not the visionary idealism of *The Princess* and other peak-paradise works, at least the bright hopefulness of youth; one could contrast to it as ambiguous or ironic the perfect mountain peak connected with the quest of death in *Sick Heart River,* and the morbid Magic-Mountain scene in Patrick Anderson's "Winter in Montreal."

The death of Miranda's bear, and the deaths in Birney's poem of first the robin and then David, are sacrificial and effective because the protagonist is giving up not another life but something of himself[14] in coming to terms with the rigor of the real world and the quality of its appropriate mercy. But perhaps it is only in romance that such acts are effective or such knowledge can be fully digested. For example, the protagonist of Hugh Garner's story "One Mile of Ice" crosses much the same threshold of experience as Conrad's Lord Jim, but in his haphazard realistic world there is no clear knowledge and accordingly no expiation or release.

The main conventions of Canadian writing are realistic, or at least demand the appearance of realism, as in "David."[15] A procession of victims makes its way through our shorter fiction, the human ones often emphasized by animal counterparts—the gasping salmon in Garner's "One, Two, Three Little Indians," the crushed butterfly in Irving Layton's "Vacation in La Voiselle," the caged owl in W. O. Mitchell's "The Owl and the Bens," the dispossessed birds in Margaret Laurence's "The Loons."[16] Useless, untransformed suffering seems to rule. Every second story in *Canadian Short Stories*, 1960, could be titled "The Trap": the farm, the city, the summer, the winter, every condition of life is an impasse, and protagonists long to escape, no matter to what alternative hell, like the frenzied, ferretlike little girl of Alice Munro's "The Time of Death." Reality, poised between the dream of romance and the nightmare of irony, seems closer to the latter. In our poetry, the ironic realm of solitude or essential disconnection is embodied in Lampman's deathless "grim idiot," in the wilderness where Heavysege's Jephthah hears only wild animals howling in answer to his prayer to God to spare his daughter, in the watery underworld of Pratt's "Silences," in the animal victims of Al Purdy's "The Death of Animals,"[17] where the wide winter distances reinforce the theme:

> Asleep or dead in the forest or the city:
> When mouse died a man coughed, stirred,
> Went to the bathroom. No connection, of course.
> When town merchant died of lobar pneumonia
> Owl was already dead. Again, no connection.
> Fox screamed, but the lady with lacquered nails
> Already owned a fur coat. No real connection.

One symbolic object moves from dreamlike beauty to brute horror, from "grace" to wrath—Pratt's iceberg, in the reverse evolution that fits it for its encounter with the *Titanic:* "no real connection."

While Canadian literature tends to show reality as grim and imprisoning, there is a more sinister level of the demonic and deluding, where all that glitters proves ice. Patrick Anderson asks in "Winter in Montreal," "O when shall we be free of the winter palace?"[18] This wartime poem looks forward to spring as a symbol of social change, the dissolution of "the capitalists' crystal"; other writers see spring as leading on a no more tolerable summer. The romantic seasonal image of desire is drawn from whatever season it doesn't happen to be at the time of writing. Here is a Canadian application of a figure we saw earlier, "the prisoner's dream":

> When every morn is fiery as the noon,
> And every eve is fiery as the morn,
> And every night a prison hot and dark,
> Where one doth sleep and dream of pleasant snow,

And winter's icicles and blessed cold,
But soon awakes, with limbs uneasy, cramped,
And garments drenched, and stifled, panting breath . . .

[Charles Mair, "August"]

Considering that winter is with us longer, and is therefore more often the enemy, one would expect in this setting some stress on the "winter pleasance"; actually this is replaced by a different symbolism less easy to characterize. The winter pleasance belongs to the celebration of love, friendship, or community, and these on the whole are only marginal or submerged Canadian topics. In earlier chapters we saw "dream" as a symbol of the idyllic state of youthful inexperience, inevitably to be shattered or dismissed; what fills that place in Canadian imagery is the unspoiled whiteness of new snow,[19] soon to be blemished or dissolved. On the other hand, in this age and setting, where extraordinarily little faith is put in the powers of art, the important, and even rescuing, imaginative creation is the dream, which when elaborated and sustained is usually—read either way—of a highly literary nature.

Let us look at the "dream" first in the seasonal context, and in its most fragile form. In earlier chapters we noted some lyrics—Waverley's poem, Wordsworth's "Lines," a group in *In Memoriam*—describing a moment just at the turning of season or time of day, or both; all these were elegiac. Canadian poetry has many such lyrics, and the favorite moment is at the point of sunset in Indian summer, late fall, or winter.[20] Often the setting is a shoreline one, thus in its way "cardinal" too. Lampman's sonnet "A Sunset at Les Eboulements" concludes:

The sun's last shaft beyond the gray sea-floor
Still dreams upon the Kamouraska shore,
And the long line of golden villages.

Typically, not only is "dream" a key word, but it is coupled with "still," as elsewhere with "yet" or "again": the dream has to do with persistence of the light after its source has vanished. Carman's "Low Tide on Grand-Pré" begins:

The sun goes down, and over all
These barren reaches by the tide
Such unelusive glories fall,
I almost dream they yet will bide
Until the coming of the tide.

Another Lampman sonnet, "Winter Evening," recalls the palaces of Prospero's speech, and perhaps too their translation to sunset visionary Venice:

To-night the very horses springing by
Toss gold from whitened nostrils. In a dream

The streets that narrow to the westward gleam
Like rows of golden palaces; and high
From all the crowded chimneys tower and die
A thousand aureoles. Down in the west
The brimming plains beneath the sunset rest,
One burning sea of gold. Soon, soon shall fly
The glorious vision, and the hours shall feel
A mightier master; soon from height to height,
With silence and the sharp unpitying stars,
Stern creeping frosts, and winds that touch like steel,
Out of the depth beyond the eastern bars,
Glittering and still shall come the awful night.

Far less explicitly than "Julian and Maddalo," or even "Winter in Montreal," the choice of words towards the end nevertheless suggests the iron-pastoral contrast between the scarcely formed dream of community and the everyday reality of social injustice and man's self-imprisonment.

"Memory" often plays a part in sinister natural descriptions, sometimes embodied in ghostly maidens who seem as much projected out of the autumnal landscape as onto it. One appears in the October Eclogue of Reaney's *A Suit of Nettles:*

> I met a green woman...
> Did I touch her?
>   Vanished.
>   Twang!
> Garnisheed
> All pulse-wage since. ...

Less succinct is Wilfred Campbell's "A Lake Memory," heavily breathing Symons and the English nineties; his phantom again is less Persephone than Eurydice, a lady of fall.

> The lake comes throbbing in with voice of pain
> Across these flats, athwart the sunset's glow.
> I see her face, I know her voice again,
> Her lips, her breath, O God, as long ago.
>
> To live the sweet past over I would fain,
> As lives the day in the red sunset's fire,
> That all these wild, wan marshlands now would stain,
> With the dawn's memories, loves and flushed desire.
>
> I call her back across the vanished years,
> Nor vain—a white-armed phantom fills her place;
> Its eyes the wind-blown sunset fires, its tears
> This rain of spray that blows about my face.

"Memory" and "dream" are both key words in some poems of Sir Charles G. D. Roberts. "The Mowing" concludes:

> The crying knives glide on; the green swath lies.
> And all noon long the sun, with chemic ray,
> Seals up each cordial essence in its cell,
> That in the dusky stalls, some winter's day,
> The spirit of June, here prisoned by his spell,
> May cheer the herds with pasture memories.

The subject of mowing is of course pastoral; pastoral too, in our sense, is the theme of the power of human arts to preserve what nature in her course both brings and takes away. The art suggested here is alchemy. Another Roberts sonnet, "In an Old Barn," concludes with a version, on a very low level of consciousness, of the winter pleasance:

> Far down, the cattle in their shadowed stalls,
> Nose-deep in clover fodder's meadowy scent,
> Forget the snows that whelm their pasture streams,
> The frost that bites the world beyond their walls.
> Warm housed, they dream of summer, well content
> In day-long contemplation of their dreams.

While "far down" hinges the octet, describing the rafter area, to the sestet on ground level, it suggests also that the cattle carry on a warm instinctive being not only surrounded by winter but beneath its blanket, like the streams under the ice. Roberts brings out a benevolent aspect of the "winter palace" in his little poem "Ice":

> When Winter scourged the meadow and the hill
> And in the withered leafage worked his will,
> The water shrank, and shuddered, and stood still,—
> Then built himself a magic house of glass,
> Irised with memories of flowers and grass,
> Wherein to sit and watch the fury pass.

From glittering prisons, scorching hells, and such human states of mind as may be represented by them, then, one brief escape is the dream or mood that momently promises to eternize an idyllic aspect of nature, or preserve its possessor from a grimmer one. A more final escape, to look at a different kind of symbol, is D. C. Scott's seachanged vessel at the end of his ballad "The Piper of Arll."[21] His theme is something like the alchemical transformation of life by art, and the end state of all concerned is neither life nor death but "dream." The jeweled structure that the vessel becomes[22] has a living element in the "quick" vine of silver leaves growing over it, like the "living" buildings mentioned in chapter 7 above. This is ark as grail, "the prize beneath water around which fish move."[23] Ralph

Gustafson's introduction to *The Penguin Book of Canadian Verse,* 1958, lists first and second among "the specifics of contemporary Canadian poetry," "the sea" and "diving." The dream, the Atlantean Arcadia or underwater paradise, and the ark are all similar and connected symbols of escape from the Canadian wilderness-world, and related to the motif mentioned at the beginning of the chapter of penetrating through the surface that conceals secret or treasure or undiscovered realm. Wilderness as flood surrounds A. M. Klein's poet in "Portrait of the Poet as Landscape," who

> lives alone, and in his secret shines
> like phosphorus. At the bottom of the sea.

Generally ark or grail is not so much created or inhabited by the poet as recognized by him in natural object[24] or, as in the sunset "dreams," in play of light. When not a mood or light-effect, the Canadian "dream" may be represented by a symbolic living creature,[25] especially fish or bird. A nightmare counterpart is the wilderness-Leviathan of Sheila Watson's novel *The Double Hook,* symbolized again and again in Jonah's phrase, "the bars of the earth"; this brute is prison rather than palace, like Anderson's frozen city. Another demonic containing creature, a Covering Cherub who has swallowed not man but man's treasure, is Douglas Le-Pan's peacock, who shares his author's name (*le paon*):

> Armoured beneath its glossy side
> Lost paradise is darkly hidden.
>
> ["The Peacock," in *The Net and the Sword*]

A native blue bird, the heron, is the embodiment of dreams in his "Image of Silenus," here representing unity and completeness of being, rather than the contradictions of the anguished "bird of pride." At the end of the poem the heron perhaps

> somewhere has found its home
> And moored
> In its nest that quietly floats on the sea-dark forest,
> Now everywhere perfectly sealed and secret.

In the old world that might have been a halcyon, or living solstice ark; a homelier version is the old goose Keziah at the end of *A Suit of Nettles,* who, with "all possible eggs inside her," carries life over from the Christmas massacre into the new year.

James Reaney speaks in an article[26] of man's power effectively to "dream his way out of his prison," and in a short story, "The Bully," has illustrated it. The story turns on the contrast between crushing reality and the liberating dream. The narrator is a young boy hoping to escape from the trap of life on the farm by becoming a schoolteacher; he is forced to drop out of high school after a few months by the cruelty of a savage

Figure 11. *Author's illustration from James Reaney,* Twelve Letters to a Small Town, *1962: chicken carrying town hall of Stratford, Ontario, on its back.*

schoolmate who completely terrorizes him, and he goes home defeated to the farm. That night he has three dreams. In the first the Bully proves to have been his strong older sister in disguise. In the second the Bully makes love to his favorite younger sister, who is "weak" like him. In the third:

> I ran away . . . across the fields into the bush. There was a round pond there surrounded by a grove of young chokecherry trees. I pushed through these and came to the edge of the pond. There lay the Bully looking almost pitiful, his arms and legs bound with green ropes made out of nettles. He was drowned dead, half in the water and half out of it, but face up. And in the dim light of the dawn I knelt down and kissed him gently on the forehead.

This reconciliation is made possible by the discovery that Cain and Abel, the strong and the weak, are brothers, and that each is so to speak the other's scapegoat. The one who can forgive most is the real victor and possesses the alchemy that transforms life. At the same time, with all the sweetness of this conclusion, Reaney no more simplifies the old Canadian topic of the relation between victims and victimizers than does Isabella Crawford, or Irving Layton, or Alden Nowlan: we know from within, from plain human nature, exactly why the Bully loathed the narrator. In his plays too, Reaney takes into account our sympathy with his demon stepmothers and tyrannical hired men in their hatred of innocence and its endless forgiveness; and in his book of lyrics *The Red Heart* he speaks eloquently for evil orphan and infant Antichrist. But in his world the power to dream is not mere passivity or escape, but is creative and transforming, a kind of art.

The creative dream appears again in P. K. Page's poem "Stories of Snow." The climates of Canada's muggy extreme west and sharp near east are transformed into imaginary tropics, hot with color, and cool Holland in winter. Its central image, of the dying swan, is close to the romantic world of the Quebec folksong "En roulant ma Boule," in which a magic duck is shot and its feathers drift down to make a featherbed for weary travelers. Comparing this poem with Purdy's "The Death of Animals" quoted above, we see that things are reversed. The world of snow and the dying animal is not remote from man but inside his head, and he can withdraw to it as if to the paradise of childhood, where hunters are winged and plumed like their quarry, where snow falls like warm feathers, and where as in the fairy tales the last act of the helpful animal is to die:

> And of the swan in death these dreamers tell
> of its last flight and how it falls, a plummet,
> pierced by the freezing bullet
> and how three feathers, loosened by the shot,
> descend like snow upon it.
> While hunters plunge their fingers in its down
> up to the neck of the wrist
> in that warm metamorphosis of snow
> as gentle as the sort that woodsmen know
> who, lost in the white circle, fall at last
> and dream their way to death.
>
> And stories of this kind are often told
> in countries where great flowers bar the roads
> with reds and blues which seal the route to snow—
> as if, in telling, raconteurs unlock
> the colour with its complement and go
> through to the area behind the eyes
> where silent, unrefractive whiteness lies.

Canadian literature is without strong individual characters on the whole, being much more forceful in its presentation of settings. Man appears rather generalized: what has character is the wilderness, the city, the snow, the sea. The symbol of quest may be the green world in or under the snow, the focal point in the waste ("Strayed"); or the treasure hidden in the earth or under the sea or inside the monster ("The City Underground," "The Peacock"); or it may be the sinister glitter of ice and the ambiguous whiteness of the snow ("Winter in Montreal"). Objects of search, we could conclude, are respectively life, transformation, and death, in approximate terms. Tasso tends to be pushed into the background by Antonio, the man of action; but if the dreamer is not important, the dream is. Again, the individual's search for love is not very important. Lampman, Scott, Pratt, and others have been accused of being unduly shy of love; perhaps the great presence of the continent dwarfs any pursuit of private fulfillment to the scale of Birney's "Slug in Woods" (despite jeweled description a distinct nontreasure):

> Azygous muted life,
> himself his viscid wife,
> foodward he noses cold beneath his sea.

The dream, as distinct from that kind of separatist somnambulism, at least points towards communion. If at worst our civilization is massminded, reflecting the qualities of nature at deadest—"their mouths full of gum, / Their eyes full of the worst winter in a hundred years"[27]— perhaps at best it is socially minded, and the search for America or True North resolves itself as the quest of community. Even "Stories of Snow," while far more tentative in its affirmation than, say, Pratt's romantic dream "The Depression Ends," assumes that the dream not only looks towards a community but is a communal possession, like the arts of wizards and fabulous bards in Morris's and Nabokov's cold kingdoms. It ends in a death that hints at communal sacrament and at metamorphosis; and, it suggests a constructive alternating rhythm of effort and dreamless rest that is nearer to Eden than whatever it is that Canadians seek in Florida.

Patrick Anderson called the unexplored continent "a gauche but beautiful mirror." Mirrors generate specters and soulmates, images of horror and desire. It's clear enough what in this landscape are Spectral forms: principally, the shapes of the possibility that the life of man takes its interests and directions only from the natural struggle—staggers round the white circle and dies without hope of renewal. The bride of desire, the elusive dream of the union of what is creative in man with what is idyllic in his vision of nature, in this setting is both the untouched wilderness retreating before him and the humane Arcadian city he hopes to shape it into.

Notes

Chapter 1

Epigraph: James Beattie, "Ode to Peace," III.3.

1 In the order of the elements, whether water is placed above earth or below it may depend on whether the writer is more aware of earth's being heavier than water or of the mutual antipathy of fire and water. In pastoral contexts, the order that places water at the bottom (*Metamorphoses* i.26–31) would seem the more useful, and it is certainly the important one for the nineteenth century.

2 Cf. Michael's prophecy about the sons of Seth (*PL* XI.621–27):

> . . . that sober Race of Men . . .
> . . . now swim in joy,
> (Erelong to swim at larg) and laugh; for which
> The world erelong a world of tears must weepe.

3 See Northrop Frye, "The Structure of Imagery in *The Faerie Queene*," in his *Fables of Identity*, pp. 69–87.

4 This "hard phrase" is adapted from Bacon's essay "Of Friendship": ". . . those that want friends to open themselves unto, are cannibals of their own hearts" (earlier he remarks that without friends "the world is but a wilderness"). Cf., besides Pythagoras's injunction "Eat not the heart" (Plutarch, *De liberis educandis* 12e), the account in *Iliad* vi.202 of how Bellerophon after his fall wandered "eating his own heart and shunning the paths of men." For a use in the period with which we shall be mainly concerned, cf. Mary Shelley, *Falkner*, 1837: "Thus . . . his soul shut up in itself—he became, in the energetic language of genius, the cannibal of his own heart" (III, 129).

5 "Winter and rough weather" (*As You Like It* [1599] II.v.8)—called "the penalty of Adam" (II.i.5)—may, as here in Shakespeare, be linked with innocence to make a hard-pastoral point (see A. O. Lovejoy and George Boas, *Primitivism and Related Ideas in Antiquity*, pp. 9–11), about the superiority of austerity to idyllic ease.

6 Quotations from the Greek pastoral poets follow the versions in *Theocritus, Bion and Moschus*, trans. Andrew Lang.

7 Quotations from Virgil are from *Works*, trans. James Lonsdale and Samuel Lee.

8 See Thomson, *Seasons*, "Summer," 12; J. Warton, *Ode to Fancy*, 41; Collins, *Passions*, 65 (with "mingled measure" at 64); Beattie, *Minstrel*, I.291.

9 These echoes are pointed out and discussed in J. B. Beer, *Coleridge the Visionary*, pp. 233–37.

10 "Primitive" is used by Milton almost invariably as a positive word, implying closeness either to the original state of man established by the Creator, or to the

state of the Church as established by Christ—never, as in Romantic writers, imputing goodness to human nature in itself. "Assuredly we bring not innocence into the world, we bring impurity much rather" (*Areopagitica*). (On this point, as on a number of others, I am indebted for guidance to F. E. L. Priestley.)

11 Beer, *Coleridge the Visionary*, p. 230, in connection with "Kubla Khan" quotes from Thomas Paine: ". . . the palaces of Kings are built on the ruins of the bowers of Paradise."

12 This example, and the structure of ideas organizing this chapter, will be found in Northrop Frye's essay "New Directions from Old" in his *Fables of Identity*, pp. 52–66.

13 Eleanor M. Sickels, *The Gloomy Egoist: Moods and Themes of Melancholy from Gray to Keats*.

14 *Sopra lo amore*, cited in Charles Lemmi, *The Classic Deities in Bacon*, p. 20. For similar formulations see below, p. 77 (*Corpus Hermeticum*); 76 (Boccaccio); chap. 3, n. 3 (Sir John Davies).

15 Creuzer, *Symbolik*, part IV, chap. v, sec. 1, p. 165, n. 2; sec. 2 passim.

Chapter 2

Epigraphs: John Milton, epigram "Ad Leonoram canentem," no. 2; Herman Melville, *Moby-Dick* i.

1 The theme of Tasso's "search" appears with the first mention of him, I.i.147–54, in a teasing speech addressed by the princess to Leonore:

> . . . we may with pleasure meet the Poet,
> Who seems to avoid us, even flees our sight,
> In quest, it seems, of some mysterious good
> Unknown to us, perhaps to him as well.
> How charming it would be if once at some
> Propitious hour he met us, and with rapture
> Beheld in us the treasure he so long
> Had sought in vain abroad through the wide world.

2 V.v.3313–14. Cf. I.iii.449–502; V.ii.3084; V.iv.3133–36.

3 The wilderness theme recurs in the "Elegie" of 1823, with specific reference to Eden.

4 The sea and shipwreck scene of Tasso's final speech has been prepared for earlier. Where previously, in keeping with the garden setting, Antonio and Leonore were both seen as serpents (II.iv.1470–71; IV.iii.2509–10), now the princess appears to Tasso a "siren," and following this he contrasts himself with galley slaves, who alone can know one another's hearts (V.v.3339–42).

5 It is characteristic of this play that relations between states or objects of the imagery seem more consistent than those between persons. At one moment it is Tasso who is removed from the storms of life, and at another the princess— this is psychologically interesting, but does not mean an alteration in essential relations. The princess and Tasso are both faint "moons" implicitly or explicitly contrasted with the "suns" of others (cf. IV.ii.2257–60; III.iii.1956–59:

these images are reinforced by Tasso's "Echo" and the princess's "pearl" in II.i.797–800, 885–87). Tasso is also the wanderer on solitary paths lit by the uncertain light of the moon, or finds himself in complete darkness on the edge of a precipice after the sun of favor and happiness has set (III.iii.1956–59, cited above, where "moon" refers to the princess; IV.i.2231–40).

6 Cf. IV.iii.2468–71. "Spinnen" in the play verges on its nineteenth- and twentieth-century colloquial meaning, to be crazy.

7 Cf. two remarks about the poetic faculty as unifying and reconciling:

His ear receives the harmony of nature . . .
His mind assembles what was widely scattered. [I.i.160, 163]

The myriad-numbered thoughts of many men,
Widely assorted, who in life and mind
Are all at variance, the poet's skill
Can comprehend in one. [V.ii.3035–38]

8 In respect of symmetry *Tasso* invites comparison with Goethe's novel *Die Wahlverwandtschaften* (Elective Affinities), 1809, whose characters are introduced in a strikingly diagrammatic arrangement.

9 Cf.: Your fathers raised these walls to stand secure,
A shelter for their dignity, providing
Sure punishment for those who broke their peace:
Exile, dungeon, death, befell the guilty. [II.iv.1505–09]

Chapter 3

Epigraph: Nathaniel Hawthorne, *The Marble Faun* xxx.

1 A specific contribution of Young's to *Tasso* may well be Tasso's differently turned image for himself of the silkworm (quoted above in chap. 2): compare *Night Thoughts* I.155–61: "How was my heart incrusted by the world! / O how self-fetter'd was my grovelling soul! / How, like a worm, was I wrapt round and round / In silken thought, which reptile fancy spun, / Till darken'd reason lay quite clouded o'er / With soft conceit of endless comfort here, / Nor yet put forth her wings to reach the skies!"

2 Nebuchadnezzar's dream (Daniel 4) represented him as a tree hewn down in divine retribution for his impiety; in Virgil's First Eclogue to see "an oak struck by heaven" was a bad omen. Scathed and blasted oaks and pines appear three times in Shelley's poems (*Wandering Jew* III.786–88; *Queen Mab* VII.259–60; *Alastor* 530–31)—the first two times implying, as in Milton, Heaven's punishment—before the vision of the "lightning-blasted almond tree" in *Prometheus Unbound* II.i.135. They recur so regularly in outdoor scenes in his romances that readers might question the following: "A scathed pine or oak, blasted by the thunderbolts of heaven, alone broke the monotonous sameness of the imagery" (*St. Irvyne*, 1811—*Complete Works* V, 165). Compare Scott, *Rokeby*, 1813, IV.iii (scenic merely); also Byron, the final lines of *Parisina*, and *Childe Harold* III.lxxviii, where the blasted tree has become assimilated to his regular symbolism of the divine fire that both inspires the exceptional man and con-

sumes him (both 1816). The hero of Maturin's *Bertram*, 1816, calls himself a "blasted tree" (IV.i); Polidori's Ernestus Berchtold (*Ernestus Berchtold, or The modern Oedipus*, 1819) declares he is now left "a scattered [sic] pine amidst this desolate scene" (89). Frankenstein, "the modern Prometheus," 1818, in III, ii (xix) declares, "But I am a blasted tree; the bolt has entered my soul": in ii it was the destruction of an oak by lightning that first excited his interest in science.

Conventional references continue: cf. Poe, "To One in Paradise," 1833. More interesting are the developments in the novel. *Jane Eyre*, 1847: "Why had the name of [Mr. Mason] . . . fallen on [Mr. Rochester] . . . as a thunderbolt might fall on an oak?" (II, viii; xx) foreshadows the remarkable part played in the story by the chestnut tree, that groans while Rochester proposes to Jane beneath it—is split by lightning the same night—later furnishes him with a comparison for his blinded and scarred state—but has already, immediately before the interrupted wedding, offered an omen for the eventual union of the pair. —While Mr. Rochester's mark of fire calls forth a reference to Vulcan, Ahab's scar, compared by Melville to a tree's lightning-seared seam (*Moby-Dick*, 1851, xxviii), is a "brand," perhaps suggesting Cain's. —In *The Mill on the Floss*, 1860, Philip, speaking of love to Maggie in a grove of Scotch firs, says, "Don't look away from me to that cloven tree; it is a bad omen" (V, iv); and Eliot calls the next chapter, in which they are separated, "The Cloven Tree."

3 This sentiment (cf. Boëthius, *De Consolatione Philosophiae* ii.4), with its attendant rhyme "find–mind," is a commonplace in Renaissance verse: cf. Wyatt's satire "My mothers maydes—" 97–99, "Then seke no more owte of thy self to fynde / The thing that thou haist sought so long before, / For thou shalt fele it sitting in thy minde . . . "; Spenser, *Amoretti* 78, where the beloved is seen in the poet's thoughts rather than in the outward world (compare Goethe's "Elegie" in chap. 4, app. 1); Vaughan, "To the Holy Bible": "Thou . . . having brought me home, didst there / Shew me that pearl I sought elsewhere." Davies's *Nosce Teipsum*, sts. 23–25, outlines the closely related theme of men's going out to gaze at natural wonders but ignoring those within (Augustine, *Confessions* x.8; cf. Browne, *Religio Medici* I, 15); in the poem's conclusion it is raised through the allegorical Narcissus (see chap. 5 above) to a religious level: "Look in thy soule, and thou shalt beauties find, / Like those which drownd Narcissus in the flood: / Honour and Pleasure both are in thy mind, / And all that in the world is counted Good" (st. 472).

4 For earlier night-wanderers, cf. "Sorceress: 'Wayward sisters, you that fright / The lonely traveller by night . . .'" (Nahum Tate, *Dido and Aeneas*, c. 1680, II.i.2); "And lonely Philomel . . . directs the Wand'rer right" (Lady Winchilsea, "A Nocturnal Reverie," 1713). For Shakespeare and Milton see below, p. 46 and note.

5 Cf. Richardson's *Clarissa* IV, letter 7, pp. 38–39:

One devious step at setting out! . . . —Which pursued, has led me so far out of my path, that I am in a wilderness of doubt and error. . . . But I, presumptuous creature! must rely so much upon my own knowledge of the right path! little apprehending that an *ignis fatuus* with its false fires (and yet I had heard enough of such) would arise to mislead me! And now, in the midst of fens and quagmires, it plays around me, . . . throwing me back again, whenever I think myself in the right track. . . .

V, letter 9, p. 22; VI, 42, p. 156, contain similar references. The deluding light becomes a prose commonplace: Louisa writes to Beckford (December 12, 1783), "The deluding meteor, that led me on to destruction, is extinguished" (Guy Chapman, *Beckford*, p. 169); or, ". . . the delusions of passion and false sentiment . . . like fascinating treacherous guides, lure along their victim by a meteor flame to the very brink of the precipice" (Charlotte Dacre, *Confessions of the Nun of St. Omer*, 1805, I, 99).

6 Notably the line, "Mislead night-wanderers, laughing at their harm" (II.i.35).

7 With Shakespeare, Burton, and Milton in this connection, we can note several seventeenth-century poets. George Sandys's *Ovids Metamorphosis*, 1632, mentions in its preliminary pages steering by "wandering stars" and "lights prov'd erring fires"; Vaughan's metaphors include false lights, and a false good luring to a precipice ("Religion" and "The Hidden Treasure," 1651); Marvell's "Mower to the Glo-Worms" speaks of "wandering Mowers" led astray by "foolish Fires"; and Rochester speaks of "Reason, an Ignis fatuus of the Mind" (*Satyr on Mankind*, 1675). Dryden links Puck and labyrinth in *Marriage-à-la-Mode*, 1673, IV.i.105–06, where Leonidas has been "wandring in a maze of fate, / Led by false fires of a fantastick glory." More personal, and moving, are lines 72–77 from *The Hind and the Panther*, 1687; for further background to the image see note on this passage in *Works*, ed. H. T. Swedenberg et al., vol. 2, *Poems 1681–84*, pp. 157–58. Dryden's *King Arthur*, 1691, a very entertaining potpourri of *A Midsummer Night's Dream*, *The Tempest*, *The Faerie Queene* II.xii, *Comus*, *Paradise Lost*, and doubtless more, contains the following song, sung by the Ariel-like Philidel to confound the Caliban-like Grimbald: "Hither, this way, this way bend, / Trust not that Malicious Fiend: / Those are false deluding Lights, / Wafted far and near by Sprights. / Trust 'em not, for they'll deceive ye; / And in Bogs and Marshes leave ye" (act II).

8 "Enchanted ground" appears in the same sense in *Aureng-Zebe*, in the prologue, line 10, and again in V.i.102–03. (In other contemporary and earlier use, e.g., Peele, *Old Wives Tale*, 596, and Bunyan, *Pilgrims Progress*, II, xii, enchanted ground does not vanish, having different magical properties.)

9 Cf. Addison, *Spectator* 413.

10 Cf. *Hamlet* I.iv.69–74.

11 The extraordinary Elizabeth Singer Rowe, 1674–1737, furnishes an early example of this image, as of most other stock items of the eighteenth-century language of sensibility: "Enchanting pleasure dances in his sight, / And tempts him forward by a treacherous light . . . / An airy phantom mocks his close embrace; / His arms in vain the sportive shade would fold, / Still like a gliding ghost it slips his fondest hold" (*Letters Moral and Entertaining*, 1733, III, letter 6, poem "On Happiness"). While Mrs. Rowe draws heavily on Shakespeare and especially Milton, her main contemporary model is Pope, above all his "Eloisa" (notably lines 317–20, describing Heaven as an Elysium of love: the *DNB* writer on Mrs. Rowe is being cautious when he speaks of her "curiously realistic expression [of] her faith in the soul's immortality"). Pope in turn

borrowed phrases from the earlier works of Mrs. Rowe (see Twickenham *Poems* II (1940), 245n., 307n., 311n.).

12 Cf. too Cowper, *The Task*, 1785, III.124–27. —The presence of the phantom among the possible troubles of travelers in the eighteenth-century poetic background may add something to our reading of Wordsworth's "She Was a Phantom of Delight," with its transition from "Phantom" to a being who is, like the rest of us, "A Traveller between life and death."

13 Prévost spent time in England in 1728–29 and again in 1733–34. Works translated by him from English include the three novels of Richardson: his own English translators include Charlotte Smith. For his English reading, see Joseph Texte, *Jean-Jacques Rousseau and the Cosmopolitan Spirit in Literature*, trans. J. W. Matthews, pp. 44–56.

14 Cf. *Faerie Queene* III.i.43.

15 The figure reappears in Byron's brief lyric addressed to the moon, "Sun of the Sleepless!"

16 Congreve is probably imitating Ovid's *Heroides* xv.123–34, a passage imitated also in classical times: cf. the dream of the deserted Ariadne in Nonnus, *Dionysiaca* xlvii.320–29.

17 In eighteenth-century imagery, the vanishing dream or vision and the phantom beloved are often indistinguishable. Cf. Mrs. Rowe's verse comment on a bride dying at the altar: "Thus airy pleasure dances in our eyes, / And spreads false images in fair disguise, / T'allure our souls; till just within our arms / The vision dies, and all the painted charms / Flee quick away from the pursuing sight, / Till they are lost in shades, and mingle with the night" (*Letters* II, 19). Again, Bishop Warburton's observation on the *Phaedo*: the reader at first is captivated, "But having thrown aside the book, grown cool, and reflected on those principles concerning *God* and the *soul* . . . , all the bright colouring disappears, and the gaudy vision shrinks from his embrace" (*Divine Legation of Moses*, in *Works*, vol. 2, bk. 3, sec. 3, pp. 61–62).

18 Milton is drawing in part on the courtly love convention of the mistress's appearing in dream at the lover's bedside: cf. Petrarch, *Rime* 342 and 359; Wyatt's "Unstable dreme"; Lodge's *Phyllis*, Sonnet 17; *Faerie Queene* I.ix.12–15; and Donne's "The Dreame." Outside the context of love, cf. Caliban's "when I wak'd / I cried to dream again" (*Tempest* III.ii.148–49).

19 An earlier version of this Virgilian description is the lines describing Orpheus's second loss of Eurydice (*Georgics* iv.499–502): both passages are in turn based on Odysseus' parting with his mother's ghost in Hades (*Odyssey* xi.204–08).

20 *Tasso* II.i.762, IV.i.2189–90; cf. I.iii.519.

21 For the passage from Fancy to Truth imaged by the departure of a dream, cf. Beattie, *The Minstrel*, 1774, II, sts. 29–30, 39–40; T. Warton, "Verses on Sir Joshua Reynolds' Painted Window at New College, Oxford," 1782, 35–38, 61–64; the passage from Mrs. Radcliffe quoted above, p. 44, 1791; Byron, "To Romance," 1807, sts. 1–2, "I Would I Were a Careless Child," st. 3; the poem from *Waverley*, 1814, quoted below, pp. 106–07.

22 A similar passage in prose fiction occurs in Smollett's *Ferdinand Count Fathom* 1753, II, lx: ". . . nightly, in his dreams, did he converse with his dear Monimia: sometimes on the verdant bank of a delightful stream . . . : sometimes reclined

within the tufted grove . . . : yet, even in these illusions, was his fancy oft alarmed for the ill-fated fair: sometimes he viewed her tottering on the brink of a steep precipice, far distant from his helping hand: at other times she seemed to sail along the boisterous tide, imploring his assistance. . . ." (Note also xliv, "dissolved the pleasing enchantment"; lxiv, "fatally misled by a faithless vapour".) Cf., with admixture of beckoning ghost, the incident of Og of Basan and the Maid of Tivoli in Beckford's *Biographical Memoirs of Extraordinary Painters*, 1780; and his letter of February 22, 1781, to Charlotte Courtenay (Chapman, *Beckford*, p. 83).

23 J. Warton, "The Enthusiast," 1740, 29–38; Akenside, *The Pleasures of Imagination*, 1744, III.546–67; Cooper, *The Power of Harmony*, 1745, II.125–40; Beattie, *The Minstrel* I, sts. 6, 22.

24 The symbolic or emblematic dream is of course a very ancient tradition, represented in the Epic of Gilgamesh and in the Bible before appearing in classical literature, e.g., in the dreams of Penelope (*Odyssey* xix.536–50) and Ceres (Claudian, *De Raptu Proserpinae* iii.67–79). Closer to our period, cf. Vittoria's dream in Webster's *The White Divel* I.ii.231–55.

25 Pope's "Eloisa" is singled out too by Thomas Warton in the Preface to his 1791 (2d) edition of Milton's *Poems upon Several Occasions:* "We find him . . . sprinkling his *Eloisa to Abelard* with epithets and phrases of a new form and sound, pilfered from *Comus* and the *Penseroso*. It is a phenomenon in the history of English poetry, that Pope, a poet not of Milton's pedigree, should be their first copier." While not precisely that, he is certainly an important transmitter.

26 Gothic warning dreams have two preferred forms, featuring either the precipice or the beloved-turned-specter. Cazotte's hero Alvare (*Le Diable amoureux*, 1772) dreams that his mother saves him from being pushed over a precipice by his deceiving beloved (p. 145). The heroine of Charlotte Dacre's *Zofloya, or the Moor*, 1806, combines the contrasting-landscapes dream of Pope, Thomson, and Young with a hint of her coming sticky end:

> Scarcely had her head reclined upon her pillow, ere the image of Zofloya swam in her sight; she slumbered, and he haunted her dreams; sometimes she wandered with him over beds of flowers, sometimes over craggy rocks, sometimes in fields of the brightest verdure, sometimes over burning sands, tottering on the ridge of some huge precipice, while the angry waters waved in the abyss below.   [p. 137]

Mary Shelley's Mathilda, again prophetically, dreams that she sees her father fleeing ahead of her towards a precipice (*Mathilda*, written 1819; ed. Elizabeth Nitchie, pp. 35–36). The precipice is of course a very familiar metaphor for danger or prospective ruin, at least back to Dryden (*Marriage-à-la-Mode* IV.i.23–24; *Aureng-Zebe* IV.51–52); in Charles Maturin's *Melmoth the Wanderer*, 1820, it occurs numerous times before the precipice is actualized at the end of the book, first in a warning dream and then as the scene of the Wanderer's death. In *Mathilda* vaguely, and emphatically in *Zofloya*, the dream-precipice prefigures the scene of the story's physical catastrophe.

The dream of an altering figure is very effectively used when Frankenstein, on the night of the Being's vivification, sees his blooming fiancée transformed in his arms to the corpse of his mother (iv in 1st ed.; v in 3d): cf. Schiller, *Kabale und Liebe* (Intrigue and Love), 1784, IV.vii; Harriet Lee, *Kruitzner*, 1801, pp. 218–19; Crabbe, *The World of Dreams*, c. 1817, sts. 30–31; Rider Haggard, *She*, 1887, ix; earlier, Sidney, New *Arcadia*, 1590, II, xxv.

The three prophetic dreams in Shelley's *St. Irvyne* involve a flowery plain suddenly exchanged for "a rugged and desolate heath" (*Complete Works* V, 159–60), two precipices with the threat of being pushed over (137–38, 183–84), and one angelic figure that becomes a threatening demon (184); thus they illustrate both our types.

Other warning dreams in Gothic contexts are Franz Moor's vision of judgment (Schiller, *Die Räuber* [The Robbers], 1781, V.i); the dreams of Lorenzo and Osmond (Lewis, *The Monk* i, *The Castle-Spectre*, 1803, IV.i); Calantha's dreams (Caroline Lamb, *Glenarvon*, 1816, II, 173, 258–60); Immalee's paradise-to-tempest dream and Melmoth's more emblematic vision before his death (*Melmoth the Wanderer* xx, xxxviii); Tatyana's dream of beasts and a robber's den (Pushkin, *Eugene Onegin*, 1831, chap. 5, sts. 11–21).

Several of these look forward in subtlety to the dream-symbolism of *In Memoriam*, *Jane Eyre*, and *The Return of the Native*, which clearly are all influenced by the emblematic Gothic dream: predictably more old-fashioned is the dream of the doomed Caroline in William Kirby's Canadian romance, *The Golden Dog*, 1887 (xlii).

27 Burton describes the state of love-melancholics who at all times imagine their mistresses present (III.ii.3): he cites Dido's passion in the *Aeneid* (iv.83: *illum absens absentem auditque videtque*): cf. Petrarch, *Rime* 158, *Epistolae Metricae* I.6. For the eighteenth century, the main source is probably two similar passages in Ovid's *Heroides* (13.103–08, 15.123–56), made current by Pope, whose translation of 15 incorporates a line from 13 (*tu mihi luce dolor, tu mihi nocte venis*: Pope's "Sappho to Phaon," 144), and who develops the topic at length in "Eloisa," 223–76. Young picks it up in *The Revenge* (acted 1719, printed 1735): I.i., "Have I not seen thee where thou hast not been? / And mad with the Idea, clasp'd the Wind, / And doated upon Nothing?" ("Idea" is Pope's word, "Eloisa," 264), and in a similar speech in *The Brothers* (acted 1724, printed 1753), act II.

Cf. Lovelace in *Clarissa*: "In and out of every place where I have seen the Beloved of my heart do I hurry; in none can I tarry; her lovely image in every one, in some lively attitude, rushing cruelly upon me, in differently remembered conversations" (V, letter 3, p. 26); "sleeping or waking, my Clarissa is always present with me" (VII, 48, p. 160). A verse summary of the plot (in "To the Author of *Clarissa*," printed at the end of VIII) comes so pat as to suggest that the state of mind described in Lovelace's letter about his dream (VII, 48) is a standard poetic topic: "Tasteless were all the pleasures that he view'd / In foreign courts; for Conscience still pursu'd: / The lost Clarissa, each succeeding night, / In starry garment, swims before his sight. . . . " By the 1780s this day-and-night haunting, whether or not attended by fear and remorse, is part of the regular language of sensibility: cf. the two Beckford passages cited above, n. 22, also Louisa's letter to Beckford of April 1782 (Chapman, *Beckford*, pp. 125–26). For a later example (1808) see Byron, "To a Beautiful Quaker," 30–36.

28 One variation in the relation between scene and observer is represented by the poems of Mrs. Radcliffe. *The Mysteries of Udolpho* is subtitled "A romance, interspersed with some pieces of poetry." (The contribution of poems and poetic snatches to their texture is one of the lines of continuity linking *Pamela, Udolpho, Waverley, Jane Eyre,* or *The Lord of the Rings* backwards to such pastoral romances as *Arcadia.*) Mrs. Radcliffe's "interspersed" poems are imitative of both poems and paintings, just as the surrounding text is: the latter aspect epitomizes her way of conceiving her main characters almost as "figures in landscape"—the former, the way in which her whole *oeuvre* can seem a by-product of contemporary poetic convention. Among hermits, shipwrecks, ruins, and fairy visions, perhaps the most constant feature in these poems is the night-wanderer, astray as often as not. Unlike the text, however, the poems show a feeling for nature and its forces that is unexpectedly subjective and also ambiguous, more nearly a Romantic than a picturesque treatment. A glowworm, a butterfly, and a sea-nymph speak from the heart of Nature's various realms, in a tone scarcely heard since Ariel's "Where the bee sucks, there suck I"; glowworm and sea-nymph, while friendly to man, can be over-ruled by the hostility towards him of, respectively, the fairies and Neptune; again, the book's first poem, "Sonnet" (i), addressing the heroine as "God-dess of this fairy scene," suggests that she is not only a *genius loci* but also what in chap. 5 we are calling the "involuntary siren"—"And who that gazes on that angel-smile, / Would fear its charm, or think it could beguile!" For a helpful comment on the "imaginative animism" of the period and its relation to the Gothic mode of terror, see N. Frye, "Towards Defining an Age of Sensibility," in his *Fables of Identity,* pp. 130–37.

29 Cf. the opening speeches of two verse tragedies: Zanga's in Young's *The Revenge:*". . . Horrors now are not displeasing to me: / I like this Rocking of the Battlements. / Rage on, ye Winds, burst Clouds, and Waters roar! / You bear a just Resemblance to my Fortune, / And suit the gloomy Habit of my Soul"; and, more pensive and less Lear-like, Lady Randolph's in Home's *Douglas,* 1757: "Ye woods and wilds, whose melancholy gloom / Accords with my soul's sadness, and draws forth / The voice of sorrow from my bursting heart, / Farewel a while. . . . "

30 *Pamela* I, 143: ". . . this large, handsome, old, and lonely Mansion, that looks made for Solitude and Mischief . . . with all its brown, nodding Horrors of lofty Elms and Pines about it": "Eloisa" 's Melancholy "breathes a browner horror on the woods" (170); for "nodding horrors," cf. the quotation from *Comus* on p. 39 above. (This is the first of those heroines' evening arrivals at significant houses that become such a reliable feature of later romance—*Udolpho, Jane Eyre, Bleak House, Uncle Silas, The Turn of the Screw*—and are parodied so early as *Northanger Abbey.*) *Pamela's* one other notably reverberating sentence is ironic in its romance reference, as the last phrase makes clear: ". . . then she may be turn'd loose to her evil Destiny, and echo to the Woods and Groves her piteous Lamentations for the Loss of her fantastical Innocence, which the romantic Idiot makes such a work about" (I, 220).

31 Curiously, Richardson's last novel, *The History of Sir Charles Grandison,* 1754, explicitly rejects what we called *Clarissa's* extension of sensibility over *Pamela* (the phrase is borrowed from A. S. P. Woodhouse on the difference between

Milton's poetry and his prose). Richardson there appears to go out of his way, in fact, to point out the foolishness of romancers (e.g., VI, letter 42, pp. 223–26), the personal unreliability of poets (e.g., II, 5, p. 30) and the emptiness of foreboding dreams (those described in V, 35, pp. 256–59 come to nothing). What poetic dimension the book has consists in a sort of phoenixism: Miss Byron is "the most amiable of women" as Grandison is "the most graceful and polite of men" (passim), and the union towards which the action (alleged) is pressing ought to have an apocalyptic dimension (see p. 212 below): however, Richardson intends in Grandison no more than an "example," and in his bride a witness of appropriate moral delicacy and discernment.

32 Mrs. Smith brings together two suggestive expressions for the presence of idyllic spots among wild scenery. With the "little green recess" "amidst the wildest horrors," cf. the Alpine landscape of *Udolpho* v, "a perfect picture of the lovely and the sublime—of 'beauty sleeping in the lap of horror' "; *Alastor's* "tranquil spot, that seemed to smile / Even in the lap of horror" (577–78); Scott, *Fair Maid of Perth*, 1828, i: "It is in such favoured regions that the traveller finds what the poet Gray, or some one else, has termed, Beauty lying in the lap of Terror." (It isn't Gray: the most nearly related passage I have met is Young, *The Brothers*, I.i: ". . . a female infant, / Amid these horrors [of carnage, not of landscape], in the cradle smiled.") The history of a related image is traced in a note (Twickenham *Poems* II, 310) on Pope's "Eloisa" 134, "And Paradise was opened in the wild." Again, the sentence from Rousseau sets echoes stirring: for one, it seems to have blended with Prospero's "rack" to form Shelley's "wreck of Paradise" and "wrecks of Eden" (*Epipsychidion* 423; *Defence—Works* VII, 128).

33 Cf. Scott, writing about Mrs. Radcliffe in *Lives of the Eminent Novelists and Dramatists*, 359: "The force . . . of the production, lies in the delineation of external incident, while the characters of the agents, like the figures in many landscapes, are entirely subordinate to the scenes in which they are placed; and are only distinguished by such outlines as make them seem appropriate to the rocks and trees, which have been the artist's principal objects."

34 The subtitle of Shelley's *Alastor, The Spirit of Solitude,* may be an echo from the first of these passages. The formula is a long-lived one: cf. in Conan Doyle's *A Study in Scarlet*, 1887, the account of the traveler in the American badlands: "His appearance was such that he might have been the very genius or demon of the region" (II, i): again, in *The Hound of the Baskervilles*, 1902 (ix), a lonely figure brooding over the moorland appears to Watson "the very spirit of that terrible place."

35 III, 49, p. 278: cf. *La Nouvelle Héloïse* I, 26, p. 89: "O Julie! que c'est un fatal présent du ciel qu'une ame sensible!"

36 Johann Georg Zimmermann's work on solitude appeared in three original versions: *Betrachtungen über die Einsamkeit*, 1756, an essay; *Von der Einsamkeit*, 1773, a monograph; and *Ueber die Einsamkeit*, 1784–85, an elaborate study in four volumes. Several English versions appeared from 1791 on, mostly based on the French translation of J. B. Mercier. The version to hand is *Solitude, or the effect of Occasional Retirement on the Mind, the Heart, General Society, in Exile, in Old Age, and on the Bed of Death . . . written originally by M. Zimmerman [sic]*, London, 1798. It consists of selections from the 1785 *Ueber die Einsamkeit*,

according to its preface (p. x), which like the text follows Mercier without acknowledgement; the translator is not identified.

Zimmermann's illustrators, Mercier, and the English translators have all added to, as well as selecting from, their original, and nearly all of the English-literary, as distinct from English-assorted, coloring comes from them. However, according to A. A. Bouvier, *J. G. Zimmermann*, 1925, the essay of 1756 commences with a quotation from Young's *Night Thoughts*—"O lost to virtue, lost to manly thought . . . / Who think it solitude, to be alone!", III.6–8 (dropped from the later German editions)—and declares enthusiasm for English writers, especially Richardson. The 1773 monograph has several *Rambler* references: 1785, treating more systematically and historically the psychological benefits and dangers of solitude, quotes Pope's ode to it but makes considerably more of Petrarch and Rousseau. While Zimmermann doesn't draw very directly on English sources, comparison between his 1773 and 1785 opening sentences illustrates the increasing openness of educated Europeans like himself and Mercier to the kind of English-influenced sensibility Goethe describes in *Dichtung und Wahrheit*—where, incidentally, Goethe speaks warmly of Zimmermann's personality, though without mentioning the works on solitude. The 1773 opening describes an alien present and nostalgia for youth and vanished domestic pleasures: that of 1785 calls up "the shades of vanished friends . . . from those days of my youth in which solitude was my only joy; in which I knew no pleasanter retreat than among cloisters and cells, untrodden mountains, deep awesome woods and ruined castles of ancient knights and nobles, and no livelier enjoyment than communication with the dead."

37 Cf. E. Panofsky on Dürer's "Melencolia": "That she rests her head on her hand is in keeping with a tradition which can be traced back to ancient Egyptian art. As an expression of brooding thought, fatigue or sorrow this attitude is found in hundreds and thousands of figures and has become a standing attribute of melancholy and 'Acedia' "—*The Life and Art of Albrecht Dürer*, p. 162. Burton notes this trait in the engraving (his remarks, conveying more sharply than Panofsky's the two-sided nature of the subject, are at I.iii.1.2): cf. in his "Argument of the Frontispiece," "Hypochondriacus leans on his arm." This becomes the standard Penseroso attitude. In Isaac Oliver's portrait miniature of Herbert of Cherbury (c. 1605–10), the head-on-hand brookside pose indicates either the poet or the philosopher; in the 1679 frontispiece of *Pilgrims Progress* (as in medieval statues, for example of either the Old Testament or the New Testament Joseph), head on hand indicates the dreamer; in eighteenth-century fanciful illustration it is the regular pose of the poet.

38 The *Zofloya* settings cited are related rather than contrasted. However, Charlotte Dacre's device of extracting and giving human expression to contrasting aspects of the same kind of scene is a recognizable development from the simpler device of Mrs. Radcliffe.

39 His widely read pastoral idyll *Paul et Virginie*, 1789, with its significant dreams and its catastrophe of storm and shipwreck, draws on the stock of images discussed in this chapter: cf. "nous ne devons point aller chercher hors de nous ce que nous pouvons trouver chez nous" (148); "la nature appelle en vain à elle le reste des hommes; chacun d'eux se fait d'elle une image qu'il revêt de

ses propres passions. Il poursuit toute sa vie ce vain fantôme qui l'égare . . . "
(171); the narrator is left at the end, as that of *Atala* will be, "comme un
voyageur qui erre sur la terre" (226).

40 Schiller's dramatic language employs such images as the following: magician
raising fairy castle out of the ground (*Kabale und Liebe*, II.i); beautiful dream and
dreadful awakening (ibid., IV.ii); fairy palace opened to exhausted pilgrim
(ibid., V.i); luring illusion (ibid., V.i: cf. dark spirit drawing one towards the
abyss, *Piccolomini* III.viii); collapsing house (*Kabale* IV.vii; cf. *Räuber* II.i);
shipwreck (*Räuber* III.ii). Note too the emblematic dreams in *Wallensteins Tod*
(The Death of Wallenstein) IV.iii, esp. 7260–67.

The proliferation of such imagery in the bourgeois tragedy *Kabale und Liebe*
perhaps reflects the influence of Lillo; however, cf. Coleridge's remarks on
Schiller's English background in his "Critique of [Maturin's Germanesque
tragedy of 1816] *Bertram*" (*Biographia Literaria* xxiii): ". . . to understand the
true character of the *Robbers*, and of the countless imitations which were its
spawn, I must . . . call to your recollection that, about that time, and for some
years before it, three of the most popular books in the German language were,
the translations of Young's *Night Thoughts*, Hervey's *Meditations*, and Richardson's *Clarissa Harlow*," etc. James Hervey, a Church of England minister
and friend of Wesley best known for the essay "Meditations among the
Tombs" included in his *Meditations and Contemplations*, 1746, was said by a
contemporary with some exaggeration to combine "the descriptive powers of
Thomson, with the sublime reflections and moral energies of Young."

Chapter 4

Epigraphs: Robert Burton, "Democritus to the Reader," *The Anatomy of Melancholy;* Thomas Carlyle, *Sartor Resartus*, II, v.

1 I am using the revised text of 1786; the differences between the two versions do
not affect the argument.

2 Cf. the early American novel *The Power of Sympathy*, 1789, by *Werther*'s admirer
William Hill Brown: ". . . now she awoke from her dream of insensibility, she
was like one who had been deluded by an *ignis fatuus* to the brink of a precipice, and there abandoned to his reflection to contemplate the horrours of
the sea beneath him, into which he was about to plunge" (quoted from *O Brave
New World: American Literature from 1600 to 1840*, ed. Leslie Fiedler and Arthur
Zeiger, pp. 488–89). The subject is the same as Goethe's, a young woman's
realization that she has been deliberately seduced; but the image has been
elaborated on in line with the available conventions.

3 In her playing and singing, Charlotte seems to draw in the sounds of the
instrument and give them back as an "echo." The sanctified quality of the
scene, and his fear of desecrating it, perhaps has something to do with the state
Werther has lost, in which earth and sky rested in his soul like the form of a
beloved woman and he felt his soul to be "the mirror of the infinite God" (May
10, 1771). Charlotte possesses, or embodies, the state in which this "mirroring" of the harmony of the universe is still possible.

4 Cf. the association of "wanderer" with destructive torrent in *Faust* I, 3348–59.

5 The prisoner's dream becomes a regular elegiac feature, found more often as an episode than as a figure of speech: examples occur in Schiller's *Die Räuber* (IV.i), Lewis's *The Castle Spectre* (V.iii), Godwin's *St. Leon* (IV, viii). Crabbe's *The Borough* (letter 23, "Prisons," ll. 275–332), *Frankenstein* (III, vi; xxiii), Pushkin's *Eugene Onegin* (chap. 1, st. 47), and more than once in Longfellow. While in the poems of the three Brontë sisters it can take horrific rather than idyllic forms, the prisoner's dream is an important constituent of their imaginative worlds: see, particularly, in Emily's "The Prisoner," "A messenger of Hope comes every night to me." Lionel Trilling notes in his essay on *Little Dorrit (The Opposing Self,* p. 53) that Freud used Moritz von Schwind's midnineteenth-century painting on this theme—"we know that he dreams of freedom because the bars on his window are shown being sawn by gnomes"—as the frontispiece to *Introductory Lectures on Psychoanalysis,* commenting on it at the end of lecture 8.

6 Prévost uses the shipwreck image, e.g., in *Manon Lescaut,* 1731, bk. I, l. 245. It is elaborately developed in two speeches by the heroine Erixene in act V of Young's tragedy *The Brothers.*

7 These motifs become actualized in numerous narratives. For shipwreck, see the catastrophes of *Paul et Virginie, David Copperfield,* and *Villette,* whose context is the rôle of destructive waters in the pastoral scene. For the collapsing house, see what happens to part of the castle of Otranto, to the House of Usher, and to Mrs. Clennam's house in *Little Dorrit:* more accommodated to the requirements of realism, and with implications weighted more towards the psychological and less towards the outright judgment of Heaven, are the burning by vengeful women of Front-de-Boeuf's castle in *Ivanhoe,* Thornfield Hall in *Jane Eyre,* and Manderley in *Rebecca.*

Chapter 5

Epigraphs: Alfred, Lord Tennyson, *In Memoriam,* iii; Robert Burton, *The Anatomy of Melancholy,* I.ii.3.1, translating Horace, *De Arte Poetica* 4.

1 *Taboo and the Perils of the Soul,* vol. III of Sir James G. Frazer, *The Golden Bough,* p. 94.

2 Pauly-Wissowa (*Paulys Realencyclopädie der classischen Altertumswissenschaft,* ed. G. Wissowa), vol. 16, article "Narkissos." An extensive survey of literary treatments of Narcissus is Louise Vinge, *The Narcissus Theme in Western Europe,* 1967.

3 Cf. Northrop Frye, *Fearful Symmetry: A Study of William Blake,* pp. 282–83, on Blake's *The Four Zoas,* Night the First. This passage was one of the starting points for the present book.

4 See Robert Graves, *The White Goddess,* p. 404; some support for this view may be found via D. W. Robertson, *A Preface to Chaucer,* p. 321. The ballad mentioned above is Child 21, "The Maid and the Palmer," with its more biblical Scandinavian versions.

5 The translation from the "Poimandres" follows that by Arthur D. Nock and A. -J. Festugière in their edition of the *Corpus Hermeticum,* I, 14–15.

6 For a suggestive discussion of this story in a different connection, see Leslie

Fiedler, "Some Contexts of Shakespeare's Sonnets," in *The Riddle of Shakespeare's Sonnets,* ed. Edward Hubler, pp. 55–90. The translation of Ovid used below is that by Mary M. Innes, pp. 103–04.

7 The first English translation, Dr. John Everard's *The Divine Pymander,* 1650, was reissued in 1657 but thereafter not till 1850. It seems probable that Blake knew this version.

8 Shelley's *Revolt of Islam,* VIII.vi, has a surprisingly similar though less mythic formulation: ". . . the shade from his own soul upthrown . . . / The Form he saw and worshipped was his own, / His likeness in the world's vast mirror shewn."

9 "My Spectre Around Me," apparently written late in the period during which Blake was elaborating *The Four Zoas,* concentrates into a lyric in dialogue the "torments of Love & Jealousy" theme of Night the First, which describes the fall of the pastoral Zoa Tharmas, who becomes a watery spirit of chaos, and the estrangement of his emanation Enion.

10 Cf. Maturin, *Melmoth the Wanderer,* xviii:

> Is the murmur of the ocean without a meaning?—Is the roll of the thunder without a voice?—Is the blasted spot on which the rage of both has been exhausted without its lesson?—Do not they all tell us some mysterious secret, which we have in vain searched our hearts for?

Shelley's more positive description at the end of "On Love" (faintly echoing *As You Like It* II.i.16–17) is closer to the mood of "sympathy," commencing, "In the motion of the very leaves of spring, in the blue air, there is . . . found a secret correspondence with our heart" (*Works* VI, 202).

11 Many Romantic villain-heroes recall Aquinas's saying, *Corruptio optimi pessima,* with its direct applicability to such fascinating figures as Shakespeare's Angelo (the epigraph to I, i. of *The Monk* suggests him as Ambrosio's original) and Milton's Satan. In his preface to *Die Räuber,* Schiller describes its hero as one whose natural powers would tend to make him either a Brutus or a Catiline, depending on the direction they received: cf. Shelley's observation in his 1817 review of *Frankenstein* (*Works* VI, 263), equally true of either of its heroes: "It is thus that, too often in society, those who are best qualified to be its benefactors and its ornaments are branded by some accident with scorn, and changed, by neglect and solitude of heart, into a scourge and a curse"; probably he is thinking as well of Godwin's Ferdinando Falkland, whom he mentions just below. It is of course of the nature of romance that its star figures are exceptionally endowed. Romantic plots often schematize this feature into noble hero and evil shadow—a plotting brother like Franz Moor or an attendant shadow-self like Mephistopheles or Mr. Hyde. We shall return to this topic below.

12 Blake, "The Grey Monk."

13 Cf. Washington Allston in his somewhat Gothic artist-romance *Monaldi,* 1841, p. 87: "With men of very vivid imaginations it would seem as if the greater charm were rather in the shadow than the substance." See further chap. 9, n. 6 below.

14 Carlos Baker in *Shelley's Major Poetry*, p. 50, quotes in connection with *Alastor* a letter written by Shelley to T. J. Hogg (August 1815) at about the time of its composition: "Yet who is there that will not pursue phantoms, spend his choicest hours in hunting after dreams, and wake only to perceive his error and regret that Death is so near?" Cf., along with the themes of delusive pursuit mentioned in chap. 3, also perhaps *Tasso* III.ii.1900–05, quoted p. 26 above.

15 Cf. 21–22, 37–38, 81–82, and the images of "fane," "secret caves," "temples." A language for "Nature" of mysteries and hidden treasures, portal, vestibule and shrine, and an initiation for the favored, goes back at least to Seneca (cf. *Naturales Quaestiones*, vii.30.6). It soon becomes enriched by reference to veiled goddess (late classical: cf. Plutarch *De Iside* 9, the inscription on the statue at Sais, "I am all that was and is and shall be, and no mortal has uncovered [*sic*] my robe": evidently her *peplos* is merely a cloak, like Isis's *palla* in Apuleius's *Golden Ass* xi.3, but from this quotation—and a much less accessible reference in Proclus to Athena's weaving the veil of Nature: see Thos. Taylor, *Mystical Hymns of Orpheus*, 1824, pp. 29–31, n. 28—comes the whole body of veiled-goddess imagery, from Spenser through Schiller and Novalis to Rider Haggard) and veiled shrine (biblical: cf. Exodus 26 : 33); the bridal veil, significant in both classical and biblical traditions, extends the erotic suggestiveness of this vocabulary, which lends itself readily to the Neoplatonizing inclinations of the period, in Germany still more than in England.

16 Some images applied to the Poet in Shelley's lament apply elsewhere more often to the object of a delusive pursuit than to its subject: "vapour" (663—cf. its equivalence to "wand'ring light" in Blake's "Little Boy Lost" and " . . . Found"); "dream" (669); "exhalation" (687—for sinister connotations see below, p. 126). Further, *Alastor* may like *Epipsychidion* reflect Shelley's interest in Shakespeare's sonnets: "But thou contracted to thine own bright eyes / Feed'st thy light's flame with self-substantial fuel" (Sonnet 1).

17 " . . . that voice / Which hither came, floating among the winds, / And led the loveliest among human forms . . . " (591 93); cf. *Adonais* 114–15, where Pleasure is "led by the gleam / Of her own dying smile instead of eyes."

18 Classical writers recognize two kinds of "narcissus": our yellow daffodil, the one referred to here, and a purple iris (cf. p. 76 above), with more Adonis-like connotations and sacred to the Furies—as Sandys elegantly puts it, translating from Bacon, " . . . what bore of it selfe no fruite, but past and was forgotten, like the way of a ship in the Sea, was consecrated of old to the infernall Deities" (*Ovids Metamorphosis*, p. 106). The yellow narcissus is also the one that beguiled Persephone (see p. 95 below and footnote).

19 *Confessions*, 1782, IX: compare, for example, Chateaubriand, *Génie du Christianisme*, 1802, II, iii, 9, "Du vague des passions"—"L'imagination est riche, abondante et merveilleuse, l'existence pauvre, sèche et désenchantée. . . . "

20 There are three passages in the poem linked by their mention of Sleep and Death and by interconnected images, all three helping to develop the "lure" theme. In the first, the Poet complains that of Sleep's "desert" and "paradise"

(cf. the contrasted types of dream described above, p. 50) he can reach only the former:

> Does the bright arch of rainbow clouds
> And pendant mountains seen in the calm lake,
> Lead only to a black and watery depth,—
> While Death's blue vault with loathliest vapours hung,
> Where every shade which the foul grave exhales
> Hides its dead eye from the detested day,
> Conducts, O Sleep, to thy delightful realms?   [213–19]

Here the attractive image leads only to gloomy vacancy, and the way to the visionary land is through charnel shades. In the second passage, the Poet is considering his quest:

> For... silent Death exposed,
> Faithless perhaps as Sleep, a shadowy lure,
> With doubtful smile mocking its own strange charms.   [293–95]

In the third, his boat follows the river into a dark and winding cavern:

> "Vision and Love!"
> The Poet cried aloud, "I have beheld
> The path of thy departure. Sleep and Death
> Shall not divide us long."   [366–69]

21 In Prévost, "evil genius" ("Notre mauvais genie travailloit pendant ce temslà à nous perdre"—*Manon Lescaut*, bk. 2, l. 1108) still means in effect no more than "evil destiny." In Romantic fiction and Gothic tales an evil genius is a human agent who in a way that seems fated either tempts one to evil or more directly brings on one's ruin (for an example, see quotation from Godwin's *Mandeville*, p. 229 below). In classical writers "alastor," probably at first a per-sonification of the fate awaiting the impious (e.g., the curse on the house of Atreus), early comes to be synonymous with the worse of the two spirits at-tending each individual—his evil rather than his good *daemon* (Greek) or *genius* (Latin). Cf. Peacock's footnote in *Nightmare Abbey*, 1817, on the philos-ophy of Mr. Toobad, describing *Manfred's* Arimanes as "the great Alastor, or [Kakos Daimon], of Persia" (*Works*, III, 31–32).

22 Coleridge, "Dejection," 47–48.

23 Cf. Freud's paper, "The Uncanny," 1919, in *Standard Edition of... S. Freud*, ed. James Strachey, XVII, 219ff.

24 For the association of Furies with narratives of fall, cf. *PL* x.619–20, "... had not the folly of Man / Let in these wasteful Furies," i.e., Sin and Death. In Du Bartas's *Devine Weekes*, tr. Joshua Sylvester, 1605, the section chronicling the first day of the second week, that following Adam's fall and expulsion, is titled, "The Furies," referring to Dearth, War, Sickness, and their train of horrors (pp. 324–54). It is evident from Milton's Trinity MS notes for a drama on his eventual epic subject that he early thought of the Fall as attended by a Pandora's-box array of evil personifications; in *Paradise Lost* these become the apparitions of Adam's lazar-house vision, XI.477–93.

25 While Wordsworth asks, "Whither is fled the visionary gleam? / Where is it now, the glory and the dream?" Shelley's Poet wakes from "his trance" to wonder,

> Whither have fled
> The hues of heaven that canopied his bower
> Of yesternight? the sounds that soothed his sleep,
> The mystery and the majesty of earth,
> The joy, the exultation? His wan eyes
> Gaze on the empty scene as vacantly
> As ocean's moon looks on the moon in heaven.   [196–202]

Some comparable passages follow, expressing in a variety of ways the departure of beauty and meaning from the outward world through an inner crisis. *Clarissa* VI, letter 53, p. 215, Lovelace to Belford: "Having lost her, my whole Soul is a blank: The whole Creation round me, the elements above, beneath, and everything I *behold* (for nothing can I *enjoy*) are a blank without her!... What is the Light, what the Air, what the Town, what the Country, what's Anything, without thee?" ("Blank" is carried over from *PL* III.48— "... for the Book of knowledg fair / Presented with a Universal blanc / Of Natures works to mee expung'd and ras'd"; its use here as synonymous with Hamlet's "flat, stale and unprofitable" illustrates how, as suggested earlier in connection with "Il Penseroso," minor Miltonic topics come to be related in other authors to the dominating theme of the loss of Paradise—in this case, considering how closely the imagery of the proems is tied to his major theme, not without some help from Milton. A still earlier use than Richardson's is Mrs. Rowe's—*Letters* III, 293—'The whole creation is a blank to me, it is all joyless and desolate" [1733].)

Werther's letter of November 3, 1772:

> Am I not still the same man who used to float about in an abundance of sensations, with a paradise attending his every step? ... When I look out from my window at the distant hills, when the morning sun breaks through the mist that covers them ... oh! when that glorious Nature lies as rigid before me as a little varnished picture....

Rousseau, *Confessions* I, i., describing his feelings following his first experience of adult injustice:

> Nous y fûmes comme on nous représente le premier homme encore dans le paradis terrestre, mais ayant cessé d'en jouir: c'étoit en apparence la même situation, et en effet tout autre manière d'être. ... La campagne même perdit à nos yeux cet attrait de douceur et de simplicité qui va au coeur: elle nous sembloit déserte et sombre; elle s'étoit comme couverte d'un voile qui nous en cachoit les beautés.

For elegiac precedents in poetry see, for example, Young, quoted p. 44 above; farther back, Petrarch's Sonnet 270, "Zefiro torna," whose gist is "Seasons return, but not to me returns" (*PL* III.41), and whose conclusion runs, in Sir William Jones's translation (*Poems*, 1772):

> The birds that warble, and the flow'rs that bloom,
> Relieve no more this solitary gloom.
> I see, where late the verdant meadow smil'd,
> A joyless desert, and a dreary wild.

26 While the maiden's "strange harp" (186) links her with poetic inspiration, her other prop, the "veil / Of woven wind" (176–77), at first sight appears to link her with the mystery of Nature (see n. 15 above): cf. Spenser's veiled Nature in "Mutabilitie," and behind that the veiled Isis of postclassical legend. At the same time the maiden's veil is closely related to her song, a "web / Of many-coloured woof and shifting hues" (156–57: cf. earlier, "woven hymns" at 48): in the *Defence of Poetry* Shelley several times uses the image of a veil or garment in connection with poetry, whose task he sees sometimes as unveiling its subjects, sometimes as veiling them. This ambiguity can perhaps be approached via an analogy in Shelley's work between nature and poetry: *natura naturans* inhabits a shrine whose impenetrable veil is *natura naturata*, the appearances of the natural world (cf. *Alastor* 38)—in the human world poetry is "that imperial faculty, whose throne is curtained within the invisible nature of man" (*Defence—Works* VII, 113), while "in a more restricted sense" the word is applied also to the instruments and products of the shaping power. (This series of connections was suggested to me by Anne Clendenning.)

27 Compare in Mary Shelley, first Safie (her name, actually from *Arabian Nights*, Night 29, recalls Sophia, Wisdom), the "sweet Arabian" with her guitar-playing and nightingalelike song, united to the happy Felix in the idyllic existence witnessed by *Frankenstein's* Being; and second Alithea (Aletheia, Truth), the "houri" lost love of *Falkner*. Behind these two figures and the "Arab maiden" of *Alastor* is perhaps a connection with *Thalaba's* Oneiza, "Arabian maid" (III, st. 33, etc.) and "Houri form" (last lines of the poem).

28 Thomson, *Castle of Indolence* I.xl: in the preceding stanza its music is characterized as "soft perdition," entangling the heart in "enchanting snares," in order to reinforce Thomson's Bower-of-Bliss view of melancholy. He finds it necessary to add a note: "this is not an imagination of the Author; there being in fact such an instrument. . . . "

29 *Alastor* 667–68, 42–44. Cf. *Castle of Indolence* I.xli: "Wild warbling nature all, above the reach of art!"; further, Coleridge, "The Eolian Harp," 1795:

> And what if all of animated nature
> Be but organic Harps diversely fram'd,
> That tremble into thought, as o'er them sweeps
> Plastic and vast, one intellectual breeze,
> At once the Soul of each, and God of all?   [44–48]

—these lines are followed immediately by Sara's "reproof" of such paganism. Shelley, *Defence*: "Man is an instrument over which a series of external and internal impressions are driven, like the alternations of an ever-changing wind over an Aeolian lyre, which move it by their motion to ever-changing melody" (*Works* VII, 109); he goes on, however, very gradually to introduce an element of conscious will into the concept.

30 Pierre-Jean de Béranger, "Le Refus: chanson addressée au Général Sébas-tiani," *Oeuvres Complètes*, II, 282. Cf. Poe's "Israfel": "In Heaven a spirit doth dwell / 'Whose heart-strings are a lute' / . . . Israfeli's fire / Is owing to that lyre / By which he sits and sings / —The trembling living wire / Of those un-usual strings." In relation to feminine rather than poetic responsiveness, com-pare *Clarissa* (V, letter 8, p. 120), Lovelace to Belford: women are "like so many musical instruments, touch but a single wire, and the dear Souls are sensible all over"; and Sterne writes to Mrs. Vesey, June 20, 1761?, "that . . . from one end to the other you are full of the sweetest tones and modulations, requires a Connoisseur of more taste and feeling—in honest truth You are a System of harmonic Vibrations—You are the sweetest and best tuned of all Instruments—O Lord!—I would give away my other Cassoc to touch you . . . " (*Letters*, ed. L. P. Curtis, p. 138). Still finer sensitivity is described in Walton's *Lives* (Donne), 4th ed., 1675, p. 31: ". . . 'tis most certain, that two Lutes, being both strung and tun'd to an equal pitch, and then, one plaid upon, the other, that is not totcht, being laid upon a Table at a fit distance, will (like an Eccho to a trumpet) warble a faint audible harmony, in answer to the same tune: yet many will not believe there is any such thing, as a *sympathy of souls*. . . . " Many writers have used this metaphor to express such a belief, from Dryden (*Aureng-Zebe* IV.76–78) to Shelley ("On Love," *Works* VI, 202).

31 Cf. Miss Howe's warning in *Clarissa* II, letter 36, p. 261): "The strings cannot long continue thus overstrained. They must break, or be relaxed" (a temporary snapping is evidenced by Clarissa's brief period of Belvidera-like decorative babble following her catastrophe); for earlier uses of this metaphor, cf. As-cham, *Toxophilus*, 1545, p. 3: ". . . I am sure that good wittes, except they be let downe like a treble string [of a lute], and unbent like a good casting bowe, they wil neuer last and be able to cōtinue in studie"; Ben Jonson, *Timber*, 1641: "The mind is like a Bow, the stronger by being unbent" (*Works* ed. Herford and Simpson, VIII, 589). Still earlier, see *Phaedo* 85d; for a variation, see Dryden's wicked queen Nourmahal on sexual pleasure: ". . . Till, like a String scru'd up with eager haste, / It breaks, and is too exquisite to last" (*Aureng-Zebe* IV.125–26).

32 Another such is Count Albert Rudolstadt in George Sand's *Consuelo*, 1843, associated like Shelley's maniac with Tasso: Count Albert has perhaps suggested some of the language of Nerval's "El Desdichado" (cf. especially chap. 45).

33 Tieck, "Der getreue Eckart" (Faithful Eckart), 1799, and Eichendorff, "Das Marmorbild" (The Marble Image), 1818, and several lyrics; a late descendant, if I get the drift of the text, is Bob Dylan's "Mister Tambourine-Man." In Stravinsky's "L'Histoire du soldat," 1918, the fiddle for which the Devil gam-bles seems to represent the hero's soul.

34 "Il Penseroso," line 62.

35 Cf. the words of Philosophy to the Muses attending Boëthius: ". . . get you gone, you Sirens pleasant even to destruction, and leave him to my Muses to be cured and healed" (*The Consolation of Philosophy*, trans. V. E. Watts, I.i).

36 Cf. the heroine of Gaston Leroux's *The Phantom of the Opera*, 1910, Christine, who also is the child of a mad violinist and becomes a gifted opera singer.

37 This conclusion is restated when Angela, the heroine of Rider Haggard's first novel, *Dawn*, 1884, rejects the magical powers offered by the sinister Lady Bellamy in favor of love and "the natural heritage of my humanity" (III, xxv, 264–66).

38 For a clear case in terms of metaphor, see Charlotte Dacre, *Confessions of the Nun of St. Omer*, III, 192: "Believe me, destruction is their [the passions'] basement; and Experience comes too late, shaking her flaming torch over the fatal havoc they have caused" (the last words of the book); cf. I, 101, "the glittering fabric I had reared," and 103–04, "too fatally were all your fairy visions overthrown, and experience pointed pale and stern to the bleak desolated heath where they had gamboled." (The main interest of this early work by the author of *Zofloya*, a domestic tale of seduction with no Gothic claims beyond its title, is that the young Shelley certainly read and remembered it; I note, to go no further, that its heroine—who at about sixteen had "a heart softened beyond the intentions of Nature from books which had refined sensibility to a pitch of agony" (I, 74)—is named Cazire: cf. P. B. and Elizabeth Shelley's youthful publication, *Original Poetry by Victor and Cazire*, 1810.)

39 This feature of pastoral has been elegantly isolated by Marie Desport in *L'Incantation virgilienne: Virgile et Orphée*, 1952.

40 The elements of this really splendid passage become the central scene of Mary Shelley's last novel, *Falkner*, recalled by a witness in terms of "a grave dug in the sands, . . . and the dark breakers of the ocean—and horses scampering away, and the lady's wet hair—" (II, 84). Cf., again, her letter of August 15, 1822, to Mrs. Gisborne describing her and Jane Williams's journey to Pisa and Leghorn for news of the *Ariel*: "It must have been fearful to see us—two poor, wild, aghast creatures driving—(like Matilda) towards the *sea* to learn if we were to be for ever doomed to misery." In view of the next *Mathilda* passage to be cited, we shall quote a later sentence: "Both LB [Byron] and the lady [Guiccioli] have told me since—that on that terrific evening I looked more like a ghost than a woman." It is partly because of their capacity to abstract their subjective presence from a scene and to, so to speak, become part of their own picturesque, that certain Romantic writers invite comparison with Narcissus.

41 Cf. in Shelley's *Zastrozzi*, 1810, v, the demon-woman Matilda:

> Her white robes floated on the night air—her shadowy and dishevelled hair flew over her form, which, as she passed the bridge, seemed to strike the boatmen below with the idea of some supernatural and ethereal form.

Cf. also *Waverley*, 1814, xxii:

> While gazing at this pass of peril [a rustic bridge 150 ft. high], which crossed, like a single black line, the small portion of blue sky not intercepted by the projecting rocks on either side, it was with a sensation of horror that Waverley beheld Flora and her attendant appear, like inhabitants of another region, propped, as it were, in mid air, upon this trembling structure. . . . The fair apparition passed on from the precarious eminence . . . and disappeared on the other side.

Apparition-maidens like these and Dicken's Estella (the brewery scene in *Great Expectations* viii) usually become fatal or impossible loves: cf. Louisa in

Polidori's *Ernestus Berchtold,* p. 31, also Adeline in Tennyson's poem of that name, who possibly has a demon lover like *Melmoth's* Immalee.

42 For bubble as object of delusive pursuit, cf. Whitney, *A Choice of Emblemes,* 1586, p. 55; Shakespeare, *As You Like It* II.vii.152–53 ("Seeking the bubble reputation / Even in the cannon's mouth"); Webster, *The Dutchesse of Malfy,* 1623, V.iv.64–66; Addison, "The Vision of Mirzah," 1711 (*Spectator* 159); Dacre, *Confessions of the Nun of St. Omer,* II, 56, 187.

43 Cf. the effect of Oothoon's plucking the "Marygold" in Blake's *Visions of the Daughters of Albion;* one wonders if his association of this flower with sexual pleasure was conceivably influenced by the English folksong "Blow Ye Winds in the Morning"—"There is a flower in our garden, / They call it marigold; / And he that will not when he may, / He shall not when he wold".—For an indication that Wordsworth's line in "Ode: Intimations," "Earth fills her lap with pleasures of her own," perhaps implies a Neoplatonic reading of Persephone's story, cf. the last stanza of his juvenile poem "The Birth of Love" (*Poetical Works,* ed. E. de Selincourt, I, 298–99), where infant Love is betrayed by a "Goddess," Enjoyment masquerading as Innocence, who "her lap with sweetmeats fill'd"—such a reading as Thomas Taylor's in his *Dissertation on the Eleusinian and Bacchic Mysteries,* 1791: "Proserpine, therefore, or the soul, at the very instant of her descent into matter, is, with the utmost propriety, represented as eagerly engaged in plucking this fatal flower; for her energies at this period are entirely conversant with a life divided about the fluctuating condition of the body" (105–06). I should regret to omit Henry Reynolds's remark, from the "Tale of Narcissus" with commentary appended to *Mythomystes,* 1632: "And they . . . feigned that Proserpine, when Pluto ravished her away as she was gathering floures, had her lap full of Narcissusses; because lazy & unbusied women are most subject unto such inconveniences" (108).

44 Outside of the range of romance that we have been concentrating on, a novel that very pointedly and successfully handles this subject is Jane Austen's *Sense and Sensibility,* 1811, in which the younger sister's indulgence in feeling keeps her childish and self-centered beyond her years.

45 *Middlemarch,* "Finale." James's review in *The Galaxy,* March 1873, is reprinted by Leon Edel in *The Future of the Novel: Essays on the Art of Fiction by Henry James,* 1956, pp. 80–89.

Chapter 6

Epigraph: William Cowper, "Verses Supposed to be Written by Alexander Selkirk."

1 The word "sylph" appears to have been coined by Paracelsus in *De Nymphis.* Abbé Montfaucon de Villars's humorous narrative *Le Comte de Gabalis,* 1670, has both "sylphe" and "sylphide," taken up by Pope in *The Rape of the Lock* (see Twickenham *Poems* II (1940), 356, appendix B, "Sylphs"). Cf. Dryden, letter to Mrs. Elizabeth Thomas, November 12, 1699, "sylph or nymph"; Rousseau, *Confessions* XI, in the spirit of de Gabalis, "Sans quelques reminiscences de jeunesse et Mad^e d'Houdetot, les amours que j'ai sentis et décrits n'auroient été qu'avec des Sylphides"; Scott, *Marmion,* 1808, II, introd. 90–93 and fre-

quently elsewhere. Cf., in *Nightmare Abbey*, Mr. Hilary's comment on Mr. Cypress's prose paraphrase of *Childe Harold* IV.121, 136: "You talk like a Rosicrucian, who will love nothing but a sylph, who does not believe in the existence of a sylph, and who yet quarrels with the whole universe for not containing a sylph" (*Works* III, 108). (De Gabalis, as his name indicates, is a Cabbalist, not a Rosicrucian; while the Rosicrucians pursued Paracelsan natural magic, the association Rosicrucian/sylph seems to be scarcely older than Pope.) "La Sylphide," first danced by Taglioni, 1832, is the essence of the "romantic" and the origin of the "white" ballet; without story, its spirit is perpetuated in "Les Sylphides," 1909.

As occultist items sylphs are associated with the element of air (cf. *Faust* I, 1275, 1287–88), and "sylphlike" maidens are often also "airy." The sylph's association with idyllic scenes can perhaps be related to the fact that air is the Paradisal element in our four-level scheme (see p. 5).

2 Plutarch, *Life* of Aristides 11.4; Festus in *Glossaria Latina* IV, sec. 107, cf. scholion on Theocritus's Idyll 13 ("Hylas"), line 44; Ovid *Fasti* iv.461: lined up with others in Pauly-Wissowa, vol. 17, pt. 2, article "Nymphai," col. 1553.

3 Carl Kerényi, *The Gods of the Greeks*, p. 159.

4 See particularly his letters to Peacock of August 16 (in which he compares nympholepsy to Plato's account in the *Phaedrus*, 245a, of the poetic fury induced by the Muses) and October 8 (referring to *Childe Harold*'s "Egeria" stanzas, IV.115–22), 1818.

5 Cf. respectively Britomart's first sight of Artegall (*Faerie Queene* III.ii.22–24); Tamino's first sight of Pamina (*Magic Flute*, I) or Ambrosio's of Matilda (*The Monk* I, ii); Arthur's of Gloriana (*Faerie Queene* I.ix.13) or Endymion's of Cynthia (*Endymion* I, 572ff.).

6 But cf. Burton I.ii.1.2: "Water-devils are those *Naiades* or Water Nymphs . . . . Such a one as Aegeria, with whom Numa was so familiar. . . ."

7 Comparable beings shed an air of mystery over other Scott novels. Shortly before her fateful walk with Cleveland on the gloomy Mermaid's beach, Minna in *The Pirate* dreams of meeting there the Mermaid, who prophesies "calamity and woe" (xix). In *The Bride of Lammermoor* the first meeting of Ravenswood and Lucy takes place beside a fountain that is the setting of a family legend. An earlier Ravenswood formed there an attachment to a mysterious lady once called an "Egeria" and three times called a "Naiad." Their relationship being interfered with by a priest, who set the clock back and so induced the otherworldly being to outstay her mystically appointed time (cf. *Der Geisterseher* for this device), the lady shrieked and disappeared into the fountain, whose bubbles then rose bloody (v). Doleful prophecies are henceforward attached to the spot, which are all worked out in the fates of Edgar and Lucy.

The elegiac fountain nymph is ironically recreated in Thomas Mann's "Tristan"; a more cheerful version is the nymph of the baths in Fellini's *8½*.

8 The mirror later becomes a common metaphor for female purity in love, as in *Kabale und Liebe* I.iv (cf. Lady Milford's variation on it in II.i) and Blake's *Visions of the Daughters of Albion*, pl. 2, ll. 15–19.

9 *Prometheus Unbound* III.ii.18; cf. the "Elysian" mirroring of sky in water in "The Magic Plant" 228–32 (*Poetical Works*, ed. H. B. Forman, III,284). From

about the date of *Paradise Lost,* the presence of a lake mirroring the scene was considered to add to the harmony of landscape or picture; cf. Christopher Hussey, *The Picturesque,* p. 26, on Dryden's "To . . . Mrs. Anne Killigrew," st. 6. A pre-Miltonic example is Sidney's description of Kalander's garden, *New Arcadia,* I, iii.

10 The savages call Rima "the daughter of the Didi," i.e., water spirit (iii): the sailors gaze at Pearl "as if a flake of the sea-foam had taken the shape of a little maid, and were gifted with a soul of the sea-fire, that flashes beneath the prow in the night-time" (xxii).

Rima is compared several times to a bird, especially in the account of her death (xix): so is Little Pearl, for example four times in xxii: cf. also the following (vi):

> Hester could not help questioning . . . whether Pearl was a human child. She seemed rather an airy sprite, which, after playing its fantastic sports for a little while upon the cottage floor, would flit away with a mocking smile. . . . It was as if she were hovering in the air, and might vanish, like a glimmering light that comes we know not whence, and goes we know not whither.

11 The last song in *The Princess,* "Come down, O maid," depicts the nymph as light-without-heat woman (cf. Tasso's princess, p. 46 above: Byron's "Lament of Tasso" 90 calls her a "crystal-girded shrine," and in Shelley's "Song" for his projected *Tasso* she appears as the "silver spirit" of a nympholeptic pursuit like that implied in his "The Two Spirits"):

> . . . cease to move so near the Heavens, and cease
> To glide a sunbeam by the blasted Pine,
> To sit a star upon the sparkling spire;
> And come, for love is of the valley . . .
>   . . . nor cares to walk
> With Death and Morning on the silver horns,
> Nor wilt thou snare him in the white ravine,
> Nor find him dropt upon the firths of ice. . . .

(This demotion of an aspiration and ideality imaged in mountaintops is connected with the reversed poetic cosmology mentioned above, p. 14.) Cf. the moonlike women of Maturin's *Bertram* III.ii and Shelley's *Epipsychidion,* the dawn-goddess of Tennyson's "Tithonus," and the moonlike maiden of Browning's "Numpholeptos."

12 This motif is treated differently in the introduction to *Marmion* I (1808):

> Stay yet, illusion, stay a while,
> My wilder'd fancy still beguile! . . .
> It will not be, it may not last,
> The vision of enchantment's past:
> Like frostwork in the morning ray,
> The fancied fabric melts away. . . .   [208–09, 220–23]

13 *The Mirror,* Edinburgh, 1780, nos. 99, 100.

14 Other significant cavern-guarded springs, besides Egeria's in *Childe Harold*

IV.cvi, occur in *PL* IV.453–55; *The Prelude* XIV.194–96; *The Triumph of Life* 310–14: all have distinct female associations.

15 Cf. the influence of Eugene Aram's "spectre," quoted p. 226 below; that of Chillingworth's presence, *Scarlet Letter*, 1850, opening of xv; and that which Esther attributes to Vholes's shadow, *Bleak House*, 1853, xlv. For black sun and shadowy rays, see Novalis, *Heinrich von Ofterdingen*, 1802, I, ix (Klingsohr's *Märchen:* cf. Jean Paul, "Traum über das All," in *Der Komet*, 1822); Mary Shelley, *The Last Man*, 1826, II, iv. Claude Pichois, *L'Image de Jean-Paul dans les lettres françaises*, pp. 283–87, shows that Nerval's "soleil noir de la Mélancolie" ("El Desdichado," 1853: cf. *Voyage en Orient*, 1851, I, 81, and *Aurélia*, II, iv) recalls his friend Gautier's reading, in some lines published in 1834, of the comet in Dürer's engraving as "un grand soleil tout noir." Earlier, cf. Blake's *Marriage*, pl. 18, and *America*, pl. 6, both 1793. In our own time a black sun, linked spiderlike to its gold counterpart, haunts the late paintings of de Chirico.

16 Two nineteenth-century chivalric tales whose heroes are comparably involved with parental rather than soulmate figures are Flaubert's *La Légende de saint Julien l'Hospitalier*, 1877, and La Motte Fouqué's *Sintram und seine Gefährten* (Sintram and His Companions), 1814, where the knight's task is to overcome the "Death and Devil" of Dürer's print ("Ritter, Tod und Teufel") that beset him, and with them his envy of an older knight and desire for his lady.

17 Arousing and then getting rid of the Shadow is the subject also of Ursula Le Guin's admirable *A Wizard of Earthsea*, 1968: we can fit in here the usurping "Shadow" that titles a Hans Andersen story.

18 The language of the climax is very reminiscent of *Alastor* or *Epipsychidion:*

> "Taji! for Yillah thou wilt hunt in vain; she is a phantom that but mocks thee; and while for her thou madly huntest, the sin thou didst cries out, and its avengers still will follow. . . . Within our hearts is all we seek. . . . "   [clxxxix]

> "I am the hunter, that never rests! the hunter without a home! She I seek, still flies before; and I will follow, though she lead me beyond the reef; through sunless seas; and into night and death."   [clxxxix]

> . . . in some mysterious way seemed Hautia and Yillah connected. But Yillah was all beauty, and innocence . . . and Hautia, my whole heart abhorred. Yillah I sought; Hautia sought me. One, openly beckoned me here; the other dimly allured me there. Yet now was I wildly dreaming to find them together. But so distracted my soul, I knew not what it was, that I thought.   [cxci]

> "Away! thy Yillah is behind thee, not before."   [cxciii]

19 This ending, like that of Mary Shelley's *The Last Man*, probably owes something to *Childe Harold* III.lxx.8–9: "But there are wanderers o'er Eternity / Whose bark drives on and on, and anchor'd ne'er shall be."

20 The combination is a favorite Gothic or decadent notion: cf. M. G. Lewis's monk Ambrosio, Hoffmann's Medardus in *Die Elixiere des Teufels* (The Devil's Elixirs, 1816), Flaubert's St. Julien, and Mann's "holy sinner" in *Der Erwählte* (The Elect). These last two recast medieval stories, *Der Erwählte* being a retelling of Hartmann von Aue's *Gregorius*, from about 1200.

Chapter 7

Epigraphs: S. T. Coleridge, "Kubla Khan"; P. B. Shelley, final chorus from *Hellas.*

1 Cf. the description of Lorna's "bower" in R. D. Blackmore's *Lorna Doone,* 1869, xix: it is a chamber in the rock with a spring and " 'chairs of living stone', as some Latin writer says, whose name has quite escaped me." Blackmore is referring to *Aeneid* i.167, or possibly *Metamorphoses* v.317: the former describes a cave of the Nymphs with a spring in it, and the latter the seats on which the Nymphs sat to judge the singing contest of the Pierides with the Muses.

2 *Tamarack Review* (Toronto) 2 (Winter 1956–57): 55–64. Interesting too are the characters: besides the narrator, these are a beautiful youth who seems to waste with the year and an older woman seen as a "Fury."

3 *Wilhelm Meister* introduces another kind of significant "good" building, the place of recognition or hallowed recollection (the "Tower" and "Hall of the Past"): cf. *Contarini Fleming's* Tower of the Future (Disraeli), *Le Juif errant's* Red Room (Eugène Sue), and *Der grüne Heinrich's* Hall of the Knights (Gottfried Keller). Their demonic opposites are those rooms ingeniously equipped for murder without trace, as in Wilkie Collins's "Terribly Strange Bed," Le Fanu's *Uncle Silas* and "Le Dragon Volant," and Conrad's "Inn of the Two Witches": these are places of recognition too, as it is by finding yourself in their place that you understand how other victims have been done in. Rooms can be the "brains" of houses, and so named by the authors: cf. the good attic in George MacDonald's *Lilith* and the bad cellar in Bulwer Lytton's "The Haunted and the Haunters." The sinister room like that in *Uncle Silas* is a close relative of the shut-up wing in Gothic fiction, from Clara Reeve's *The Old English Baron* on.

4 Du Maurier in *Peter Ibbetson* tries to raise his dream-house above any such suspicion by introducing, "to make it real," dust (II, v).

5 Cf. Eino Railo, *The Haunted Castle,* p. 10. (I came on this book too late to make much use of it, but have found it for my purposes easily the most illuminating and congenial work on Gothicism and related subjects, and consider the present study respectfully as something of a sequel.)

6 The House of Busyrane's "Be bold" motif comes from the British equivalent of Perrault's "La Barbe Bleue"—"Mr. Fox"—and is the earliest known reference to it. Later in the history of English fiction, significant mention of Bluebeard is made by, among others, Godwin in relation to *Caleb Williams* (see chap. 11, n. 10 below), Charlotte Brontë in *Jane Eyre,* and Dickens in *Bleak House.*

7 Close to these are a number of double-natured palaces in Morris's *The Earthly Paradise,* e.g., that in "The Man Who Never Laughed Again, "whose grounds contain a small iron door leading to a kind of hell, like that through which Ignorance is bundled at the end of *Pilgrims Progress.* Perhaps we can see an extension of such structures in certain houses whose otherwise attractive surroundings include some strikingly dismal spot—usually a stretch of dreary shoreline: cf. Mary Shelley's *Falkner,* Wilkie Collins's *The Moonstone* and *The Woman in White,* Daphne Du Maurier's *Rebecca.*

8 Milton's "shining Rock," *PL* IV.283; "Rock / Of Alablaster," 543–44: cf. the rock as smooth as brass on which Tennyson's palace stands, also the "mount of

diamond" to which Shelley compares Athens's visionary foundations in "Ode to Liberty," st. 6.

9 For discussion see Milton Wilson, *Shelley's Later Poetry*, pp. 22–25.

10 See Railo, *Haunted Castle*, p. vii. The background to this subject includes, first, bride-claiming ballads like "King Estmere" (Child no. 60—Lewis imitates the type in "Alonzo the Brave and Fair Imogine" in *The Monk*); second, such personages of the drama as Banquo's ghost and the Stone Guest of Tirso de Molina. "The Armenian," Melmoth, and Edgar Ravenswood interrupt wedding or engagement celebrations (*Der Geisterseher*, episode of Lorenzo and Jeronymo; *Melmoth* vii; *Bride of Lammermoor* xxxii–xxxiii); so does Apollonius in *Lamia*. Other kinds of festivity are broken into in *Udolpho* (II, vii; xx) and Poe's "Shadow" and "Masque of the Red Death." Waverley's ancestor and Ivanhoe both return home disguised as palmers (iv in both books), the latter heralded appropriately by an epigraph from the *Odyssey* xxi, describing Odysseus' return. The theme is developed further, perhaps with some help from *Lara*, which depicts, so to speak, the outsider from inside (but cf. especially I. 3), in the Tennysonian unwanted revenant, present already in "The Lotos-Eaters," Choric Song st. 6, and in *In Mem.* xc before its full-length treatment in "Enoch Arden."

11 If 1860 seems late for a "Romantic" document, let us add that Hawthorne's Rome is substantially that of Mme de Staël (*Corinne*, 1807): he has clearly borrowed in many places, including such important scenes as, besides that at the Trevi fountain, those set in the sculptor's studio and in St. Peter's. Some backgrounds and parallels to Corinne's elegiac Rome (II, iii) and her Italy are noted in Camillo von Klenze, *The Interpretation of Italy*.

12 For more threads connecting "The Assignation" with Byron, cf. Byron's letter to Moore of November 17, 1816: "It is my intention to remain at Venice during the winter, probably, as it has always been (next to the East) the greenest island of my imagination. . . . I have been familiar with ruins for too long to dislike desolation. Besides, I have fallen in love, which, next to falling in the canal, (which would be no use, as I can swim), is the best or the worst thing I could do. Marianna . . . has . . . large, black, oriental eyes . . . " (*Letters and Journals*, ed. Leslie Marchand V, 129–30). The letter was first published by Moore in 1830.

13 Cf. the dreamlike mood and sunset-vision scene in *Little Dorrit's* Venice, XI, iii (end).

14 ". . . this mighty enchantress . . . waving her wand over the world of wonder and imagination . . ." (Scott, *Miscellaneous Works* III, 345–46).

15 These lines (*Tempest* IV.i.151–56) are quoted by Mrs. Piozzi, one of Mrs. Radcliffe's main sources for picturesque Italian scenery, on leaving *Naples* and its environs, just after a paragraph mentioning Circe and "such enchantresses": *Observations and Reflections*, II, 94. On Venice, Mrs. Piozzi gives her translation of Sannazaro's epigram dismissing the famous buildings of Rome (*Illam homines dices, hanc posuisse Deos*): "While human hands those glittering fabrics frame, / By touch celestial beauteous Venice came" (II, 186). Rather than Prospero's magic, Byron may have thought of Comus's, hence "structures" and not "fabrics": "the brute Earth would lend her nerves, and

shake, / Till all thy magic structures rear'd so high, / Were shatter'd into heaps o're thy false head" (796–98).

  William Beckford's *Italy*, 1834, commences its "Advertisement" thus: "Some justly admired Authors having condescended to glean a few stray thoughts from these Letters . . . ; I have been at length emboldened to lay them before the public." In its earlier version, *Dreams*, we may note a couple of Venetian references: "To behold at one glance these stately fabrics, so illustrious in the records of former ages . . . " (letter 8, p. 90); ". . . we drew near to Venice, and saw its world of domes rising out of the waters" ("Additional Letters," letter 3, p. 287).

16 For the associations of this phrase, cf. the following: *The Wandering Jew*, 1810, II.345–46: after the passing of a storm, "Light baseless mists were all that fled, / Above the weary traveller's head"; *St. Irvyne* xi: "this, perhaps, baseless dream of . . . happiness might fade"; *Zastrozzi* xiv: in the "fairy scene" of Venice (cf. *Udolpho* II.ii; xv), "All the air-built visions of delight . . . faded away . . . every oath of fidelity . . . , like a baseless cloud, dissolved away. . . . " "Baseless," clearly still Prospero's word, for the unrealized resolution of self-fulfilling friendship in "Julian and Maddalo" seems to imply that it is of the nature of the Venetian cloud-vision ideal that its promise is *not* realized. Such a resolution taken in Shelley's Athens, for all its likeness to the ideal Venice, would probably have been carried out ("Ode to Liberty," sts. 5–6); as was once pointed out to me by Milton Wilson, the anchor word stabilizing the cloud palace is probably, in particular, "pavilions," carried down from *PL.* II.959–61 via Collins's "Ode to Liberty," 1747, 103–06, 116. Compare Wordsworth's Solitary's sunset vision in *The Excursion*, 1814, II. 827–55 (containing both "fabric" and "pavilions"), linked by the repeated line "Glory beyond all glory ever seen" to the "golden palace" of French revolutionary hopes, III.714.

17 "Venice," 9–14: cf. *In Mem.* lxx, "Cloud-towers by ghostly masons wrought"; Browning, *Fifine at the Fair*, secs. 106, 110–11.

18 Turner captioned many of his paintings with quotations from the poets, especially Thomson, but often Milton and later also Byron. From 1812 he draws as well on *The Fallacies of Hope*, his own labored Thomsonian MS opus, which again and again illustrates its theme from the ever-changing lights of earth. A "Venice" fragment of 1843 contrasts the fisherman's bright morning departure with the grim fate lurking to meet him in the evening: other passages, not recorded, accompanied four Venetian paintings shown in 1845—"Evening . . . ," "Morning . . . ," "Noon," and "Sunset, a Fisher." He seems to have produced more fragments as he needed captions, up to 1846 or even 1850: surely the latest conceivable date for work on a poem of this kind. From Shelley, to whose perceptions of light his are often compared, no quotations are recorded: in the world of words Turner was extremely conservative. See further Walter Thornbury, *Life of Turner*, appendix, pp. 567–83. Jack Lindsay in *The Sunset Ship* has published all of Turner's available and decipherable poems with a very illuminating essay.

19 *Observations*, II, "Naples," p. 9.

20 Before ever seeing Venice, Mrs. Radcliffe's Emily, on being told of a young Piedmontese peasant who is going there to the carnival to earn some money by

his fiddle, "could not forbear silently lamenting, that he should be drawn from the innocence and beauty of those scenes, to the corrupt ones of that voluptuous city" (*Udolpho* II.i; xiv). Byron's letters confirm that twenty-five years later this reputation was not undeserved.

21 Thomas Coryat, in his *Crudities: hastily gobled up in five moneths travells in . . . Italy . . .* , 1611, II, 262–63.

22 "Facino Cane," 1836, republished 1844 in *Scènes de la Vie parisienne,* vol. II.

23 Browning, "A Toccata of Galuppi's," 1855.

24 *T. S. Eliot's Poetry and Plays,* p. 51.

25 Similar in spirit and in the poetic language used to describe them are the Venetian dream-cities of August Graf von Platen's *Sonette aus Venedig,* 1824, and Proust's *A la Recherche du temps perdu,* especially *Albertine disparue,* 1925.

26 No connection is made by writers between this theme and the famous Venetian glass manufacture, except that sometimes a significant mirror, e.g., that in Gautier's "Spirite," is said to come from Venice. (See, however, the remark on *The Tales of Hoffmann,* p. 135 above.) James Howell, *A Survay of the Signorie of Venice* (London, 1651), says, "They have a saying there, that the first hansom Woman was made out of Venice Glasse, which implies beauty but brittlenes withall, and Venice is not unfurnished with Creatures of that mould" (39). No doubt other Renaissance jokes of the same kind exist, considering how numerous are the joking associations between glass and women: cf. Webster, *The Dutchesse of Malfy,* 1623, II.ii.6–12; II.iv.13–15; IV.ii.77–79.

27 From its sharp, cold, duck-shooting opening, Hemingway's novel presents a very fresh-air Venice with the wind blowing: the place and the story have a winter idyll quality, frost dispelling all brooding and miasmas. Descriptions and conversations are highly literary: Shakespeare echoes are prominent, mostly from *Othello.* The hero, who three times stands pondering his battered façade in hotel mirrors, has loved Venice from his boyhood, or at least is proud of having defended her when he was eighteen. The main tradition of the Venetian past emphasized is that of upright soldiering, now departed from here as from everywhere else: this elegiac motif expresses itself also in his sense that the modern army has no place for him, and hence his occupation is gone. The soulmate Renata (literally "reborn," as in Scaliger's line, quoted in Coryat, that Venice is a new Rome reborn in the midst of the sea—*in medio Roma renata mari*) is descended from the Venetian nobility. The colonel calls her "Daughter," and jokes about incest (98). From *Der Geisterseher* to "The Aspern Papers," being a portrait is a regular mode of Venetian existence: Renata says of hers, painted by a pederast with false teeth, "It is very romantic. My hair is twice as long as it has ever been and I look as though I were rising from the sea without the head wet" (97). Like Coryat's and Mann's, this book also has a demon boatman, this one "over-liberated" and therefore refractory when carrying a man in a battle-dress jacket. (Coryat's willful gondoliers carry unsuspecting tourists to courtesans' houses, being in league with the system of prostitution.)

28 Venice as in-between world is to be noted in one particularly narcissistic connection, that of sexual ambivalence. Volpone keeps an androgyne as a household pet; the hero of 'The Assignation," and its narrator, admire (while mis-

locating) the one passage in Politian's *L'Orfeo* that is "tainted with impurity"; the composer of Vernon Lee's "A Wicked Voice" is pursued in Venice by the siren warblings of a highly sinister castrato; Arthur Symons's "Alvisi Contarini" (*Poems*, II, 271–72) has a Salome-like dancer on one side of him and a painted punk on the other; Proust's Marcel dreams in Venice of carrying on his pursuit of Mme Putbus's sexually versatile maid; the love-object of Rolfe, Baron Corvo's *Desire and Pursuit of the Whole* is a boyish girl with a boy's name and dress; and Hemingway's old soldier addresses his Renata's picture as "Boy or daughter or my one true love" (173). Venice is a favorite resort of the mother-ridden aged youth of Tennessee Williams's *Suddenly Last Summer*. In real life, Beckford, von Platen, John Addington Symonds, and Rolfe all appear to have pursued homosexual adventures there. Still farther from literature, *Leggi e memorie Venete sulla prostituzione* cites numerous lurid sodomitic episodes, notwithstanding a public declaration in August 1464 that Venice should be especially wary of this particular sin, seeing that from her topographical situation the Lord would find it all too easy to carry out on her the punishment of the Cities of the Plain.

29 Quotations are essentially from the translation by H. T. Lowe-Porter.
30 Two other entrapped souls unable to leave Venice are Byron's Jacopo Foscari and the hero of Browning's lyric "Rawdon Brown"; the latter like Aschenbach gets packed up to leave, but then is beguiled by the view. Cf. von Platen, Sonnet 25: "Week after week I feel go gliding by me, / And cannot, Venice, bring myself to leave thee."
31 "Der fremde Gott" of the dream is very much the Dionysus of Euripides' *Bacchae*.
32 Cf. von Platen, Sonnet 26: "Here Art expanded like a tulip-flower, / Risen in gorgeous colours from the sea; / Here on bright clouds she seems to flit and flee / With a mirage's soft beguiling power."
33 Cf. Heine's account in *Französische Zustände*, 1832, article 6, of the arrival of the cholera in Paris at the mid-Lenten break:

> Since this was the day of mid-Lent and the weather was sunny and pleasant, the Parisians crowded the more merrily onto the boulevards, where one even saw masked characters who, in caricatured discoloration and deformity, mocked at the fear of cholera and sickness. The same evening the masquerades were more frequented than ever; the loudest music was all but drowned out by hectic laughter; people grew heated in the chahût, a rather unambiguous dance, and swallowed down ices and assorted cold drinks; when suddenly the merriest of the harlequins felt an excessive chill in his bones, and took off his mask, and to the amazement of all revealed a face of a violet blue. It was soon realized that this was no game, and the laughter died away, and several carriages full of people were driven from the masquerade straight to the Hôtel-Dieu, the central hospital, where, arriving in their fantastic costumes, they immediately died. Since in the first dismay everyone thought of infection, and the patients already in the Hôtel-Dieu set up a terrible cry of fear, it is said that these dead were buried so quickly that their chequered fools' costumes were not even taken off them, and as they lived merrily, so they lie merrily in their graves.

Earlier than this historical reality is Mary Shelley's juxtaposition in *The Last Man*, 1826, of the first news of the plague with a children's masquerade, II, vi. Accounts combining plague and revelry go back as far as Thucydides on the plague at Athens (ii.7.53, recalled by Jean Paul in *Titan*, 1800–03, jublee 20, cycle 86).

34 E. Welsford, *The Fool*, plate facing p. 321.

35 Since solitude is not conducive to catching the so-called social diseases (the misadventure in i belongs to an earlier period), what he actually gets is nervous prostration.

36 Venice was one of the main trading cities through which during the early Renaissance pearls reached Europe from the East: cf. the paintings of Veronese, whose Venices and Venuses and other secular ladies are all lavishly decked with them. Gautier's "Sur les Lagunes" contains the lines, "Sur une gamme chromatique, / Le sein de perles ruisselant, / La Vénus de l'Adriatique / Sort de l'eau son corps rose et blanc." Other conspicuously pearl-necklaced maternal ladies with youths attached are Colette's Léa in *Chéri* and Tennessee Williams's Mrs. Venable in *Suddenly Last Summer* IV: "Yes, something had broken, that string of pearls that old mothers hold their sons by, like a . . . sort of—umbilical cord."

37 For a full treatment of these and others, including E. M. Forster and D. H. Lawrence, see Patricia Merivale, *Pan the Goat-God*, 1969. The subject of the survival or return of the classical gods is developed in Germany before it comes to England. Schiller's "Die Götter Griechenlands," 1788, 1800; Eichendorff's "Götterdämmerung," 1818; Heine's "Die Götter Griechenlands," 1826, all lyrically lament or rejoice over (Eichendorff) their overthrow by Christianity; Tieck, Eichendorff, and Heine handle the medieval legend of Tannhäuser before Wagner's 1845 opera or Swinburne's "Laus Veneris" of 1866 ("Der getreue Eckart"; "Das Marmorbild," for which the "Götterdämmerung" lyrics were written; "Tannhäuser," a ballad of 1836); in Heine's essays *Elementargeister*, 1835, and *Die Götter im Exil*, 1853, the gods are alive and active, and in *Die Göttin Diana*, 1846, a narrative for ballet, Diana, Venus, and Dionysus triumphantly return.

38 "Dans une ineffable ambiguité, le délire alterne avec l'extase, l'ardeur avec la liesse, la saltation guerrière avec la jubilation nuptiale . . . " (*Le Martyre de St. Sébastien*, I).

39 Yeats in setting up his opposed primary and antithetic cycles seems to be the heir on the one hand of Irish romantic last-phase myths that confront ruddy heroes with ascetic saints, and on the other of this kind of aesthetic myth of history.

40 Evidently named after the "honest man" who was for twenty years James I's ambassador in Venice.

41 Other characters in whom soul is either dead or temporarily suspended, besides those we shall meet as captives of the Alchemist, are Dickens's Haunted Man, Hawthorne's Artist of the Beautiful and the soulless man of "The Christmas Banquet," and Du Maurier's Little Billee in *Trilby* (see below, chap. 10).

Chapter 8

Epigraphs: Gérard de Nerval, Introduction to Heine's "Intermezzo," *Oeuvres complémentaires,* I, 89; Søren Kierkegaard, *Journals,* ed. A. Dru, no. 88, p. 34.

1 Described in W. E. Collin's paper, itself unpublished, "The Unpublished Novels of Frederick Philip Grove," read to the Royal Society of Canada in Toronto in 1955. Cf. Ibsen's *When We Dead Awaken,* 1899.

2 An artist's obsessive passion for perfection is symbolized without mention of love in Balzac's "Le chef d'oeuvre inconnu," in which a mad painter paints so long at his masterpiece that it disappears to all eyes but his own.

3 The supernatural female sitter appears to be an invention of W. H. Wackenroder ("Raffaels Erscheinung" in *Herzensergiessungen eines Kunstliebenden Klosterbruders* [Raphael's Vision in *Outpourings of an Artloving Friar*], 1797, followed by Herder in "Legenden," 1797 (*Sämmtliche Werke,* ed. Bernard Suphan, XXVIII, 192–94): cf. D. G. Rossetti's story "Hand and Soul," 1850, and the second sentence of *Middlemarch.*

4 The story of the "ring given to Venus" and the statue's claiming her bridegroom (cf. William of Malmesbury, *Gesta Regum Anglorum* bk. II, sec. 5; Burton, *Anat.* III.ii.1.1) is used also in Moore's early ballad "The Statue," Eichendorff's novella "Das Marmorbild," Heine's *Elementargeister,* and Morris's *The Earthly Paradise.*

5 A cheerful Pygmalion story is Hawthorne's "Drowne's Wooden Image"; a very sad one is Hazlitt's *Liber Amoris, or the New Pygmalion,* 1823.

6 Active and passive are the important categories in, for example, *Christabel, Vanity Fair* (Thackeray's drawings, incidentally, distinguish Amelia and Becky as dark and fair more clearly than the text), *Richard Feverel, The Egoist,* and a more recent artist-in-displaced-Venice novel, Durrell's *Justine.*

7 *Corinne* was a favorite novel of the nineteenth century. Mary Shelley read it three times between 1815 and 1820, she and Shelley both reading it in Naples in December 1818. Hunsden Yorke's romance in *The Professor,* xxv, and the contrast between his Lucia and Crimsworth's Frances, recall it: Charlotte Brontë could have read it so near home as the Keighley Mechanics' Institute library. George Eliot cites it in *The Mill on the Floss,* V, iv (see p. 239 below); for Hawthorne, see chap. 7, n. 12 above. (Jean Paul's Liane, in *Titan,* precedes Corinne in bequeathing her lover to another woman. A much later novel strongly reminiscent of *Corinne,* not least in the narcissistic treatment of its poet-hero, is D'Annunzio's *Il Fuoco* [The Flame], 1900.)

8 A dark Cora earlier than Cooper's is the Indian wife of a Spaniard in Marmontel's novel *Les Incas,* 1777, on which is based Kotzebue's tragedy *Die Spanier in Peru,* 1795, translated by M. G. Lewis as *Rolla, or the Peruvian Hero* and adapted by Sheridan as *Pizarro,* both in 1799. The MSS of Coleridge's "Lewti," 1798, show that he first tried out the names Mary and Cora. The original Corinna was a Greek poetess contemporary with Pindar.

9 Scott's Mordaunt Mertoun (*The Pirate,* iii), divided between two sisters, "was sometimes heard to say that Minna never looked so lovely as when her lighthearted sister had induced her, for the time, to forget her habitual gravity; or

Brenda so interesting as when she sat listening, a subdued and affected par-
taker of the deep pathos of her sister Minna."

10 See *Poems of Tennyson,* ed. C. Ricks, headnote p. 603.

11 The renouncing lady—released by death from the bond that divided her from
her real love but for reasons of delicacy or scruple unwilling to marry him—
seems to originate in French fiction. Besides her appearance in *La Nouvelle
Héloïse,* she occurs in Mme de La Fayette's *La Princess de Clèves,* 1678, Godwin's
Italian Letters, 1784, and Swinburne's *Love's Cross-Currents* (first published,
1877, as *A Year's Letters,* and closer in spirit to *Les Liaisons dangereuses* than to
anything in English). Variations on this situation contribute to the endings of
Daniel Deronda and *Portrait of a Lady.*

12 The "angel or devil" question, appropriate to beings so far beyond ordinary human measure as many of our characters, is in fact put to several, as in Caroline
Lamb's *Glenarvon* (III, 43–44) and Mary Shelley's *The Last Man* (I, iv [A]), where
both characters addressed represent Byron; so does the "ange, ou démon" of
Lamartine's *Méditations poétiques* I.ii, "L'Homme, à Lord Byron," 1820. Hugo
picks up the phrase in *Les Orientales* 40, "Lui," 1828, addressing Napoleon. It is
attached to more purely fictional characters in his *Hernani,* 1830 (I.ii.152), and
in the opening lines of George Sand's *Lélia,* 1833. Heine raises the question
about Herodias (*Atta Troll,* 1841, caput 19), and appears thereby to have inspired Nerval's question (however, compare Hoffmann, Postscript to *Die
Abenteuer der Silvesternacht* [New Year's Night Adventures], "O Julie—
Giulietta—heavenly image—hellish spirit": cf. n. 18 below). John Fenton asks
it of Milady in *The Three Musketeers,* 1844, xlv; so does victim of vampire in "La
Morte Amoureuse," 1857. Melville's Pierre has already exclaimed to Isabel,
"Girl! wife or sister, saint or fiend!" (XXVI, vi, 1852). Both "angel" and "devil"
are possible translations for *daimon* or *genius* (cf. *Anthony and Cleopatra* II.iii, "thy
daemon," "thy angel," "thy spirit"): heavenly and hellish colorings aside,
bringing the two terms together seems appropriate in describing the over-
lifesize and equivocal energies of the Romantic fatal man or woman.

13 This reference to the scenes at Lake Leman where St-Preux and Julie fell in love
is typical of the very literary texture of *Sylvie.*

14 We can note some background to this thoroughly Hoffmannesque theme.
Nerval published in 1831 a translation of the first and third chapters of
Hoffmann's *Silvesternacht,* in which the narrator meets again "la bien-aimée,"
now married to a hideous other, and then in a dream sees her transformed into
a temptress, the instrument of the Devil. In 1840 he sketched out a scenario
based on a Hoffmann story—"Le Magnétiseur"; however, for the villain Alban
and heroine Maria he substitutes the names Médard and Aurélie, from
Hoffmann's *Die Elixiere des Teufels,* of which at one time he commenced a
French version. As Aurélia is to become the name of Nerval's most comprehensive ideal female figure, we can note further that, while the Aurelie of
Die Elixiere has the rôles of sensitive maiden / victim / saving goddess (Nerval
finished his translation of Goethe's *Faust* in 1840, and the transformation of
Gretchen from lost maiden to mediatrix is an important strand in his mythology), in an untitled story in the *Serapionsbrüder* another Aurelie, again an
innocent girl, becomes a vampire; while her name and her demon mother link

her story with that of the *Elixiere*, the name of the man who loves her, Hippolyt, is that of Maria's lover in *Der Magnetiseur*, renamed Maurice by Nerval. The spectrum of fiend / victim (Maria merely dies) / near-saint in these three connected stories sums up much that is common to the mythologies of Hoffmann and Nerval. (The main Nervalian element not conspicuous in Hoffmann—the lady as actress or singer—is supplied in the Barbier-Carré version of Hoffmann—see n. 18 below: it's hard to believe that Gérard didn't sit down with the collaborators some night in some pub in the winter of 1850–51.)

15 *Selected Writings of Gérard de Nerval*, p. 253. The symbolism of dark and fair is pervasive in Nerval's work. The title of his most famous poem, "El Desdichado," comes from Scott's *Ivanhoe* (viii or ix—editions vary), whose contrasted heroines Rebecca and Rowena are the most familiar and popular example of such a pairing (for "tour abolie" see some six pages back).

16 We have mentioned the Neapolitan settings of Mrs. Piozzi, *The Italian*, *Corinne*, and *Zanoni* : other notable ones occur in Cazotte (*Le Diable amoureux*, admired by Nerval), Beckford (*Dreams*, letter 23), the Shelleys (*The Last Man* commences with a visit to the Sibyl's cave), and Gautier ("Jettatura," 1857).

17 The gamut of female types is a Romantic feature: cf. *Wilhelm Meister* (see p. 164 above), Jean Paul's *Titan*, and the male gallery in George Sand's *Lélia* (this term is borrowed from Marvell's poem "The Gallery"); in poetry, Byron's *Don Juan*, Tennyson's "Dream of Fair Women" and poems on women's names, and the poems titled "Verschiedene" (Various Women) in Heine's *Neue Gedichte*, 1833. Fellini's *8½* is a recent version.

18 I am following the fullest version of the libretto that I know in print (*The Authentic Librettos of the French and German Operas*, pp. 195–251): followed in the Opera Festival Company of Toronto's production of 1958, it has always seemed to me a very satisfying work. Since the complete libretto produced by Jules Barbier around 1875 from his and Carré's play of 1851 is no longer extant, Colin Graham and Edmund Tracey, in their efforts to approximate the original one for the Sadler's Wells Opera 1970 production, made the following changes, all but the first in line with the play: five acts become three with a prologue and epilogue; the Muse introduces herself in the prologue before appearing as Nicklausse; the Antonia episode precedes that with Giulietta, and some emphasis is given to Antonia's selfishness in desiring a singing career, to imply a movement downwards from Olympia's blankness towards Giulietta's depravity; Stella goes off with Lindorf in the epilogue only after Hoffmann has rejected her, and the epiphany of the Muse follows her departure.

The stories on which the opera is based are the *Silvesternacht* (frame and Giulietta), "Der Sandmann" (The Sandman—Olympia), "Rat Krespel" and "Der Magnetiseur" (Councillor Crespel and The Mesmerist—Antonia), and "Signor Formica" (the figure of Pitichinaccio). In addition, the point that the Artist by not marrying his Ideal preserves it is made at the end of "Die Fermate" and "Die Doppeltgänger"—in the latter, by a Berthold wiser than the painter of the "Jesuiterkirche."

19 With this theme the story recalls a note in Hoffmann's journal, January 19,

1812: "... Ktch—Ktch—Ktch   O Satanas—Satanas   I believe that something highly poetical is lurking behind this demon, and in that respect Ktch should be regarded only as a mask—demasquez vous donc, mon petit Monsieur!" Ktch, from Kleist's devoted and mediumistic child-heroine Käthchen von Heilbronn, was Hoffmann's code name for his fifteen-year-old singing pupil Julchen Mark, here a "mask" for both Satan and the Muse. The journal entry suggests many relationships in Hoffmann's yet-to-be-written fiction, where a Julie may seem to mask a Giulietta (*Silvesternacht*), or a Julia or Maria is practiced upon by estranging dark powers (*Kater Murr* [Tomcat Murr], "Magnetiseur").

20 Cf. the relations existing between Blake's Albion and his daughter Jerusalem, or Shelley's brother-sister pairs Laon and Cythna, Prometheus and Asia.

21 For a modern and specifically homosexual variant, see Gore Vidal's *The City and the Pillar*, 1949, with its reference to Sodom and Gomorrah and the fate of Lot's wife. The "Afterword" of 1965 remarks, "From too much looking back, [the hero] was destroyed, an unsophisticated Humbert Humbert trying to recreate an idyll that never truly existed except in his own imagination." The idyllic scene, complete with reflections of the beloved and a stream that metaphorically reaches the sea in the last pages, is in line with Brick's more mythologically explicit love affair with Echo Spring in Tennessee Williams's *Cat on a Hot Tin Roof*, 1955, act 1.

22 Cf. above, p. 90, the experience of *Zanoni*'s Viola.

23 The Tennyson-Hallam-Emily relationship in *In Memoriam* is one of several elements bringing that poem close to Victorian fiction. For a note on the sentiment involved, cf. Jean Paul, *Titan*, trans. C. T. Brooks, jubilee 3, cycle 20, p. 127: "... for every one, if it is only half practicable, loves to spin himself into one chrysalis with the sister of his friend."

24 A vampirism handled more within realistic conventions destroys Fitzgerald's Dick Diver in *Tender is the Night*—Rosamund and Lydgate again, perhaps.

25 In another Romantic context this mood is expressed in the Wilis, the dead maidens who entrap young men in their moonlight dances. Gautier with a collaborator developed from Heine's account of them in *Florentinische Nächte* and *Elementargeister*, both 1835, the ballet "Giselle, ou les Wilis," adding the motif of the maidens' deaths being caused by betrayal: "Giselle" with Grisi, 1841, replaced in popular favor "La Sylphide" with Taglioni, 1832. (*Elementargeister* is a remarkable compendium of Romantic legends about otherworldly attachments.)

26 Much closer to Shelley, cf. the opening of the incantation in *Manfred* following the brief apparition that presages the appearance of the phantom of Astarte: "When the Moon is on the wave, / And the glow-worm in the grass, / And the meteor on the grave, / And the wisp on the morass ... " (I.i.192–95). Without will-o'-the-wisp associations, beguiling female visions waylay night wanderers in German lyrics of the period, and slightly later in some of the paintings of Moritz von Schwind. The theme returns in *Lolita*, I, v: to "certain bewitched travelers" (cf. "Enchanted Hunters," I, xxi) some maidens "reveal their true nature, which is not human, but nymphic (that is, demoniac)."

27 Recollection of this picture probably enters into *The Tales of Hoffmann,* act I, where Hoffmann before describing his own loves makes fun of the mistresses of his three friends: "Oui, Léonor, ta virtuose! . . . / Oui, Gretchen, ta poupée inerte, au coeur glacé! / Et ta Fausta, pauvre insensé . . . / La courtisane au front d'airain!" He appears unconscious of the parallel these present with Antonia, Olympia, and Giulietta as he goes on to sing of Stella, "trois femmes dans la même femme! / Artiste, jeune fille, et courtisane!"

28 *Faerie Queene* IV.v.15: for connotations of this term see below, pp. 198–99.

29 In Nabokov's *Pale Fire,* the Muse of John Shade's poem is his daughter, the drowned maiden Hazel; both her elegiac nature and the sexual ambiguity of the mirror worlds of the book are pointed up in the extraordinarily touching evocation of Goethe's "Erlkönig":

> Who rides so late in the night and the wind?
> It is the writer's grief. It is the wild
> March wind. It is the father with his child.   [ll. 662–64]

30 For comparable moods and figures, besides the "unborn" children whose "faces shine / Beside the never-lighted fire" in *In Mem.* lxxxiv, compare Werther's ghostlike Charlotte (above, p. 66) and the phantom Yillah of *Mardi* (above, p. 114): also *Ernest Maltravers,* "that morning dream haunted by the vision of the lost and dim-remembered Alice" (IX, vii), and *Alice,* "haunted by the mournful memory of my lost Alice" (VIII, i); also, from De Quincey's Prefatory Notice to the 1856 edition of the *Opium-Eater:*

> The search after the lost features of Ann, which I spoke of as pursued in the crowds of London, was in a more proper sense pursued through many a year in dreams. The general idea of a search and a chase reproduced itself in many shapes. The person, the rank, the age, the scenical position, all varied themselves for ever; but the same leading traits more or less faintly remained of a lost Pariah woman, and of some shadowy malice which withdrew her, or attempted to withdraw her, from restoration and hope.

Poe's Ulalume, Annabel Lee, and Marchesa Aphrodite belong to the same family, which we could call, following the epigraph of *Aurélia* II, that of Eurydice.

Chapter 9

Epigraphs: Herman Melville, *Moby-Dick* i; Eliphalet Oram Lyte, before 1891.

1 Cf., for example, Beattie in "The Triumph of Melancholy": "Even while the careless disencumber'd soul / Dissolving sinks to joy's oblivious dream, / Even then to time's tremendous verge we roll / With haste impetuous down life's surgy stream."

2 *Alastor* 505, 569: cf. *The Excursion* III, last lines. Such a precipice or waterfall often figures as "threshold symbol" in an adventure story—*Typee, The Water Babies, Lorna Doone.* In three more that occur to me, the sense of symbolic action

is heightened by the relationships of the characters concerned as subject and alter ego. In George MacDonald's *The Flight of the Shadow,* identical twins fight for a demon-woman on the lip of an Alpine cataract and each supposes he has pushed the other over. In Rider Haggard's *Ayesha* the bosom friends and complements (see next chapter) Leo and Holly take the plunge in Tibet, each prepared to die for the other. And at the end of *The Memoirs of Sherlock Holmes,* in "The Final Problem," Holmes and his evil opposite Moriarty are assumed to have rolled together over another Alp-edge, locked in a last dreadful embrace, as the saying is.

3 Cf. Elizabeth Rowe, *Letters* I, letter 2; Smollett, *The Regicide,* III.vi, Eleonora's speech about "love's deceitful voyage"; Young, *Night Thoughts* V.344–49; Johnson, *Vanity of Human Wishes* 344–45: "Must helpless man, in ignorance sedate, / Roll darkling down the torrent of his fate?" More Wertherian is Frankenstein's statement, ". . . when I would account to myself for the birth of that passion, which afterwards ruled my destiny, I find it arise, like a mountain river, from ignoble and forgotten sources; but, swelling as it proceeded, it became the torrent which, in its course, has swept away all my hopes and joys" (ii). See too Isaac Watts, *Hymns and Spiritual Songs,* 1707, bk. 2, no. 11, "Parting with Carnal Joys"—"I Send the Joys of Earth away" (ed. Selma Bishop, p. 165).

4 For a comparable symbolic use of water elsewhere in George Eliot, cf. *Romola* lxi, "Drifting Away," and lxviii, "Romola's Waking." Her boat, like others we shall meet, is of the coffin–cradle variety.

5 A poem which Blake illustrated links pleasure in one's own reflection with pensive fishing: Gray's "Ode on the Death of a Favourite Cat."

6 Compare the following: Shelley, "On Love" (VI, 201–02):

> We are born into the world, and there is something within us which, from the instant that we live, more and more thirsts after its likeness. . . . We dimly see within our intellectual nature a miniature as it were of our entire self, yet deprived of all that we condemn or despise, . . . a mirror whose surface reflects only the forms of purity and brightness; a soul within our soul that describes a circle around its proper paradise, which pain and sorrow and evil dare not overleap.

Hawthorne (besides the remarks on reflections in the introduction to *Mosses from an Old Manse*), *The Scarlet Letter,* xix, "The Child at the Brook-side":

> Just where [Pearl] had paused, the brook chanced to form a pool so smooth and quiet that it reflected a perfect image of her little figure, with all the brilliant picturesqueness of her beauty, in its adornment of flowers and wreathed foliage, but more refined and spiritualized than the reality.

MacDonald, *Phantastes,* x:

> Why are all reflections lovelier than what we call the reality?—not so grand or strong, it may be, but always lovelier? Fair as is the gliding sloop on the shining sea, the wavering, trembling, unresting sail below is fairer still. Yea, the reflecting ocean itself, reflected in the mirror, has a wondrousness about its waters that somewhat vanishes when I turn toward itself. All mirrors are magic mirrors. The commonest room is a room in a poem when

I turn to the glass. . . . In whatever way it may be accounted for, of one thing we may be sure, that this feeling is no cheat; for there is no cheating in nature and the simple, unsought feelings of the soul. There must be a truth involved in it, though we may but in part lay hold of the meaning. Even the memories of past pain are beautiful; and past delights, though beheld only through clefts in the grey clouds of sorrow, are lovely as Fairy-land. But how have I wandered into the deeper fairy-land of the soul, while as yet I only float toward the fairy palace of Fairyland! The moon, which is the lovelier memory or reflex of the down-gone sun, the joyous day seen in the faint mirror of the brooding night, had rapt me away.

Reflection becomes sealed-off paradise with water as barrier in Housman, *A Shropshire Lad*, no. 20; cf. Traherne's poem "Shadows in the Water."

7 For a cruder but not irrelevant association of a maiden with a glassy surface, cf. *Pericles* IV.vi.150–51: "Boult, take her away, use her at thy pleasure, crack the glass of her virginity, and make the rest malleable." Snow-White's name, sleep, and glass coffin are all negative symbols of virginity: snow-, stone-, and mer-maidens are in some respects analogous.

8 Cf. the "elf locks" and "eyes . . . hollow and wild" of Verney near the end of *The Last Man* (III, x).

9 Compare three Canadian poems: Patrick Anderson's "Winter in Montreal," with its fantasy of "the winter palace" and "those who live in the capitalists' crystal"; Anne Hébert's "Vie de château": "L'enchantement pervers de ces lieux / Est tout dans ses miroirs polis. / La seule occupation possible ici / Consiste à se mirer jour et nuit" (in *Le Tombeau des rois*); and Daryl Hine's "Bluebeard's Wife," with its castle containing in "the room of artifice" "Vene-tian glass that counterfeited ice" (in *The Wooden Horse*). South of the border, there is Scott Fitzgerald's story "The Ice Palace," 1920.

10 Their names, Pearl and Jasper, suggest the underwater-treasure symbolism discussed below, chap. 10, n. 2, and chap. 12, pp. 261–62.

11 The magical aura of these poems, the feeling that earth and heaven are briefly in a special mutual alignment, is paralleled in Poe's "The Domain of Arn-heim," 1842. "From his cradle to his grave, a wave of prosperity bore my friend Ellison along. Nor do I use the word prosperity in its mere worldly sense. I mean it as synonymous with happiness. . . . In the widest and noblest sense he was a poet. . . . It seemed to my friend that the creation of the landscape-garden offered to the proper Muse the most magnificent of oppor-tunities." Ellison's garden is so designed as to exclude all the signs of mortality and imperfection that mark our world as fallen. The approach to this paradise is by boat through a winding gorge: "At every instant the vessel seemed imprisoned within an enchanted circle, having insuperable and impenetrable walls of foliage, a roof of ultramarine satin, and *no* floor—the keel balancing itself with admirable nicety on that of a phantom bark which, by some accident having been turned upside down, floated in constant company with the sub-stantial one, for the purpose of sustaining it." Eventually, after transferring to a self-moving "fairy bark," the traveler arrives just at sunset at his destination and beholds "upspringing [a Miltonic and Tennysonian word] confusedly from amid all, a mass of semi-Gothic, semi-Saracenic architecture, sustaining

itself as if by miracle in midair, glittering in the red sunlight with a hundred oriels, minarets, and pinnacles, and seeming the phantom handiwork, conjointly, of the Sylphs, of the Fairies, of the Genii, and of the Gnomes." This sunset vision has a Prospero; it is a combined fairy palace, castle in Spain, and Venetian rapture (cf. Dickens's description of St. Mark's in *Pictures from Italy*); and the conclusion makes the four elements all contribute. The fairy or reflected bark is found in other Poe idyllic landscapes: cf. "Landor's Cottage" and especially "The Island of the Fay," which adapts the cyclical symbolism of *De Antro Nympharum,* Porphyry's commentary on Homer's description of the place to which Odysseus was carried by what Poe in "To Helen" calls "those Nicéan barks of yore," the intelligent ships of the Phaeacians.

12 Surviving now mainly as a proper name, "pleasance" is equivalent to *locus amoenus* or *Lustort*, as in Willard Trask's translation of E. R. Curtius's *European Literature and the Latin Middle Ages,* x, sec. 6.

13 Mrs. Gaskell's other notable winter piece is "The Old Nurse's Story," in which winter embodies demonic separation, not idyllic community: as a result of the mutual hatred of two sisters a generation before the story opens, a living child is enticed out into the snow by a spectral child. Besides recalling the ghostly Cathy at the window in *Wuthering Heights* and foreshadowing the governess's struggle in "The Turn of the Screw," the story makes a striking complement to "Half-Brothers": both, incidentally, have the figure of the saving shepherd.

14 Cf. Milton, "Epitaphium Damonis" 45–49:

> quis me lenire docebit
> Mordaces curas, quis longam fallere noctem
> Dulcibus alloquiis, grato cum sibilat igni
> Molle pyrum, & nucibus strepitat focus, at malus auster
> Miscet cuncta foris, & desuper intonat ulmo.

("Who will teach me to lighten consuming cares, who to beguile the long nights with sweet converse, when the mellow pears shall be set hissing by the cheery fire, and the hearth shall crackle with the nuts, while the evil South Wind confounds all the world outdoors, and thunders down through the elm?"—trans. Skeat.) A possible parallel is Horace, *Odes* i.9. Cf. also the opening of Drayton's verse letter to Reynolds; Lovelace, "The Grasshopper"; Wordsworth, "Written in Germany"; the end of Shelley's "Letter to Maria Gisborne"; De Quincey, *English Opium Eater*—"Introduction to the Pains of Opium," where he cites the winter pleasance raised by evil magic in *Castle of Indolence* I.43; *In Mem.* cvii.

15 For the gondola as coffin–cradle (Goethe, *Venezianische Epigramme* 8; Mme de Staël, *Corinne* xv, 7; Shelley, letter to Peacock, October 8, 1818), see Milton Wilson, "Travellers' Venice: Some Images for Byron and Shelley," *University of Toronto Quarterly* 43 (1974): 93–120.

16 Tennyson in *In Memoriam,* for example in lxxv–lxxvii, absolutely rejects any notion of constructing his poem as a vessel of Hallam's ongoing life or even his proper monument; its composition is intended only, in the words of "Lycidas," "to interpose a little ease." It is a matter of moral will to him that he will not ascribe to art any but the most limited and commonsense powers,

admitting nothing mystic or magical. His death-ships are not in our sense arks. He twice uses the expression "mortal ark," in *In Mem.* xii and in "The Two Voices": in the first it is his body and in the second his whole self which the negative voice seeks to "wreck," but the usage is very much the traditional medieval and Renaissance one suggesting the pathos and fragility of human life afloat on the perilous flood. The most positive of his ships, suggesting Grail-ship or landing ark, is the Christmas ship bringing Arthur back to England in the dream concluding "The Epic": it images the powers not of poetry but of a social idealism rooted like that of Blithedale in a fireside communal feeling.

Chapter 10

Epigraphs: William Wordsworth, Preface to *Lyrical Ballads;* Mary Shelley, *Frankenstein,* I, iv in 1st ed., v in 3d; Lord Byron, *Manfred,* I.i.12 (adapting *Faust* I, 2038–39).

1 Other connections may be the caverned magicians of Collins's "Ode on the Popular Superstitions of the Highlands" and Scott's *Marmion,* introduction to canto I.

The source of Godwin's romance, according to his preface, was *Hermippus Redivivus* [*or, The Sage's Triumph over Old Age and the Grave,* trans.] by John Campbell [from the German of J. H. Cohausen (London, 1744)], one of many speculative works in the area of alchemy-Rosicrucianism-Freemasonry that occupy the gap between the folklore world of Faust and more or less highbrow alchemical fiction. *Hermippus* relates among other episodes that of the mysterious signor Gualdi, who at Venice in 1687 admitted to a guest that he was the subject as well as the owner of a certain Titian portrait, and left the city before he could be questioned further: this story gave Godwin the idea for his own.

2 A particularly relevant symbol for happiness or fulfillment is "pearl," with its underwater associations and its use as a woman's name (cf. Margaret and Marguerite). In Christ's parable (Matthew 13) it is a quest-object and symbol of immense value. In Elizabethan literature it can suggest the biblical and alchemical "stone" unrecognized and trampled underfoot: besides Othello as "base Indian," cf. Nashe, *Anatomie of Absurditie* (*Elizabethan Critical Essays,* ed. Gregory Smith, I, 333): "He that will seeke for a Pearle must first learn to know it when he sees it, least he neglect it when he findes it, or make a nought worth peeble his Jewell." "Perle" in *Tasso* is a symbol of the princess, but with the suggestion that the treasure sought for is inward and spiritual: speaking of his first meeting with her in a quiet chamber of the bustling palace, Tasso says: "Though eager, inexperienced desire / At first went straying forth a thousand ways, / Now, struck with shame, I to myself returned, / And learned at last to know what's truly worthy. / So one might seek along the broad sea-sands / In vain a pearl, that, hidden from his gaze, / Rests silently, closed up within its shell" (II.i.881–87).

3 The ironic theme of the substitute reappears in Stevenson's "The Bottle Imp": in Wagner's *Flying Dutchman,* as in Longfellow's *The Golden Legend* and

Gerhart Hauptmann's *Der arme Heinrich* (Poor Henry)—both retellings of
Hartmann von Aue's medieval tale of a knight whose leprosy is to be cured by
a maiden's sacrifice—the theme is romantic.

4 This particular dramatic moment, the instant on which depend life and death,
described by Godwin and Shelley ("Raking the cinders of a crucible / For life
and power, even when his fevered hand / Shakes in its last decay") and
Bulwer Lytton, recurs three times in *The Man Who Could Cheat Death* (by Barre
Lyndon, 1959), and is recalled in a speech of the Jesuit Rodin in *Le Juif errant*, at
the instant at which mortal sickness seizes him: "comme l'alchimiste penché
sur son creuset, où bouillonne une mixture qui peut lui donner des trésors ou
la mort . . . moi seul je puis, à cette heure . . . " (VII, xi, 186–87). A few chapters
later, Rodin at the point of death is recovered by an incredibly (it is stressed)
painful operation that suggests ritual magic. Rather than recount the appalling
details, let us notice the author's expressions: "On eût dit un cadavre, sans
deux ardentes étincelles qui brillaient dans l'ombre formée par la profondeur
des orbites" (VIII, iv, 60). "Ainsi qu'un cadavre soumis à l'action de la pile
voltaïque se meut par soubresauts brusques et étranges, ainsi Rodin . . . " (v,
68). "La santé . . . la vie . . . et tout à l'heure encore Rodin entendait parler des
funérailles solonelles qu'on allait lui faire. . . . Eh bien! la santé! la vie, il les
aura, il se le dit. Oui . . . il a voulu vivre jusque-là . . . et il a vécu. . . . Il vivra
donc! . . . il le veut!" (viii, 96–97). Within a page he leaps up "comme s'il eût été
mû par un ressort" and crosses the room, trailing his sheet "comme un suaire,
derrière ce corps livide et décharné . . . ," and extending "un de ses bras de
squelette, dur comme du fer." The watching priests speak of "miracle" and of
the raising of Lazarus. During the operation, which consists of burning his
flesh, his corpselike appearance is twice more mentioned. After the crisis, in
which he is "miraculeusement rappelé à la vie" (x, 122), "En entendant dire
qu'il était sauvé, Rodin, quoique ses souffrances fussent peut-être les plus
vives qu'il eût encore ressenties, car le feu arrivait à la dernière couche de
l'épiderme, Rodin fut réellement beau, d'une beauté infernale. A travers la
pénible contraction de ses traits éclatait l'orgueil d'un farouche triomphe; on
voyait que ce monstre se sentait redevenir fort et puissant, et qu'il avait conscience des maux terribles que sa funeste résurrection allait causer" (ix, 119).
To complete the effect, this satanic parody of a resurrected Christ-phoenix
complacently counts off on his body five fire-inflicted wounds, representing to
him the five victims he is going to devote his renewed life to destroying.

5 In *Caleb Williams* and *Mandeville*, the ironic recognition already has the kind of
intensity developed by the discoveries of Poe's "William Wilson" or Hawthorne's "Ethan Brand."

6 Frankenstein swears an oath of vengeance on the graves of his brother, father,
and bride, calling on their spirits to assist him. He sees them in his dreams and
continually assumes they are with him: e.g., "a slight repose, during which
the spirits of the dead hovered round and instigated me to toil and revenge"
(III, vii; xxiv—cf. *Thalaba* XII.v). While victims more often haunt their murderer (*Richard III*, the Don Juan tradition, *Die Räuber*), another Hamlet-style
haunted avenger appears in Conan Doyle's *A Study in Scarlet* (II, v): "As I
drove, I could see old John Ferrier and sweet Lucy looking at me out of the

darkness and smiling at me. . . . All the way they were ahead of me, one on each side, until I pulled up at the house in the Brixton Road."

7 St. Leon speaks of the "melancholy" attaching to his transformation:

> I still bore the figure and lineaments of a human creature; but I knew that I was not what I seemed. There was a greater distance between me and the best constructed and most consummate of the human species, than there is betweeen him and an ant or a muskito, crushed by the first accidental tread, or consumed by the first spark wafted by the wind. I can no longer cheat my fancy; I know that I am alone. The creature does not exist with whom I have any common language, or any genuine sympathies. . . .
>
> [IV, i]

Here is Melmoth after losing his bride:

> . . . there was but one human chord that vibrated in my heart—it is broken to-night, and for ever! I will never tempt woman more! Why should the whirlwind, that can shake mountains, and overwhelm cities with its breath, descend to scatter the leaves of the rosebud?   [xxxv]

Zanoni addresses Viola:

> Yes, Viola, I might love thee; but in that love what sorrow and what change! The flower gives perfume to the rock on whose heart it grows. A little while, and the flower is dead; but the rock still endures, the snow at its breast, the sunshine on its summit. Pause, think well . . . learn . . . , sweet flower, that there are more genial resting-places than the rock.
>
> [II, iii]

> A moment in the life of ages, a bubble on the shoreless sea. What else to me can be human love?   [III, vii]

The same complaints are made by female mages: cf. "The Witch of Atlas" st. 24, Rider Haggard's *Ayesha* xviii. To take the theme down to modern times, the century-and-a-half-old doctor of *The Man Who Could Cheat Death* also grows weary of solitude, and he resolves to perform his rejuvenating operation on a woman, thus precipitating the story's calamity.

8 "Gambler's Luck": gambling themes are close to those of alchemy and magic, and are often used to lead into them: cf. *St. Leon*, Pushkin's "Queen of Spades," and "The Bottle-Imp, a tale from the German" (and set in Venice—*Romancist and Novelist's Library*, I [1839]—a descendant, like Stevenson's story of 1891, from the anonymous "Bottle Imp" melodrama of 1828).

9 Cf. Wordsworth's corrupt Oswald, who, seeing in the innocent Marmaduke "a mirror of my former self," resolves to make him a "shadow" of his present self (*The Borderers*, ll. 1864, 2008-09). For "happy valley" and related terms, cf. *Rasselas*; *Udolpho's* La Vallée; Poe's "The Haunted Palace" and "Eleonora" (Valley of Many-Coloured Grasses); *Rebecca*.

10 The once-benevolent misanthrope, or "misery made me a fiend" character, like Timon, Godwin's Bethlem Gabor (*St. Leon*) or Mandeville, Scott's Black Dwarf, and to some extent Heathcliff, is to be distinguished from the natural villain—Iago or Edmund, Moore's Zeluco, numerous post-Shakespearean wicked brothers. Early examples of the former are the Moor Zanga (much

admired by the young Byron) in Young's tragedy *The Revenge* and Sade's Dolmancé in *La Philosophie dans le boudoir,* 1793. M. G. Lewis in *The Castle-Spectre,* 1798, goes beyond two of his obvious sources, *The Revenge* and Schiller's *Die Räuber,* in his development of both types of villain. Osmond has been a fiend from birth: his excuse, "Nature formed me the slave of wild desires" (II.iii), recalls (besides Schiller's Franz Moor, who in turn recalls Richard III) Miss Howe on "the nature of the beast" (*Clarissa* III, letter 40, p. 230, a remarkable passage) and Sade's heroes almost everywhere. His black servant Hassan like Zanga was born free and generous: "My heart once was gentle, once was good! But sorrows have broken it, insults have made it hard! I have been dragged from my native land . . . in that bitter moment did I banish humanity from my breast. I . . . vowed aloud endless hatred to mankind" (I, ii). Lewis in an appended note "To the Reader" defends among other features

> my misanthropic Negro. He has been compared to Zanga; but Young's Hero differs widely from what I meant in Hassan. Zanga's hatred is confined to one object; to destroy the happiness of that object is his sole aim, and his vengeance is no sooner accomplished than he repents its gratification. Hassan is a man of violent passions, and warm feelings, whose bosom is filled with the milk of human kindness, but that milk is soured by despair; whose nature was susceptible of the tenderest affections, but who feels that all the chains of his affections are broken for ever. He has lost every thing, even hope; he has no single object against which he can direct his vengeance, and he directs it at large against mankind. He hates all the world, hates even himself; for he feels that in all the world there is no one that loves him. [Hassan could not] hate with such inveteracy, if he had not loved with extreme affection.

The treacherous negro Babo of Melville's "Benito Cereno" seems to belong rather with the natural villains.

11 An equivocal effect is produced by the directions and supplies left by the monster for Frankenstein in III, vii; xxiv: Frankenstein, who since his illness has become something of a fiend himself, receives them with execrations. On his deathbed his last words are full of self-justification. He warns Walton that the Being is "eloquent and persuasive," and Walton then refuses to be "touched by the expressions of his misery," devoting all his compassion and admiration to the dead Frankenstein: however, the reader may well find both Walton and Frankenstein at this point excessively self-righteous.

12 "O, there are spirits of the air." Cf. our theme of calamitous separation between body and soul (p. 145 above), and such variations on it as the situations of Poe's "William Wilson" and Stevenson's *Dr. Jekyll and Mr. Hyde,* or more recently Hesse's *Steppenwolf.*

13 "We are coupled by a chain of adamant," Oswald has already said to Marmaduke after their crime (*Borderers,* 1. 1854).

14 Like the newly created Eve, the Being sees himself reflected in a pool: "I had admired the perfect forms of my cottagers—their grace, beauty, and delicate complexions, but how was I terrified when I viewed myself in a transparent pool! At first I started back, unable to believe that it was indeed I who was

reflected in the mirror, and when I became fully convinced that I was in reality the monster that I am, I was filled with the bitterest sensations of despondence and mortification" (II, i; xii). "I cherished hope, it is true, but it vanished when I beheld my person reflected in water, or my shadow in the moonshine, even as that frail image and that inconstant shade" (II, vii; xv). Along with Byron's Arnold (*The Deformed Transformed* 46–52) and Rider Haggard's Holly (*She* i), the Being is an anti-Narcissus or perhaps Polyphemus (Theocritus, *Idylls* xi). His ugliness like Holly's or that of Blake's Ugly Man (*Descriptive Catalogue*) suggests his incompleteness, his need to be joined with an appropriate complement (cf. the relation of hero and friend in Rostand's *Cyrano de Bergerac*): perhaps too he is a disguised Eros, like Beauty's Beast or the Phantom of the Opera.

15 Vercors, *You Shall Know Them*, 1952; Brigid Brophy, *Hackenfeller's Ape*, 1953; closest to our line, John Collier, *His Monkey Wife*, 1939, in which the dark woman of romance, pitted against the blonde Amy, is in fact an ape, and personifies the mystery of Nature, instinct, poetry, and Africa. A precursor is Rider Haggard, *Allan's Wife*, 1889.

16 Caliban would seem to be behind Clon and Clov, the clod-servants of Pierre Andrézel's *The Angelic Avengers*, 1946, and Beckett's *Endgame*, besides John Fowles's collector, Clegg.

17 Cf. Miriam's bond with the underworld in *The Marble Faun* (iv, titled "The Spectre of the Catacomb") and Isabel Archer's commitment to return to the deadly Osmond at the end of *Portrait of a Lady*.

18 Related to this theme is "scientific experimentation," especially on those closest to one, as a regular sadistic topic: cf. Sade's Rodin in *Justine*, 1791; Borel's Vésalius in *L'Anatomiste*, 1833; doctor and chemist in Féval, *Les Mystères de Londres*, 1844 (described in Praz, *Romantic Agony*, p. 416); Machen, *The Great God Pan* and *The Inmost Light*, 1894: Maturin's Melmoth (xxxiv) seems to be considering his expected child as a fit object for his own kind of "fearful experiment."

19 It is a short step from here to sinister Utopias or science fiction parables—like John Wyndham's "The Compassion Circuit" or the film *Invasion of the Body-Snatchers*—where hero or society is tempted to exchange human pain and weakness for an apparently superior existence without feeling.

20 In part 1 Trilby is taken to see "La Dame aux camélias," and the story makes her cry: her own as it unfolds greatly resembles that of Marguérite, with her lover's mother rather than father as the indignant parent.

21   [Svengali] had but to say *"Dors!"* and she suddenly became an unconscious Trilby of marble, who could produce wonderful sounds—just the sounds he wanted, and nothing else—and think his thoughts and wish his wishes —and love him at his bidding with a strange, unreal, factitious love . . . just his own love for himself turned inside out—*à l'envers*—and reflected back on him, as from a mirror . . . *un écho, un simulacre, quoi! pas autre chose!* . . .
                                                             [viii, 357]

To the relation between Svengali and his wife we could compare that between Kurtz and his "intended" in *Heart of Darkness*:

... a long time after I heard once more, not his own voice, but the echo of his magnificent eloquence thrown to me from a soul as translucently pure as a cliff of crystal.

22 She is not really insane, but the author wants this special touch added to her pathos, doubtless on the model of Ophelia.

23 In the background is Nodier's "Trilby," telling of the sacrificial love of a brownie for the wife of a Scottish boatman: I owe the fishy remarks that follow to Milton Wilson. Such a siren as Trilby is not is presented with great exuberance in *Vanity Fair,* lxiv.

24 Principally from Irenaeus, *Adversus Haereses* 1.23.2: see further Hans Jonas, *The Gnostic Religion,* 1958, iv; note on pp. 104–05 the quotation from Hippolytus that seems to link Simon with the Narcissus-myth of the "Poimandres" (p. 77 above).

25 See P. M. Palmer and R. P. More, *The Sources of the Faust Tradition,* 1936.

26 Woman as "lure" or "bait" is a sinister theme in our examples so far: cf. Hoffmann's mad painter in "Die Jesuiterkirche in G-," "The Devil lures us with puppets, to which he glues angels' wings"; a description of La Comnena in D'Annunzio's *La Gloria* (quoted in Praz, *Romantic Agony,* p. 261), "Thou wast trailed like a bait through all the sloughs of vice. . . . " Positive cases exist, however, as in those medieval interpretations of the unicorn hunt where the maiden's trapping the unicorn represents Mary's conception of Christ, and in Dylan Thomas's "Ballad of the Long-Legged Bait."

27 Like Jay Gatsby, the hero of this film is last seen floating in the swimming pool with a bullet in him; both works thus feature adaptations of the house built on water. A third American great-house romance, *Citizen Kane,* set largely in Kane's Florida mansion, Xanadu, reveals as the secret of its cellar the sled that embodies the house's antithesis, the winters of his boyhood.

28 The professor of *The Blue Angel* (film, 1929, based on Heinrich Mann's *Professor Unrat,* 1905) is another who descends to being an animal man; he is consoled by the demon showman while the fatal lady goes off with his rival, the Strong Man or natural brute—a lineup rather like that of the characters in "Petrouchka." Cf., for rivalry of Strong Man and intellectual, Browning's *Fifine at the Fair,* sec. 25. The professor has his prophetic double in the sad-faced clown whose rôle he inherits.

29 Cf. numerous expressions in "The Murders in the Rue Morgue": "the wild fervour and the vivid freshness of his imagination"—"the rather fantastic gloom of our common temper"—living in "a time-eaten and grotesque mansion . . . tottering to its fall"—Dupin and the narrator could be "regarded as madmen"—"our seclusion was perfect," "locality . . . carefully kept a secret." "It was a freak of fancy in my friend . . . to be enamoured of the Night. . . . [W]e could counterfeit her presence. At the first dawn of the morning we closed all the massy shutters of our old building; lighted a couple of tapers which . . . threw out only the ghastliest and feeblest of rays. By the aid of these we then busied our souls in dreams."

30 In "The Greek Interpreter" Holmes tells Watson that his gifts are traceable to his "grandmother, who was the sister of Vernet, the French artist. Art in the blood is liable to take the strangest forms . . . ": so, doubtless, is the French

connection. While Poe does nothing to develop for us the character of his narrator, Holmes's Watson, the dumb but feeling chum, provides a needed balance: "When one tries to rise above Nature one is liable to fall below it. The highest type of man may revert to the animal if he leaves the straight road of destiny" ("The Creeping Man"); "I am a brain, Watson; the rest of me is appendix" ("The Mazarin Stone").

31 Cf. Zschokke's *Aballino* (1794), *The Monk*, Hoffmann's *Das Fräulein von Scuderi* and *Die Elixiere des Teufels*: see Railo, *Haunted Castle*, pp. 183–88.

32 Cf. "The Murders in the Rue Morgue": "Observing Dupin in these moods, I often dwelt meditatively upon the old theory of the Bi-Part Soul, and amused myself with the fancy of a double Dupin—the creative and the resolvent."

33 That Dupin and D—are brothers or doubles is suggested in Richard Wilbur's essay on Poe in *Major Writers of America*, I, 379–80.

34 Conan Doyle is particularly clear about this in his preface to *The Case-Book of Sherlock Holmes*, 1927:

> One likes to think that there is some fantastic limbo for the children of imagination, some strange impossible place where the beaux of Fielding may still make love to the belles of Richardson, where Scott's heroes still may strut, Dickens' delightful Cockneys still raise a laugh, and Thackeray's worldlings continue to carry on their reprehensible careers. . . . And so, reader, farewell to Sherlock Holmes! I thank you for your past constancy, and can but hope that some return has been made in the shape of that distraction from the worries of life and stimulating change of thought which can only be found in the fairy kingdom of romance.

While his sense of other literature is a little vague, his grasp of the appropriate conventions is not.

35 Connected with this theme is the significant relation between characters and art subjects: it starts with the visit to Canova's studio in *Corinne* (VIII, ii), where Oswald is found to resemble a figure intended for a tomb—"'le génie de la douleur appuyé sur un lion, emblème de la force"; continuing in *The Marble Faun* ii and xiv, with Donatello's resemblance to an antique faun and Miriam's to Kenyon's Cleopatra; in *Pierre* xxiv, with Lucy's attraction to a copy of Reni's Beatrice Cenci and Pierre's and Isabel's to a "Stranger"; in Elsie Venner's connection with the Laöcoön, and Milly Theale's (James, *The Wings of a Dove*) with the Bronzino portrait.

36 Cf. Burton, *Anat.* I.iii.1.1.:

> Parrhasius a painter of Athens, amongst those Olynthian captives Philip of Macedon brought home to sell, bought one very old man; and when he had him at Athens, put him to extreme torture and torment, the better by his example to express the pains and passions of his Prometheus, whom he was then about to paint. I need not be so barbarous, unhumane, curious, or cruell for this purpose to torture any poor melancholy man; their symptomes are plain, obvious and familiar. . . .

He names his source, the *Controversiae* of Seneca the Elder, x.5. Cf. Young's sonnet "On Michael Angelo's famous piece of the Crucifixion: who is said to have stabbed a person that he might draw it more naturally." Another such story is told of Goya. Zola's artist Claude in *L'Oeuvre* paints the dead body of his child; this repeats an incident in the life of Luca Signorelli.

37 Job 8 : 14, the hypocrite's "trust shall be a spider's web."

38 Cf. III, letter 62, p. 347, "the joy of having such a charming Fly entangled in my web"; V, 34, p. 321, more spider and fly after Clarissa's fall.

39 *Ivanhoe* xv (xvi in some editions); *Le Juif errant* VII, xi; *Alice* X, iv; *Hunchback of Notre-Dame* VII, v; *Master of Ballantrae* iv. A web-spinner and poison-brewer whose "type" is an actual monstrous spider is Hawthorne's Dr. Portsoaken in *Septimius Felton* (Centenary Edition XIII, *The Elixir of Life Mss.* [1977], pp. 133–34, 193, 528).

40 "My bountiful winepress for a while," is Dracula's elegant phrase (xxi). Here and in the Dreyer film *Vampyr* (ostensibly based on Le Fanu's "Carmilla," where it is the vampire who appears to sleepwalk), the victim's tendency to somnambulism and trance assists the monster, whose relation to her is thus like that of magus to dummy-woman.

41 Cf. *Alastor:* "The spirit of sweet human love has sent / A vision to the sleep of him who spurned / Her choicest gifts. He eagerly pursues / Beyond the realms of dream that fleeting shade; / . . . Lost, lost, for ever lost . . . " (203–05, 209).

42 Cf. Zanoni's renunciation of his powers to save his wife, and Monte Cristo's renunciation of his vengeance before it is completed in order both to save the life of his friend's fiancée and to attend to his own love story.

43 This topic becomes the supernatural or science fiction theme of the revolt against man of animals, birds, insects, or machines, whether or not in vengeance for ill-treatment. Early examples are Arthur Machen's *The Terror,* 1917; Karel Čapek's *R.U.R.* and *War with the Newts,* 1923 and 1937: later ones are Philip Macdonald, "Our Feathered Friends," Daphne Du Maurier, *The Birds* (basis of the Hitchcock film), and Irving Layton, "The Ants" (poem).

44 Simon Magus; Faustus; the Monk; *Zofloya's* Victoria; Melmoth; Michael Scot (in James Hogg's *Three Perils of Man,* 1822).

45 "The Bell-Tower," in *Piazza Tales,* 1856; H. G. Wells, *The Island of Doctor Moreau,* 1896.

46 For this traditional form of female vengeance see above, chap. 4, n. 7.

47 Both titles refer to the same figure, a long-lived woman of occult powers.

48 On the journey in, their boat is wrecked in a river; all are drowned but the persons needed to carry on the story, and Holly saves Leo's life. The party is guided blindfold into Ayesha's home valley, an old volcanic crater; Leo alone is not blindfolded, being too ill to observe; Ayesha recovers him from his death-agony with a potion. After the catastrophe in the heart of the mountain, their outward way leads over a chasm whose bridging plank was knocked away on the journey in; they jump, and here Holly's life is saved by Leo. When they emerge, Leo's golden hair is snow-white, and Holly sees reflected in a pool the "wild look" that henceforward never leaves him.

49 Traveling across swampland towards Ayesha's realm, Holly compares man's earthly wanderings to the movements of fireballs in the marsh (x); Ayesha later (xvii) says she has been "led on only down [her] dreary road by the marsh lights of Hope": when Holly refuses her offered gift of immortality, she blames him (xxii): " . . . man can never be content with that which his hand

may pluck. If a lamp be in his reach to light him through the darkness, straightway he casts it down because it is no star. Happiness dances ever a pace before him, like the marsh-fire in the swamps, and he must catch the fire, and he must win the star!"

50 Besides the fiery fountain and well of *Adonais* and "The Witch of Atlas" (cf. Southey, *Thalaba* II.xxv; Lady Morgan, *The Missionary* II, 207–08), an obvious source for *She* and *Ayesha* is the last two chapters of *A Strange Story*, where the magus Margrave is attended by two oriental familiars, a skeletonlike animal man, "Juma the Strangler," and Ayesha the Arabian "Veiled Woman." She is not the magician's dummy—Lilian is that—but maternal or nurselike, and last seen mourning over the dead Margrave lying in her lap; at the same time she personifies some deeper wisdom than Margrave's. Corresponding to *She's* veiled-maiden statue, *Ayesha's* mountain shrine has a draped maternal form comforting a child; Ayesha in that book is last seen on the mountain in pietà attitudes mourning over Leo.

51 While otherworldly resolutions of the love-and-friendship triangle are unusual, obviously Romantic patterning requires that they be possible. We might compare the apostrophe of Hölderlin's Hyperion (*Hyperion,* 1799) to his (by now presumably dead) friend about the (now certainly dead) love on whose account they parted: "Poor Alabanda! now she belongs to us both!" (II, ii).

52 A descendant is John Buchan's last novel, *Sick Heart River,* 1945. Sir Edward Leithen, aging and mortally ill, undertakes a journey into the Canadian north to find a missing man, though essentially what he wants is just to die working. Having found the man, he discovers he must do more to restore him sane to his friends: the quest has an unexpected inward dimension, so Leithen feels obliged to resist the desire to stay and die where he is. Like Conway he is called on first of all to get someone out of a prison-paradise, his own place of temptation, by a tricky bit of mountaineering that only he can perform; then the party travels "out" to a starving Indian village, where the rescued man (like Romola) finds himself in saving others, while Leithen dies so radiantly that the local priest is sure he will be as welcome in heaven as a Catholic would. While Leithen's loneliness and his friendship for the younger rescued Galliard have played some part, the real inspiration of the quest seems to be his regard for Galliard's wife, Felicity: it is to save Galliard for her, and not really on account of the Indians, that he throws away his chance of recovery by staying in the infected village. Hilton, by decreasing his hero's aura of sanctity towards the end where Buchan intensifies it, though not a better writer is able to achieve a more suggestive and much less cloying final effect.

53 Besides *The Princess* and *The Blithedale Romance,* where schemes of social reform are conspicuous, social idealism is relevant to, for example, *Frankenstein* with its connection with the ideas of Godwin and Shelley, and *Zanoni,* where main topics in addition to magic are the pursuit of beauty in art and the fated course of the French Revolution as a wrongly conceived search for social justice.

54 Such displays sometimes feature in horror films: never better, in my view, than in *The Black Cat,* 1934, where an engineer and master builder (Boris Karloff) shows a visitor (Bela Lugosi) his cellar stocked with embalmed

blondes in glass cases. Earlier, female magicians conserve dead lovers—especially Antinéa in Pierre Benoit's *L'Atlantide,* 1919, a kitschy derivative from *She.*

55 "Ill usage and length of years have driven me from [my country], and estranged me from [my home]." His "inducement" to this journey was "a kind of nervous restlessness which haunted [him] like a fiend." He has earlier "imbibed the shadows of fallen columns at Balbec, and Tadmore, and Persepolis, until [his] very soul has become a ruin." Shortly before the end, he says: ". . . a curiosity to penetrate the mysteries of these awful regions predominates even over my despair, and will reconcile me to the most hideous aspect of death. It is evident that we are hurrying onwards to some exciting knowledge—some never-to-be-imparted secret, whose attainment is destruction."

56 The Terrible Journey Out is combined with illness at the end of *Green Mansions,* and to all practical purposes replaced by it in *Ayesha* (opening of i), *Heart of Darkness, Lost Horizon, Frankenstein* (xxiii, preparatory to climactic Terrible Journey In in xxiv). In a novel of self-discovery without exotic wanderings, such as *Great Expectations,* the illness may have the same value in the design.

57 Published complete in *Blackwood's,* August 1859. Bulwer Lytton shortened the ending for republication in his collected works, because of its similarity to some of the incidents of *A Strange Story,* published two years later.

Chapter 11

Epigraphs: John Milton, *Paradise Lost,* IX.171–72; Gérard de Nerval, "Antéros"; Senator Barry Goldwater, presidential nomination acceptance speech, July 16, 1964.

1 For the term *misanthrope,* cf. Burton, *Anat.* I.ii.2.6:

> . . . this solitude undoeth us, *pugnat cum vitâ sociali;* 'tis a destructive solitariness. These men are Devils alone, as the saying is, *Homo solus aut Deus, aut Daemon:* a man alone, is either a Saint or a Devil, . . . and . . . woe be to him that is so alone. These wretches do frequently degenerate from men, and of sociable creatures become beasts, monsters, inhumane, ugly to behold, *Misanthropi;* they do even loath themselves, and hate the company of men, as so many Timons, Nebuchadnezars; by too much indulging to these pleasing humors, and through their own default.

Also Byron's early lyric, "Love's Last Adieu": "Oh! who is yon misanthrope, shunning mankind? / From cities to caves of the forest he flew: / There, raving, he howls his complaint to the wind; / The mountains reverberate love's last adieu!"

2 Cf. *Alastor:* ". . . he would linger long / In lonesome vales, making the wild his home, / Until the doves and squirrels would partake / From his innocuous hand his bloodless food, / Lured by the gentle meaning of his looks, / And the wild antelope, that starts whene'er / The dry leaf rustles in the brake, suspend / Her timid steps to gaze upon a form / More graceful than her own" (98–106). In Arnold's "Scholar-Gipsy," as in some Wordsworth poems, this

type is absorbed into the landscape as a kind of nature spirit. Female equivalents are the outdoor-haunting "nymphs," like Wordsworth's Lucy, Hudson's Rima, and the young girl of Felix Salten's *Bambi*.

3 This image comes from a remark of Chateaubriand: "Le coeur le plus serein en apparence ressemble au puits naturel de la Savane Alachua; la surface en paraît calme et pure, mais quand vous regardez au fond du bassin, vous apercevez un large crocodile": I am quoting F. L. Lucas, *Decline and Fall of the Romantic Ideal*, p. 101.

4 Thomas Campbell, *Gertrude of Wyoming* III.v.: cf. chap. 9 above, n. 1.

5 Cf. Caroline Lamb, *Glenarvon* I, 258–60.

6 While the law forbidding marriage to a deceased wife's sister was not repealed until 1906, Tess assures Angel that such marriages are frequent where she comes from (lviii).

7 There are two kinds of case in which the (or a) hero dies simultaneously with the villain, sometimes combined: hero and villain constitute a Gothic pair, like Frankenstein and the Being, Jekyll and Hyde, Holmes and Moriarty, the Master of Ballantrae and his brother; or, as in *Dracula*, an element of sacrifice is needed if evil is to be destroyed.

8 Eugene appears still more a pastoral figure in those editions of the novel that include the original Eugene Aram's essay "The Melsupper and Shouting the Churn," linking English harvest customs with those of the ancient Hebrews.

9 A different imagery, like that of chap. 7 above, appears in V, v.: "I have read somewhere of an enchanted land where the inmates walked along voluptuous gardens, and built palaces, and heard music, and made merry, while around and within the land were deep caverns, where the gnomes and the fiends dwelt, and ever and anon their groans and laughter, and the sounds of their unutterable toils or ghastly revels, travelled to the upper air, mixing in an awful strangeness with the summer festivity and buoyant occupation of those above. And this is the picture of human life!"

10 Review of *Frankenstein, Works* VI, 264. Two more literary strains may be noted. Caleb as a shrinking sensibility in a large house with an inscrutable master inspiring both hate and love recalls Pamela or Psyche; Godwin's 1832 preface mentions a related story type—"Falkland was my Bluebeard . . . Caleb Williams was the wife who . . . persisted in his attempts to discover the forbidden secret." The seeker for justice or revenge who afterwards repents, exemplified in Caleb and in Frankenstein's Being, seems to go back to the conclusion of Young's drama *The Revenge*, where Zanga, the Iago-like Moor who has been dishonored by a blow, exclaims over the dead body of his victim, "Oh Vengeance! I have follow'd thee too far."

11 Amid the numerous references to the supposed properties of the spider, we may note the words addressed to Henrietta by her guardian in III, 228: "In your cradle, as in that of Plato, a swarm of bees seems to have gathered round your lips, and the persuasion of moral wisdom and rectitude falls irresistibly from your tongue."

12 The Oxford episode is rather like the card-sharping incident that Poe later puts into "William Wilson," another narrative whose gloomy protagonist chooses to hate instead of love his better genius.

13 For Mezentius, an early Italian ruler who comes into the *Aeneid,* cf. Milton, *Doctrine and Discipline of Divorce* II, xvi; the whole paragraph in Godwin's narrative of the seventeenth century draws on Milton's passage.

The concluding expression is of a kind with remarks by characters in Mme de Lafayette, Prévost, and Richardson who feel themselves singled out for special afflictions—Lovelace in one of his last letters says he will always be "the most miserable of beings", and the opening lines of the first of Rousseau's *Rêveries,* 1778, declare the speaker to be cut off from the human species. In line with the way in which we have seen figures of speech take on substance, this kind of rhetoric can be said to culminate in the Byronic hero, who is conceived of as being tragically placed beyond mankind.

14 The words in which she announces her decision to Mandeville recall those Evil-be-thou-my-good reversals that connect the book with Brockden Brown's *Wieland* before it and Hogg's *Confessions of a Justified Sinner* after:

> "Mandeville! . . . you are my greatest enemy. . . . Most remorseless of brothers!
>
> > Beautiful tyrant! fiend angelical!
> > Dove-feathered raven! wolfish, ravening lamb!
>
> since I cannot escape you, since I have no hope to move you, I will fly from your envenomed hostility—into your arms! You are my only destroyer! therefore I will love none but you! That shall be my revenge: so will I satiate all the just and deep resentment, with which your unkindness has filled me. . . . Therefore all my days and nights shall be devoted to the increase of your comforts. I will talk to you all day, and smooth your pillow by night. . . . I will weep for your sorrows, when my heart is bursting with my own." [III, 269–71]

The verse quotation, from *Romeo and Juliet* III.ii.75–76, is in the spirit of Amalia's exclamation at the climax of *Die Räuber* (V.ii): "Murderer! Devil! I cannot leave thee, angel." Cf. "angel or devil" in chap. 8, n. 12 above.

15 Shelley recalls this speech for a not much more unnatural situation, the cursing of Beatrice Cenci by her father (*Cenci* IV.i).

16 A similar episode, but with fewer overtones, is the cut given Sir Hargrave Pollexfen by Sir Charles Grandison in defence of Miss Byron—"the disgrace the wretch must carry in his face to the grave" (I, letter 39, p. 320). Cf. Shelley, "On Godwin's *Mandeville*" (VI, 223): "The noun *Smorfia* comes at last, and touches some nerve, which jars the inmost soul, and grates as it were along the blood; and we can scarcely believe that the grin, which must accompany Mandeville to the grave, is not stamped upon our own visage."

17 He shares his name with the author of *The Fable of the Bees,* 1724, a satirist and social realist much denounced by his age for cynicism: Lovelace cites him as "my worthy friend Mandeville" (V, 21, 240–41); Mr. Flosky in *Nightmare Abbey* (Peacock, *Works* III, 39) opens a parcel of books : " 'Devilman, a novel'. Hm. Hatred—revenge—misanthropy—and quotations from the Bible"; he is not the first to break the name down.

18 Cf. the reference to the Old Man of the Mountain, II, 73.

19 The Justified Sinner stands midway between the outright religious hypocrite like Le Fanu's Uncle Silas, or more recently Mr. Pennhallow in Andrézel's *The Angelic Avengers* and the Preacher in Davis Grubb's *Night of the Hunter,* 1953, and the sincere but sinister religious idealist like Ibsen's Brand, 1866.

20 A comparable grotesque is the speaker of Browning's "Johannes Agricola in Meditation," grouped under the title *Madhouse Cells* with "Porphyria's Lover," whose speaker is a demon of our aesthete type.

21 *Aids to Reflection,* 1825, 220n.; quoted in Beer, *Coleridge the Visionary,* pp. 123–24. De Quincey's essay "The Apparition of the Brocken" in *Suspiria de Profundis* makes of it "the dark symbolic mirror for reflection to the daylight what else must be hidden forever": Tennyson uses the "glory" in *In Mem.* xcvii, "My love has talk'd with rocks and trees." Hogg discusses the physical phenomenon in his essay "Nature's Magic Lantern" (*Tales and Sketches* V, 352–60).

22 For evidence that Bergman's conventions sometimes overlap with ours, cf. further the rôles of dark and fair women in *Virgin Spring* and *The Silence;* demon artist (novelist watching the progress of his daughter's insanity) in *Through a Glass Darkly;* the saving servant, earthy and unspiritual—close to our animal man types—in *Cries and Whispers.*

23 In Staël and Disraeli, as in Thomas Mann's *Death in Venice* and "Tonio Kröger," his moral rigor is associated with northern scenery, as against the lassitude or self-indulgence of the south. This view of racial types is propounded by Mme de Staël in *De la Littérature,* 1800 (and cf. the North-South intelligence-imagination parentage that Novalis's notes provide for Heinrich von Ofterdingen).

24 A more troubling quality emerges in the endings of some recent works—Arthur Miller's *A View from the Bridge,* 1955, Orson Welles's film *Touch of Evil,* 1958 (about a justice-obsessed D.A. who takes to faking evidence against the guilty), and John Arden's impressive *Serjeant Musgrave's Dance,* 1960. Exasperated policemen exacting retribution outside the law have supplied many film plots of the seventies, from TV quickies like *Death Squad,* 1974, to better-class thrillers like *The Cop* (Le Condé), 1971.

25 Jean Rhys revives these interests in *Wide Sargasso Sea,* 1968, a novel about *Jane Eyre's* Bertha Mason.

26 Not only are hero and heroine the last of their Moorish and Spanish noble lines, but the father of the one killed the father of the other in battle, making their marriage impossible: cf. Nerval's "Emilie," 1854, where the indignant brother of Emilie learns that her fiancé killed their father in an engagement against the Prussians, or Kirby's *The Golden Dog,* where the heroine's brother is manipulated into murdering the father of her fiancé. In the later nineteenth century this kind of irremovable obstacle to marriage comes to replace the (mostly merely apparent) incest impasse.

27 Starting serial publication in 1859, the book was published as a whole in 1861.

28 A common biblical tradition accounts for the striking applicability of lines 19–25 of Marvell's "Coronet," "But thou who only could'st the Serpent tame. . . ." Again, Elsie resembles Beatrice Rappaccini, whose evil emblem is the poison-tree (likewise a basically biblical image) and who dies of an antidote

administered by ignorant love. While Hawthorne's story is by several years the earlier, Holmes mentions of his (in the 1883 preface) only *The Marble Faun*.

29 This last rôle (cf. *Zastrozzi*, De Quincey's story "The Avenger") has a particular development in stories and films concerning the American West, from Karl May's *Winnetou*, 1892, on. It suits Deerslayer-type heroes, who are the soul of honor and justice but don't want much actual truck with live women.

30 Her words in the judgment scene would fit Judith's case as well: "What strange beings you men are . . . ! It is the simplest thing in the world with you to bring a woman before your secret tribunals, and judge and condemn her unheard, and then tell her to go free without a sentence. The misfortune is that this same secret tribunal chances to be the only judgment-seat that a true woman stands in awe of, and any verdict short of acquittal is equivalent to a death-sentence!" (*The Blithedale Romance*, xxv).

31 "With a cry of anguish I started to my feet, and was about to rush away towards the village when a dazzling flash of lightning made me pause for a moment. When it vanished, I turned a last look on the girl, and her face was deathly pale, and her hair looked blacker than night; and as she looked she held out her arms towards me and uttered a low, wailing cry. 'Good-bye for ever!' I murmured, and turning once more from her, rushed like one crazed into the wood" (vi). Cf. the Eurydice figures mentioned above (p. 49, also chap. 8, n. 30), and a later one in Galsworthy's short story "The Apple-Tree" (*Five Tales*, 1918): Ashurst is about to forsake dark Megan for fair Stella, but feels as he sits by the sea and thinks of her a prophetic compunction (she later drowns herself): ". . . it was as if her arms and all of her were slipping slowly, slowly down from him, into the pool, to be carried away out to sea; and her face looking up, her lost face with beseeching eyes, and dark, wet hair— possessed, haunted, tortured him!" (247)

32 Cf. the trance of Contarini's Alceste, p. 131 above.

33 Cf. Melville's Billy Budd, whose execution is placed between two allusions (opening of xxvi, end of xxviii) to dawn clouds as fleecy vapor; also *The Confidence-Man* i, the "man in cream-color": "His cheek was fair, his chin downy, his hair flaxen, his hat a white fur one, with a long fleecy nap. . . . Gradually overtaken by slumber, his flaxen head drooped, his whole lamb-like figure relaxed, and . . . lay motionless, as some sugar-snow in March, which, softly stealing down over night, with its white placidity startles the brown farmer peering out from his threshold at daybreak." For Billy's stammer and the lamblike man's being a mute, cf. Isaiah 53 : 7: ". . . he is brought as a lamb to the slaughter, and as a sheep before her shearers is dumb, so he openeth not his mouth."

34 Collins dedicated *The Frozen Deep* in 1874 to Holmes, "in sincere admiration of his genius as poet, novelist, essayist, and in cordial remembrance of our inter- course during my visit to America."

35 In C. M. Yonge's *The Heir of Redclyffe*, 1853, the hero's inherited passion and vengefulness, emblematized in his resemblance to the portrait of a turbulent ancestor, is his particular form of original sin; the transformation of character that he achieves is imaged in a sketch made of him shortly before his death by an artist who wants to use it for his Sir Galahad.

36 This interest continues, e.g., in William March, *The Bad Seed*, 1954, in which a young woman discovers her mother to have been a murderess and her own little blonde daughter to be a return to the type. The alien child, sometimes a sinister cuckoo-chick like Kleist's "Foundling" or Heathcliff, figures with or without explanatory heredity in modern horror fiction: cf. John Wyndham's *The Midwych Cuckoos* (their destruction requires a sacrifice, cf. n. 7 above), John Collier and Ray Bradbury practically passim, and Ira Levin's *Rosemary's Baby*.

37 These two pairs represent a combination of the motif of sisters dark and fair or active and passive with that of Cain-and-Abel brothers. We have seen two sets of these latter, in this chapter and the last, in *Confessions of a Justified Sinner* and *The Master of Ballantrae*. Not to go so far back as *Hamlet* or *Lear* or Otway's *The Orphan*, 1680, we can start the line with Young's tragedy *The Brothers*, c. 1724 (an adaptation of Thomas Corneille's *Persée et Démétrius*, 1662, from Livy): of two brother princes, rivals in love, the younger is destroyed by the elder's shameless plotting. (In *Tom Jones*, e.g., a similar device is merely a feature of dramatic construction, without strong emotional overtones.) Conflicts of love and ambition drive violent younger brothers to murder their more passive and peaceable elders in two German tragedies of 1775, Leisewitz's *Julius von Tarent* and Klinger's *Die Zwillinge* (The Twins); in both, as in *The Brothers*, the father then executes the murderer. A bright youth and gloomy plotter, closer to the *Brothers* pair, are the brothers Moor in Schiller's *Die Räuber*, 1781; these return in *Der Geisterseher*'s story of Lorenzo and Jeronymo, later adapted by Mrs. Radcliffe (*The Italian*), Coleridge (*Remorse*), Byron ("Oscar of Alva"), Catharine Smith (*Barozzi*), and Maturin (*The Fatal Revenge*). In Scott's *Pirate*, the sisters Brenda and Minna are balanced by Mertoun and Cleveland, innocent youth and criminal, who turn out to be half-brothers.

38 Dickens's "Author's Preface" begins, "When I was acting, with my children and friends, in Mr. Wilkie Collins' drama of *The Frozen Deep*, I first conceived the main idea of this story." Collins's preface to *The Frozen Deep* in novel form recalls that it first saw the light as a three-act play, in 1856, and was produced the next year with Dickens as Richard Wardour and Collins as Frank Aldersley. I have not seen the acting text, but in the novel, which is mostly in the present tense and appears to follow it all too closely, some of Wardour's last expressions are much like Carton's famous lines. The wasteland imagery used for Dickens's France replaces Collins's horrific Arctic setting. Dickens's obvious other fictional source for the ending, not mentioned by him, is *Zanoni*, in which the magister takes his wife's place at the guillotine.

39 For example, cf. the tradition that the man in the moon is Cain gathering thorns, and the rôle of the thornbush as the tree of a blasted pastoral landscape. Briars and thorns accompany curses on the land in the Old Testament (see above, pp. 9–10). To be caught among thorns is a regular symbol of suffering through guilt, as in the English folksong: "Oh, the briary bush! that pricks my heart so sore: / If once I get out of the briary bush, I'll never get in any more." The presence of thorns beside or surrounding the rose belongs to the curse on love. Cf. also *In Mem.* lxix, with its blasted landscape ("Spring no more"), its mourner wearing a crown of thorns that marks him as in effect an outcast, and the gesture of the angel suggesting among other things forgive-

ness of sin (the purport of the similar miracle in the Tannhäuser legend). *In Memoriam* tends regularly to associate guilt with sorrow: iii, "vice of blood," vii, "like a guilty thing," etc.

40 We noted earlier (p. 104 above) that vampirism can parody marriage: in addition, "Carmilla" and *Dracula* both have expressions suggesting demonic versions of the essential transactions of the Bible: Carmilla tells her victim, "Love will have its sacrifices. No sacrifice without blood" (vi), and *Dracula*'s Renfield declares, "The blood is the life!" (xi: cf. Genesis 9 : 4).

41 Much more than remotely Christian is the saving shepherd Gregory of "The Half-Brothers." Odder is what has become of "Frankenstein's monster" since Mary Shelley finished with him. Boris Karloff's makeup and manner in the film series carrying on the tradition could at times be reflectively melancholy to an awesome degree. The Karloff tragic mask emphasizes forehead clamps and sutures so as to suggest man of sorrows with wounded brow: *The Bride of Frankenstein*, 1935, has a scene suggesting the monster's crucifixion. In the British TV version of 1973, "the Creature" is conceived first and last as a newborn Adam—beautiful, innocent, trusting, joyful (screenplay published as *Frankenstein: The True Story*, by Christopher Isherwood and Don Bachardy).

42 Comparable mechanics operate in other eighteenth-century works. Lovelace undertakes the seduction of Clarissa in pursuance of a vow of vengeance taken against her sex; she in turn fears the operation of her father's curse on her. The plot of *Otranto* reflects the working-out of a doomful prophecy. Harriet Lee's *Kruitzner* (the source of Byron's play *Werner*), persuasively describes the fulfillment of a curse which is reinforced by a father's bad example to his son.

43 I.iii and III.vi.1 (and see Hallam Tennyson's note on the latter) suggest the course of a year, from March to March. These two indications of season are distinctly elegiac, referring to "the shining daffodil dead, and Orion low in his grave," and connected with Maud, first as an apparition in dreams, later as a blessed form from the dead.

44 Hallam Tennyson's introductory note on *Maud*. For further connections between the avenger and the man of sensibility, see pp. 155–56 above, on *Ernest Maltravers*.

45 The subject of demonic honor, not stressed in *Maud*, needs more comment. The best-known passage of Tasso's pastoral drama *L'Aminta*, commencing "O bella età de l'oro," characterizes "Onor" as "Quell' idolo d'errori, idol d'inganno": Mrs. Rowe, *Letters Moral and Entertaining* I, 7, translates (via a French version which she quotes and which uses the same term), ". . . Honour, phantom of controul, / False airy idol, tyrant of the soul," and Lovelace in VIII, 35 calls honor a "phantom" (cf. phantom duty in *La Princesse de Clèves*, phantom Philosophy in *Clèveland*, phantom caution in Smollett's *Regicide*, phantom virtue in *La Nouvelle Héloïse*); so does the repentant Spanish avenger in *Ferdinand Count Fathom*, and cf. *The Man of Feeling* xxi, "You have substituted the shadow Honour, instead of the substance Virtue." The phantom becomes murderous in *Caleb Williams*, in what we could call the Foreign Legion romance (George MacDonald, "The Broken Sword"; P. C. Wren, *Beau Geste*; A. E. W. Mason, *The Four Feathers*), and in a range of works from *Eugene Onegin* via *The Ordeal of Richard Feverel* to Schnitzler's *Liebelei*, where the duelling code

imposes an obligation opposed to the values of real life. The real victim here is usually, as in *Maud,* a woman, a pastoral figure to whom the iron world of manly honor seems nightmarishly unreal. Criticism of duelling is a standard literary topic (the regular terms are "gothic" and "barbarous") from Addison (*Spectator* 99) down through Richardson (*Grandison*) and Godwin (*Italian Letters*).

46 Cf. an early connection between Cain and the man who travels to escape the past in one of Clarissa's last letters (VII, letter 89, pp. 367–68): "If that part of Cain's curse were Mr. Lovelace's, *To be a fugitive & vagabond in the earth;* that is to say, if it meant no more harm to him, than that he should be obliged to travel . . . then should I be easy. . . . "

47 Cain in Jewish legend is not subject to natural death—like the Wandering Jew in Christian legend, to whose tradition he contributes early and late (cf. *The Monk* iv, where the Wandering Jew's forehead is marked with a burning cross).

48 Several books introduce devices which make this clear. In *The Hunchback of Notre-Dame, The Three Musketeers, A Tale of Two Cities,* and *Lorna Doone,* God is the real punisher of Frollo, Milady, Mme Defarge, and Carver Doone; and some sympathetic criminals, like Magwitch and the avenger of *A Study in Scarlet,* die of illness before they can be hanged, and are considered to have been judged by a higher (and more worthy) tribunal than that of man.

Chapter 12

The chapter title is from Patrick Anderson's "Winter in Montreal." *Epigraph:* Rosanna Leprohon, *Antoinette de Mirecourt . . . A Canadian Tale,* 1864, preface.

1 Douglas LePan, "A Country without a Mythology." Most poems cited in this chapter will be found in *The Book of Canadian Poetry, A Critical and Historical Anthology,* ed. A. J. M. Smith, 3d ed., 1957.

2 Charles Sangster, *The St. Lawrence and the Saguenay,* 1856.

3 With four exceptions, all stories mentioned are printed in one or both of: *Canadian Short Stories,* ed. Robert Weaver and Helen James, 1952; *Canadian Short Stories,* ed. R. Weaver, 1960. The first prints only stories broadcast by the CBC in the years 1946–51, while the second ranges from 1895 to 1957. These collections and the Smith poetry anthology mentioned above were textbooks in the Canadian literature course I inherited from Northrop Frye at Victoria College in the late 1950s. Very much in this essay comes from him.

4 Following, naturally, Joseph Scriven's "What a Friend we have in Jesus" and Col. John McCrae's "In Flanders Fields," in that order.

5 "True North" is Tennyson's phrase, from the epilogue "To the Queen" that concludes *Idylls of the King,* where he comments on a British movement around 1870–72 to encourage the newly formed Dominion of Canada to separate to save expense to the Empire: "that true North, whereof we lately heard / A strain to shame us . . . " (14–15); it was taken up by his main informant on the Canadian response, William Kirby, soon to publish *The Golden Dog,* and others before being enshrined in the English translation of the (originally French) national anthem. See Lorne Pierce, *Tennyson / Kirby Unpublished Correspon-*

dence, 1929, 41–50, 66–68. "True" here means "faithful"; the magnetic pole's location in Canada is merely a happy coincidence.

6 In *Twice to Flame,* 1961.

7 R. G. Everson, "Fish in a Store-Window Tank," in *A Lattice for Momos,* 1958; Earle Birney, "Images in Place of Logging," in *Trial of a City and other verse,* 1952; Patrick Anderson, "Country Station," in *The Colour as Naked,* 1953.

8 "Invocation to the Muse of Satire," in *A Suit of Nettles,* 1958. Cf. two short stories: Alice Munro's "Thanks for the Ride," in her *Dance of the Happy Shades,* and Larry Thomas's "The King-Size Deal," published by *The Raven* (University of British Columbia student magazine) in January 1960; again, James Reaney's "Granny Crack," from *One-Man Masque,* 1960 (in *The Killdeer and Other Plays)*—"We dozen scoundrels laid you / For a quarter each in the ditch / To each you gave the sensation / That we were the exploited bitch."

9 Usually present as simile or metaphor, rather than physically as in "The Nymph Complaining": cf. *Aeneid* IV.68–73; Petrarch, *Rime* 209; Surrey, "If care do cause men cry"; *Faerie Queene* I.ii.24; *Hamlet* III.ii.274; Burton, *Anat.* I.iii.1.2; Richardson, *Clarissa* VII, letter 50, p. 170; Cowper, *Task* III.108–11; M. Shelley, *Frankenstein* II.i (ix); Scott, *Bride of Lammermoor* xxxi; Shelley, *Adonais* 297.

10 Alan Walker, "The Mighty Hunters," *Acta Victoriana* 86 (1962): 2.

11 "The Rural Mail," in *The Deficit Made Flesh,* 1958.

12 The title describes the child's world of reverie: his underground city, based on pictures in the *National Geographic,* combines the romance of Venice with the sobriety of Holland. At the end of the story he is planning to teach his imaginary citizens the arts of civil defence.

13 Avrom is explicitly developed as an Old Testament patriarchal figure. In Yves Thériault's short story "Jeannette," David, who kills himself and his pregnant daughter, is a fisherman, like the avenging father in Balzac's "Un Drame au bord de la mer." In literature in general, this latter kind of patriarchal morality belongs either to the world of shepherds and fishermen or to a clan society with a rigorous code of honor, like that of Gogol's Cossacks ("Taras Bulba"), Mérimée's Corsicans (*Colomba,* "Matteo Falcone"), or Mark Twain's southern Grangerfords and Shepherdsons in *Huckleberry Finn.*

14 Cf. Ringuet, "The Heritage," in *Canadian Short Stories,* 1960.

15 The extreme, even manipulating, care of the design is somewhat glossed over by the diction, intended to make us forget that it is not reality but romance that requires that we kill our best friends, and romance of a rather decadent kind (cf. Chamisso's lyric "Der Soldat"). A late comment on the idyll of male friendship (see Leslie Fiedler, *Love and Death in the American Novel,* passim), or the love-and-friendship debate, is made by love's martyr, Branwell, in Reaney's *A Suit of Nettles,* January Eclogue: "Your favourite land is better, I agree— / What a round concrete continent of snows! / But too round and too continent for me. . . . "

16 Published in her *A Bird in the House,* 1970.

17 As printed in *The Blur In Between,* 1963.

18 Cf. Canadian glass- or ice-houses cited above, chap. 9, n. 9.

19 At the time of writing, every group of very naïve Canadian poems—high school poetry contest entries, say—would yield a significant proportion of works presenting a snow-covered winter wonderland, deploring the way man strewed his crude footprints (etc.) all over it, and consoling the reader at length with the thought that God would send more snow.

20 Cf. Roberts's "The Solitary Woodsman"; Campbell's "How One Winter Came in the Lake Region"; Anderson's "Ballad of the Young Man" (in *The Colour as Naked*, 1953).

21 For more discussion see Milton Wilson's article "Klein's Drowned Poet," *Canadian Literature* 6 (Autumn 1960): 5–17, and Germaine Warkentin, "[F. R.] Scott's 'Lakeshore' and its Tradition," *Canadian Literature* 87 (Winter 1980): 42–50.

22 The mythology of translucent boats is explored in an eccentric but suggestive book, *The Ancient Secret: In Search of the Holy Grail*, by Flavia Anderson, 1953. Add: Southey, *Madoc*, 1805: "or beneath / The mid-sea waters, did that crystal Ark / Down to the secret depths of Ocean plunge / Its fated crew?" (I.xi.117–20, and note); Edward Davies, *Mythology and Rites of the British Druids*, 1809, pp. 211–12; Wallace Stevens, "Prologues to What is Possible."

23 Daryl Hine, "The Boat," in *The Carnal and the Crane*, 1957.

24 Cf. Louis Dudek, "The Pomegranate," the fruit enclosing a Persephone as interior paramour: "The jewelled mine of the pomegranate . . . / Gleaming without a sun—what art where no eyes were!— / Till broken by my hand, this palace of unbroken tears."

25 Cf. also the magic half-breed, first imaged in Crawford's *Malcolm's Katie* V, 1884—"a child with yellow locks, / And lake-like eyes of mystic Indian brown"—and reappearing as Hugh, the hero of her unfinished long poem known as "Narrative Two" (see Dorothy Livesay, "The Hunters Twain," in *Canadian Literature* 55 [Winter 1973]: 75–98); D. C. Scott's short story "Tête Jaune," 1939, republished in *The Circle of Affection*, 1947; Howard O'Hagan's *Tay John*, 1939 (same title, same year).

26 "The Third Eye," *Canadian Literature* 3 (Winter 1960): 23–34.

27 Patrick Anderson, "Poem on Canada," in *The White Centre*, 1947, the source also of the quotation below.

A Short Finding List

I. Primary

Allston, Washington. *Monaldi: A Tale*. Boston: Little, Brown, 1841.

Anderson, Patrick. *A Tent for April*. Montreal: First Statement, 1945.

——. *The White Centre*. Montreal: First Statement, 1947.

——. *The Colour as Naked*. Toronto: McClelland & Stewart, 1953.

Ascham, Roger. *Toxophilus: The Schole of Shootinge*. 1545. Reprint (facsimile). The English Experience, no. 79. Amsterdam: Da Capo Press, 1969.

Bacon, Sir Francis. *Works*. Edited by James Spedding, R. L. Ellis, and Douglas Denon Heath. 14 vols. London: Longman, 1857–74.

——. *The Twoo Bookes of the Proficience and Advancement of Learning, Divine and Humane*. London, 1605. Reprint (facsimile). The English Experience, no. 218. Amsterdam: Da Capo Press, 1970.

[Barbier, Jules.] "The Tales of Hoffmann." In *The Authentic Librettos of the French and German Operas*, pp. 195–251. New York: Crown [c. 1939].

Beckford, William. *Dreams, Waking Thoughts, and Incidents: In a Series of Letters from Various Parts of Europe*. London, 1783.

Benson, E. F. "The Man who Went Too Far." In his *The Room in the Tower*, pp. 205–37. 2d ed. London: Alfred Knopf, 1929.

Béranger, Pierre-Jean de. *Oeuvres complètes*. 2 vols. Paris: Perrotin, 1857.

Birney, Earle. *Trial of a City, and Other Verse*. Toronto: Ryerson Press, 1952.

Boëthius. *The Consolation of Philosophy*. Translated by V. E. Watts. Harmondsworth: Penguin Books, 1976.

Burton, Robert. *The Anatomy of Melancholy*. 6th ed. London: Henry Cripps, 1652.

Byron, George Gordon, Lord. *Byron's Letters and Journals*. Edited by Leslie A. Marchand. London: John Murray, 1973–.

Cazotte, Jacques. *Le Diable amoureux*. 1772. Reprint. Paris: Quantin, 1878.

Coleridge, S. T. *Notebooks*. Edited by Kathleen Coburn. Bollingen Series L. New York: Pantheon Books, 1957–.

Corpus Hermeticum. Edited by Arthur D. Nock and A. -J. Festugière. 2 vols. Paris: Les Belles Lettres, 1945.

Coryat, Thomas. *Crudities: Hastily Gobled Up in Five Moneths Travells in France, Savoy, Italy, Rhetia. . . .* 1611. Reprint. 2 vols. Glasgow: James MacLehose & Sons, 1905.

Creuzer, Friedrich. *Symbolik und Mythologie der alten Völker, besonders der Griechen*. 4 vols. Leipzig: Leske, 1837–43.

Dacre, Charlotte [Rosa Matilda]. *Confessions of the Nun of St. Omer*. 3 vols. London: J. F. Hughes, 1805.

————. *Zofloya, or the Moor.* 1806. Reprint. Edited by Montague Summers. London: Fortune Press [1928].

Davies, Edward, *Mythology and Rites of the British Druids.* London: J. Booth, 1809.

Davies, Sir John. *Poems.* Edited by Robert Krueger. Oxford: Clarendon Press, 1975.

Doyle, Sir Arthur Conan. *The Memoirs of Sherlock Holmes.* London: John Murray, 1924.

————. *The Case-Book of Sherlock Holmes.* London: John Murray, 1927.

Dryden, John. *The Works of John Dryden.* Edited by H. T. Swedenberg. 8 vols. Berkeley and Los Angeles: University of California Press, 1956–62.

Du Maurier, George. *Trilby,* with the author's illustrations. 1894. Reprint. Everyman's Library. London: J. M. Dent, 1931.

Everson, R. G. *A Lattice for Momos.* Toronto: Contact Press, 1958.

Galsworthy, John. "The Apple Tree." In his *Five Tales,* pp. 185–286. London: Heinemann, 1918.

Gascoigne, George. *Complete Works.* Edited by J. W. Cunliffe. 2 vols. Cambridge: Cambridge University Press, 1907–10.

Gérard de Nerval. *Oeuvres complémentaires.* Edited by Jean Richer. Paris: Minard, 1959–.

Glassco, John. *The Deficit Made Flesh.* Toronto: McClelland & Stewart, 1958.

Godwin, William. *St. Leon: A Tale of the Sixteenth Century.* 4 vols. London, 1799.

————. *Mandeville: A Tale of the Seventeenth Century.* 3 vols. London, 1817.

Goethe, Johann Wolfgang von. *Works of Goethe.* 7 vols. London: Robertson, Ashford & Bentley [c. 1902]. Vol. 7, *Poetical Works.*

Gogol, Nicolai. *Tales of Good and Evil.* Assembled and translated by David Magarshack. New York: Doubleday Anchor, 1957.

Hawthorne, Nathaniel. *The Centenary Edition of the Works of Nathaniel Hawthorne.* Edited by William Charvat and others. 14 vols. Columbus: Ohio State University Press [c. 1962–80].

Hébert, Anne. *Le Tombeau des rois.* Québec: L'Institut Littéraire, 1953.

Hemingway, Ernest. *Across the River and Into the Trees.* New York: Scribner, 1950.

Herder, Johann Gottfried. *Sämmtliche Werke.* Edited by Bernard Suphan. 33 vols. Berlin: Weidmann, 1877–1913.

Hine, Daryl. *The Carnal and the Crane.* McGill Poetry Series 2. Toronto: Contact Press, 1957.

————. *The Wooden Horse.* New York: Atheneum, 1965.

Hogg, James. *Private Memoirs and Confessions of a Justified Sinner.* 1824. Reprint, edited by John Carey. Oxford English Novels. London: Oxford University Press, 1969.

————. *Tales and Sketches.* 6 vols. London and Edinburgh: W. Nimmo, 1878.

Jonson, Ben. *Ben Jonson.* Edited by C. H. Herford and Percy Simpson. 11 vols. Oxford: Clarendon Press, 1925–52.

Kesey, Ken. *One Flew Over the Cuckoo's Nest.* New York: Viking, 1962.

Kierkegaard, Søren. *Journals.* Selected and edited by Alexander Dru. 1938. Reprint. London: Oxford University Press, 1959.

Klein, A. M. *The Rocking Chair and Other Poems.* Toronto: Ryerson Press, 1948.

Lamb, Lady Caroline. *Glenarvon.* 3 vols. 2d ed. London: Colburn, 1816.

Laurence, Margaret. *A Bird in the House*. Toronto: McClelland & Stewart, 1970.

Lee, Harriet. *Kruitzner: or, The German's Tale*. 1801. 5th ed. London: John Murray, 1823.

LePan, Douglas. *The Net and the Sword*. Toronto: Clarke, Irwin, 1953.

Leprohon, Rosanna. *Antoinette de Mirecourt, or, Secret Marrying and Secret Sorrowing: A Canadian Tale*. Montreal: John Lovell, 1864.

Lyndon, Barre, and Sangster, J. *The Man Who Could Cheat Death*. New York: Avon Books, 1959.

Lytton, Edward Bulwer, 1st baron. *Works*. 15 vols. Illustrated Sterling Edition. Boston: Dana Estes [n.d.].

Mann, Thomas. *Death in Venice: Tristan: Tonio Kröger*. Translated by H. T. Lowe-Porter. Harmondsworth: Penguin Books, 1959.

Morgan, Lady Sidney [Owenson]. *The Missionary: An Indian Tale*. 3 vols. 2d ed. London, 1811.

Munro, Alice. *Dance of the Happy Shades*. Toronto: Ryerson Press, 1968.

O'Hagan. Howard. *Tay John*. London: Laidlaw & Laidlaw, 1939.

Ovid. *The Metamorphoses*. Translated by Mary M. Innes. Harmondsworth: Penguin Books, 1974.

Peacock, Thomas Love. *The Works of Thomas Love Peacock*. The Halliford Edition. Edited by H. F. B. Brett-Smith and C. E. Jones. 10 vols. London: Constable, 1924–34.

Pierce, Lorne. *Tennyson/Kirby Unpublished Correspondence*. Toronto: Macmillan, 1929.

Piozzi, Hester Lynch. *Observations and Reflections made in the Course of a Journey through France, Italy, and Germany*. 2 vols. London, 1789.

Pope, Alexander. *Poems*. Twickenham Edition. Edited by John Butt. 11 vols. London: Methuen, 1940–69.

Prévost d'Exiles, Antoine-François. *Histoire du Chevalier des Grieux et de Manon Lescaut*. 1731. Reprint. Edited by Georges Matoré. Textes Littéraires Françaises. Geneva: Librairie Droz, 1953.

———. *Le Philosophe anglois, ou histoire de monsieur Cléveland, fils natural de Cromwel*. 1731–39. 2d complete ed. 8 vols. Amsterdam, 1757.

Purdy, Alfred W. *The Blur In Between: Poems 1960–61*. Toronto: Emblem Books, 196[3].

Reaney, James. *A Suit of Nettles*. Toronto: Macmillan, 1958.

———. *The Killdeer and Other Plays*. Toronto: Macmillan, 1962.

Richardson, Samuel. *Pamela: or, Virtue Rewarded*. 1740. Reprint. 4 vols. Stratford-upon-Avon: Shakespeare Head, 1929.

———. *Clarissa: or, The History of a Young Lady*. 1747–48. Reprint. 8 vols. Stratford-upon Avon: Shakespeare Head, 1930.

———. *The History of Sir Charles Grandison*. 1754. Reprint. 6 vols. Oxford: Blackwell for Shakespeare Head, 1931.

Richter, Johann Paul Friedrich [Jean Paul]. *Titan*. 1800–03. Translated by Charles T. Brooks. Boston: Ticknor and Fields, 1862.

Rilke, Rainer Maria. *Neue Gedichte*. Leipzig, 1908.

Roberts, Dorothy. *Dazzle*. Ryerson Poetry Chapbooks. Toronto: Ryerson Press, 1957.

Rousseau, Jean-Jacques. *Julie, ou la Nouvelle Héloïse.* 1760. Reprint. Vol. 2 of *Oeuvres complètes,* edited by Bernard Gagnebin and Marcel Raymond in 4 vols. Bibliothèque de la Pléiade. Paris: Gallimard [c. 1959–69].

St-Pierre, J. H. Bernardin de. *Paul et Virginie.* 1789. Reprint. Edited by Maurice Souriau. Les Textes Français. Paris: Société Les Belles Lettres, 1952.

Sandys, George. *Ovid's Metamorphosis Englished, Mythologized, and Represented in Figures.* 1632. 2d ed. London, 1640.

Scott, Duncan Campbell. "Tête Jaune." In his *The Circle of Affection,* pp. 36–48. Toronto: McClelland & Stewart, 1947.

Shelley, Mary. *Mathilda.* Edited by Elizabeth Nitchie. Chapel Hill: University of North Carolina Press, 1959.

Shelley, Percy Bysshe. *Complete Works.* Edited by Roger Ingpen and Walter E. Peck. 10 vols. London: Ernest Benn, 1926–30.

———. *Poetical Works.* Edited by H. B. Forman. 4 vols. London: Reeves & Turner, 1876.

Smith, Charlotte. *Celestina.* 2d ed. 4 vols. London, 1791.

Sterne, Laurence. *The Letters of Laurence Sterne.* Edited by Lewis P. Curtis. Oxford: Clarendon Press, 1935.

Sue, Eugène. *Le Juif errant.* 10 vols. in 5. Brussels: Méline, Cans, 1844–45.

Swift, Jonathan. *Prose Works.* Edited by Herbert Davis. 13 vols. Oxford: Blackwell, 1939–62.

Symons, Arthur. *Poems.* 3 vols. London: Martin Secker, 1924.

Tennyson, Alfred Lord. *Poems.* Edited by Christopher Ricks. London: Collins, 1968.

Virgil. *Works.* Translated by J. Lonsdale and S. Lee. London: Macmillan, 1890.

Warburton, William. *Works.* 7 vols. London, 1788–94.

Watts, Isaac. *Hymns and Spiritual Songs 1707–1748.* Edited by Selma L. Bishop. London: Faith Press, 1962.

William of Malmesbury. *Gesta Regum Anglorum.* Edited by W. Stubbs. 2 vols. London: Her Majesty's Stationery Office, 1887.

Wordsworth, William. *Poetical Works.* Edited by Ernest de Selincourt. 5 vols. Oxford: Clarendon Press, 1940–49.

Wyatt, Sir Thomas. *The Poems of Sir Thomas Wiat.* Edited by A. K. Foxwell. 2 vols. London: University of London Press, 1913.

Zola, Emile. *L'Oeuvre.* 1886. Vol. 4 of his *Les Rougon-Macquart: Histoire naturelle et sociale d'une famille sous le second empire.* 5 vols. Complete edition under the general editorship of Armand Lanoux. Bibliothèque de la Pléiade. Paris: Gallimard [c. 1960–67].

II. Secondary

Anderson, Flavia. *The Ancient Secret: In Search of the Holy Grail.* London: Gollancz, 1953.

Baker, Carlos. *Shelley's Major Poetry: The Fabric of a Vision.* 1948. Reprint. New York: Russell & Russell, 1961.

Beer, John B. *Coleridge the Visionary.* London: Chatto & Windus, 1959.

Bouvier, Auguste A. *J. G. Zimmermann: un représentant suisse du cosmopolitisme littéraire au XVIIIe siecle.* Geneva: Georg, 1925.

Chapman, Guy. *Beckford.* London: Jonathan Cape, 1937.

Child, Francis James. *The English and Scottish Popular Ballads.* 5 vols. Boston and New York: Houghton Mifflin, 1883–98.

Cody, Richard. *The Landscape of the Mind: Pastoralism and Platonic Theory in Tasso's Aminta and Shakespeare's Early Comedies.* Oxford: Clarendon Press, 1969.

Curtius, Ernst Robert. *European Literature and the Latin Middle Ages.* Translated by Willard Trask. London: Kegan Paul, 1953.

Desport, Marie. *L'Incantation virgilienne: Virgile et Orphée.* Bordeaux: Delmas, 1952.

Fiedler, Leslie. *Love and Death in the American Novel.* New York: Criterion [c. 1960].

———. "Some Contexts of Shakespeare's Sonnets." In *The Riddle of Shakespeare's Sonnets,* edited by Edward Hubler, pp. 55–90. New York: Basic Books [1962].

Fiedler, Leslie, and Zeiger, Arthur, eds. *O Brave New World: American Literature from 1600 to 1840.* New York: Dell [1968].

Frazer, Sir James G. *The Golden Bough: A Study in Magic and Religion.* 12 vols. London: Macmillan, 1911–15.

Freud, Sigmund. *Standard Edition of the Complete Psychological Works of Sigmund Freud.* Edited by James Strachey. 24 vols. 1953. Reprint. London: Hogarth Press [1973–74].

Frye, Northrop. *Fearful Symmetry: A Study of William Blake.* Princeton: Princeton University Press, 1947.

———. *Fables of Identity: Studies in Poetic Mythology.* New York: Harcourt Brace, 1963.

Graves, Robert. *The White Goddess: A Historical Grammar of Poetic Myth.* London: Faber & Faber, 1948.

Gustafson, Ralph, ed. *The Penguin Book of Canadian Verse.* Harmondsworth: Penguin Books, 1958.

Henkel, Arthur, and Schöne, Albrecht, eds. *Emblemata: Handbuch zur Sinnbildkunst des 16. und 17. Jahrhunderts.* Stuttgart: J. B. Metzler [c. 1967].

Hussey, Christopher. *The Picturesque: Studies in a Point of View.* London: G. P. Putnam's Sons, 1927.

James, Henry. *The Future of the Novel: Essays on the Art of Fiction by Henry James.* Edited by Leon Edel. New York: Vintage, 1956.

Jonas, Hans. *The Gnostic Religion: The Message of the Alien God and the Beginnings of Christianity.* Boston: Beacon Press, 1958.

Kerényi, Carl. *The Gods of the Greeks.* Translated by Norman Cameron. 1951. Reprint. Harmondsworth: Penguin Books, 1958.

Klenze, Camillo von. *The Interpretation of Italy during the Last Two Centuries: A Contribution to the Study of Goethe's "Italienische Reise."* Chicago: University of Chicago Press, 1907.

Lang, Andrew. *Theocritus, Bion, and Moschus, Rendered into English Prose with an Introductory Essay.* London: Macmillan, 1880.

Leggi e Memorie Venete sulla Prostituzione, fine alla Caduta della Republica. Venice: Printed for the Earl of Orford, 1870–72.

Lemmi, Charles. *The Classic Deities in Bacon: A Study in Mythological Symbolism.* Baltimore: Johns Hopkins University Press, 1933.

Lindsay, Jack, ed. *The Sunset Ship: The Poems of J. M. W. Turner.* [Lowestoft, England:] Scorpion Press [1966].

Lovejoy, Arthur O., and Boas, George. *Primitivism and Related Ideas in Antiquity.* Baltimore: Johns Hopkins University Press, 1935.

Lucas, F. L. *The Decline and Fall of the Romantic Ideal.* Cambridge: Cambridge University Press, 1937.

Merivale, Patricia. *Pan the Goat-God.* Cambridge: Harvard University Press, 1969.

Panofsky, Erwin. *The Life and Art of Albrecht Dürer.* 4th ed. Princeton: Princeton University Press, 1955.

Pauly, August Friedrich von. *Paulys Realencyclopädie der classischen Altertumswissenschaft.* New edition by Georg Wissowa. 34 vols. in 68. Stuttgart: Druckenmüller, 1893–1972.

Pichois, Claude. *L'Image de Jean-Paul dans les lettres françaises.* Paris: Corti [1963].

Praz, Mario. *The Romantic Agony.* Translated by Angus Davidson. 1933. Reprint. New York: Meridian, 1956.

Railo, Eino. *The Haunted Castle: A Study of the Elements of English Romanticism.* London: Routledge, 1927.

Robertson, D. W. *A Preface to Chaucer.* Princeton: Princeton University Press, 1962.

Scott, Sir Walter. *Biographical Memoirs of Eminent Novelists.* Vols. 3–4 in *Miscellaneous Prose Works.* 30 vols. Edinburgh: Cadell, 1834.

Sickels, Eleanor M. *The Gloomy Egoist: Moods and Themes of Melancholy from Gray to Keats.* Columbia University Studies in English and Comparative Literature. New York: Columbia University Press, 1932.

Smith, A. J. M., ed. *The Book of Canadian Poetry, A Critical and Historical Anthology.* 3d ed. Toronto: Gage, 1957.

Smith, Gregory, ed. *Elizabethan Critical Essays.* 2 vols. London: Oxford University Press, 1904.

Smith, Grover C. *T. S. Eliot's Poetry and Plays: A Study in Sources and Meaning.* Chicago: University of Chicago Press, 1958.

Texte, Joseph. *Jean-Jacques Rousseau and the Cosmopolitan Spirit in Literature: A Study of the Literary Relations between France and England.* Translated by J. W. Matthews. London: Duckworth, 1899.

Thornbury, George Walter. *The Life of J. M. W. Turner, R. A.* 1862. New ed. London: Chatto & Windus, 1904.

Trilling, Lionel. *The Opposing Self.* 1955. Reprint. New York: Viking, 1959.

Vinge, Louise. *The Narcissus Theme in Western Europe up to the Early Nineteenth Century.* Lund: Gleerups, 1967.

Wagner, Geoffrey. Introduction to *Selected Writings of Gérard de Nerval*, pp. 5–46. New York: Grove Press, 1957.

Weaver, Robert, ed. *Canadian Short Stories.* World's Classics. London: Oxford University Press, 1960.

Weaver, Robert, and James, Helen, eds. *Canadian Short Stories.* Toronto: Oxford University Press, 1952.

Welsford, Enid. *The Fool: His Social and Literary History.* London: Faber & Faber, 1935.

Wilbur, Richard. "Edgar Allan Poe." In *Major Writers of America,* edited by Perry Miller, vol. 1, pp. 369–82. 2 vols. New York: Harcourt Brace [1962].

Wilson, Milton. *Shelley's Later Poetry: A Study of His Prophetic Imagination.* New York: Columbia University Press, 1959.

Index

Figures and Topics

torrent, 41, 64, 190, 278, 302

traveler: 43, 46–47; 34 (*Tasso*), 62 (*Werther*), 165 (Shelley), 272 (Wordsworth), 278 (*Paul et Virginie*), 293 (Shelley), 300 (*Lolita*). *See also* night-wanderer; wanderer

treasure: 3, 184, 281: *Tasso*, 26–27; in Canada, 250, 264

treasure, underwater: 171, 261–62, 303. *See also* pearl

trickster, 194

True North, 321

turn of season, 109, 169, 259

tyrant's solitude, 14, 125

uninvited guest, 127, 142, 292

Upas-tree, 6, 206, 229

vampire house, 127

vampire, vampirism: 207, 312, 320; 104 (*Dracula*), 300 (Fitzgerald); Gautier, 135, 298

vampiric love: 96, 151, 168; 140 (*Death in Venice*), 231 (*Mandeville*)

vegetation, hellish, 5, 6, 249. *See also* Upas-tree

vegetation, wilderness, 5, 319

veil, 184, 211, 281, 284, 313

Venice: 127, 128–44, 292–96, 304; 91 (*Zanoni*); dream-city, 129, 138, 170–71; sunset vision, 131–32, 175; seductions, 135–37, 294; in Canadian writers, 259, 322

Venus: 16; 144 (Vernon Lee), 148 (Zola), 158 (Nerval), 297 (ring story); and Venice, 128, 296

victim, substitute, 246–47, 305, 319

victim, victimization, 207, 238, 258, 264. *See also* sacrifice; scapegoat

villain-hero, 280

violin. *See* stringed instruments

vision, desolating, xiii, 84, 220–21. *See also* delusive pursuit; nympholepsy

vision, disappearing, 12, 44, 47, 81, 289. *See also* fairy vision

wanderer: 58; 67 (*Werther*), 70 (lieder-cycles), 278 (*Faust*), 290 (*Childe Harold*); *Tasso*, 26, 269; and alchemist, 213–14

wandering goddess, 105

Wandering Jew, 182–84, 213, 243, 321

water: 4–5 (*Paradise Lost*), 35 (*Tasso*), 71 (lieder-cycles), 191 (*Frankenstein*), 198 (*Trilby*); *Alice* books, 173–74, 177–78; *Eugene Aram*, 223, 226; in pastoral myth, 4, 17, 279; as symbol and metaphor, 169–70, 300, 301, 302. *See also* brookside vision; mirror-world; reflection, &c.

water-fairy: 98, 103; and Narcissus, 17, 75, 76, 92. *See also* mermaid; siren

Whore of Babylon, 76, 130, 149

Wife of Bath, 77

wilderness: 58, 68, 246; 5 (*Paradise Lost*), 35 (*Tasso*), 43 (Burton), 44 (Akenside), 99 (*Childe Harold*), 191 (*Frankenstein*), 213 (*Donovan's Brain*), 239 (*Pierre*), 286 (Dacre); "Elegie," 69–70, 268; in Canada, 250, 252, 258, 262

Wilis, 300

will-o'-the-wisp: 41, 42, 270–71, 281; 59 (*Julie*), 71 ("Winterreise"), 135 (*R. Feverel*), 157 (*Sylvie*), 166 (Shelley), 278 (*Power of Sympathy*), 300 (*Manfred*); *She*, 210, 312–13

winter vision, 177–78, 247

woman of Samaria, 76

women idealists, 104